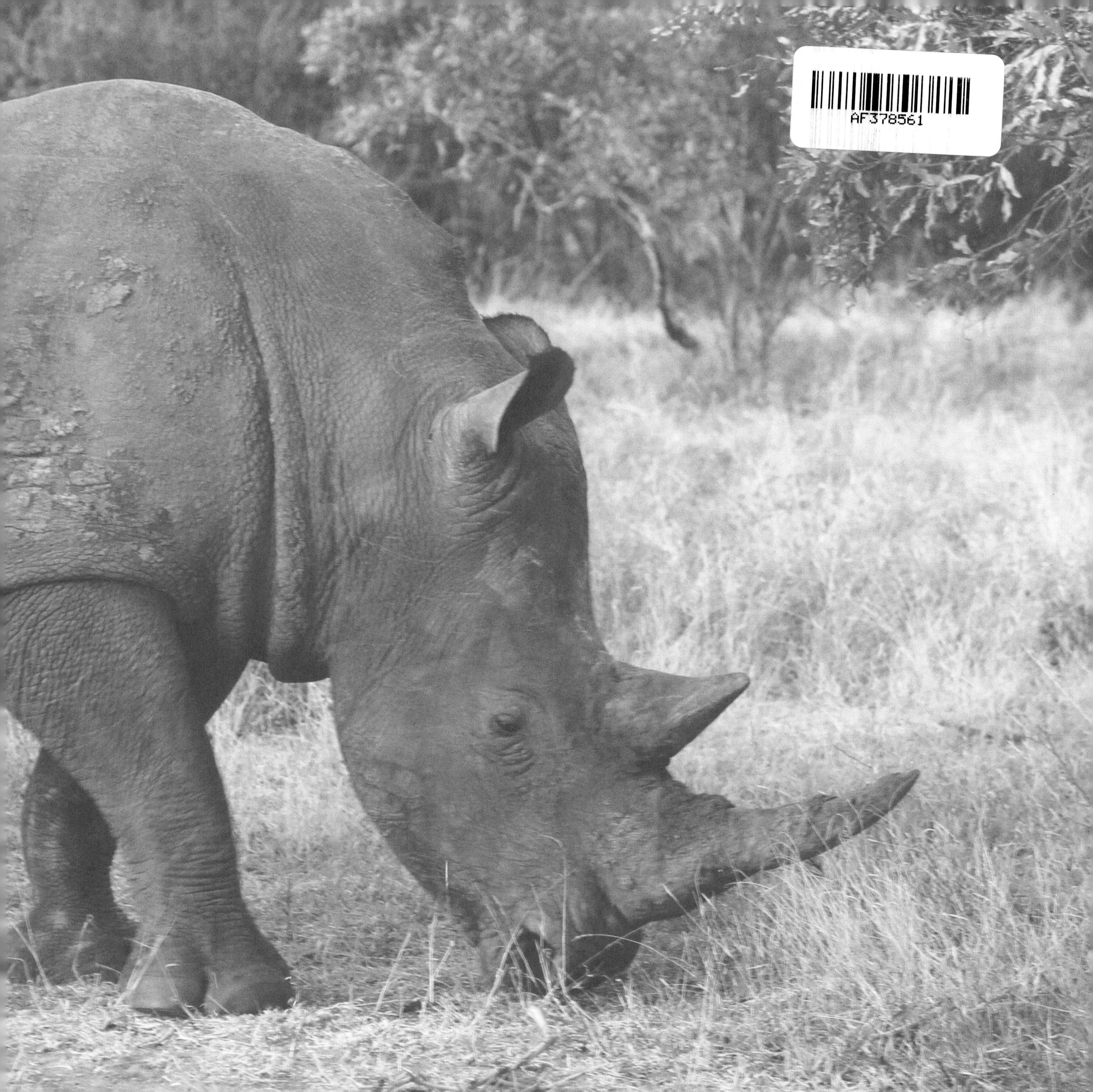

AF378561

# AFRICA *Serena*

I dedicate this book to my husband Sandy, who has supported
me every step of the way to make this dream come true.

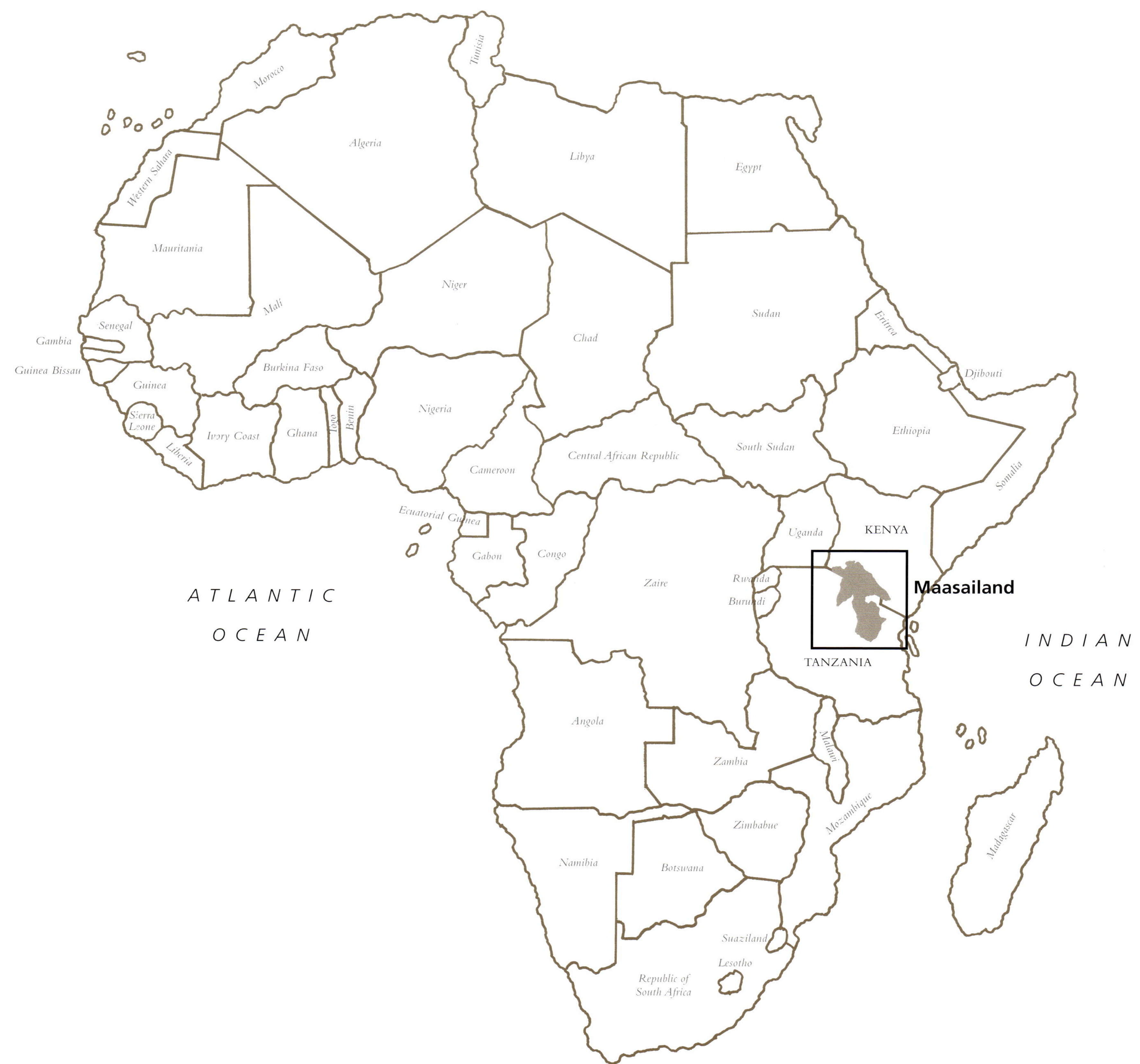

Morocco
Tunisia
Western Sahara
Algeria
Libya
Egypt
Mauritania
Mali
Niger
Sudan
Eritrea
Gambia
Senegal
Guinea Bissau
Guinea
Sierra Leone
Liberia
Ivory Coast
Burkina Faso
Ghana
Togo
Benin
Nigeria
Chad
Djibouti
Ethiopia
Somalia
Central African Republic
South Sudan
Cameroon
Ecuatorial Guinea
Gabon
Congo
Zaire
Uganda
KENYA
Rwanda
Burundi
Maasailand
TANZANIA
Angola
Zambia
Malawi
Mozambique
Zimbabue
Namibia
Botswana
Madagascar
Suaziland
Lesotho
Republic of
South Africa
ATLANTIC
OCEAN
INDIAN
OCEAN

# AFRICA *Serena*
## 30 Years Later

CLARA MARTINEZ THEDY

*Africa changes you forever, like nowhere on earth. Once you have been there, you will never be the same. But how do you begin to describe its magic to someone who has never felt it?*

BRIAN JACKMAN

SCRIPTUM EDITIONS

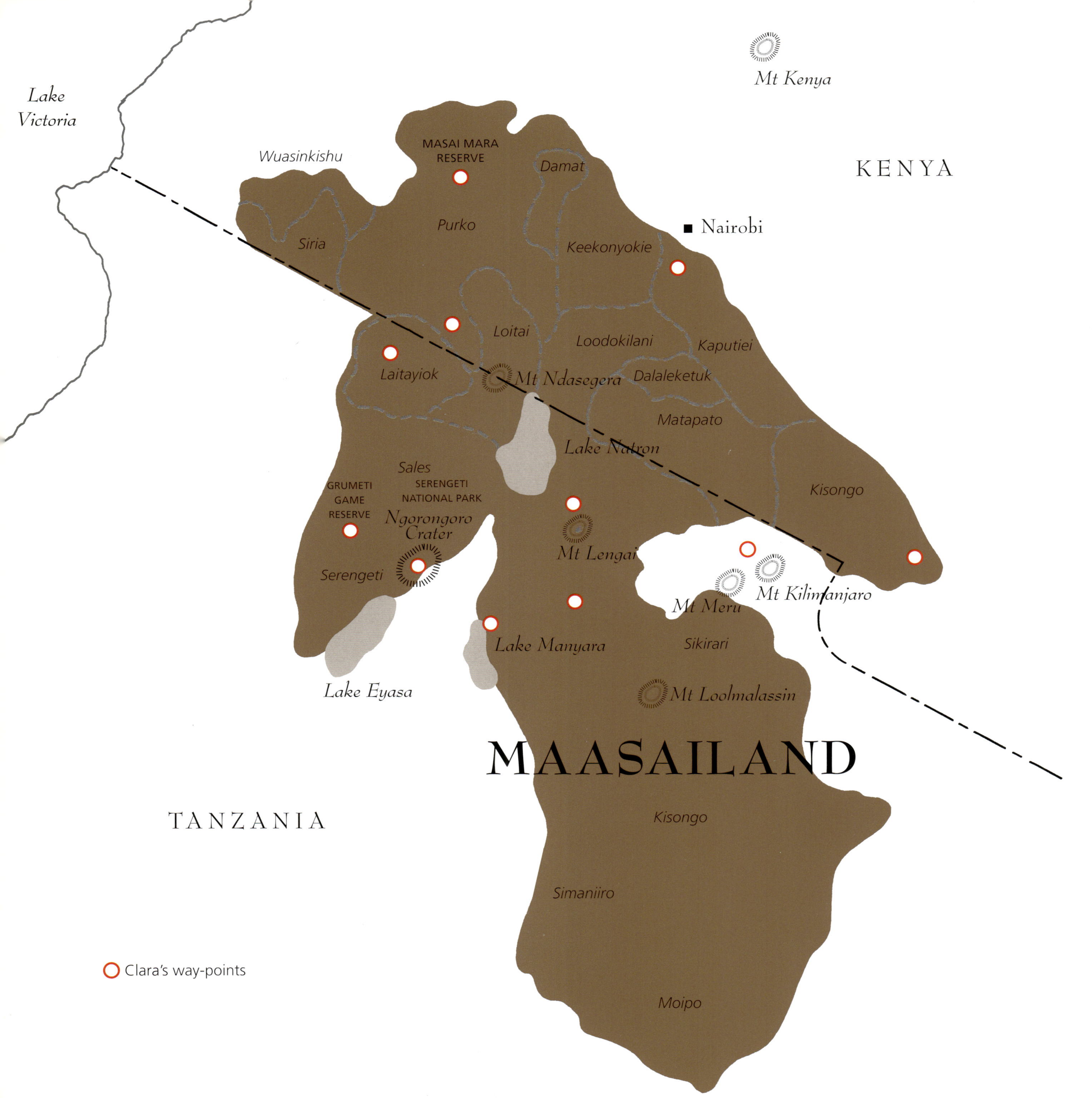

Lake Victoria
Mt Kenya
Wuasinkishu
MASAI MARA RESERVE
Damat
KENYA
Purko
Siria
Nairobi
Keekonyokie
Loitai
Loodokilani
Kaputiei
Laitayiok
Mt Ndasegera
Dalaleketuk
Matapato
Lake Natron
Sales
Kisongo
GRUMETI GAME RESERVE
SERENGETI NATIONAL PARK
Ngorongoro Crater
Mt Lengai
Serengeti
Mt Meru
Mt Kilimanjaro
Lake Manyara
Sikirari
Lake Eyasa
Mt Loolmalassin
MAASAILAND
TANZANIA
Kisongo
Simaniiro
Moipo
Clara's way-points

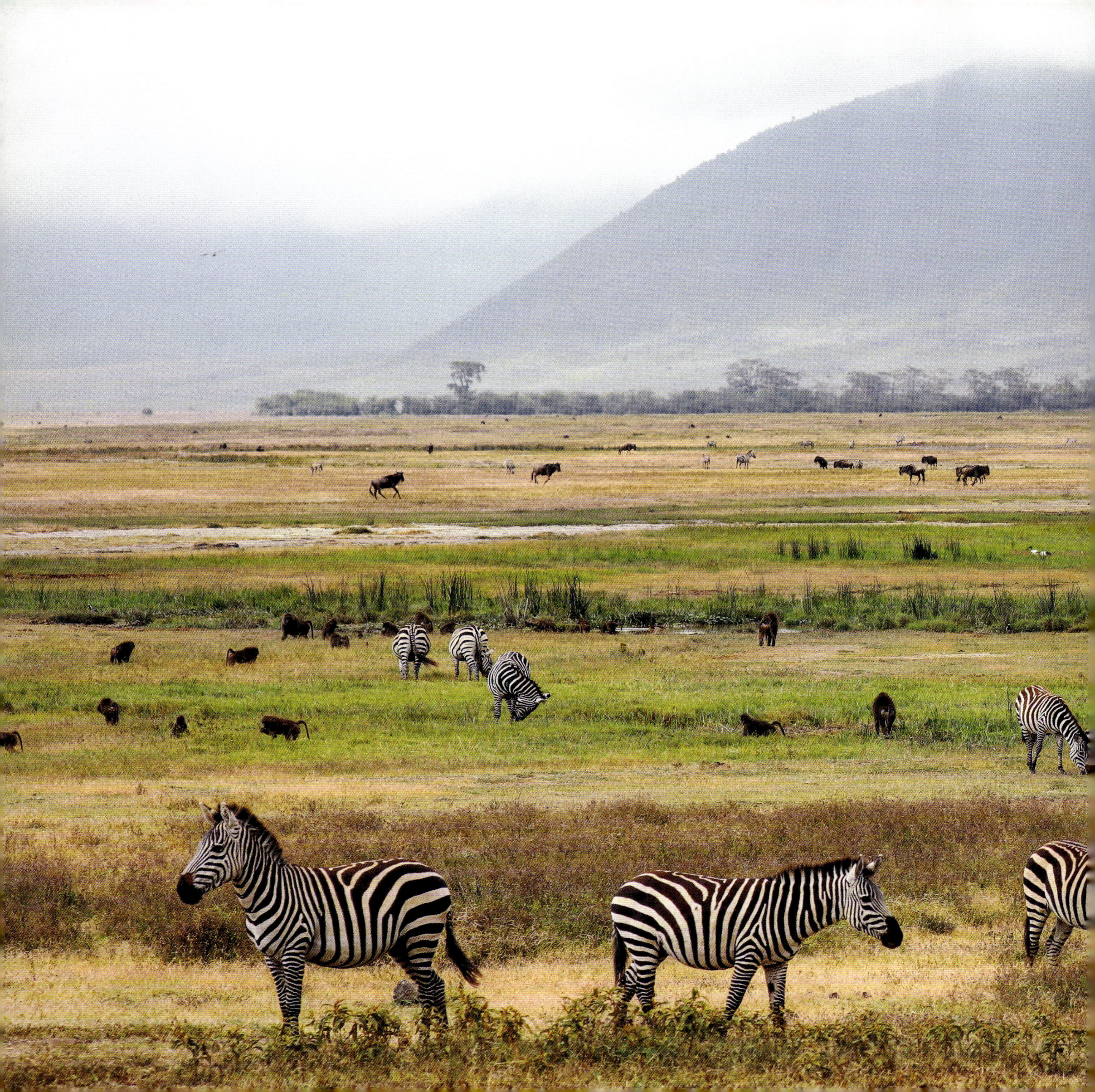

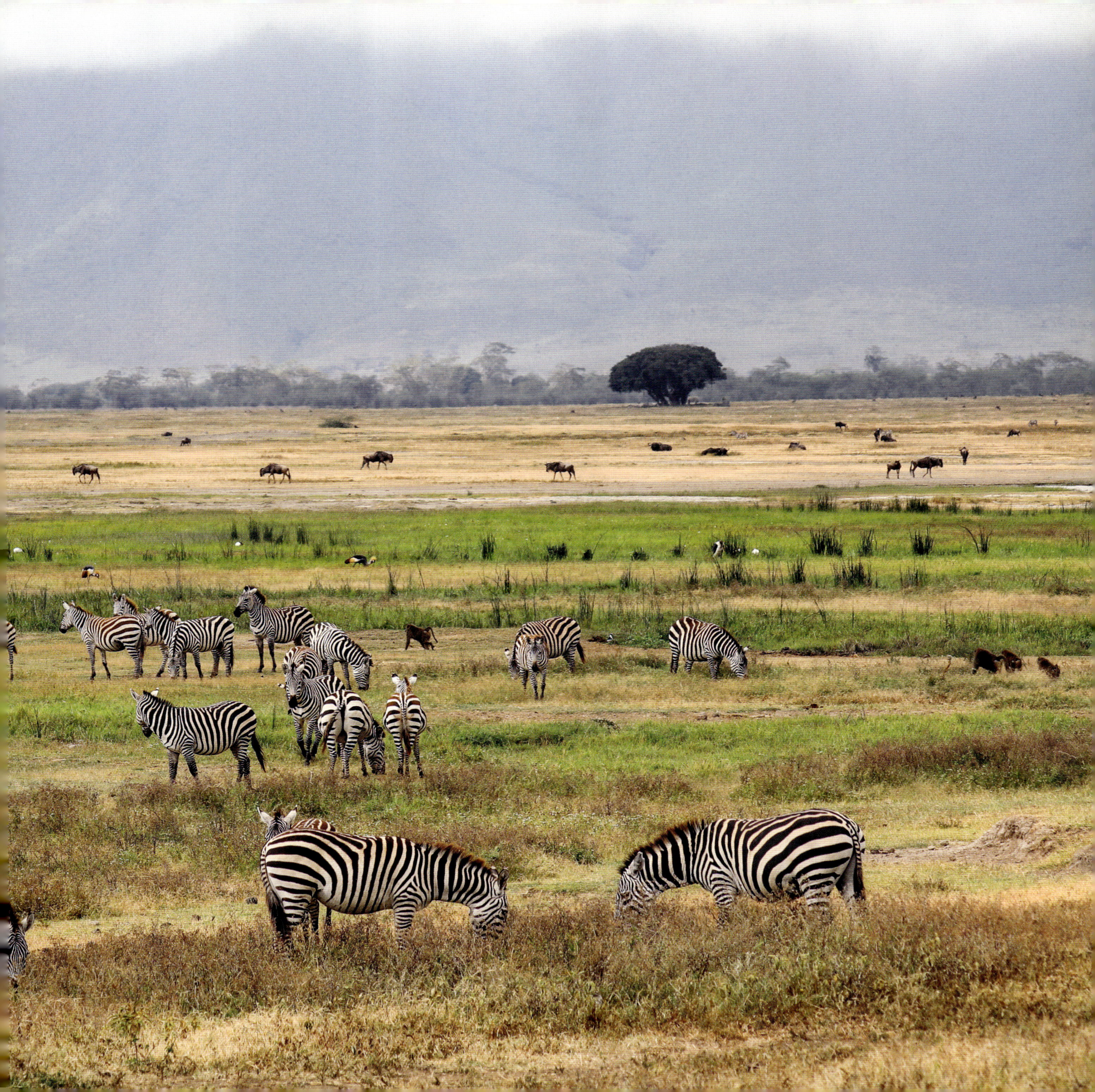

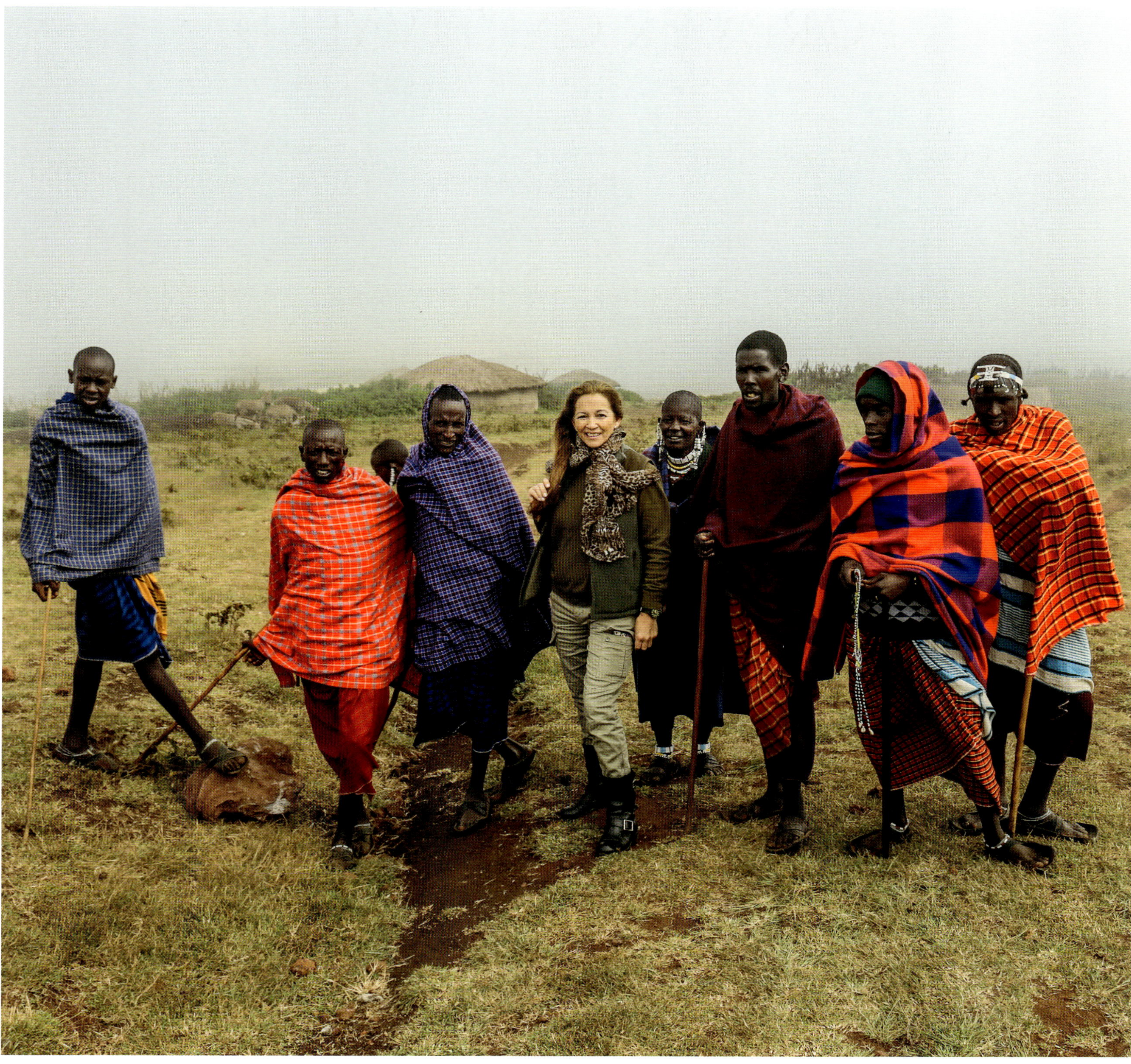

# FOREVER CAPTIVATED
## CLARA MARTÍNEZ THEDY



Africa truly has one of the richest and most diverse geographies of all the continents. It is credited with being the cradle of humankind: the hominids and anthropoids that gave rise to human beings are said to descend from there.

In 1987 I visited the legendary savannas of Kenya, and from the first moment I had the impression I was gazing upon a Garden of Eden, for its endless plains are home to thousands of species that live among a diverse and exuberant vegetation. One animal in particular caught my attention, not just because of its unmistakable profile and prehistoric features, but also because, despite its robust proportions, it is so vulnerable, in danger of extinction: the rhinoceros. I had the opportunity to touch these animals and admire them up close during my visit to the Daphne Sheldrick Elephant Orphanage, named after the project's founder, with whom I shared my first experiences in this fascinating land.

But seeing this abundance of wildlife is just part of the great beauty of this region. Meeting the Maasai tribe was undoubtedly what crowned one of the greatest experiences of my life. Learning about their customs, their lifestyle, their beliefs and their infinite humility captivated me forever.

I never imagined, returning three decades later, that I would once again find the land that I had so often dreamed of almost unchanged. I was pleasantly surprised to still find animals in great numbers; that humans had not managed to completely destroy, or radically change, the landscape; and, above all, I was delighted to see that the Maasai tribe still preserved its traditions. They continue to lead a semi-nomadic life, rearing the bovine herds, sheep and goats that sustain their unique way of life, and still live in settlements called *bomas*, which consist of a circle of huts made from branches and mud, surrounded by a barrier of thorny shrubs to protect the livestock from predators.

Thirty years on, I also had the opportunity to discover more about the Maasai and develop my understanding of their home, this time in the Serengeti National Park. It was an experience that heightened my admiration for these people even more, and for this place – such a special and unique part of the world.

My first encounter with this idyllic land left an indelible mark on me, which was why I returned again and again and immersed myself in its abundance and majesty. Contrary to what many people think, there is a serene Africa, an Africa filled with peace where everything seems to revolve around a celestial orbit.

These lands are an echo of the world's primitive animal and plant life, and I live in hope that the next generations will safeguard them so they may always exist.

# A RETURN JOURNEY

## CARLOS ACERO RUIZ

*Artist and curator, vice chair of the International Association of Art Critics (AICA)*

In 1987, Clara Martínez Thedy embarked on a journey to Africa which was destined to change the course of her life. She had set out to fulfil a dream cherished since childhood: to travel deep into the African plains to meet the Maasai tribe and discover the wildlife of this mysterious continent. Her travels resulted in her first solo exhibition, *África: luz y sombra* (*Africa: light and shadow*), held in October of the same year at La Galería Art Centre in Santo Domingo. The time she spent there unlocked her true passion and vocation for photography, which began at the early age of 15, when her first camera came into her possession.

Born in Colombia to a Uruguayan father and an Argentine mother, she arrived in the Dominican Republic in October 1966, still a child, when her father was appointed ambassador of the Oriental Republic of Uruguay. She made the country her own and virtually her entire artistic career unfolded there, until she was appointed ambassador of the Dominican Republic to the United Arab Emirates, a position she holds to this day.

After her first exhibition, in which her work focused primarily on both the human and the animal, with the beautiful and colourful African landscapes as her background, she began an ever-ascending career as a photographer, both at home and overseas. After completing her studies at the International Center of Photography in New York, she continued her training in Paris alongside George Fevre, a professional black-and-white-photograph printer who worked for many years with Henri Cartier-Bresson and Josef Koudelka. This fertile photographic experience led Martínez Thedy to centre her work on black and white technique, at a time when the emergence of the new digital technology was pure science fiction. Hard-working and dedicated in the darkroom, she mastered the art of chemical photography like few photographers had in the Dominican Republic. In the early years, she toured the world with the traveller's eye that characterises much of her work.

In 1990, she received her first photographic award, followed by a succession of prizes before finally winning the Acquisition Award in the Santo Domingo National Visual Arts Biennial, the most important event organised by the Dominican Republic since 1942. Clara Martínez Thedy and Miriam Calzada were the first photographers to receive awards in the 21st National Biennial, after photography was included as an artistic discipline in the competition in 1979.

Childhood is a subject that Clara Martínez Thedy has dealt with at length, particularly in her first decade as a professional artist, not just because of her affinity with children, but also as a way to raise awareness of the plight of the young people who in many societies live in unfavourable conditions, where many teenagers' futures are destroyed by untimely pregnancies. Her hope is that the so-called cycle of poverty can be broken. At the same time, women have also been a great source of inspiration for the artist, who, with huge sensitivity, examines the various societies in which they live and the different roles they play in each of them. It was with this subject matter that she took part in photographic groups that revitalised the photography scene in the Dominican Republic in the 1990s, first with the mixed group Objetivo 10, and then with Visiones x Ocho, a group made up of female photographers. With both groups, she participated in several successful collective exhibitions.

The Dominican Republic carnival is another source of inspiration for Martínez Thedy. She has captured this pre-Lent festivities with true devotion, delving beyond the masks, makeup and costumes to produce portraits that form an anthropological study of the festival, exploring the symbolism of these popular celebrations which have been so important across the Caribbean islands since colonial times – one of the most significant European cultural legacies inherited by the new continent.

Popular religiosity, processions and Marian worship have also been a focus of attention for the artist, both in the Americas and Europe, where her lens has recorded a number of mostly Catholic pilgrimages and manifestations.

Among her most important solo exhibitions were those held in Santo Domingo, Miami, La Romana, London, Paris, Abu Dhabi, Rochefort and Mayenne, covering the themes mentioned above in a fruitful artistic career spanning thirty years. Her work has also been exhibited in collective exhibitions in China, the United Arab Emirates, Dominican Republic, Argentina, Cuba, Germany, USA, France, Spain and Belgium.

The nostalgia and desire to return to Africa expressed by the artist herself was not fulfilled until she travelled there once more in 2016 and again in 2017. Photographers often make several trips, since each provides a different challenge. Every journey stirs up the same feeling of expectation, the excitement of not knowing what they will see through the viewfinder or how they will connect once again with the wild environment.

In this long-awaited, and no less dreamed of reunion, Clara Martínez Thedy, this time returning to Africa as an experienced photographer, manages to draw a photographic comparison between then and now, as this book entitled *Africa Serena, 30 Years Later* illustrates in its

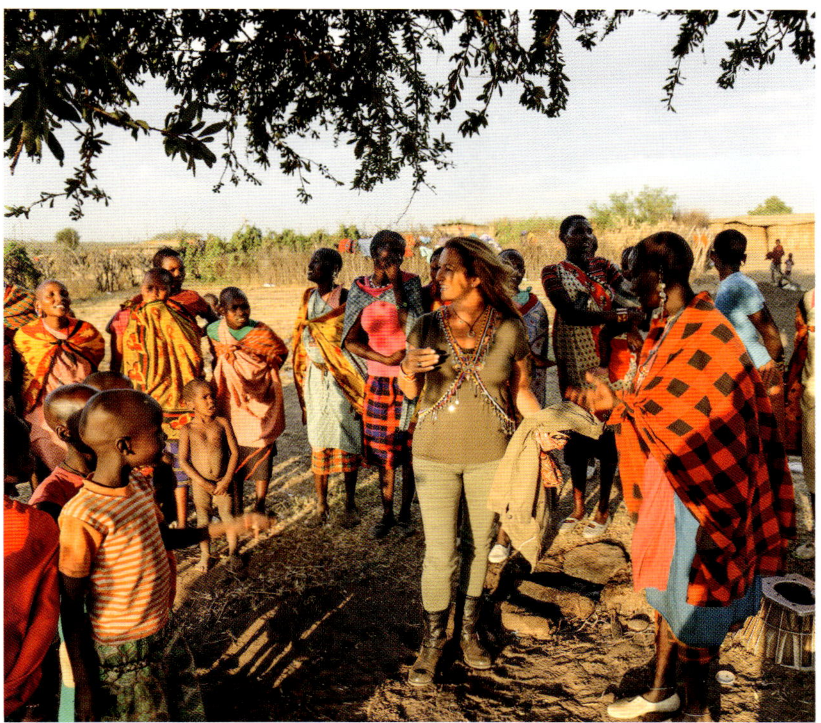

▲ 2016                                    2017 ▼



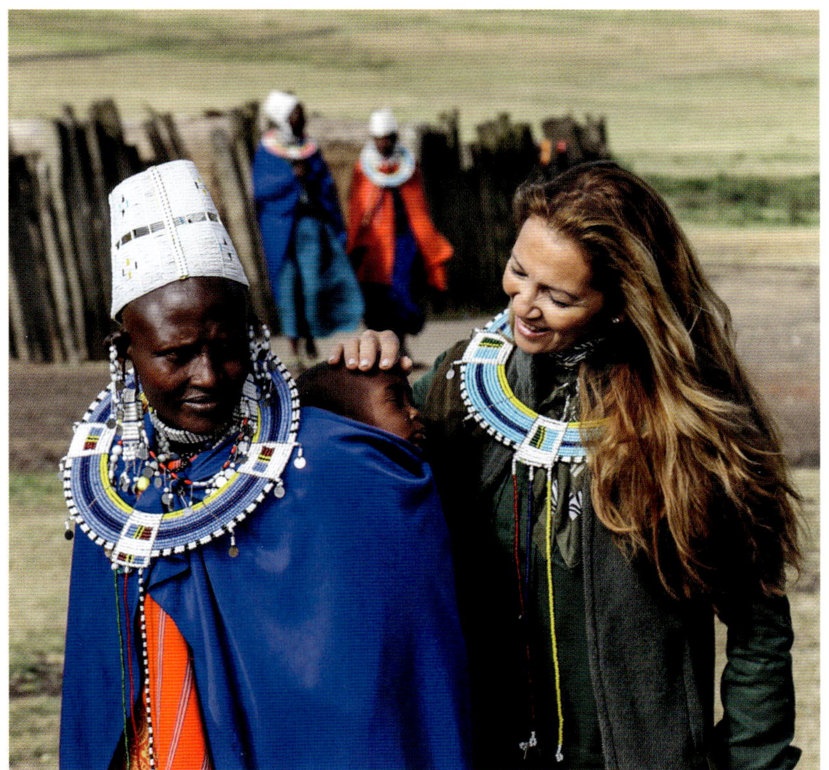

opening pages. These images are testament to the fact that this area of East Africa, home to the Maasai, remains practically intact as this tribe reaffirms, day after day, its vocation to remain a semi-nomadic, warrior people, attached to their rituals and ancestral customs.

The Maasai live to the west of the Rift Valley, in a region spanning Tanzania and Kenya: great plains that are now a national park on the banks of the Mara River. Hunting was permitted in the region until the late 1970s, but for political and conservational reasons was then banned. The Maasai Mara Reserve was created and covered some 1,500 square kilometres, an area roughly the size of Greater London. It was at this time that the safaris began, enabling people to visit and photograph a region renowned for its extraordinary wildlife and unique vegetation. The Maasai are permitted to graze their herds and hunt on the reserve, since they are a people that depend to a large extent on the health and abundance of their animals. On rare occasions, in very specific festivities, they kill livestock for food, including sheep, goats or perhaps an old ox. Their animals, tended by the men of the tribe, provide them with the staples of their diet: milk and blood. They use tanned skins for their clothing and footwear. They are not farmers, given the semi-nomadic life they lead, but they do gather plants that they find while they travel with their livestock.

The status of the tribesmen depends on the number of animals and children they possess. They are permitted to have several wives, who, along with their offspring, help protect and take care of the family livestock. The women of the tribe are responsible for building the family home, as well as the rudimentary palisades, some of them interwoven, whose function is to prevent the animals from escaping the herd, as well as to protect them from predators. Wide shots, showing hills and grasslands dotted with livestock and tribespeople, also offer a glimpse of these semi-nomadic settlements, where the tribe's simple huts stand out among their surroundings.

For these peoples who have maintained their traditions through the ages in the heart of the African savannah, the various ceremonies held within the tribe are important. Among the most frequent are the festive dances they perform at night, by firelight. In the images

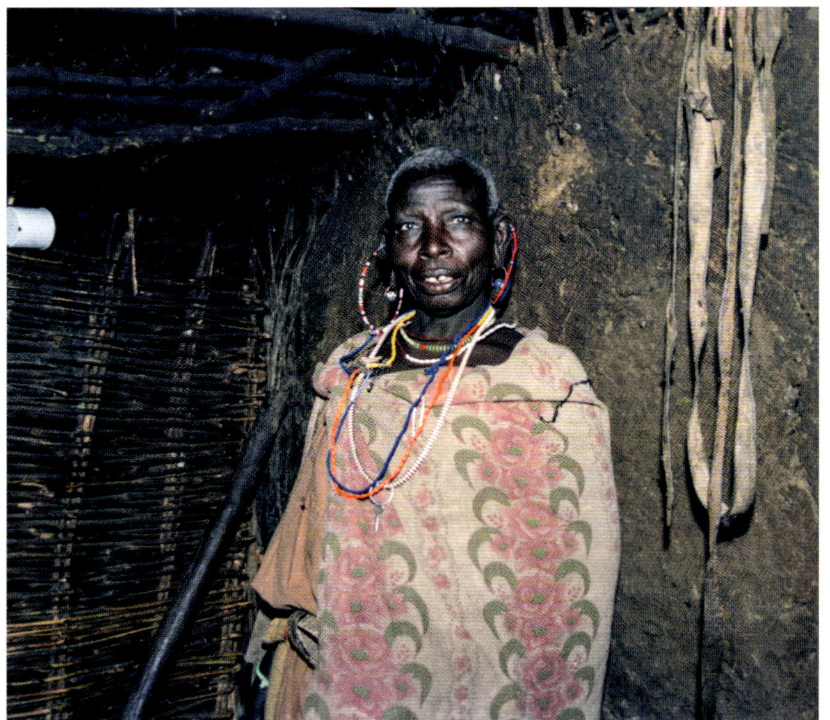

▲ 1987

2017 ▼

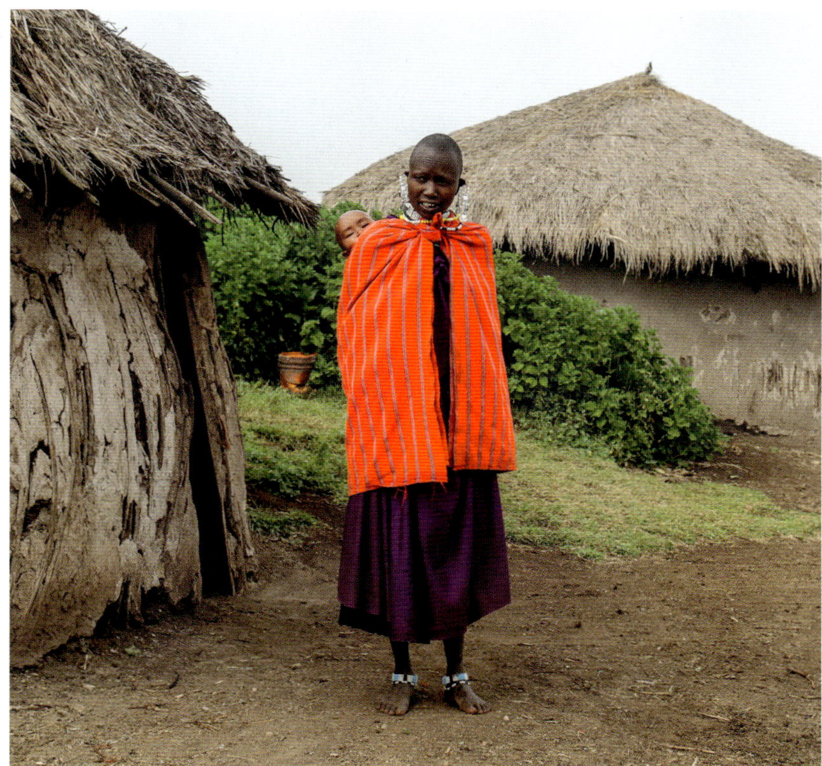

captured brilliantly by the Matinez Thedy, we can appreciate these dances in all their splendour. The women dress in beautiful accessories whose beads accompany the lilting rhythm, while the men dance in a series of vertical leaps, giving the celebration a very unique character.

They often lengthen their ear lobes, the accessories used by the women perhaps the most attractive, as Martínez Thedy's portraits illustrate. These photographs are taken using natural light and with no special tricks or technological accessories. The beautiful features of these people and their colourful dress can be seen in these images, a reddish colour predominating. The loose garments are also a characteristic feature of the tribe. Attractive necklaces and a whole range of accessories for the hair, as well as headdresses, are worn by both men and women.

This part of East Africa, characterised by rolling grasslands, is visited by tourists and locals, mainly during the winter, to admire the great migration of animals that leave the dry plains of Tanzania from June to October in a desperate search for water and greener pastures in the northern region. This circular migration offers an exceptional and unique visual spectacle, because of the large concentration of animals making the journey. Clara Martínez Thedy has captured this phenomenon in a selective way, sometimes showing us large herds on the African plains, sometimes other smaller flocks, as well as close-ups, when she has had permission to approach the animals. These idyllic scenes reveal the animals' habitat and life in the wild.

The depiction of animals goes back to the ancient prehistoric drawings found in caves, some preserved to this day. In art, the animal world has always been a source of inspiration for artists, who have portrayed it alternately with themes of power relations, fear, submission and admiration. Photographers, since the dawn of cameras, have also depicted animals, whether for scientific reasons, as hunting trophies, or capturing the way in which they relate to humans in the everyday life of a household.

In these last thirty years, the technology has changed more rapidly than in previous periods. The dramatic change in photography from the analogue to the digital system is the best example of how new technology has revolutionised the way in which we communicate, and how we share all kinds of information. The difficulties that photographers experienced for years, with storing, protecting and transporting negative and reversal films in order to prevent the latent image from being exposed, have now been completely overcome by the digital camera, which enables the user to store a huge quantity of photographs on easily transportable devices and take better shots in low-light conditions. All of this, along with advances in optics, have resulted in some stunning close-ups of animals in their natural habitat, where each day is a fierce battle for survival.

Clara Martínez Thedy's strong interest in animals is evident in the way she chooses to photograph them: with dignity, respect and great subtlety. Very few shots capture hunting scenes or predators in action, and this is precisely what the title of the book, *Africa Serena,* refers to, because the author wants to show us a peaceful, gentle Africa – an Africa that is in stark contrast with the violent one that is so often portrayed: silhouettes of giraffes in front of magical sunsets, while others rest under leafy trees; zebras, antelopes and elephants, whose forms are repeated in patterns that create exquisite compositional rhythms; lions, wildebeest, rhinoceroses and leopards under a burning sun at its zenith, accompanied by beautiful birds to create a sublime scene in which the dense vegetation and animals coexist harmoniously; hippopotamuses frolicking in the river, while crocodiles lie in wait ready to catch their prey.

This captivating book features a stunning hand-picked selection of images of the ancient civilisation of the Maasai, and also captures the innocence and vulnerability of innumerable wild animals in an environment in which only the strongest survive, in the constant struggle between life and death. It is also an impassioned call to protect the many endangered species, and to raise awareness of the never-ending conflict between the natural world and the expansion of urban areas in the pursuit of human progress. The photographer's sensitive eye proposes a balance of power between humans and animals in this lost paradise where time seems to have stood still, the Eden to which she gained access on her return journey.

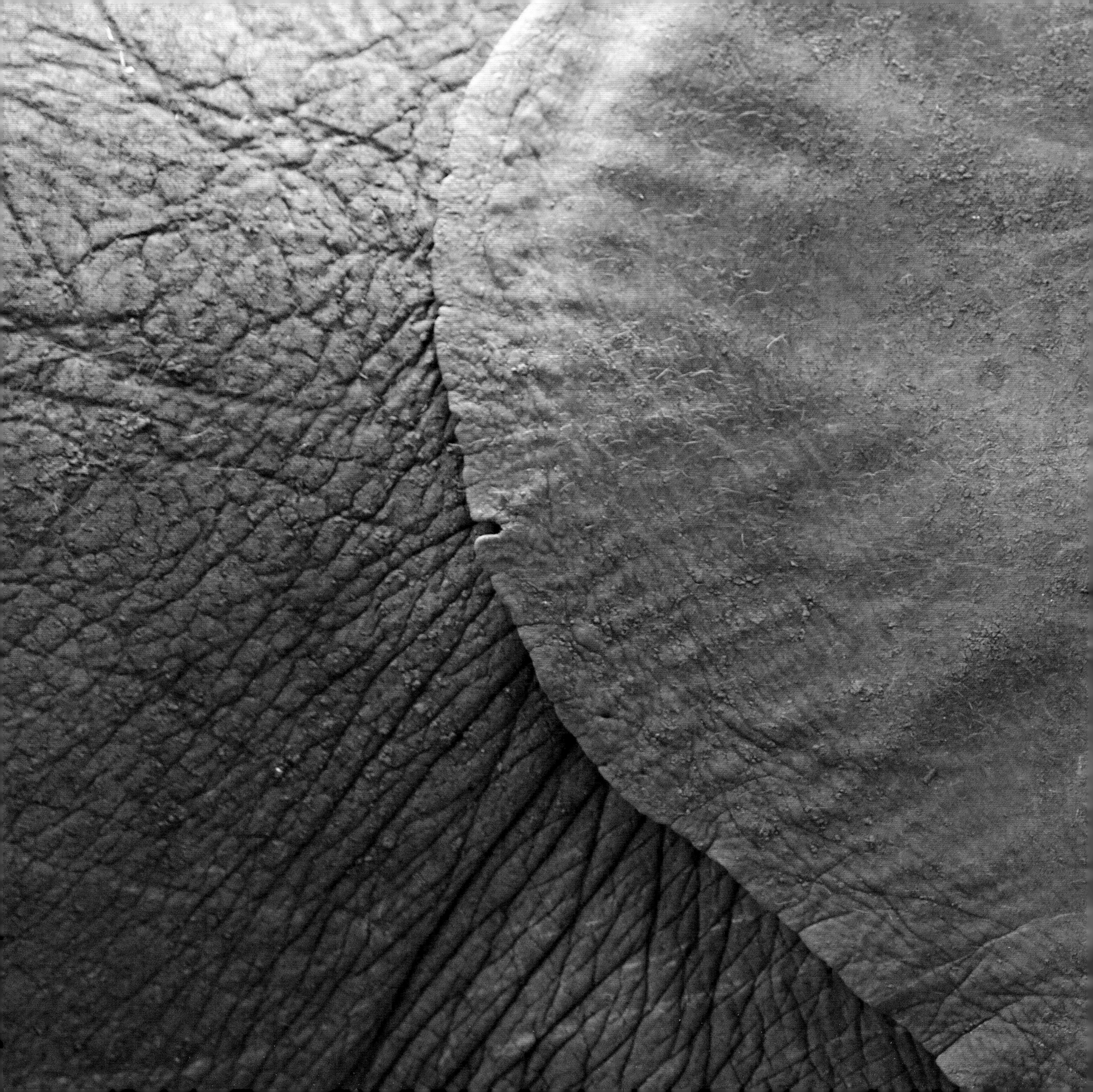

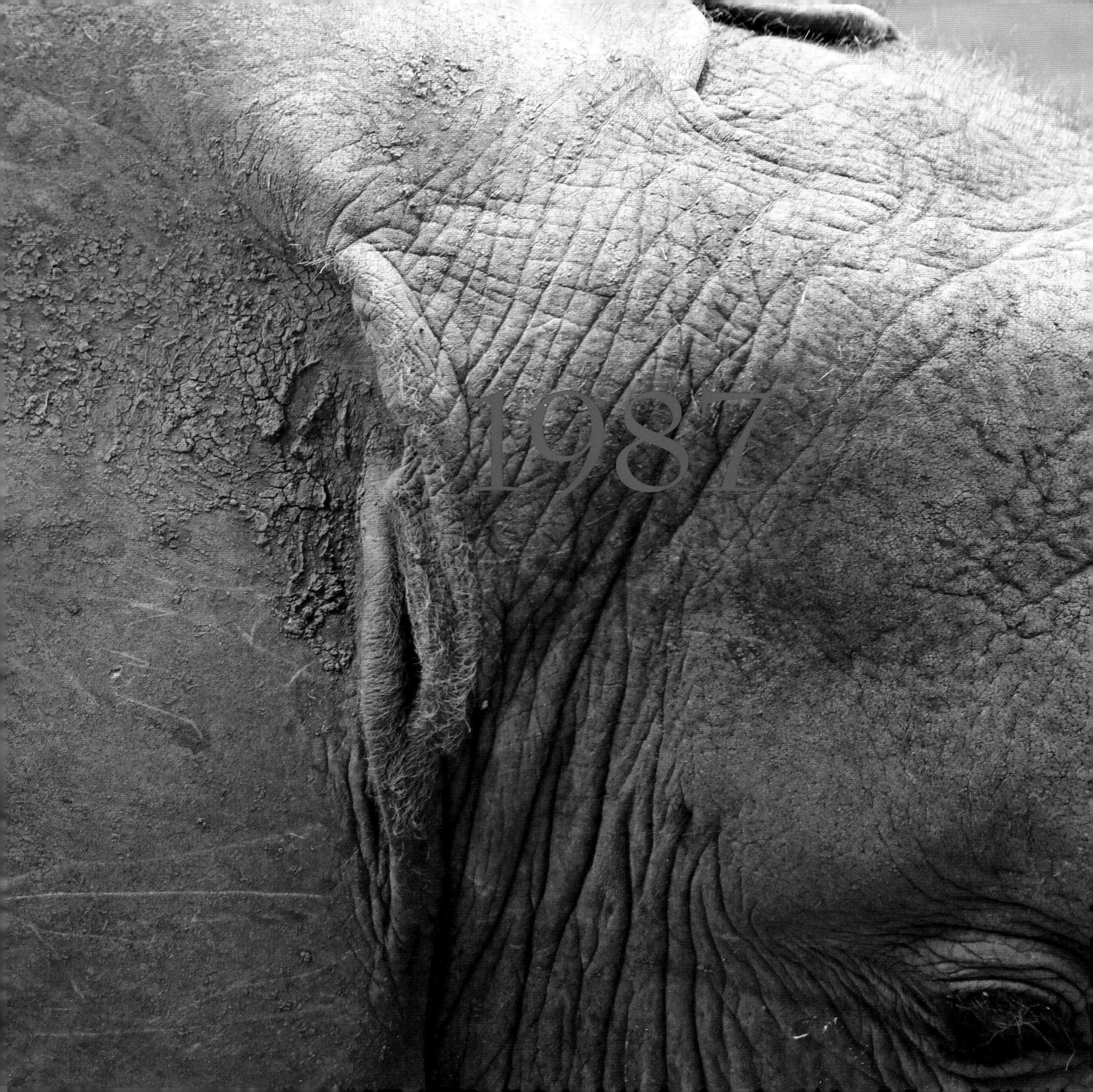
1987

# AFRICA
# Light and Shadow

MARIANNE DE TOLENTINO • OCTOBER 1987

*Director of the National Gallery of Fine Arts, Dominican Republic*

A tribal elder explained the essence of Africa to a young researcher in these terms: 'If you want to know who I am, if you want me to show you what I know, give up what you are for a moment and forget what you know.' When Clara Martínez Thedy, in the company of some members of her family, embarked on her journey to Africa, she followed a route through Kenya and, in her own words, settled in a "rustic camp". A new world was revealed to her and for a moment she stopped being who she was … but she was unable to completely forget everything she knew, because it was that knowledge that enabled her to capture the images that we can see today. Clara's moving story and her photographs make it clear that, during that unforgettable stay in Africa, she identified with concepts, values and dimensions that were different. She wanted to transmit the strength and integrity of the people, of the animals, of nature; of a place where the sun goes down with more lyricism and drama than in any other continent. This is palpable in the incandescent images that seem to fulfil one of the African people's aspirations: to stop time and reign over the night.

A young photographer, Martínez Thedy's work contains an understandable element of personal development and memories transported with enthusiasm from the Maasailand region to the Dominican Republic. However, it is neither the entertainment and pleasure, nor the demonstration of growing skill with the camera, that play the leading role here. What stands out most about the photographer's work is her wonder at some incredible sights and discoveries, at the originality and beauty of the natural environment that surrounded her for fifteen days.

As expected, themes gradually arose in response to the successive scenarios provided by East Africa, a region that scientists consider the global centre for research on life, the environment and the origin of man. Human beings, unsurprisingly, also attracted her. The Maasai tribe, with their noble and elegant typology, had a big impact on her due to the colours – dominated by red – of their clothing. The photographer's portraits, anonymous to us, are physical and psychological studies that show us various attitudes, exhibiting varying degrees of trust in the strange tourists … They are also an opportunity to admire the splendid body ornaments – chokers, necklaces, pectorals, giant earrings – which are an essential part of the traditional dress and local rituals.

As far as the Maasai themselves allowed her, Clara Martínez Thedy endeavoured to offer a testimony, an ethnographic and anthropological document, which manages, stealthily, to reveal the simple and yet peculiar life of the tribe. We can observe the importance of motherhood, the primary function of women across Africa. One repeated, disturbing detail arouses an unpleasant feeling: the constant presence of flies which delight in the skin of the children's faces. The flies – reminding us of the terrible plague of the tsetse flies – are indicative of the surrounding conditions and symbols of the many deficiencies in hygiene and health.

The photographs illustrate the exceptionally pure preservation of tradition, of the way of life and cultural identity of a pastoral group oblivious to foreign influences. The livestock, for its milk and blood – its meat is rarely eaten – is the cornerstone of the Maasai economy

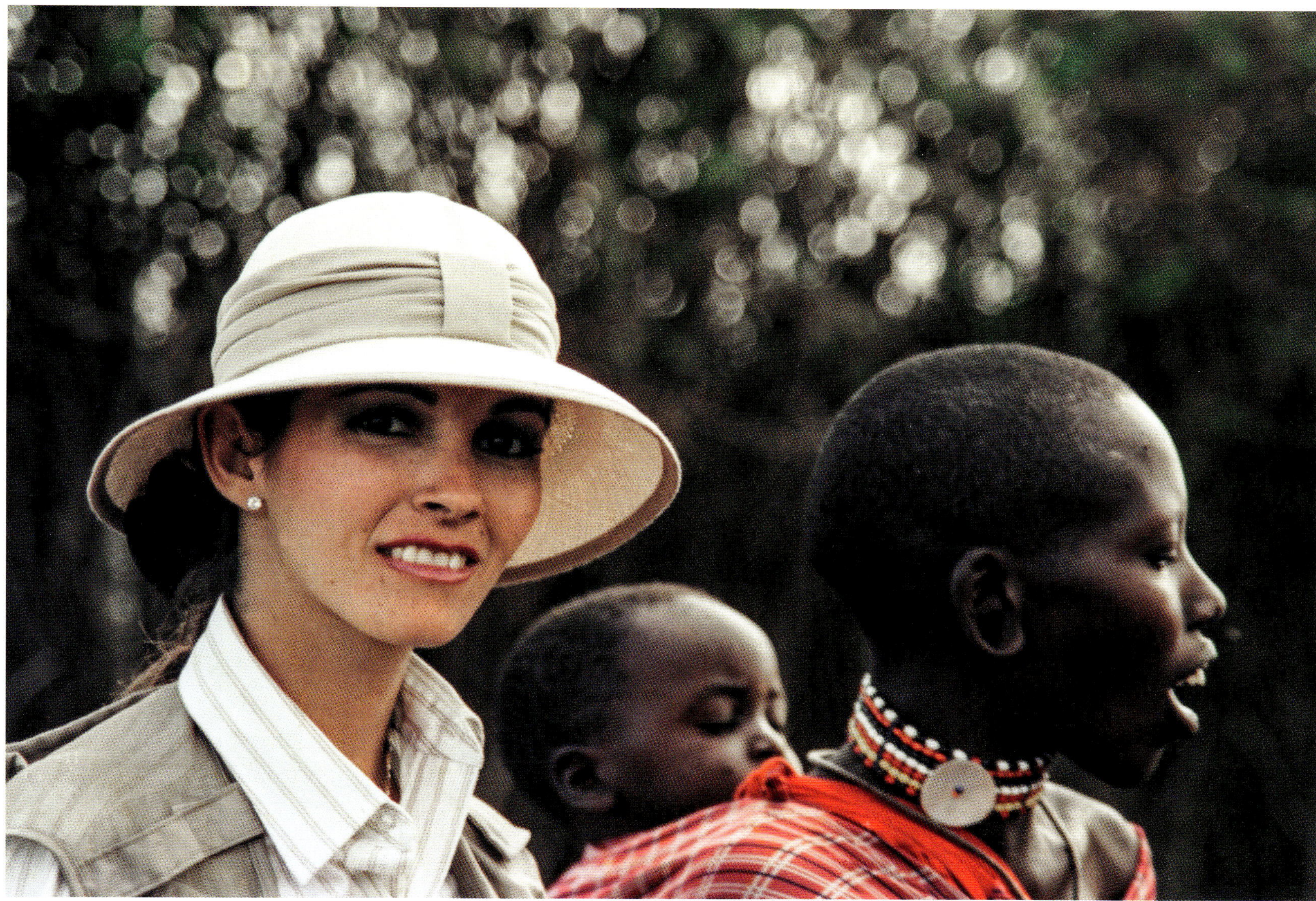

and their basic food source. However, in images shot with good timing and an interesting composition, we are also shown the wildlife of a national reserve that is seeking to protect species that are in danger of extinction. The photography sends a message of ecological reflection. Clara gives expression to the abundance of animal resources, their richness and variety, with an eye that has managed to capture both the cruel sights – wild beasts feasting – and the poetry and tenderness of the heron on the elephant's back. Lions, elephants, buffalo, giraffes, zebras, antelopes, gazelles, monkeys, rhinoceroses, birds of prey …

and herons 'parade' in herds, pairs or as solitary specimens. It becomes clear that there is a battle for survival, fought by these animals under threat of extermination by man. And naturally, Clara Martínez Thedy has photographed the physical environment of Kenya: its mighty geography of savannahs, highlands and river basins, under an endless, clear blue sky. The landscapes show the topography with a mixture of uniformity and definition. In addition to her technical achievements and aesthetic concerns, Clara Martínez Thedy's photographs also fulfil the triple function of reportage, documentation and souvenir.

# AFRICA
## *Light and Shadow*

CLARA MARTINEZ THEDY • OCTOBER 1987

*Fantasy of a land that came true,*
*since I was a child I dreamed of you*
*asleep and awake*
*through a dim, hazy veil;*
*lions and tribes*
*stirred my curiosity*
*until one day I suddenly found myself*
*in the middle of your immensity.*

*Africa, mysterious, colourful*
*alien, vast,*
*enigmatic,*
*superstitious,*
*hot.*

*Your beating jungle,*
*the roar of lions,*
*the flutter of birds,*
*the dazzling drums;*
*all within an immense fauna*
*and a grand spectacle of flora.*

*With my camera I captured*
*something of your extraordinary aura*
*so that those who cannot reach you*
*may get to know you*
*and I shall stay …*
*with nostalgia and hope*
*that one day I will return.*

Translated from the Spanish.

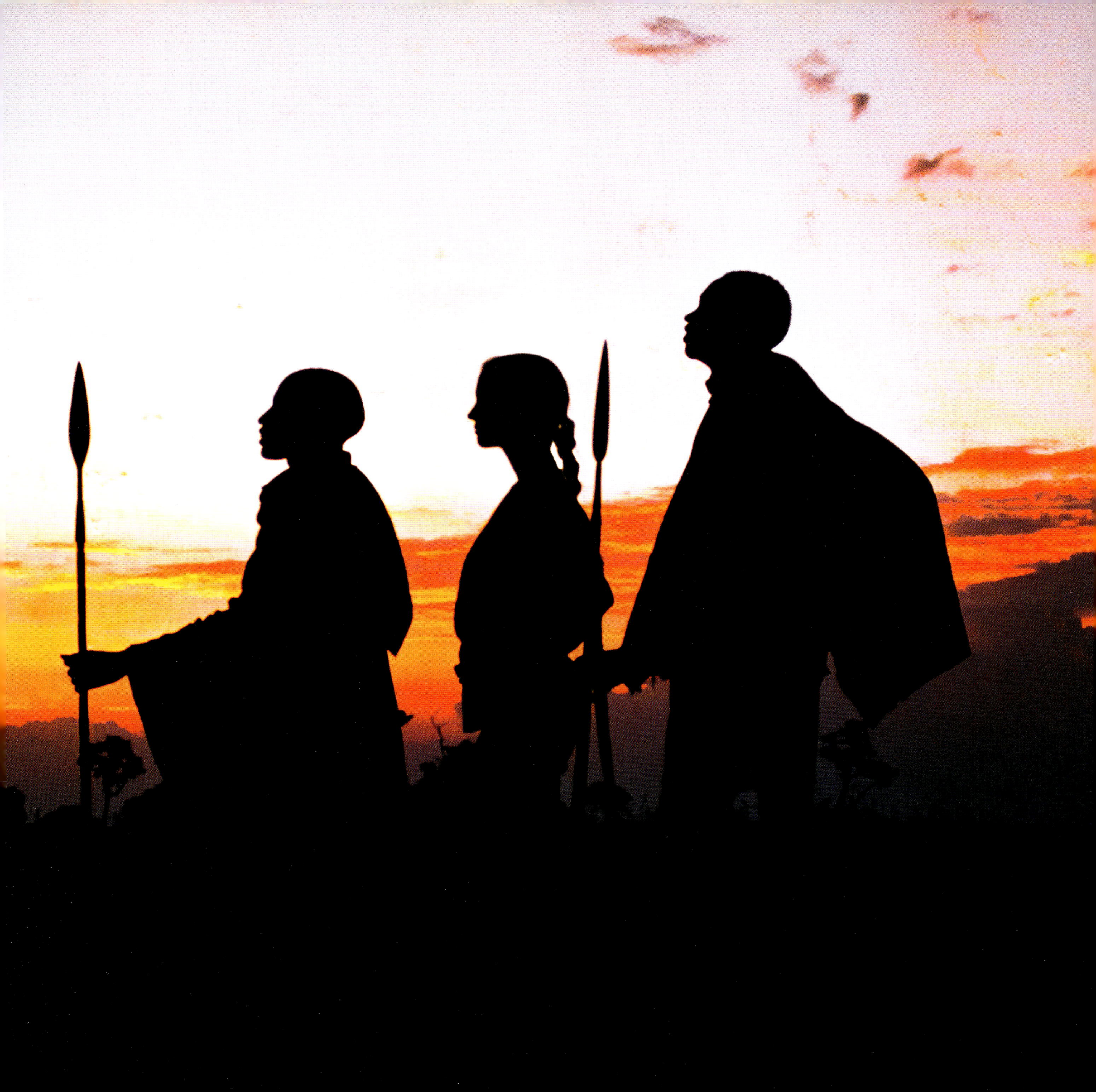

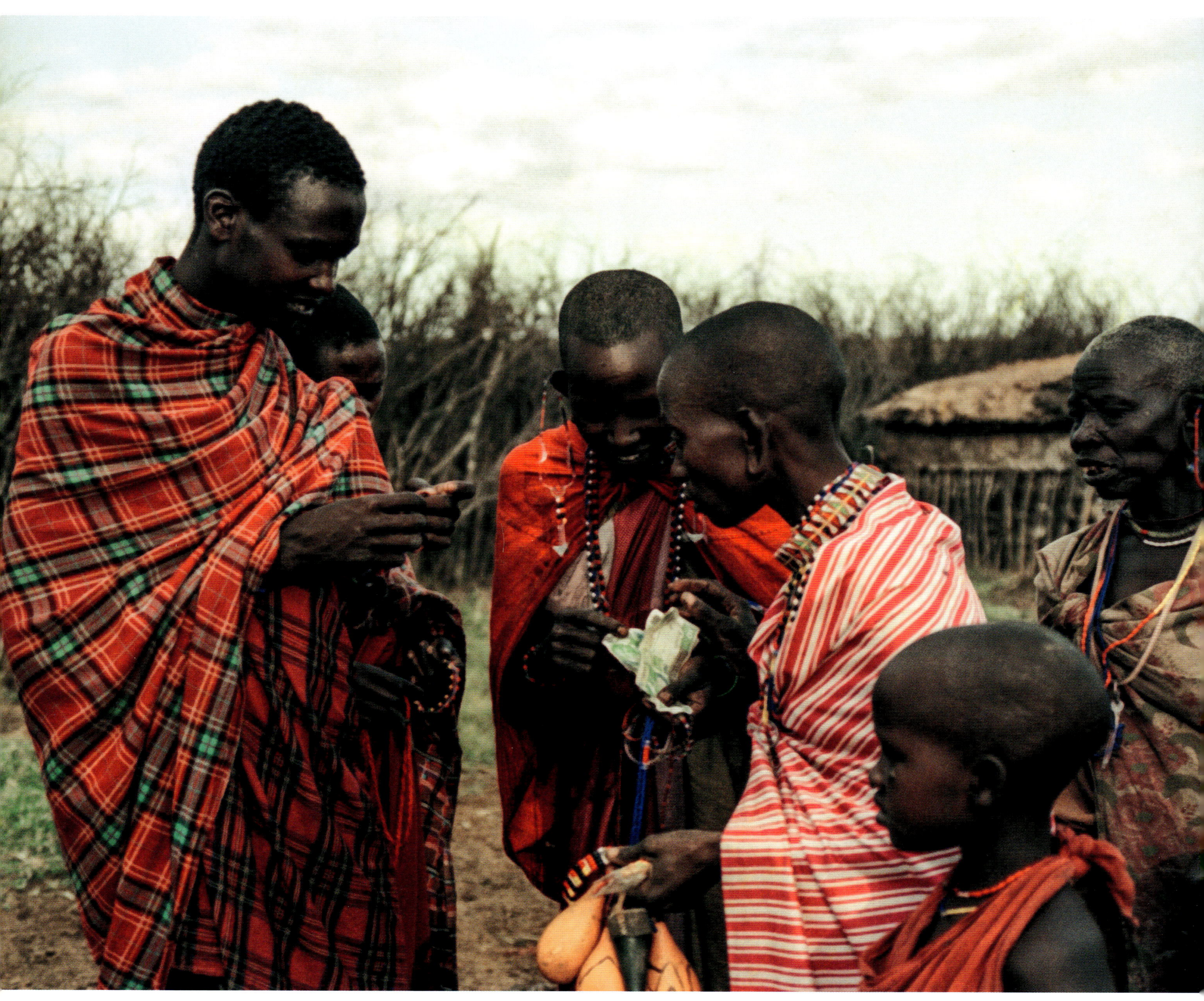

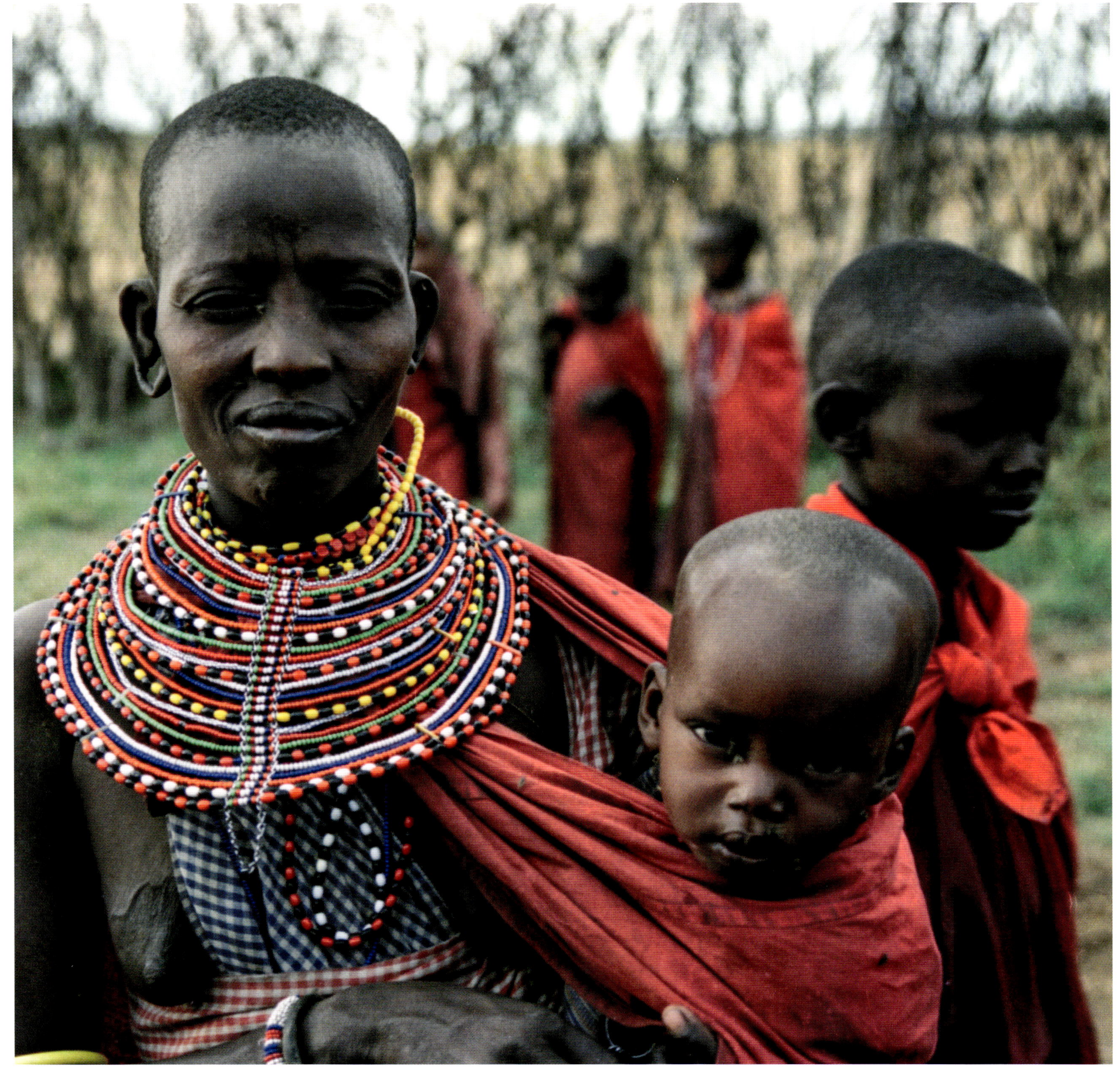

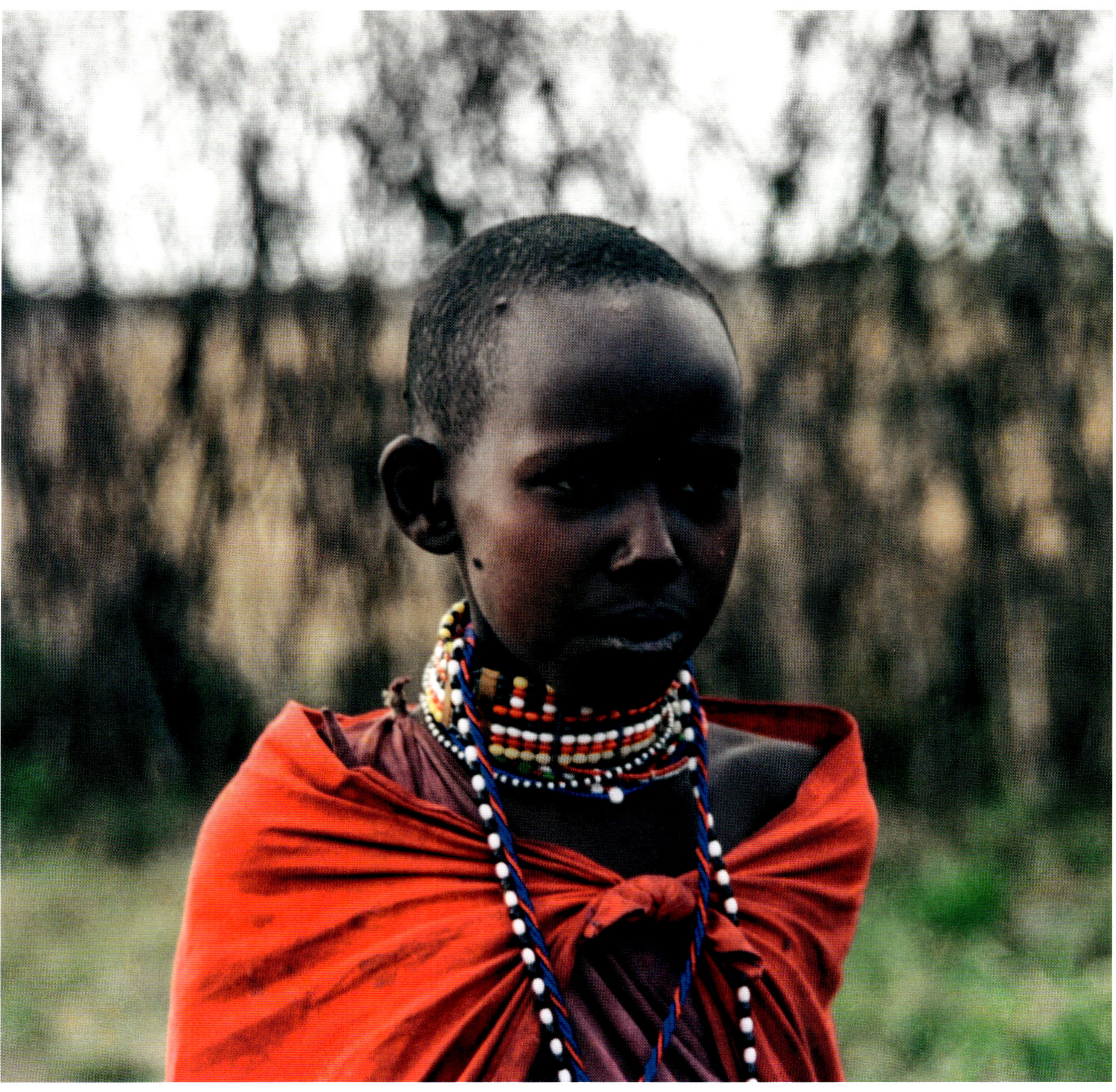

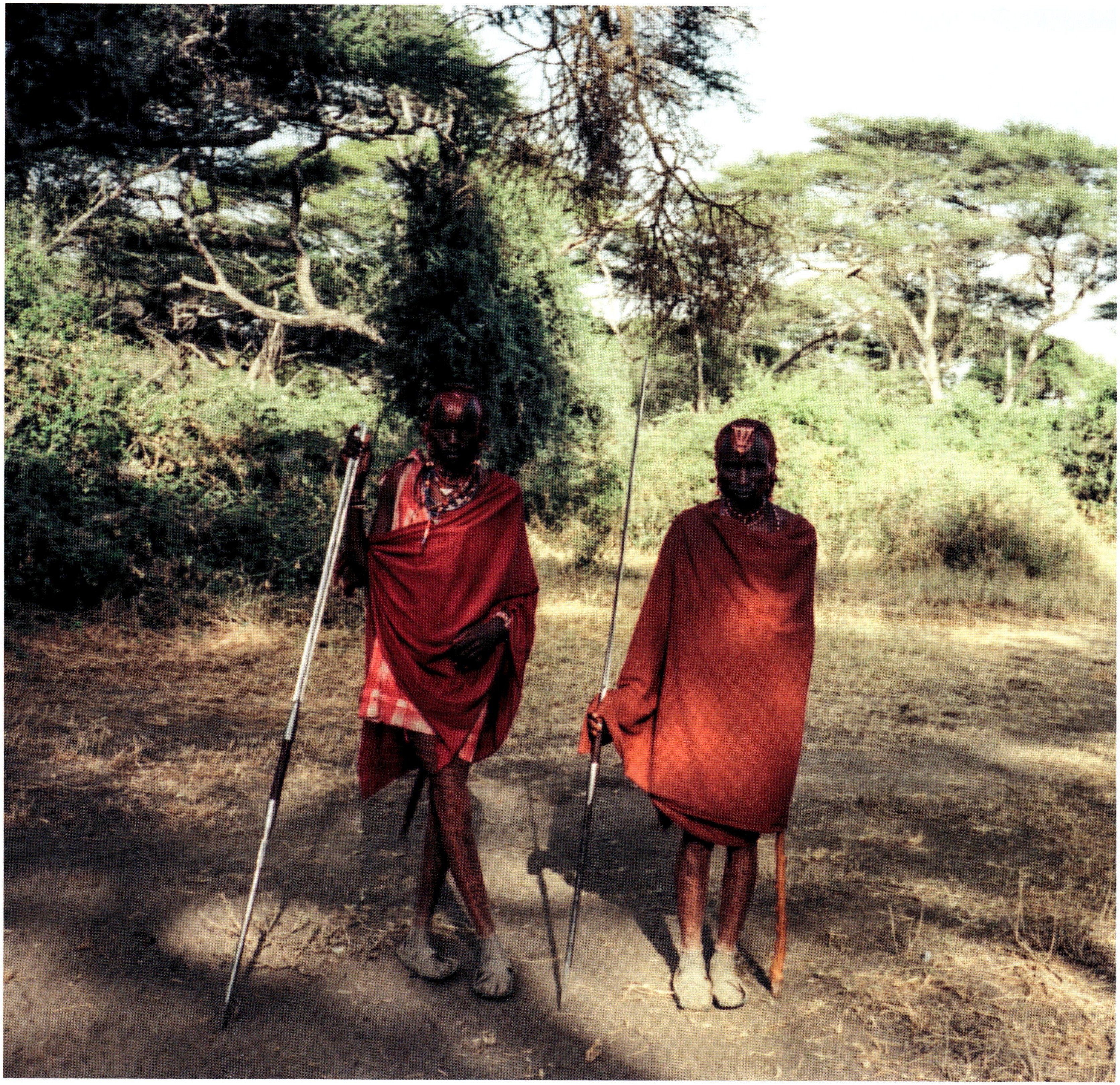

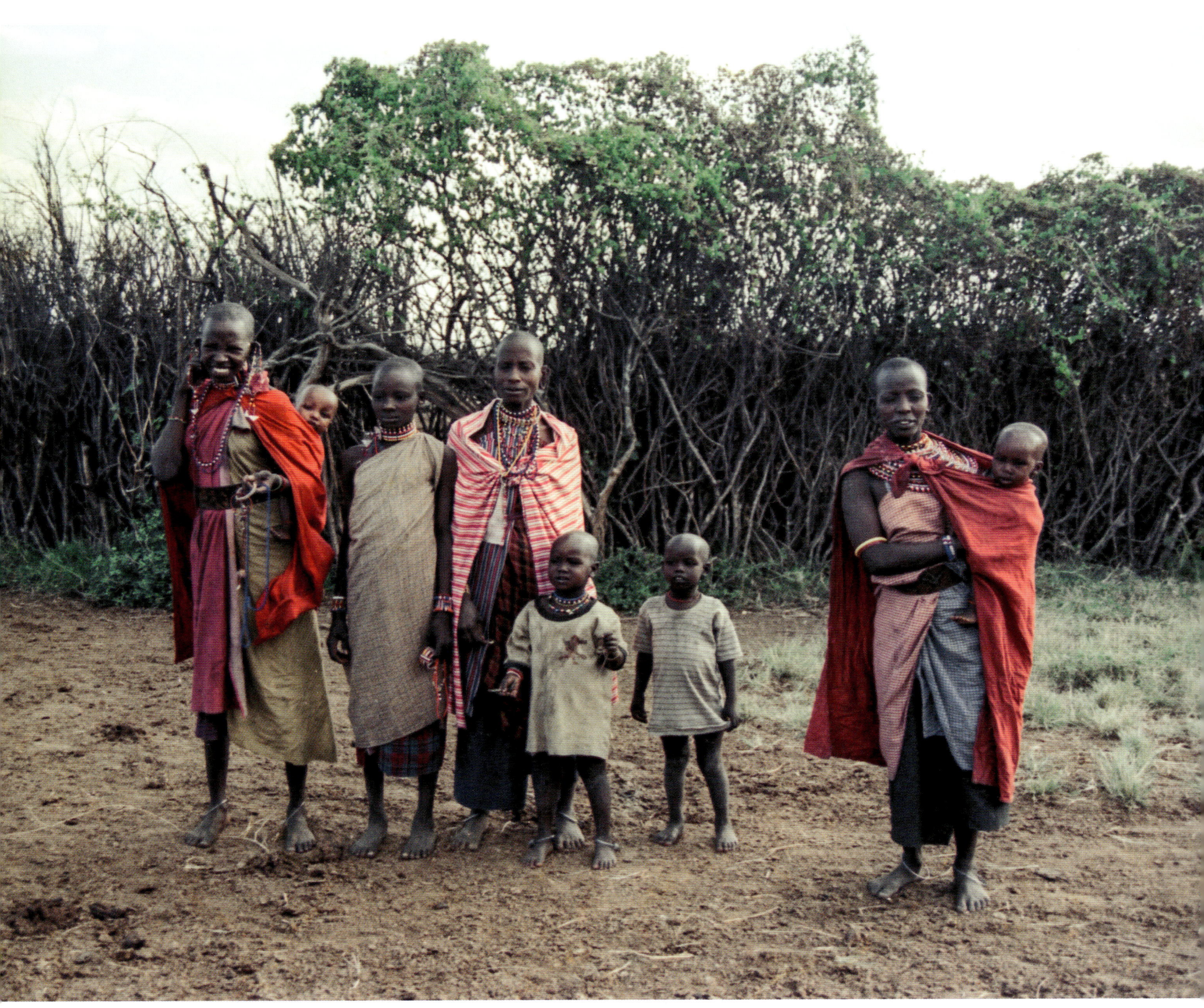

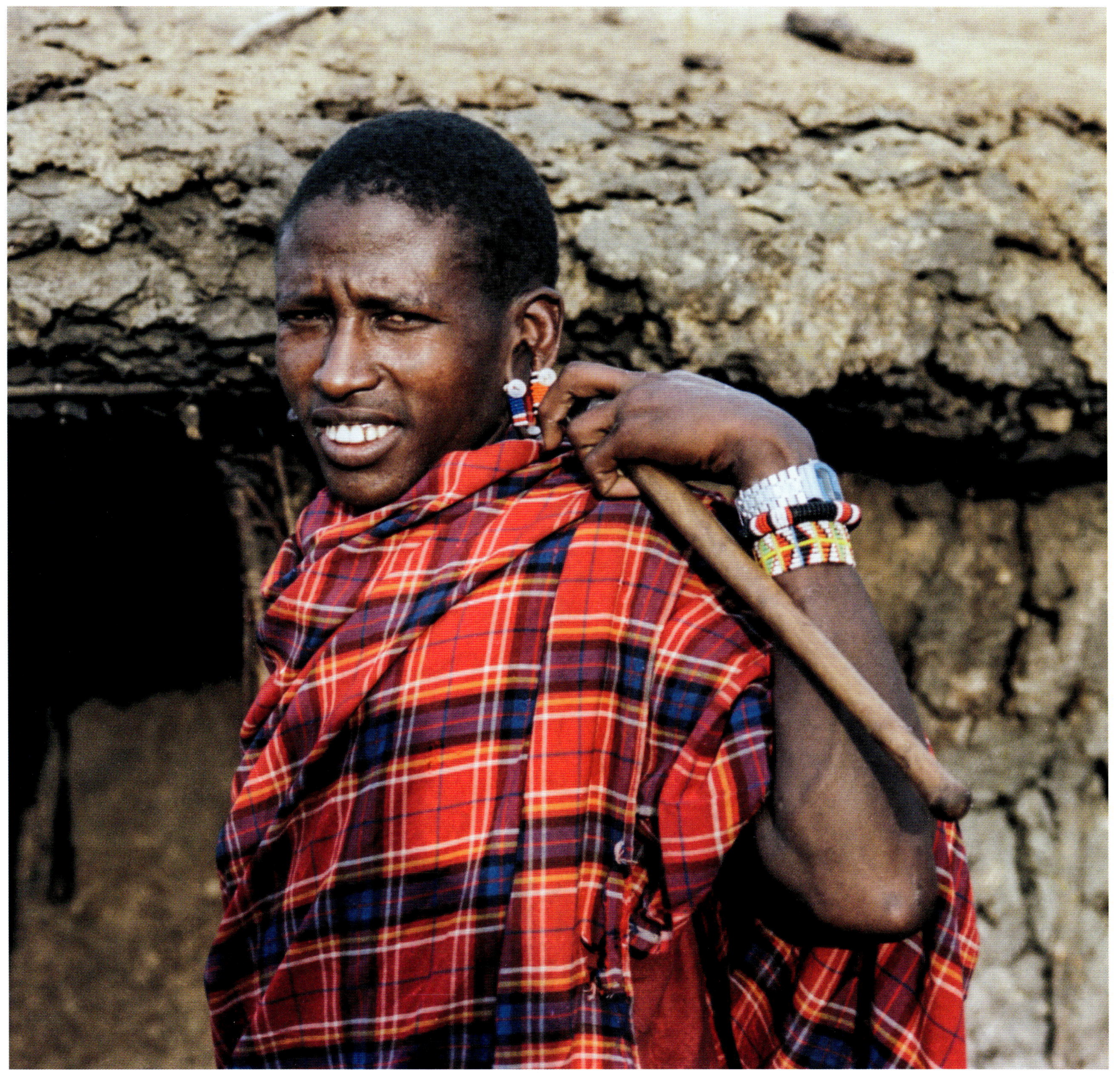

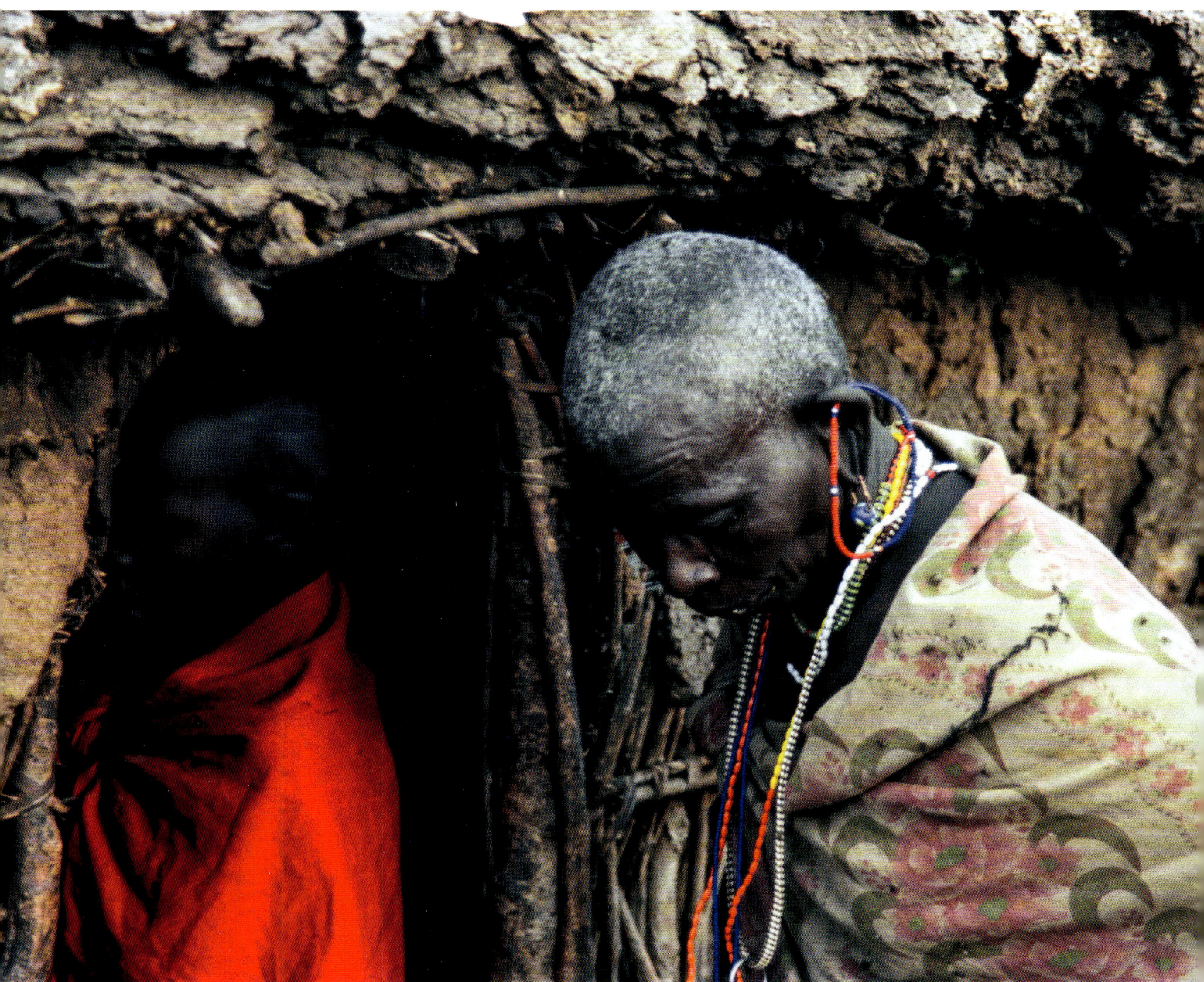

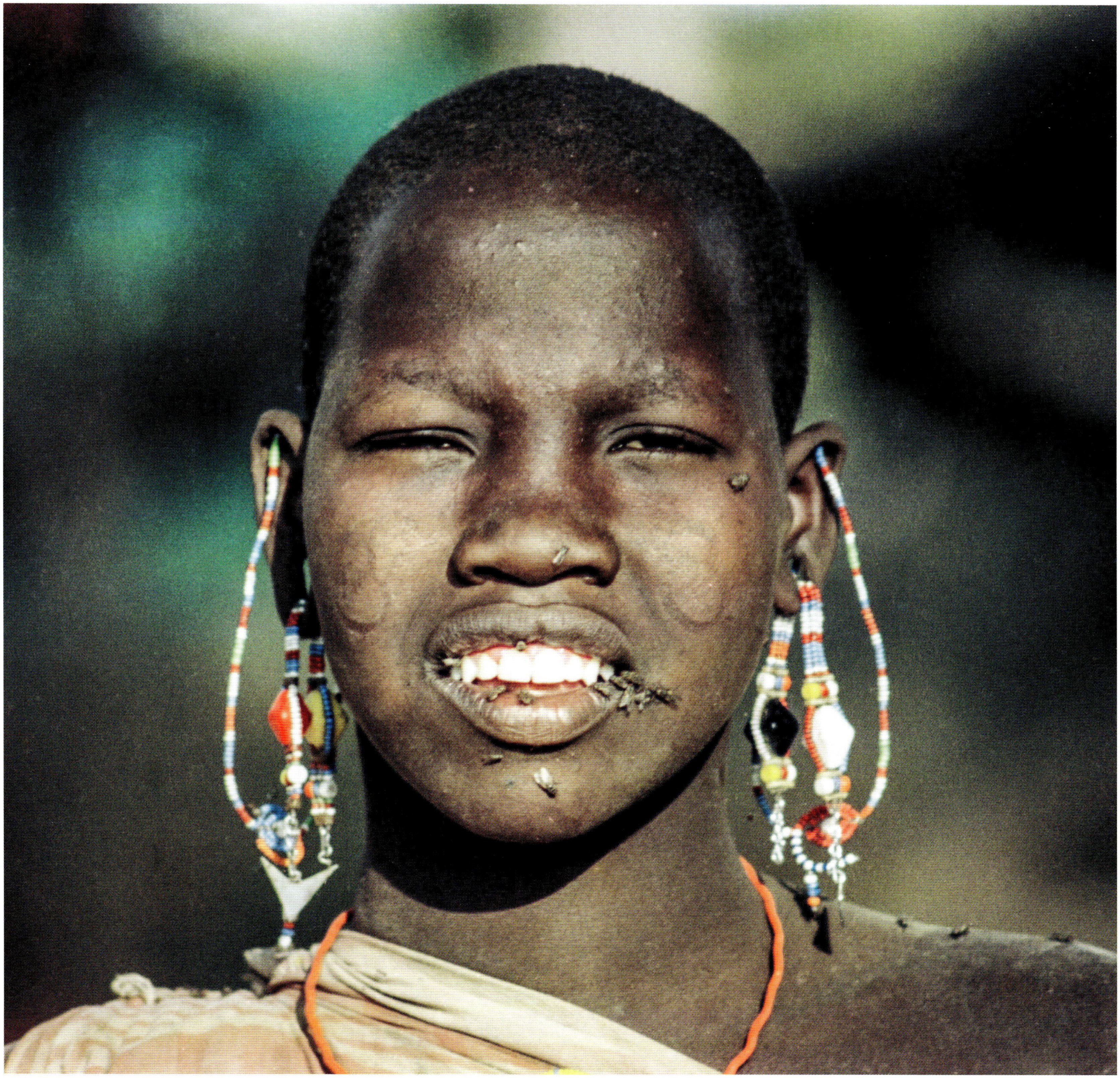

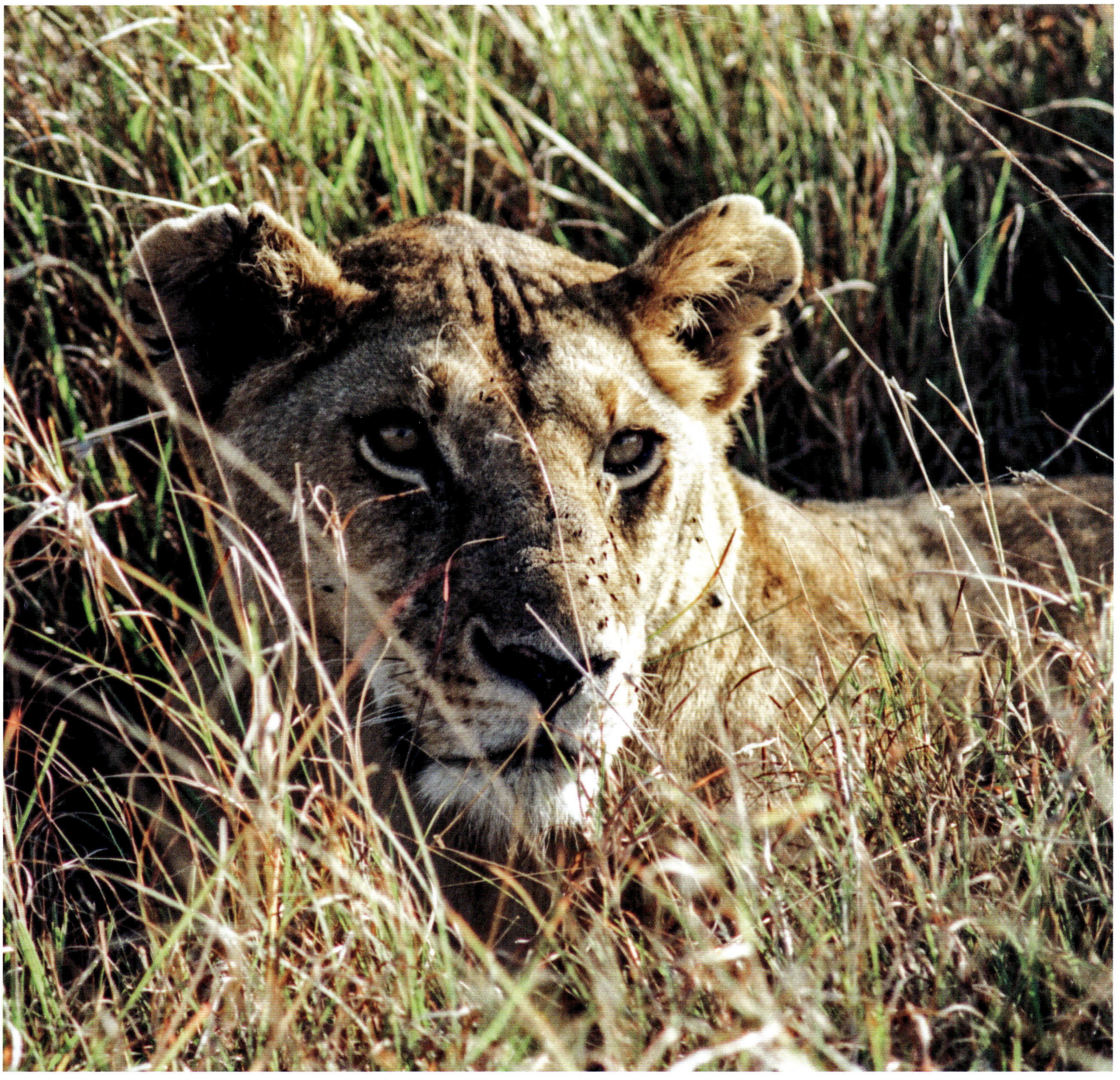

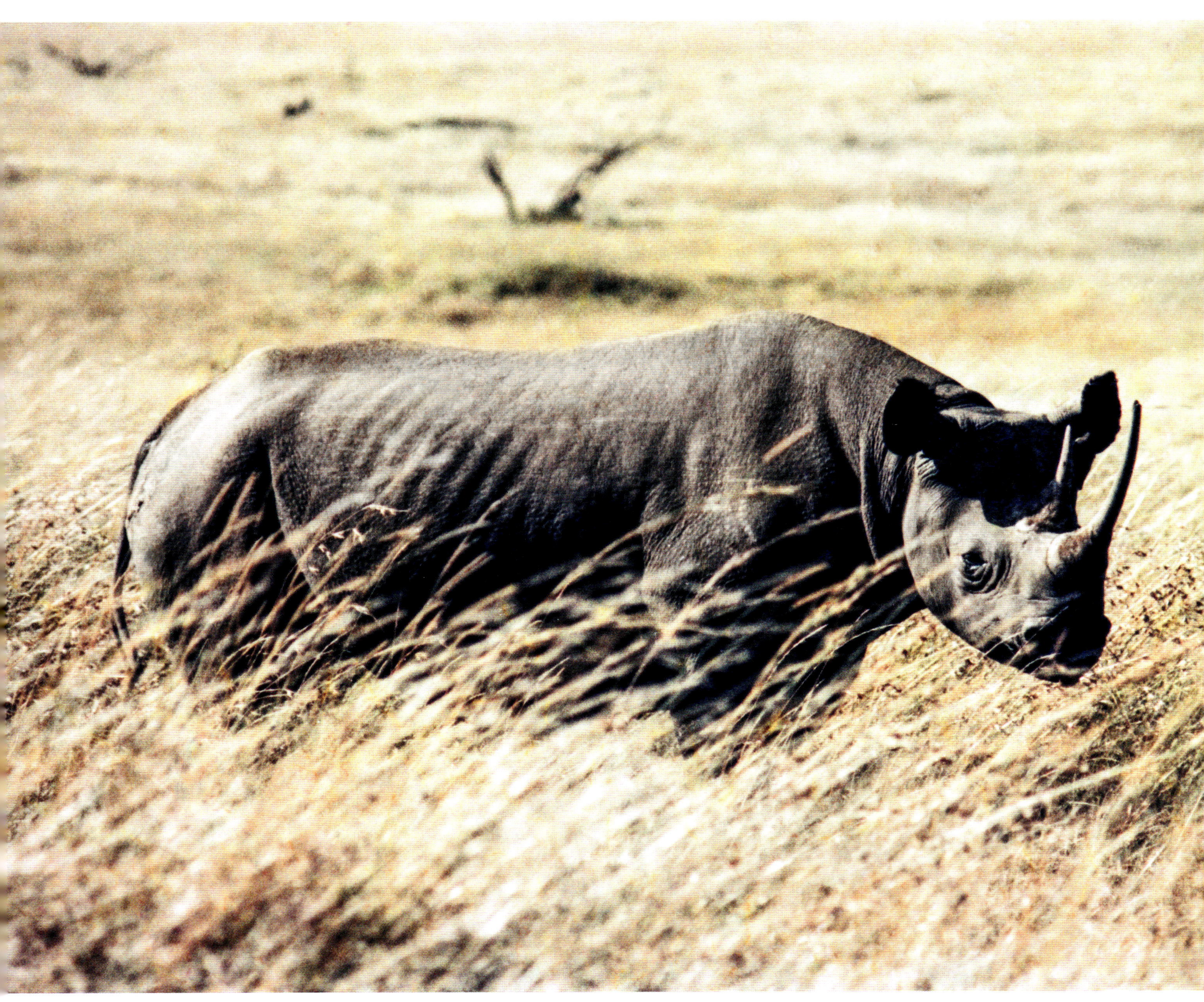

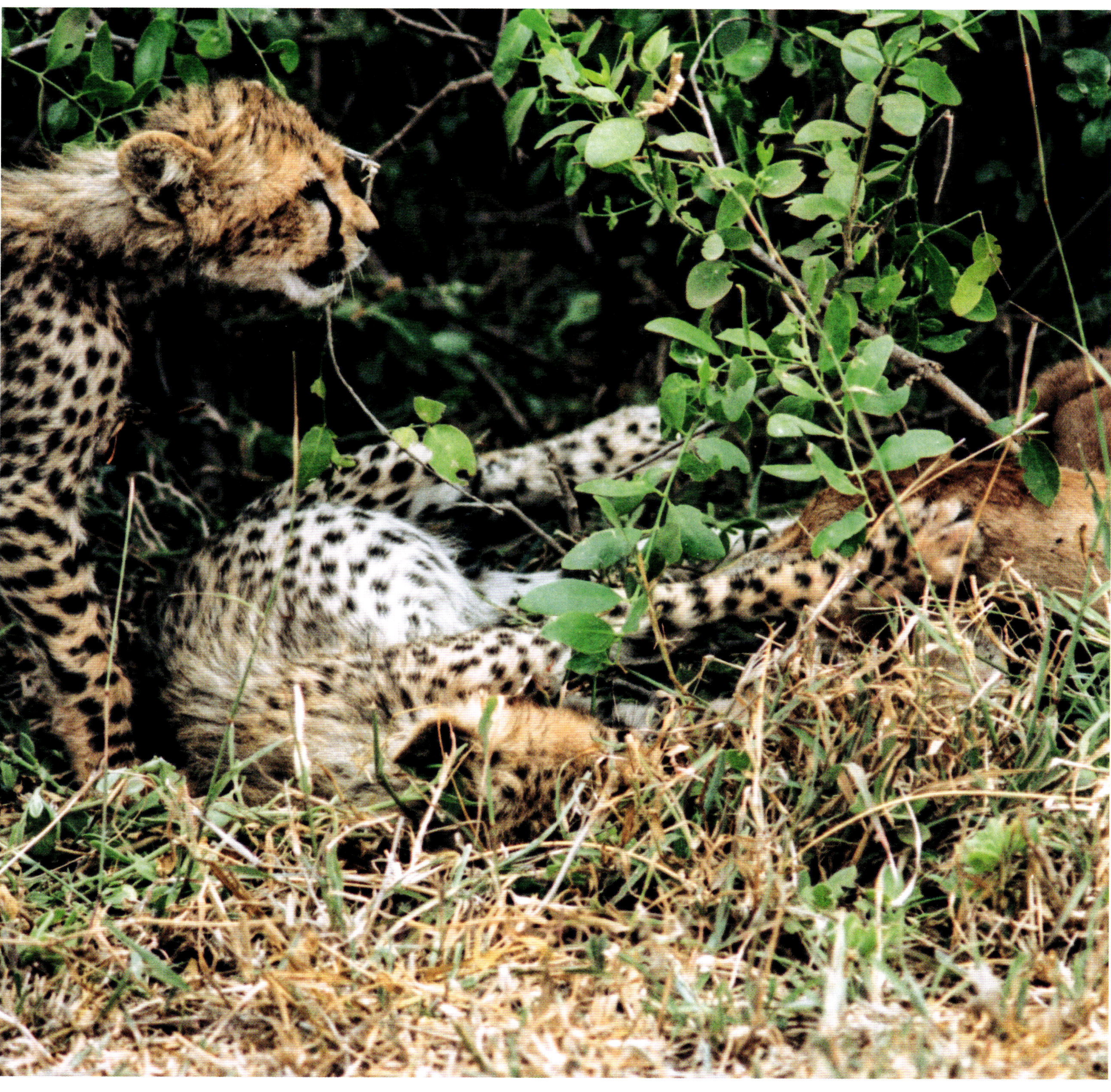

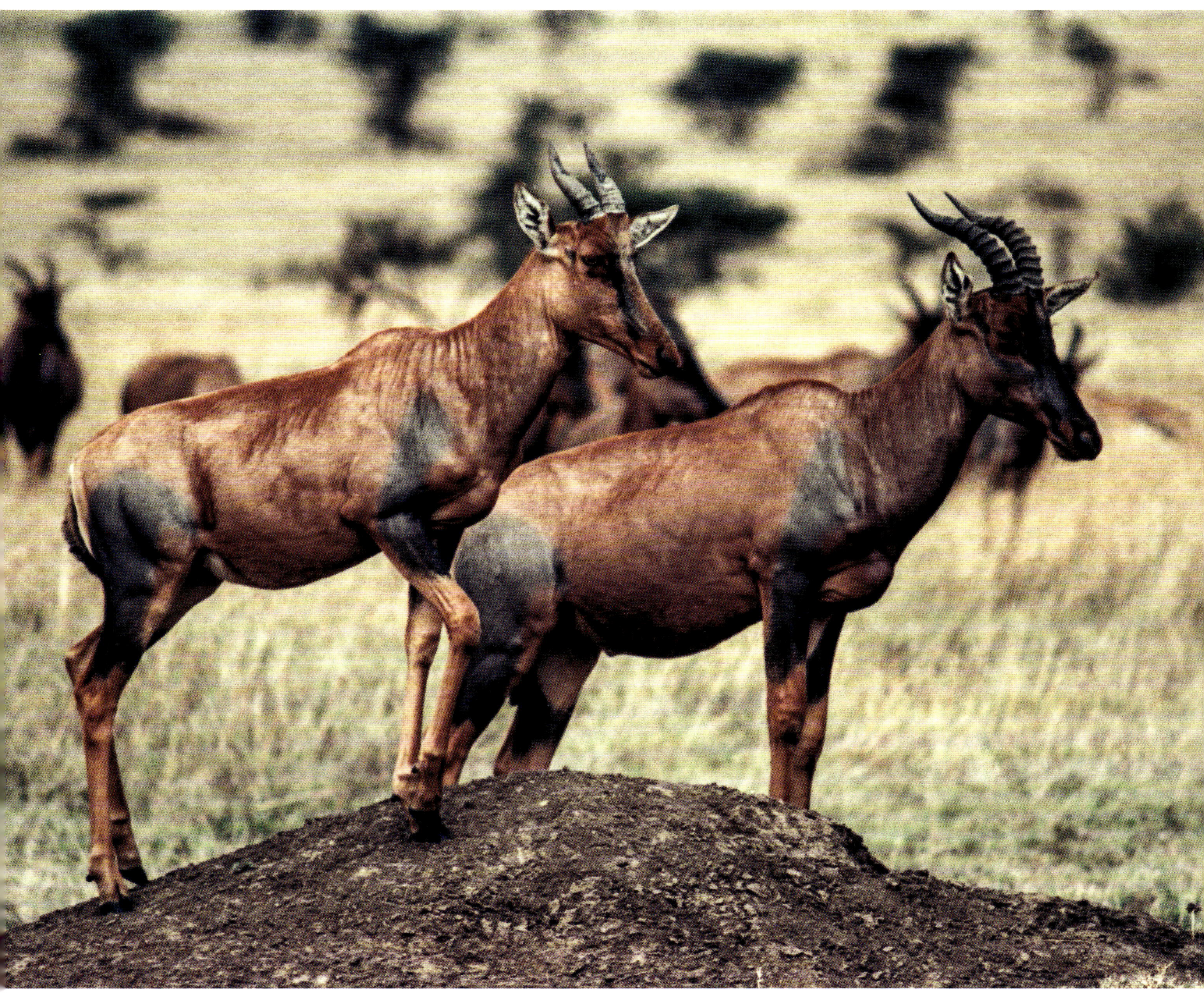

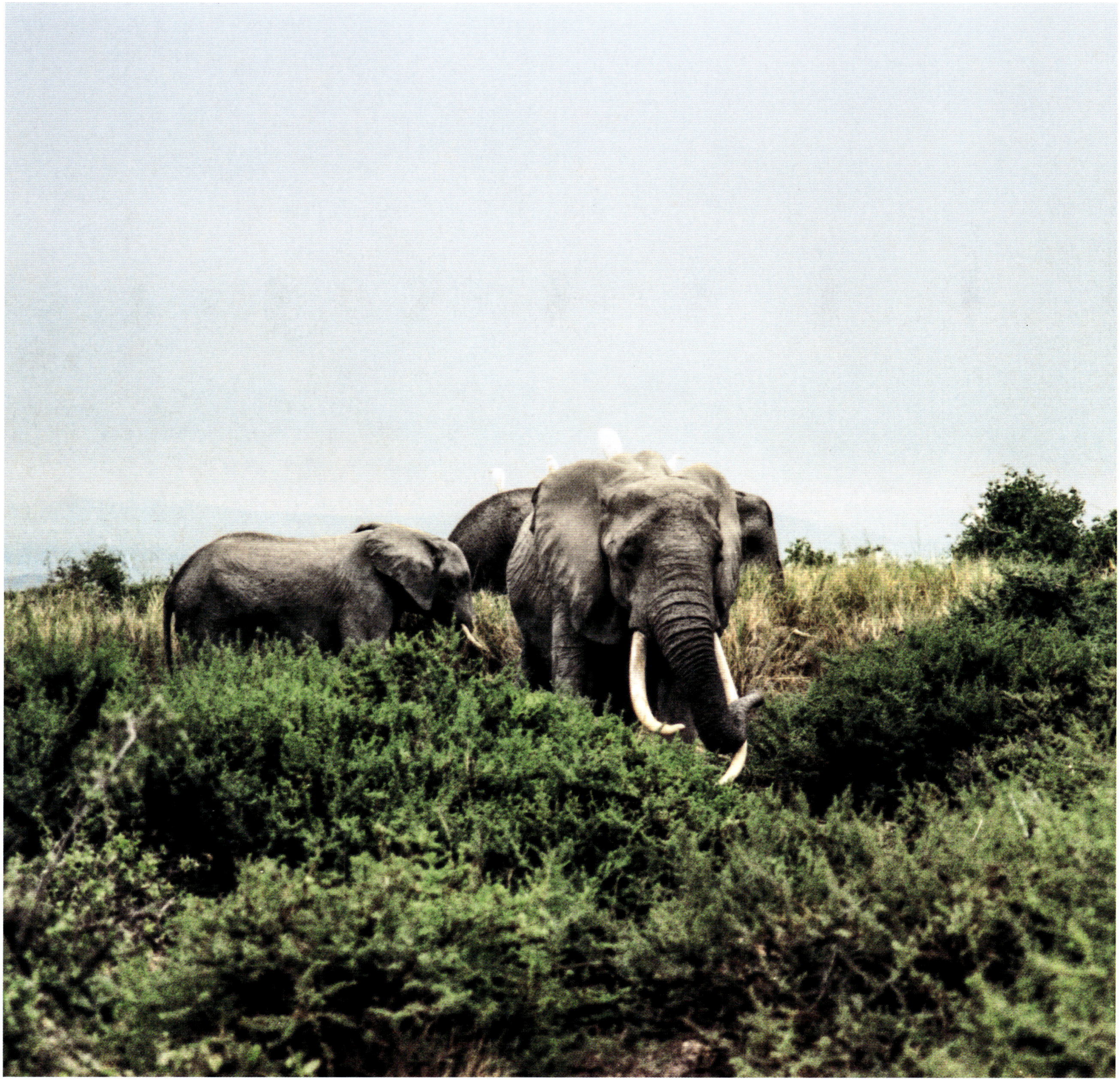

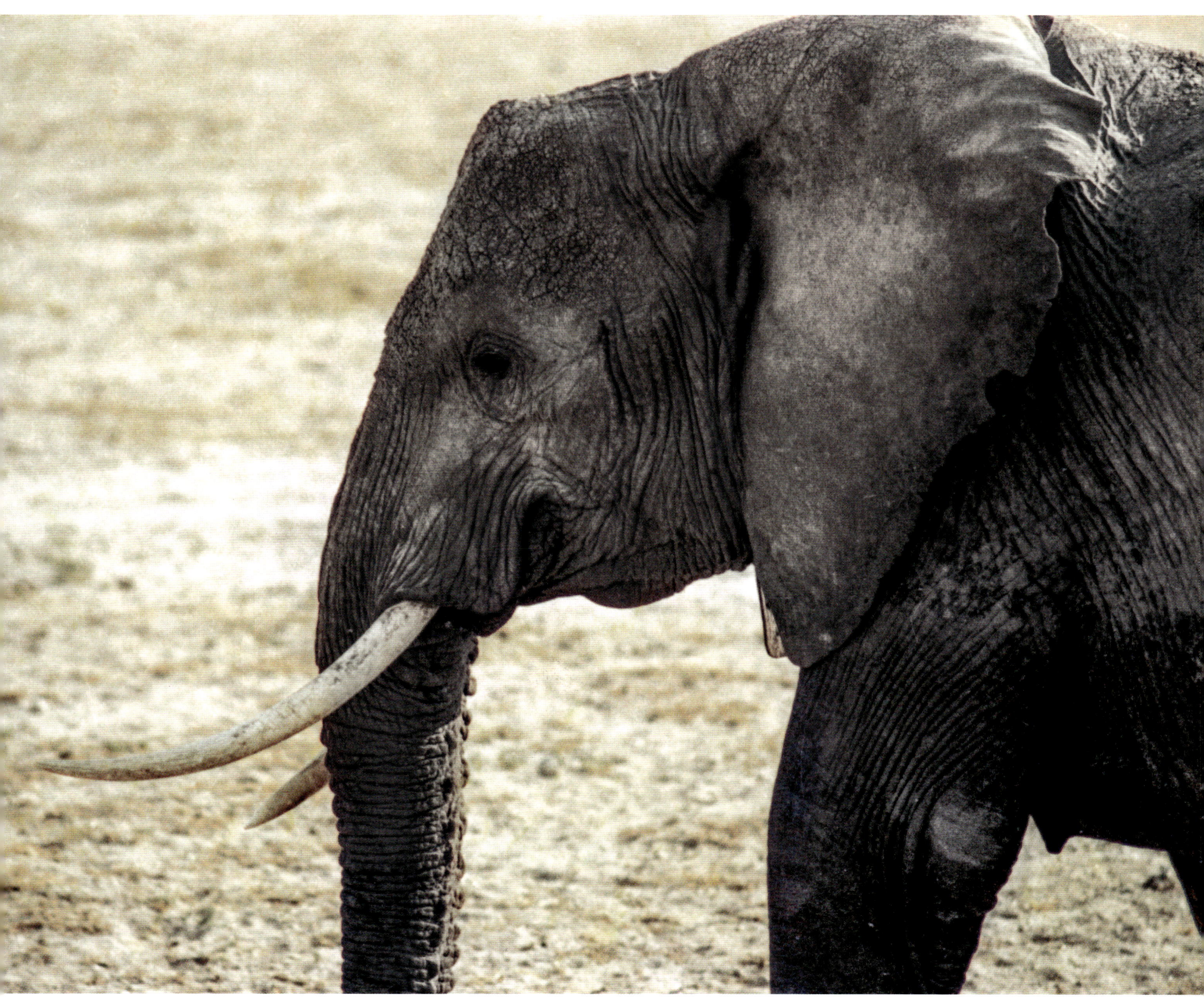

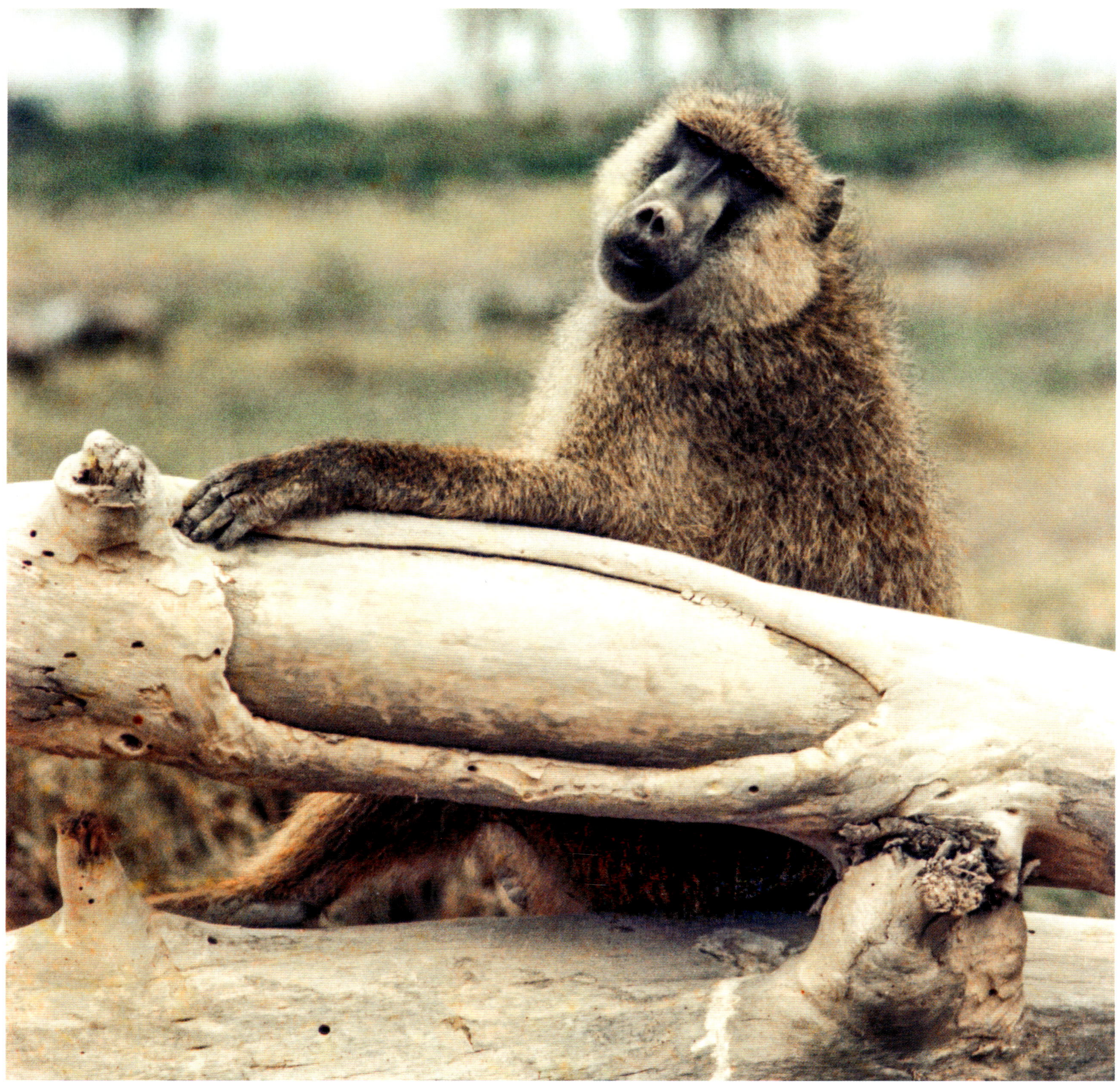

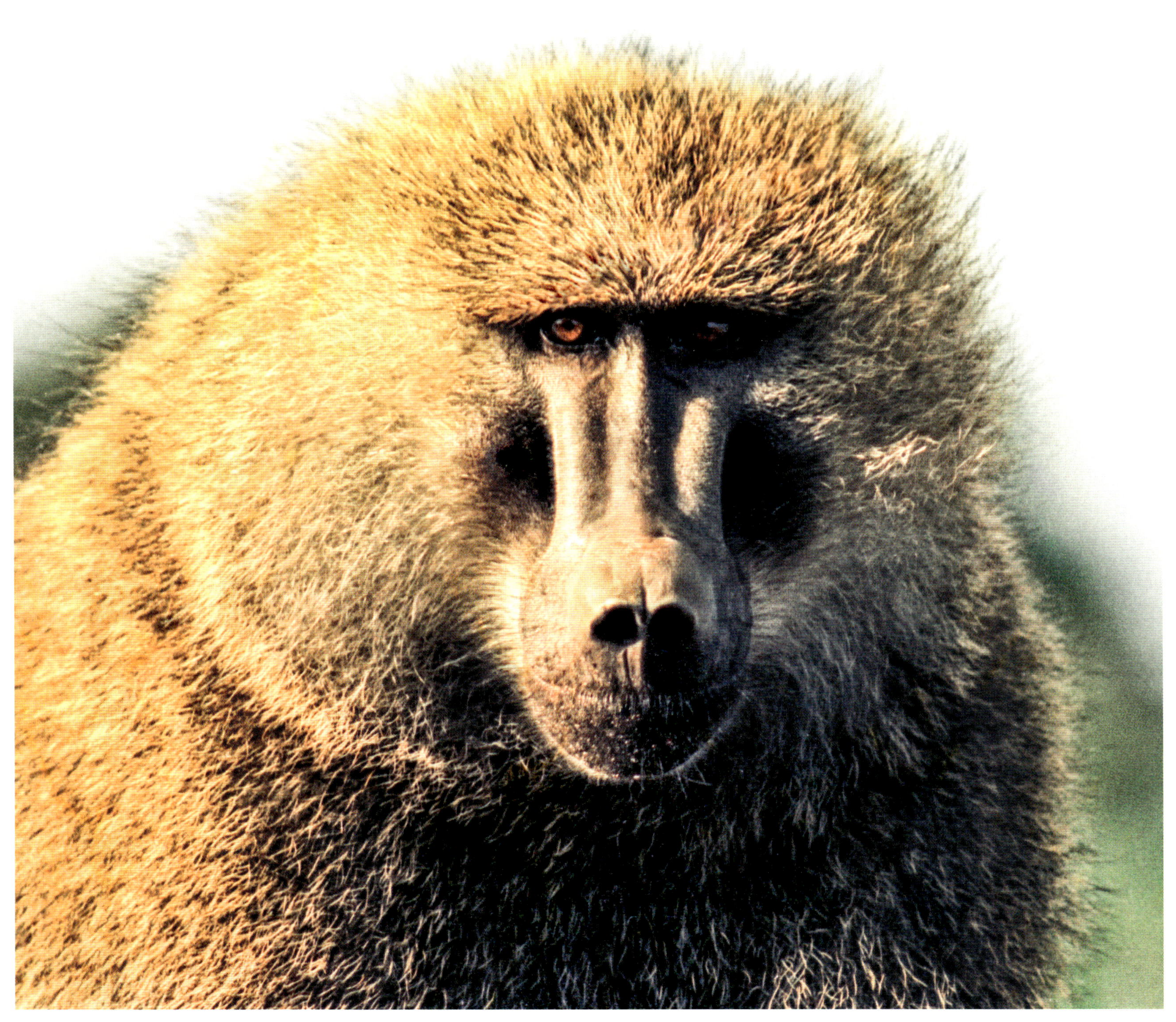

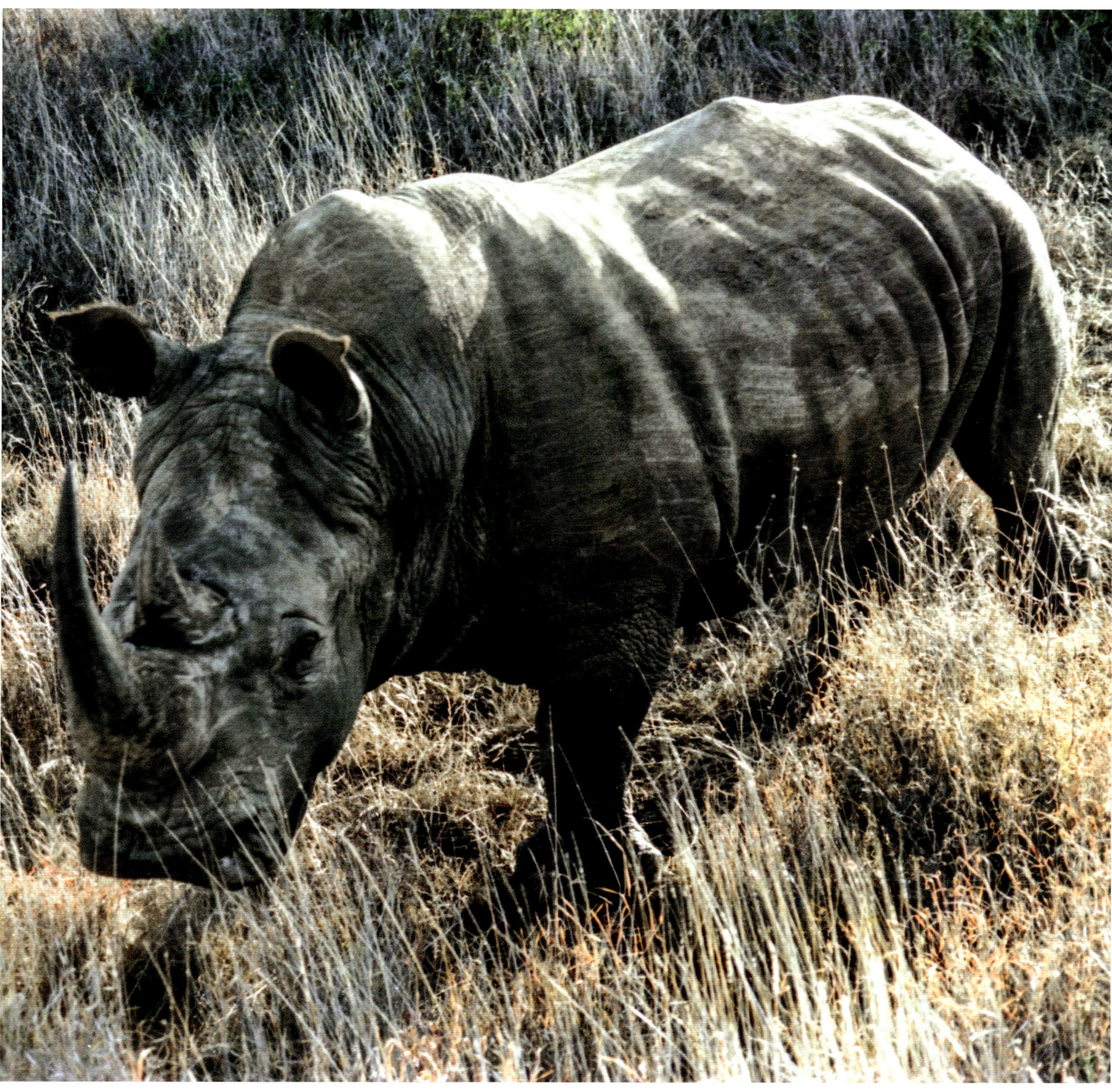

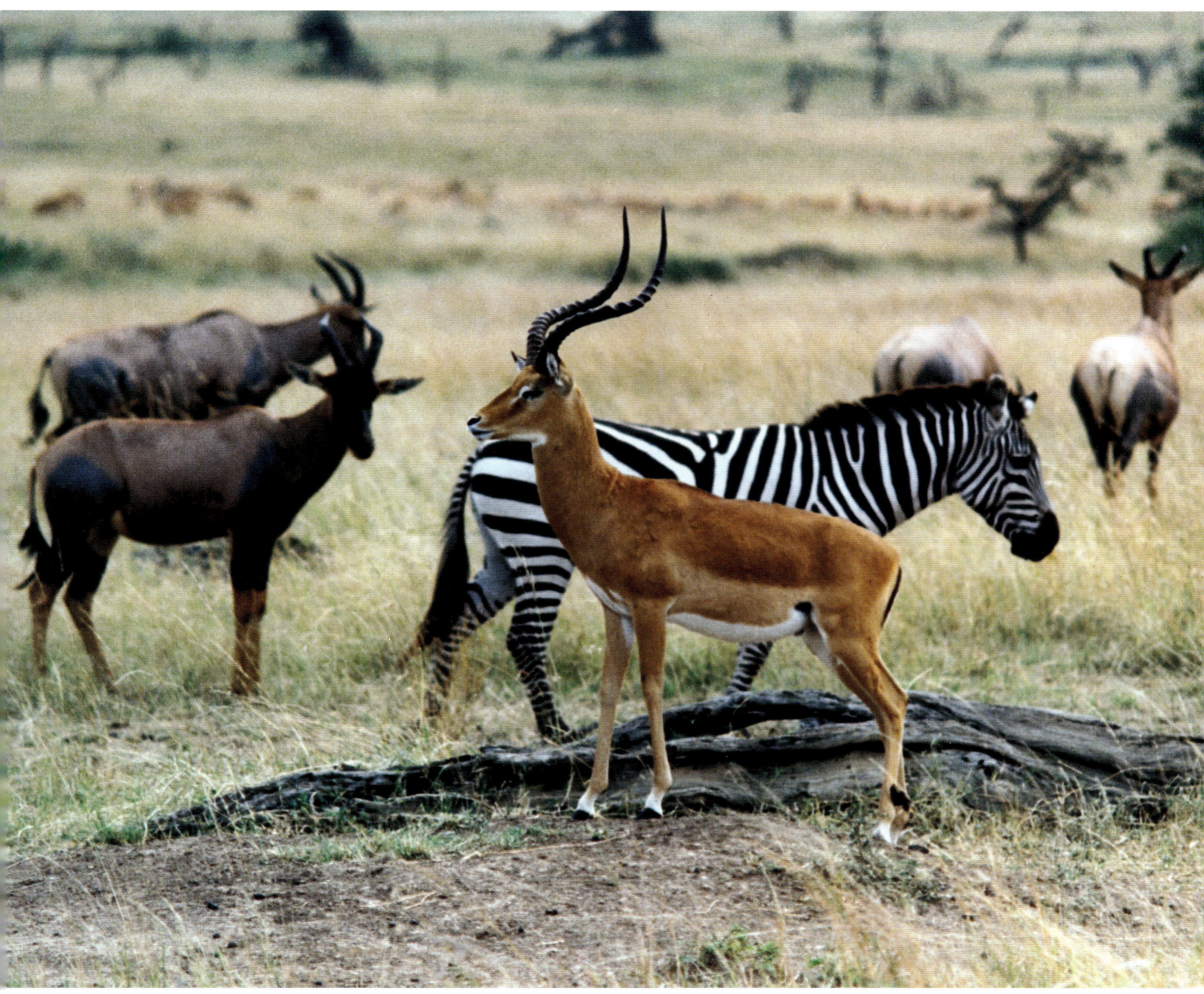

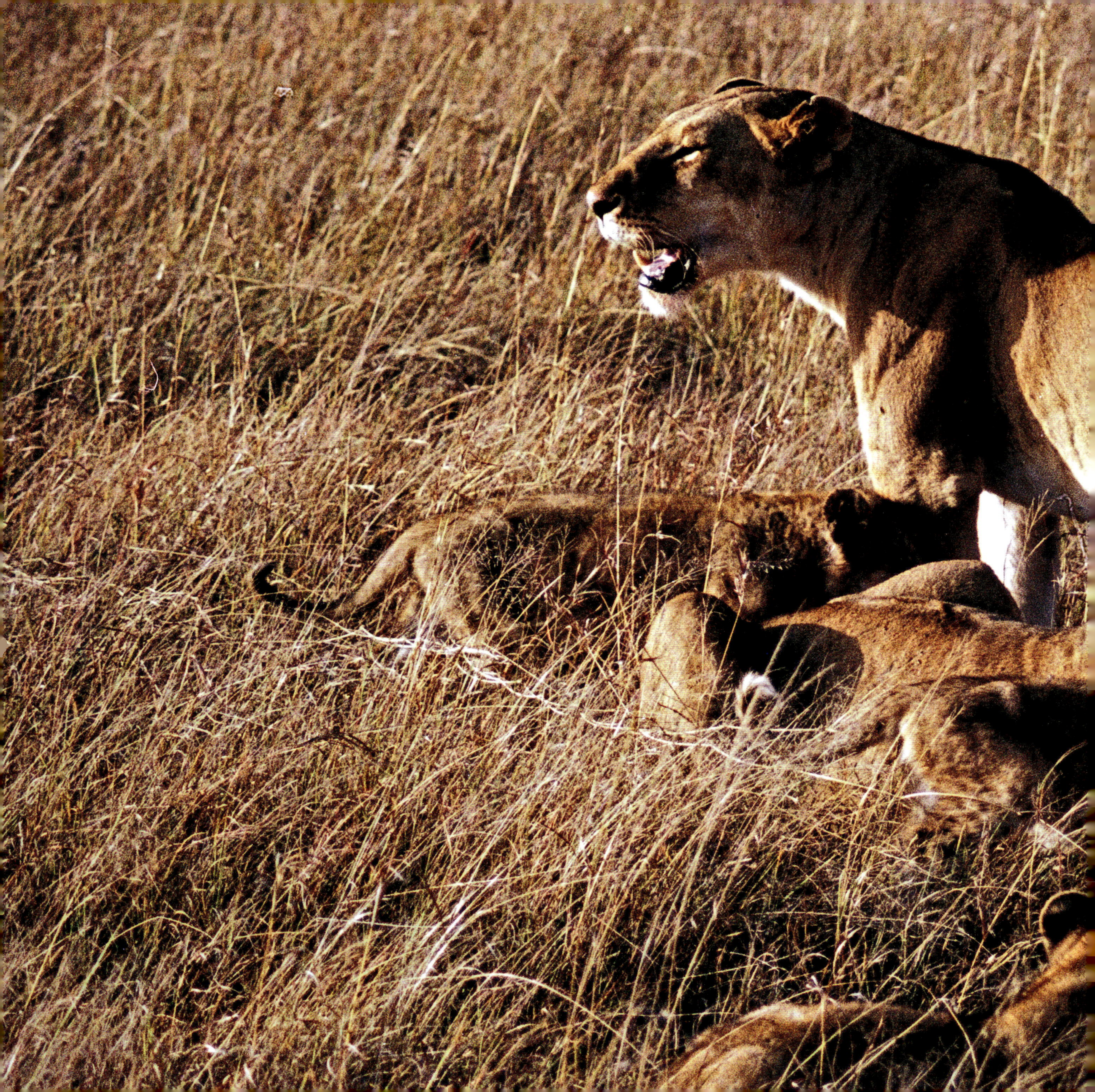

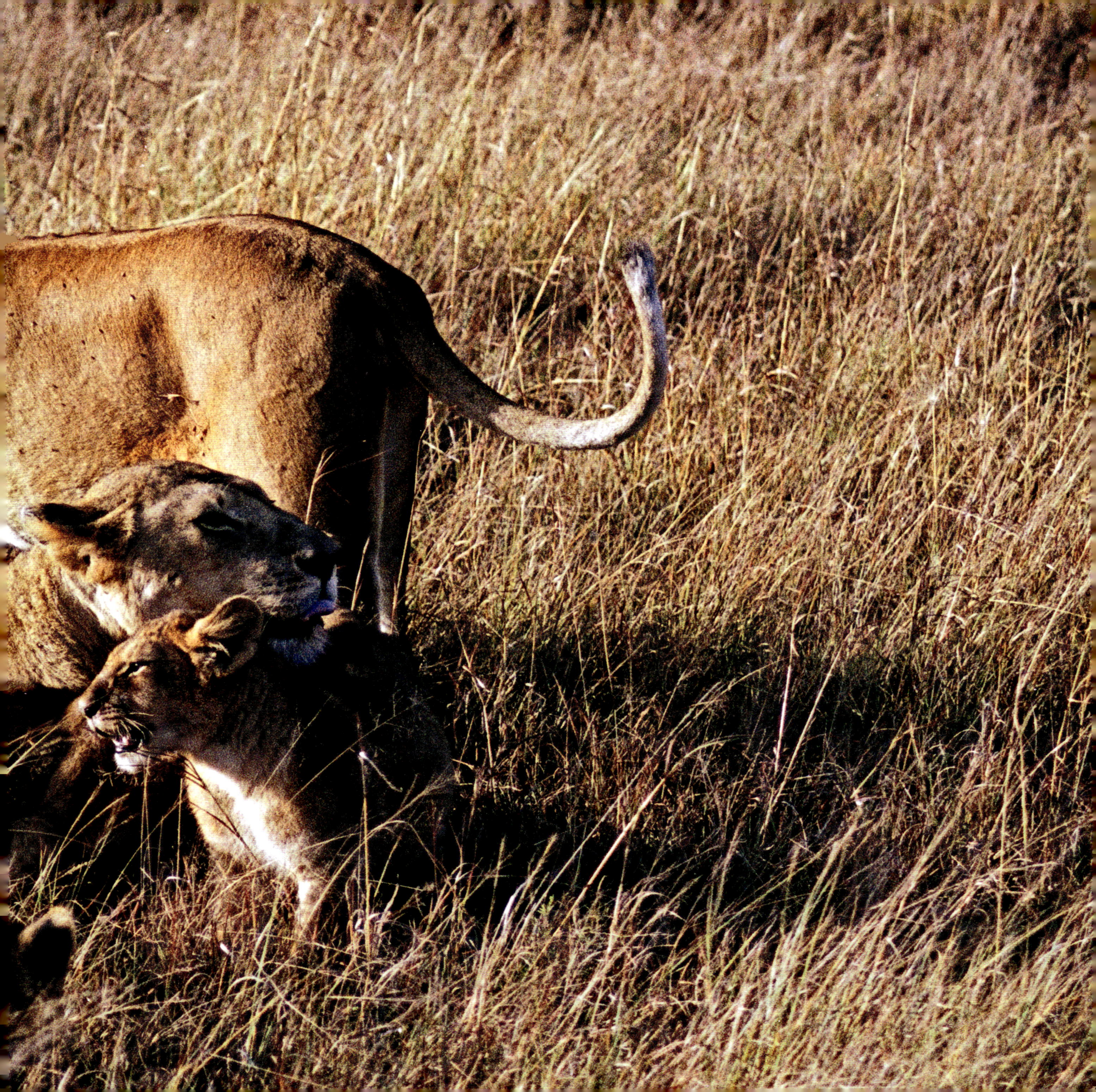

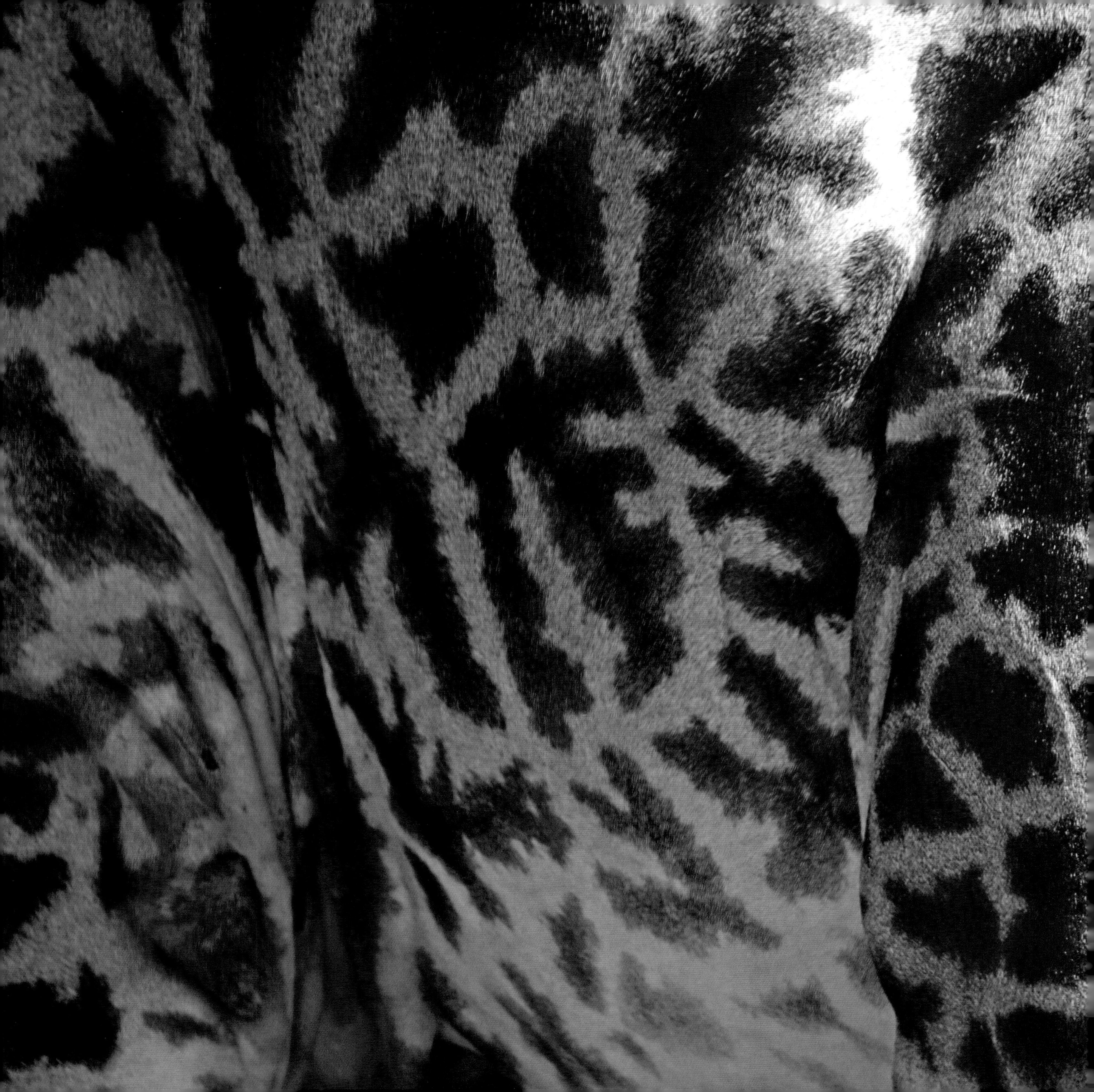

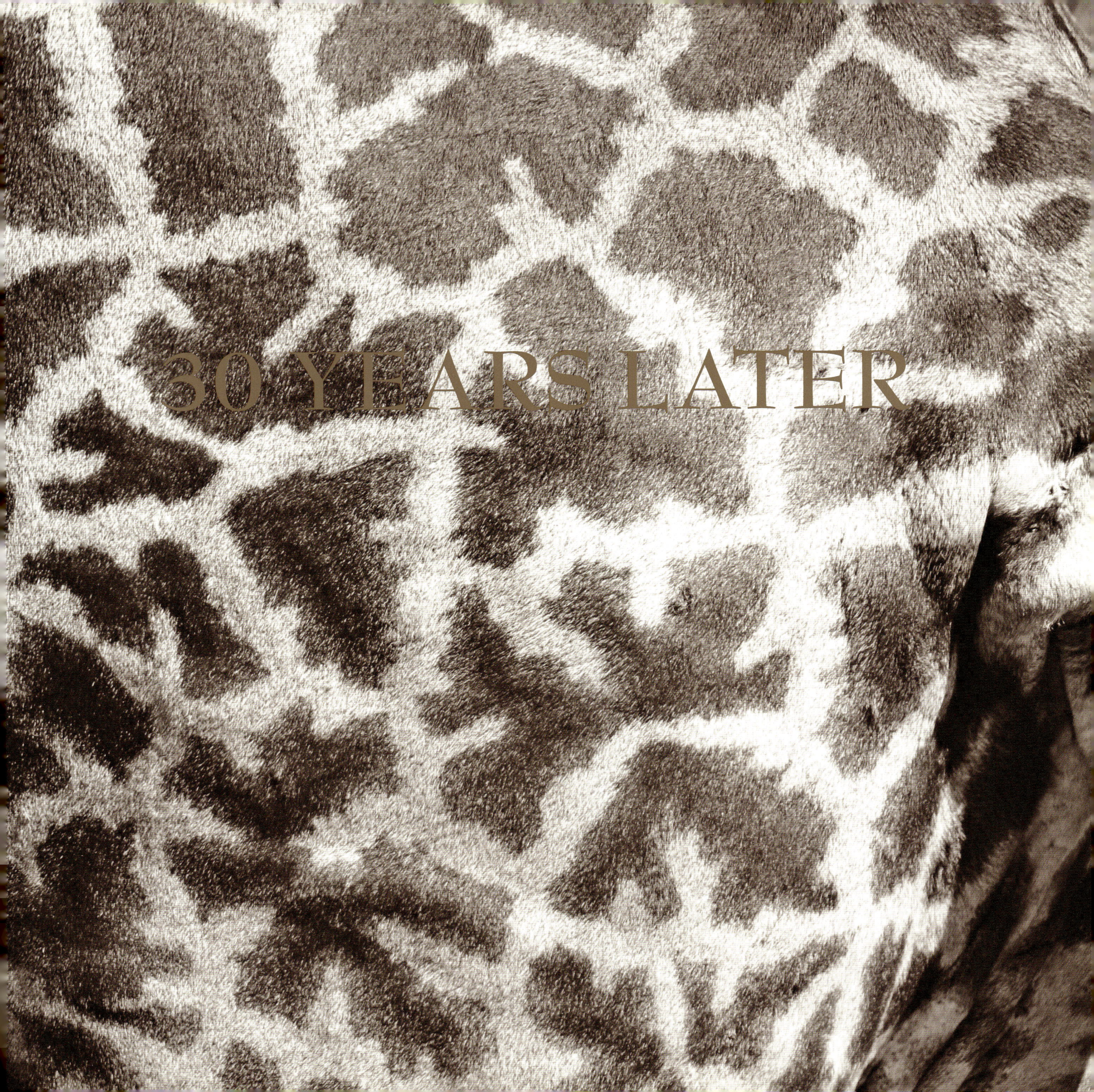
30 YEARS LATER

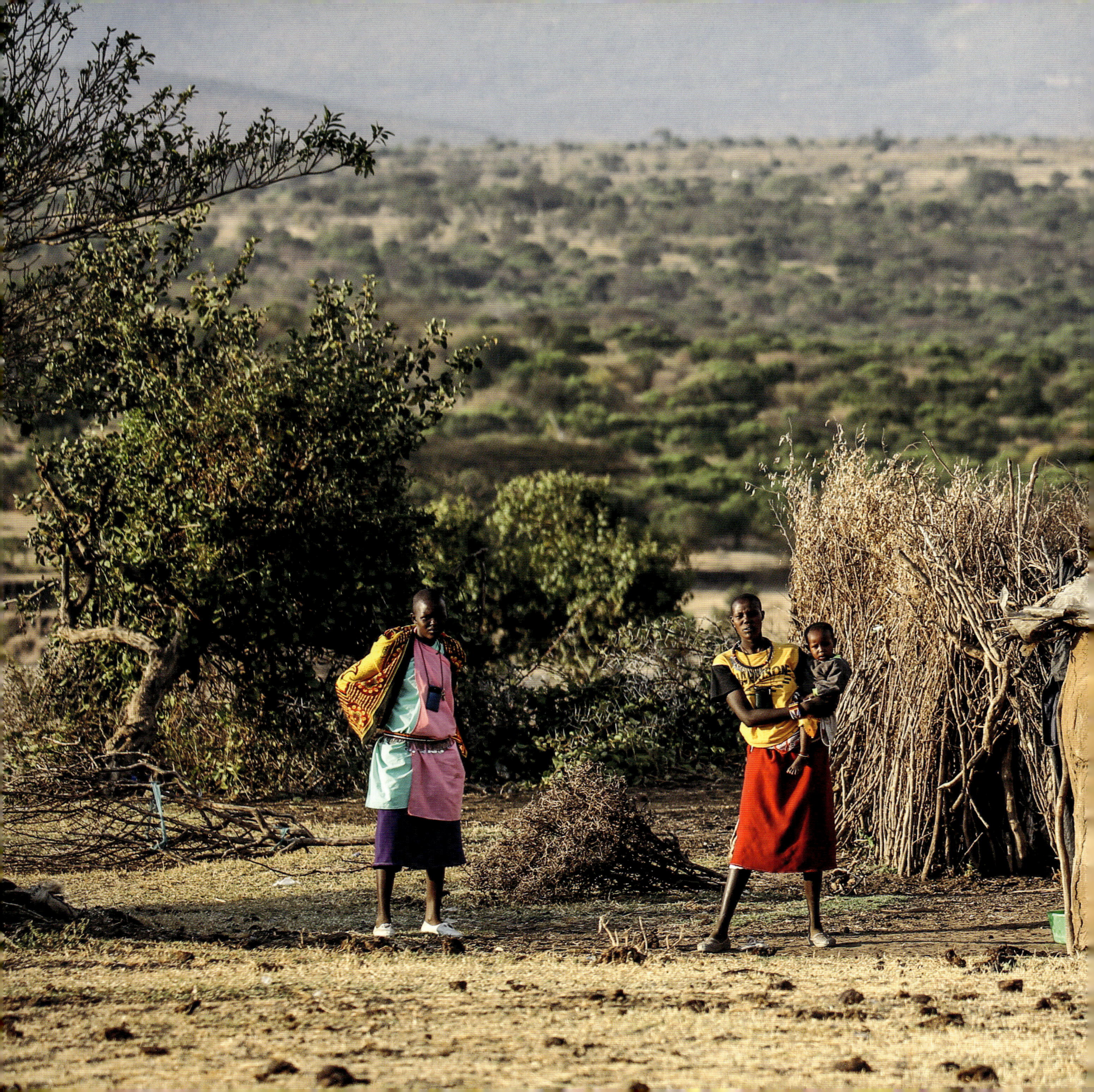

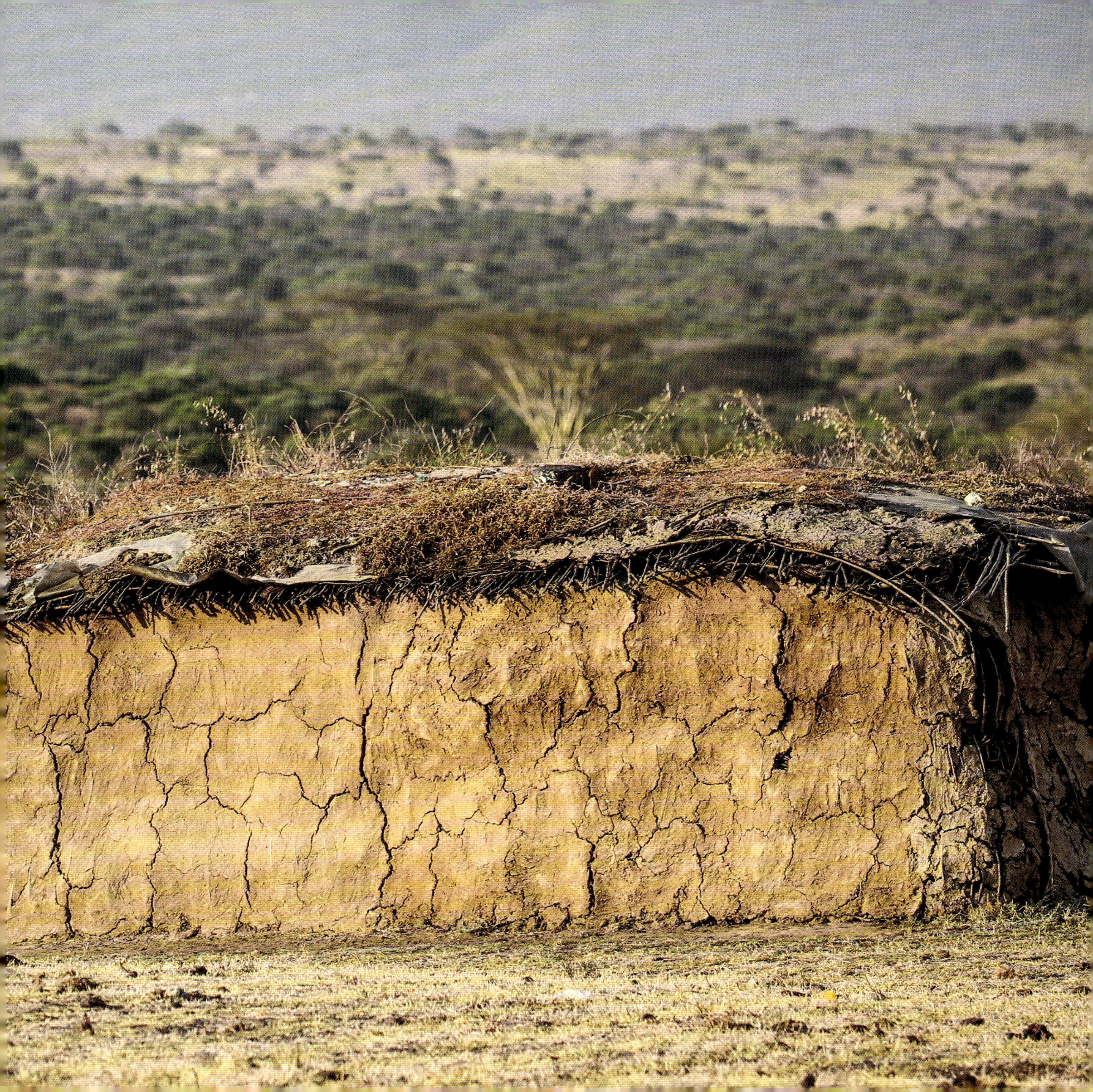

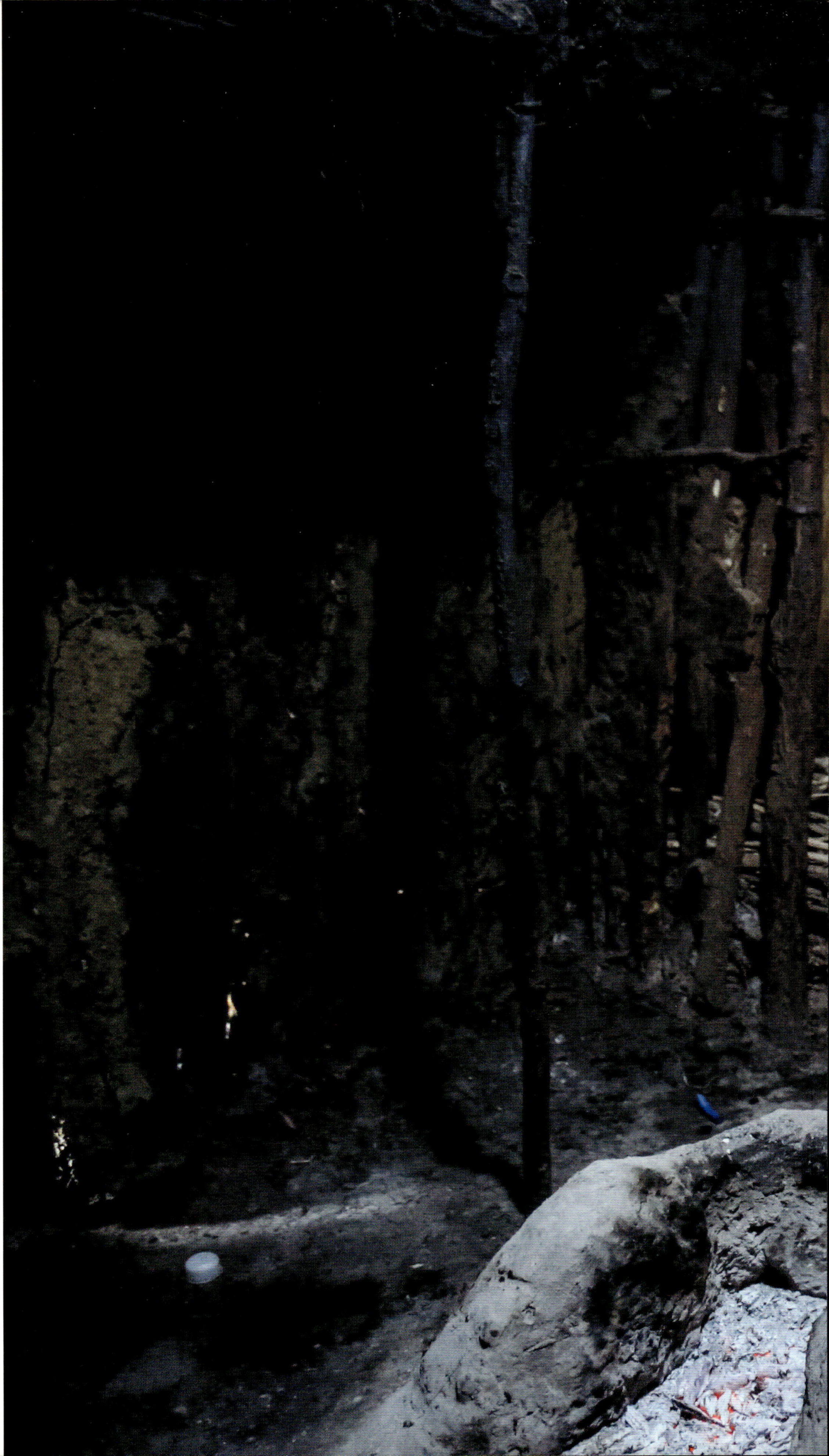

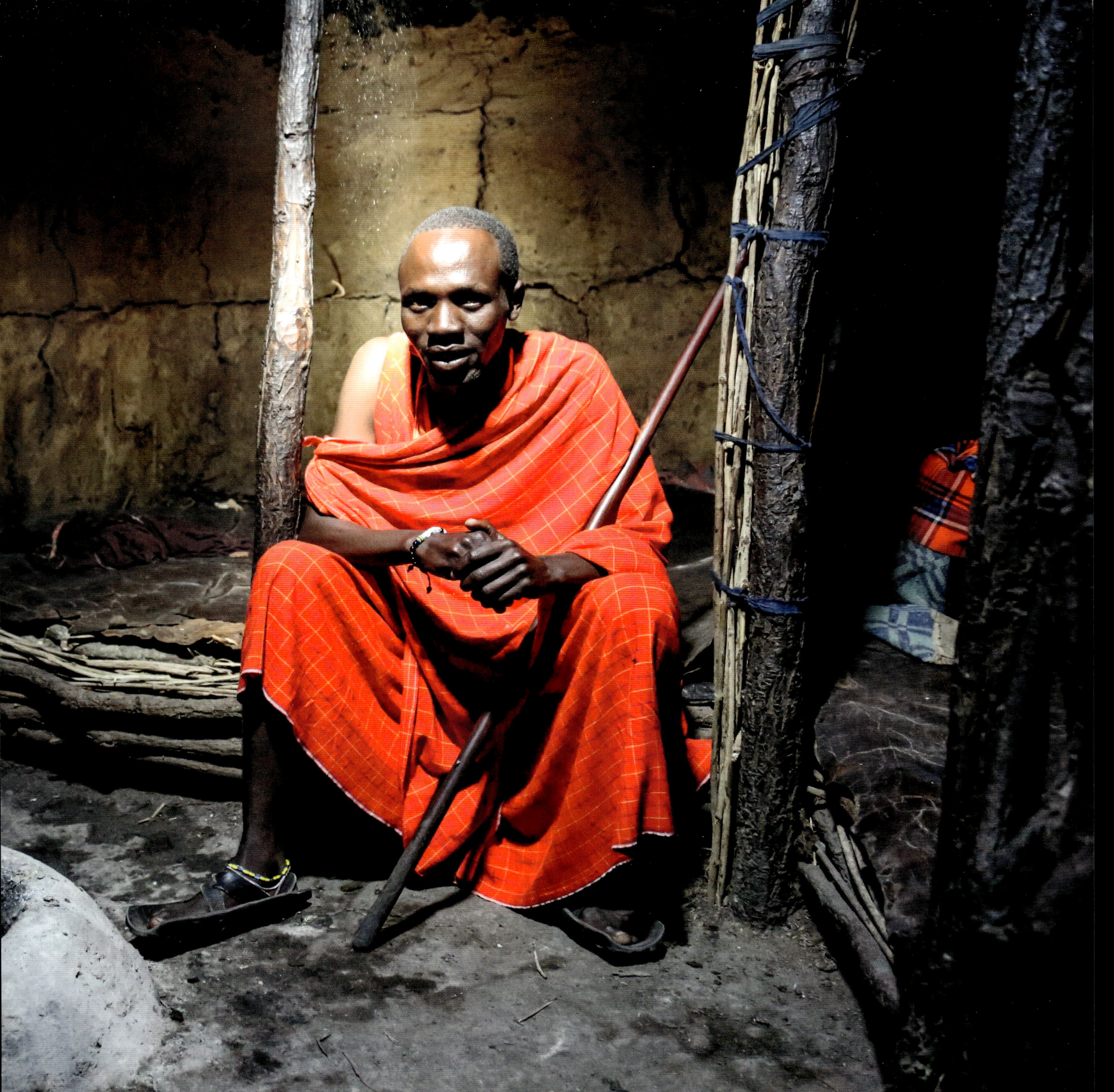

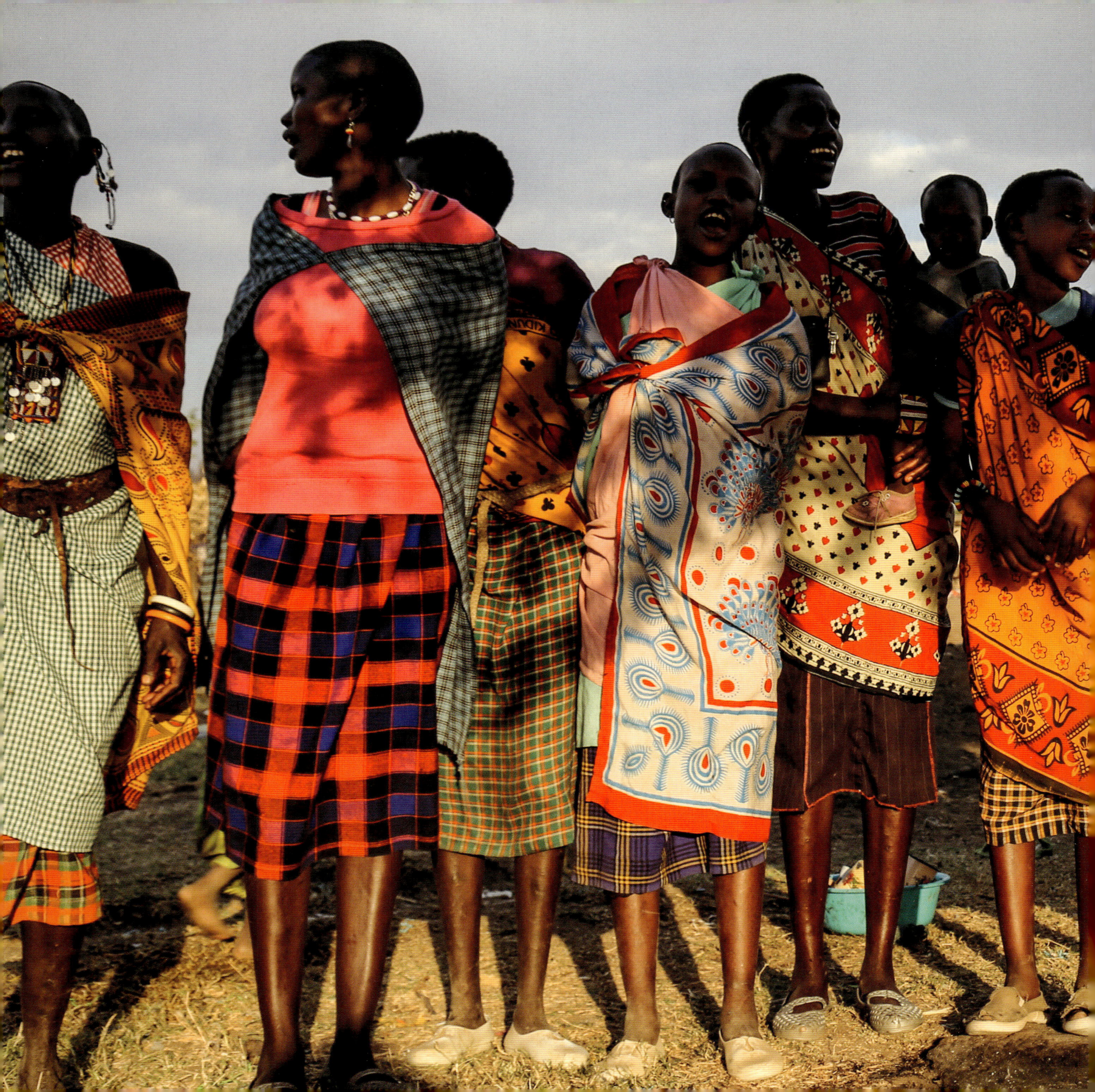

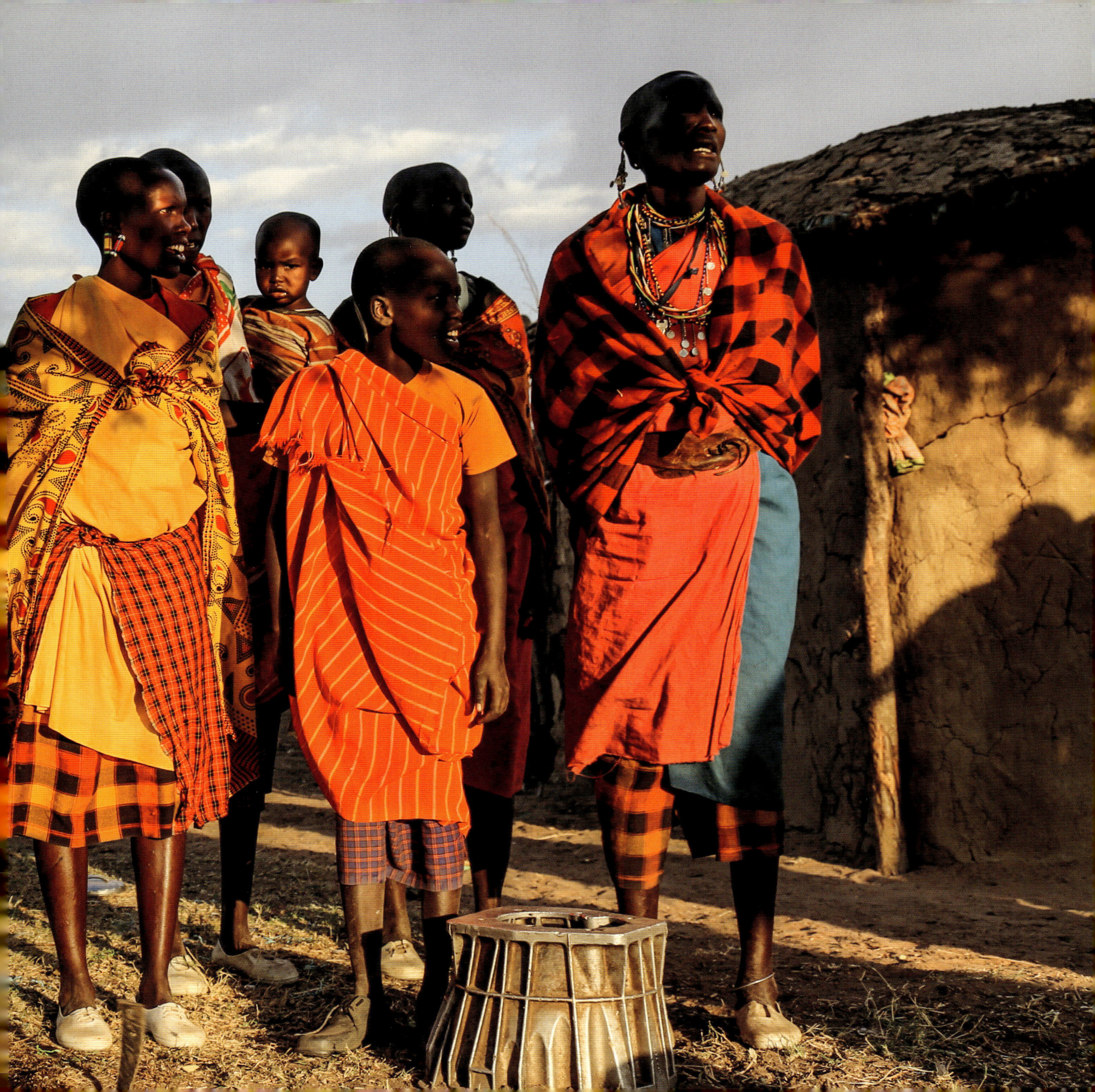

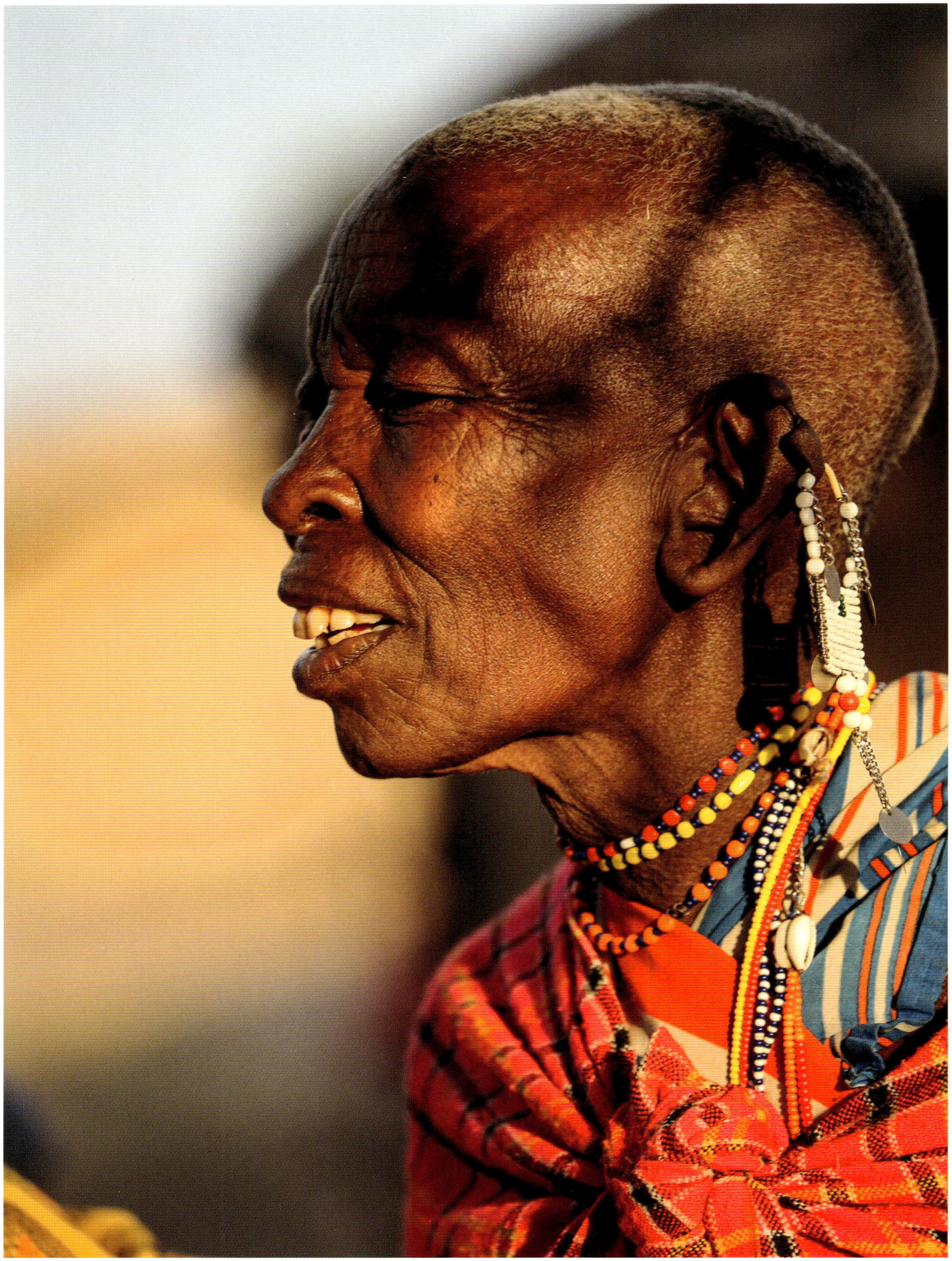

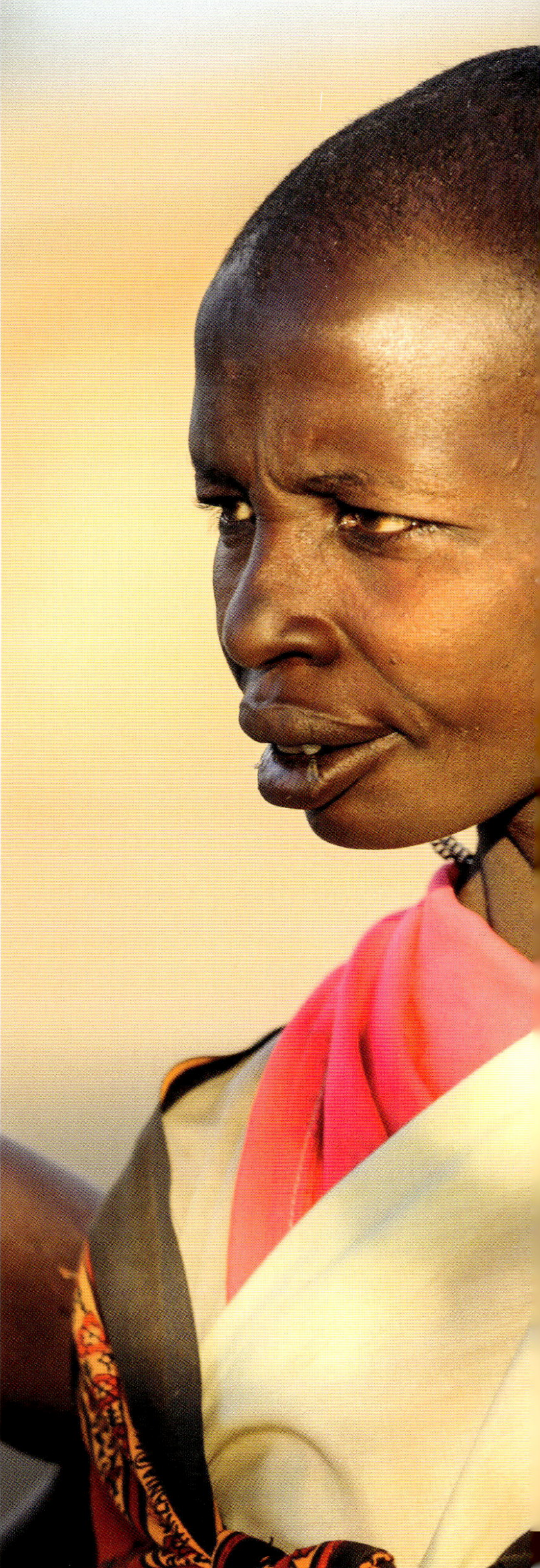

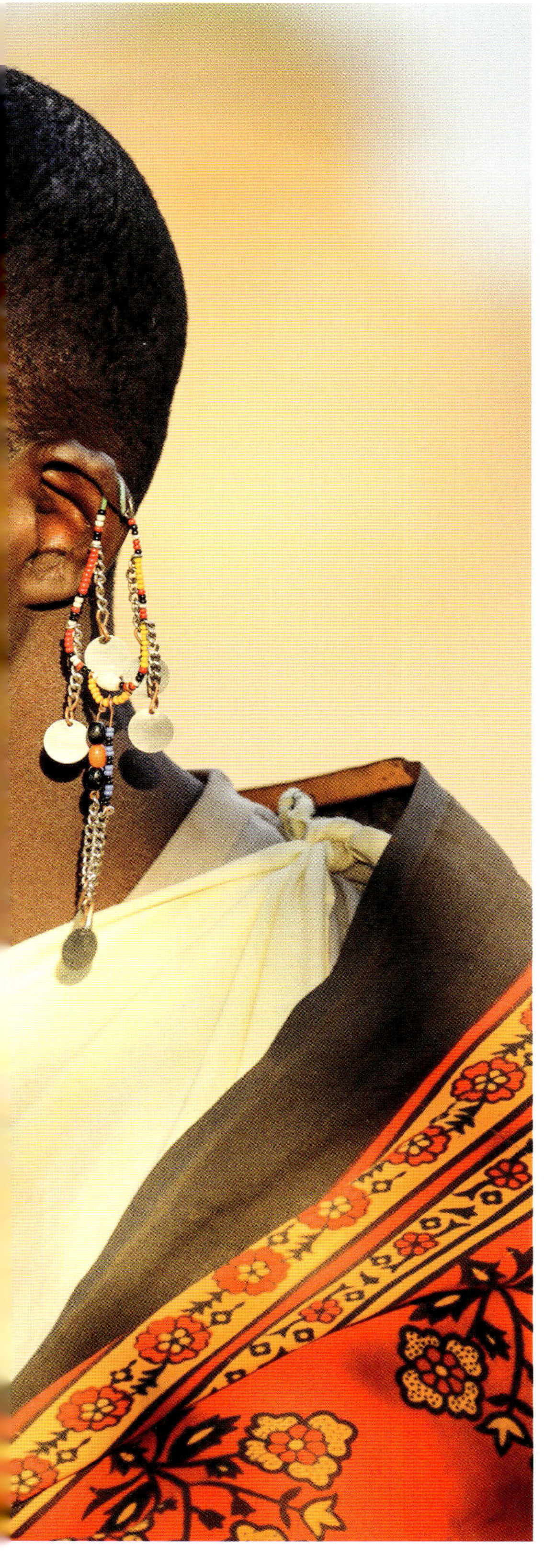

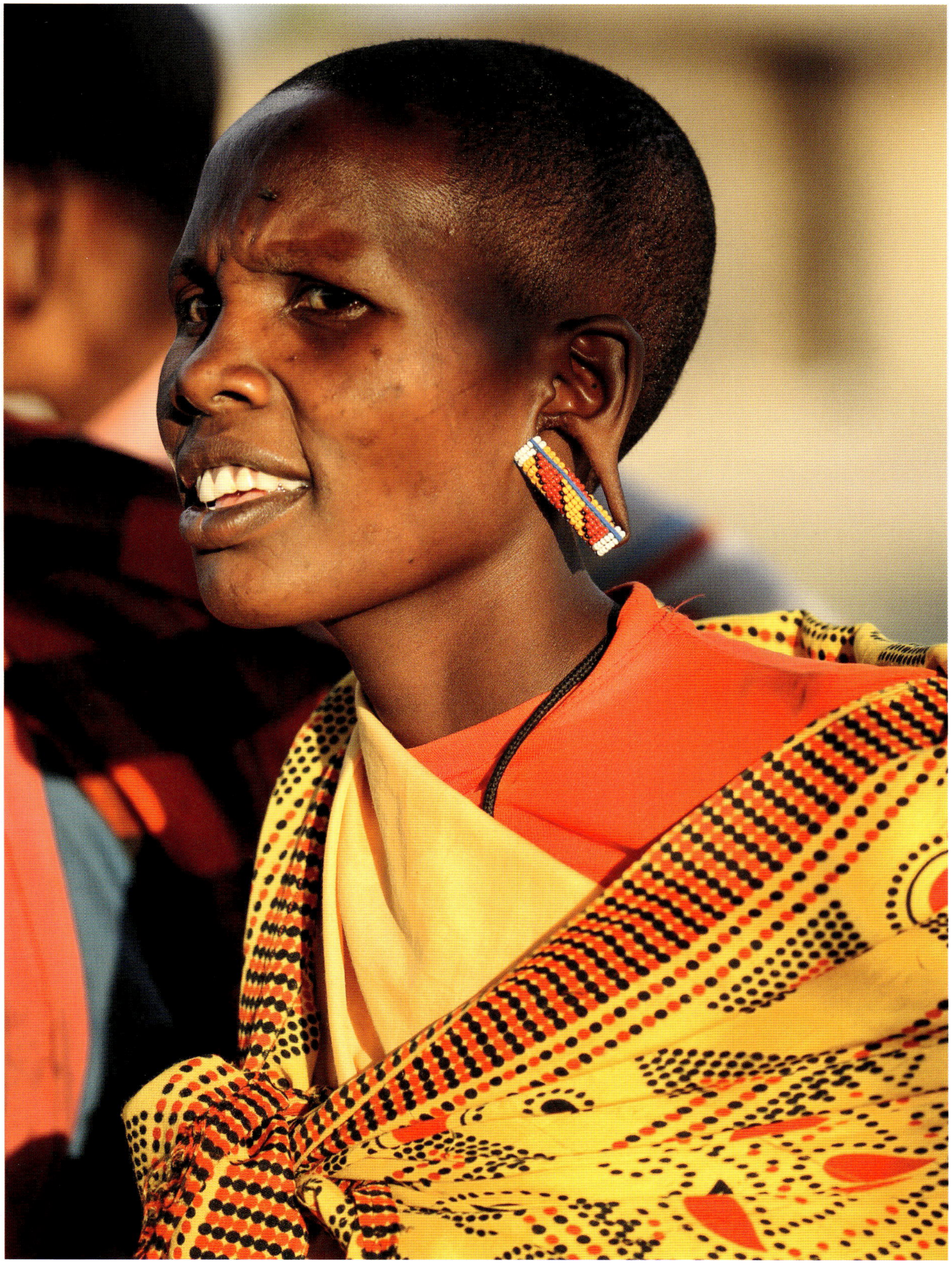

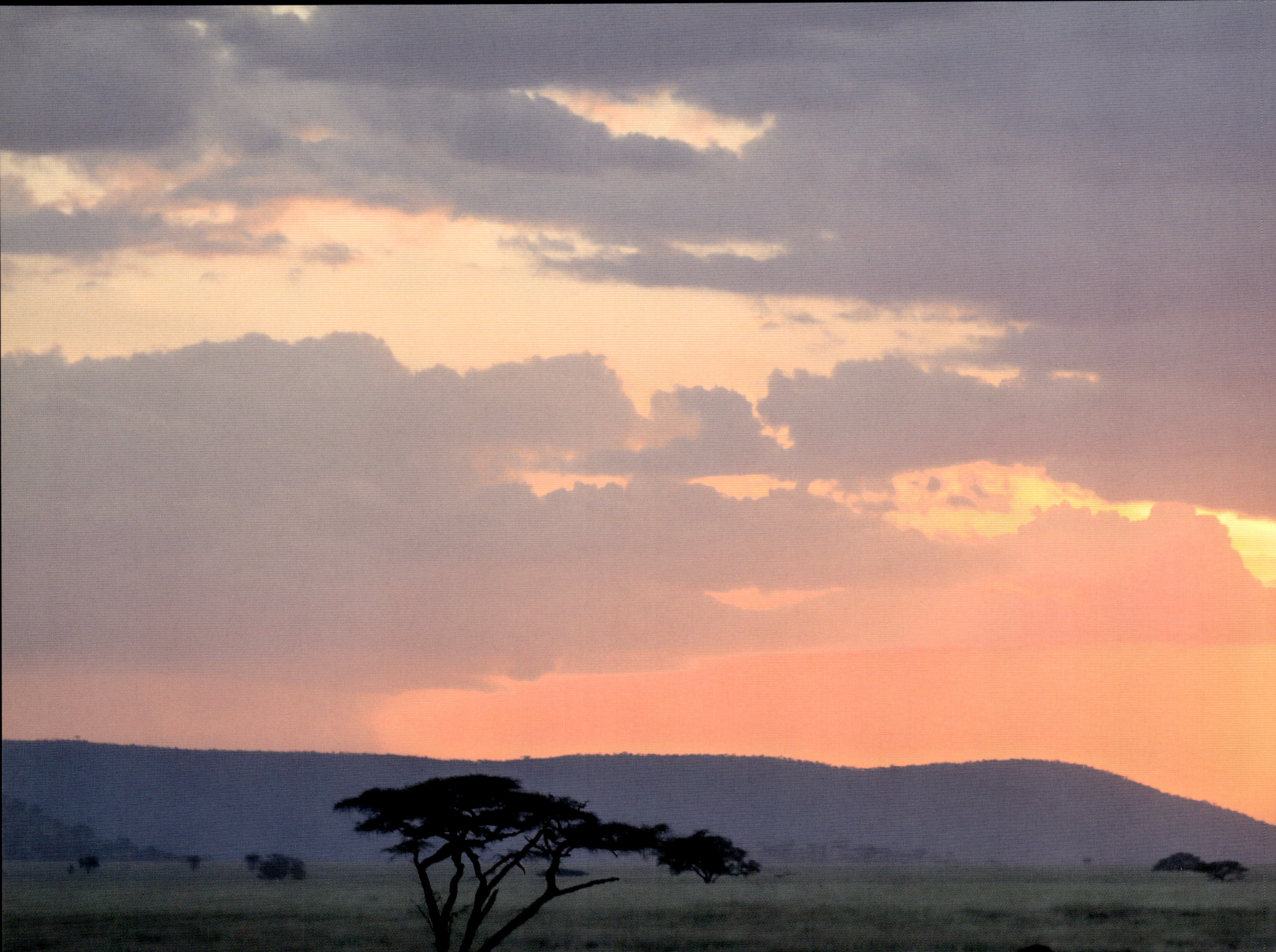

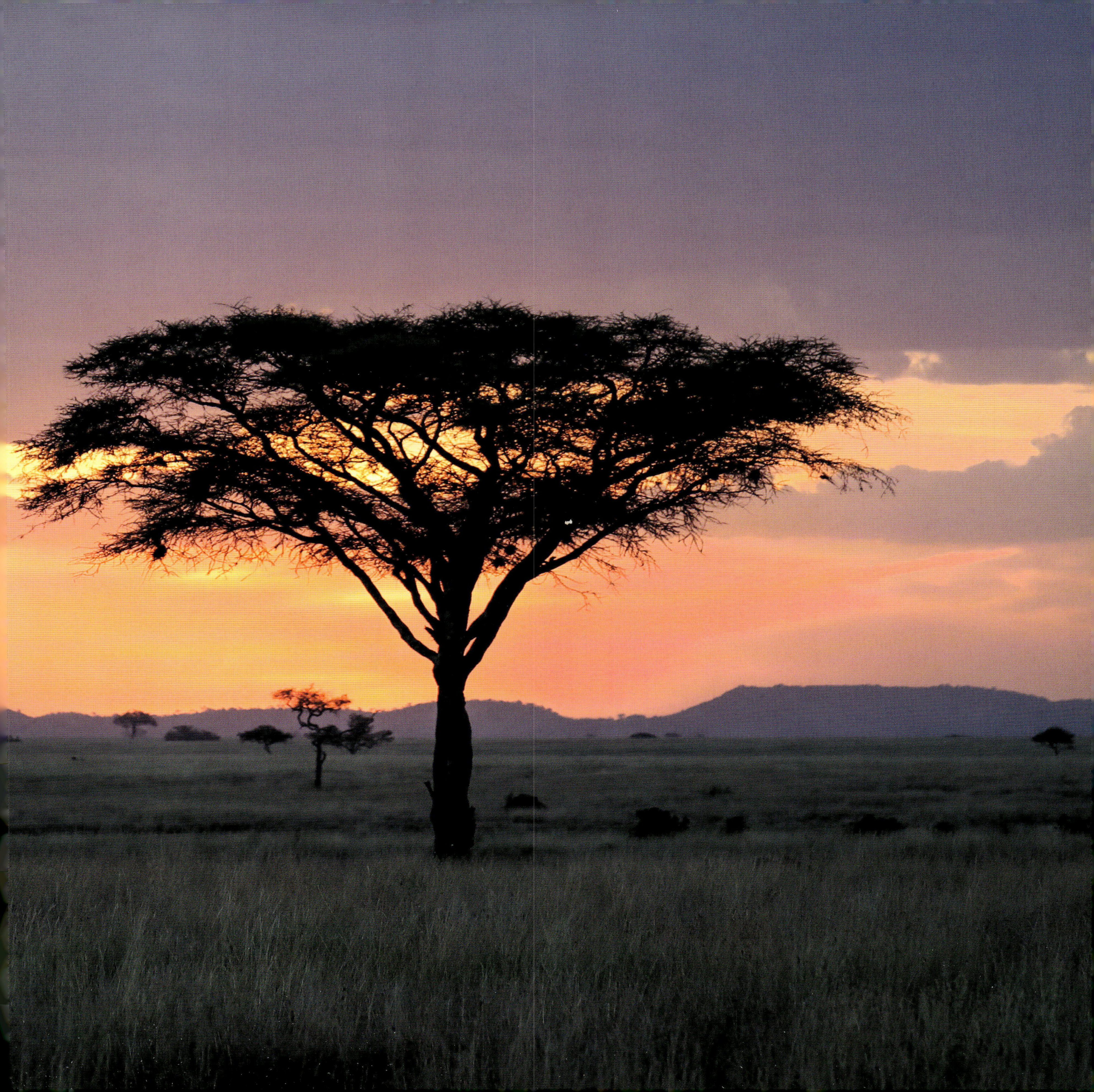

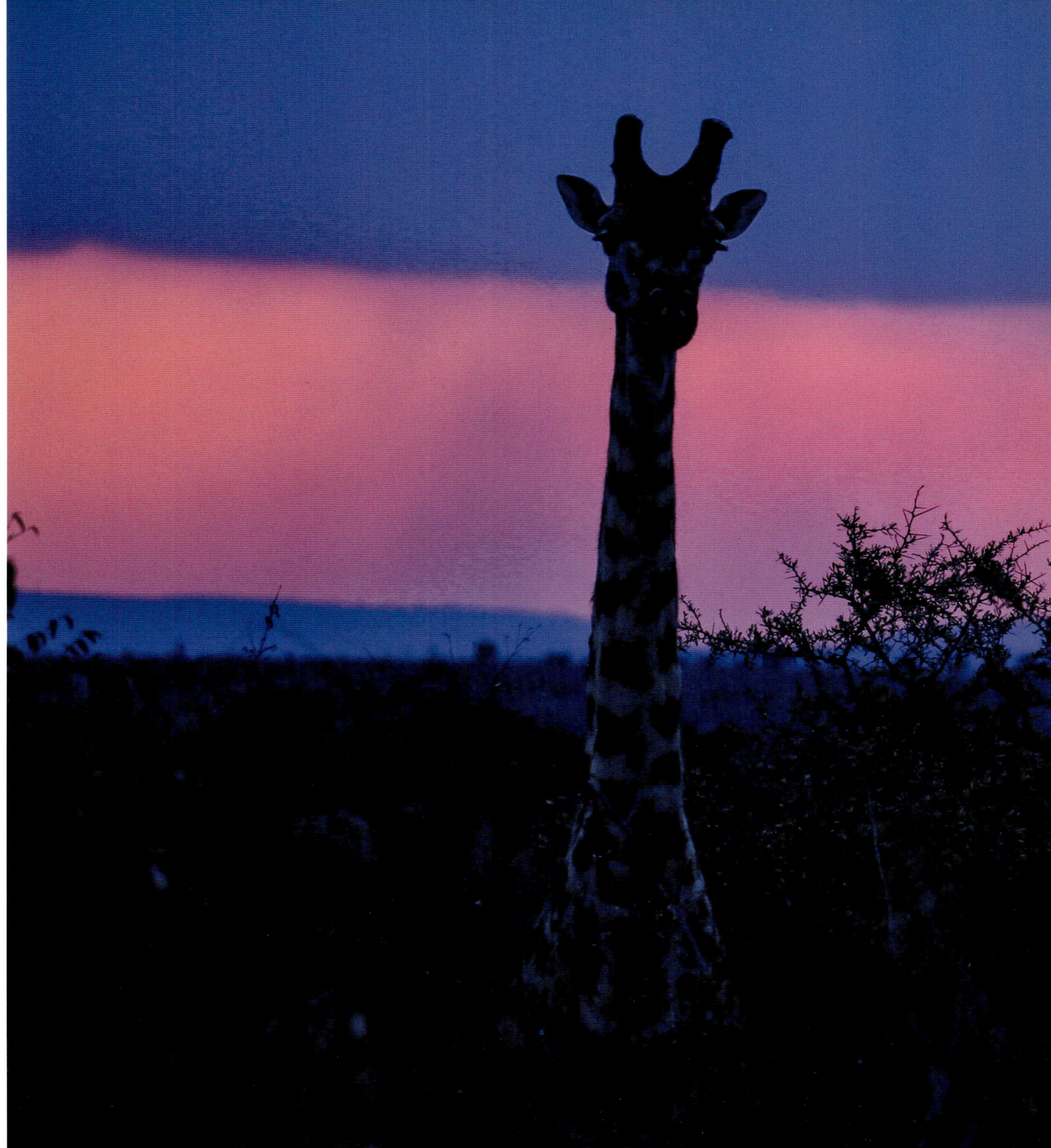

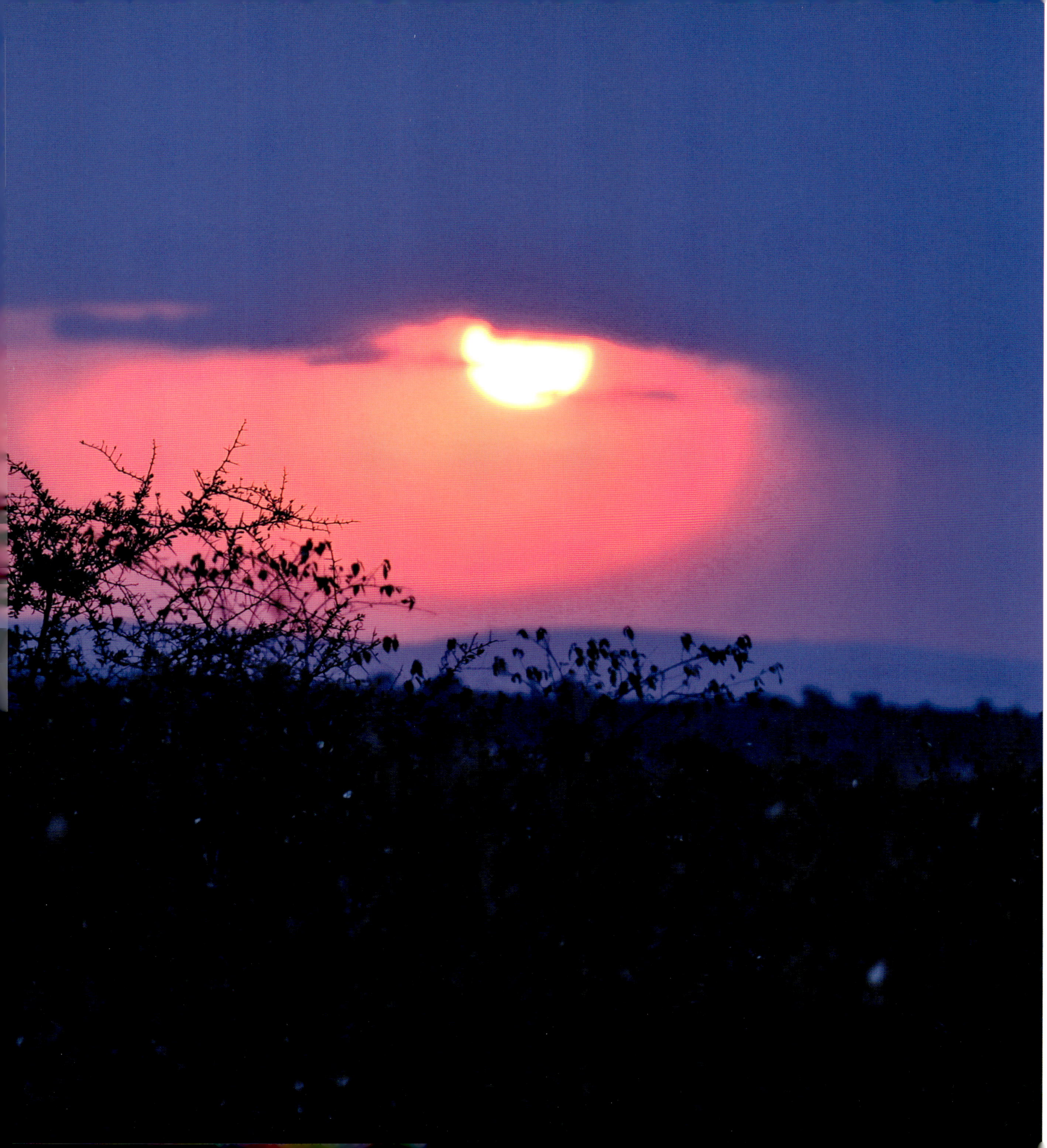

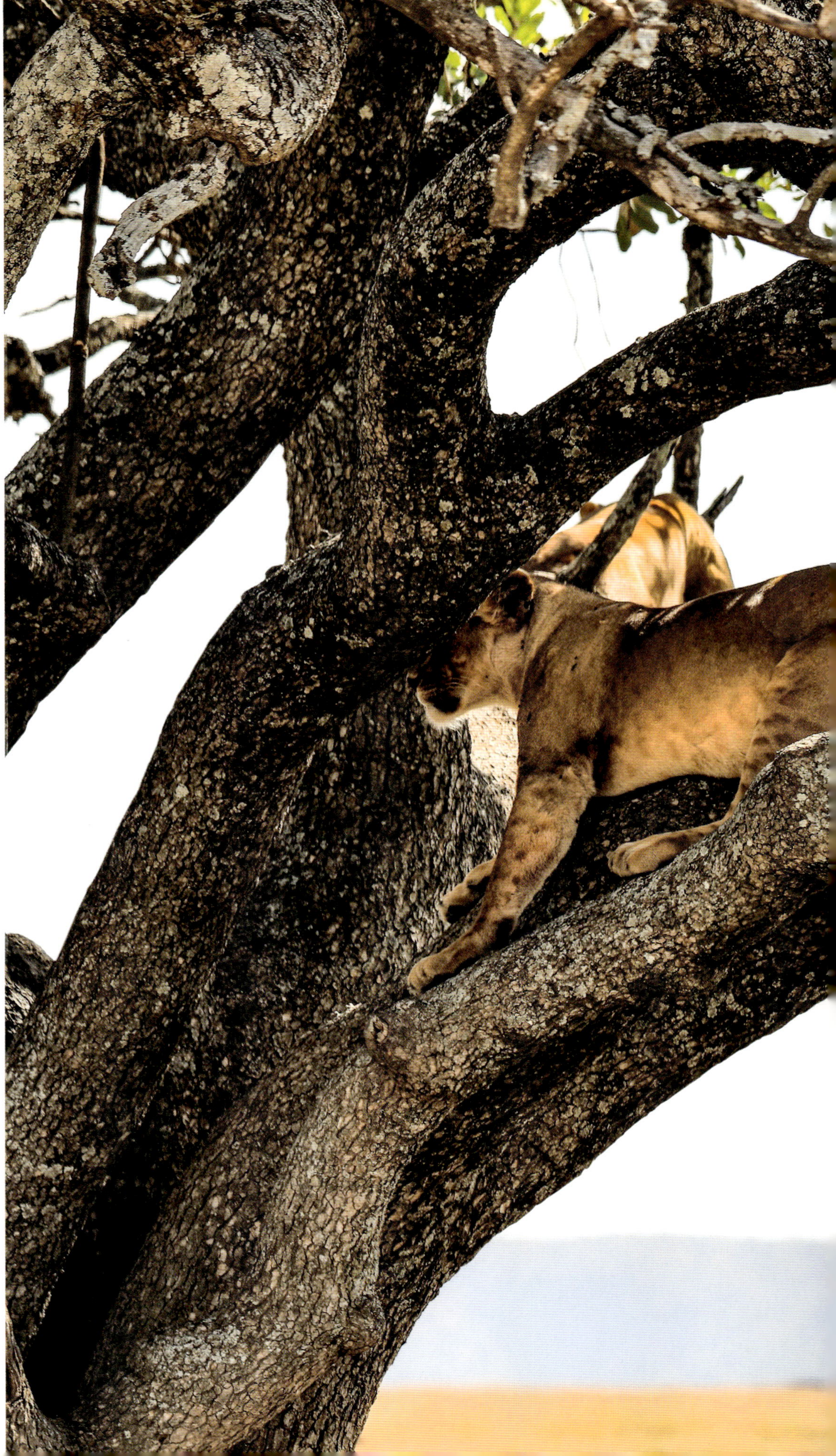

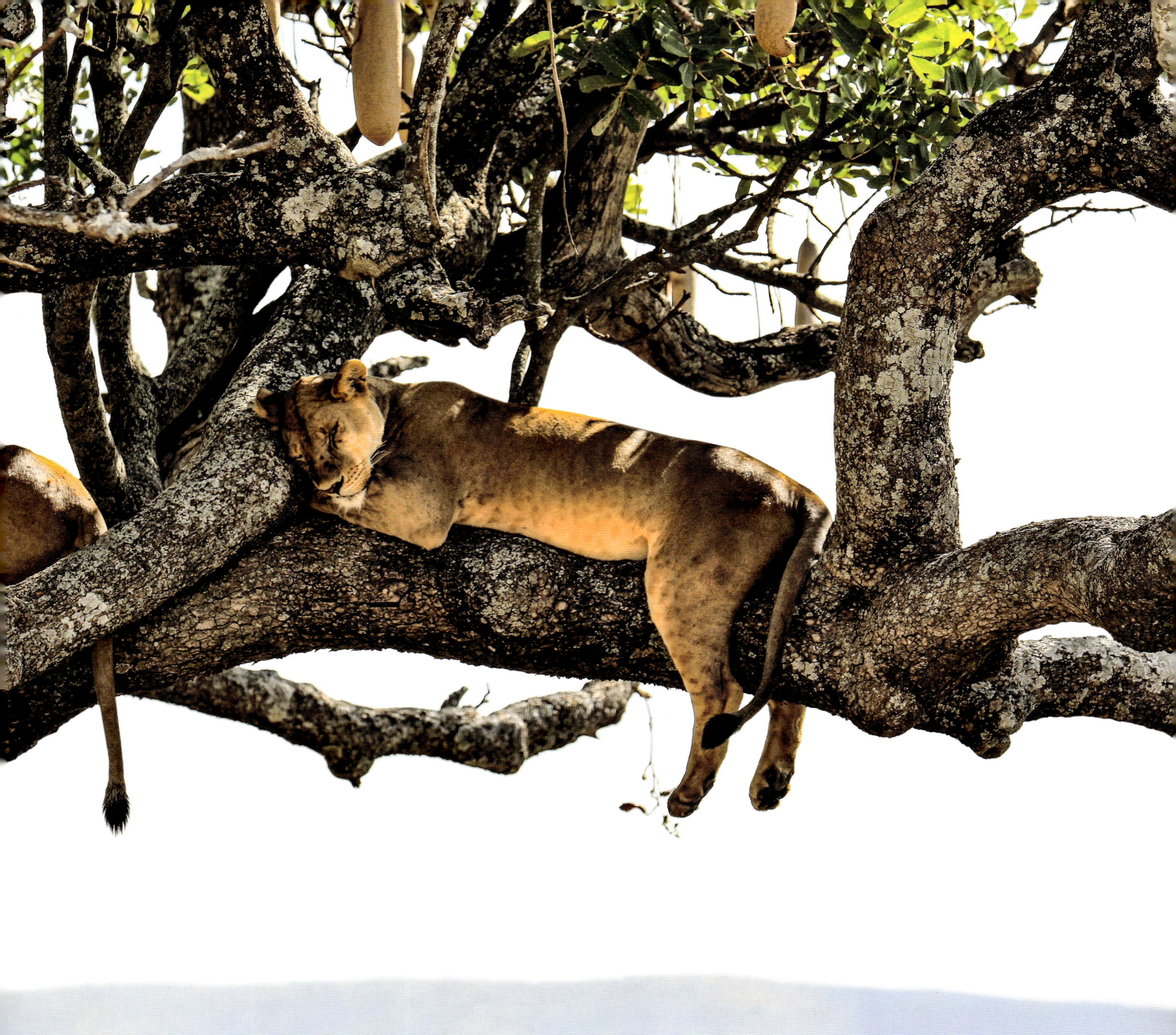

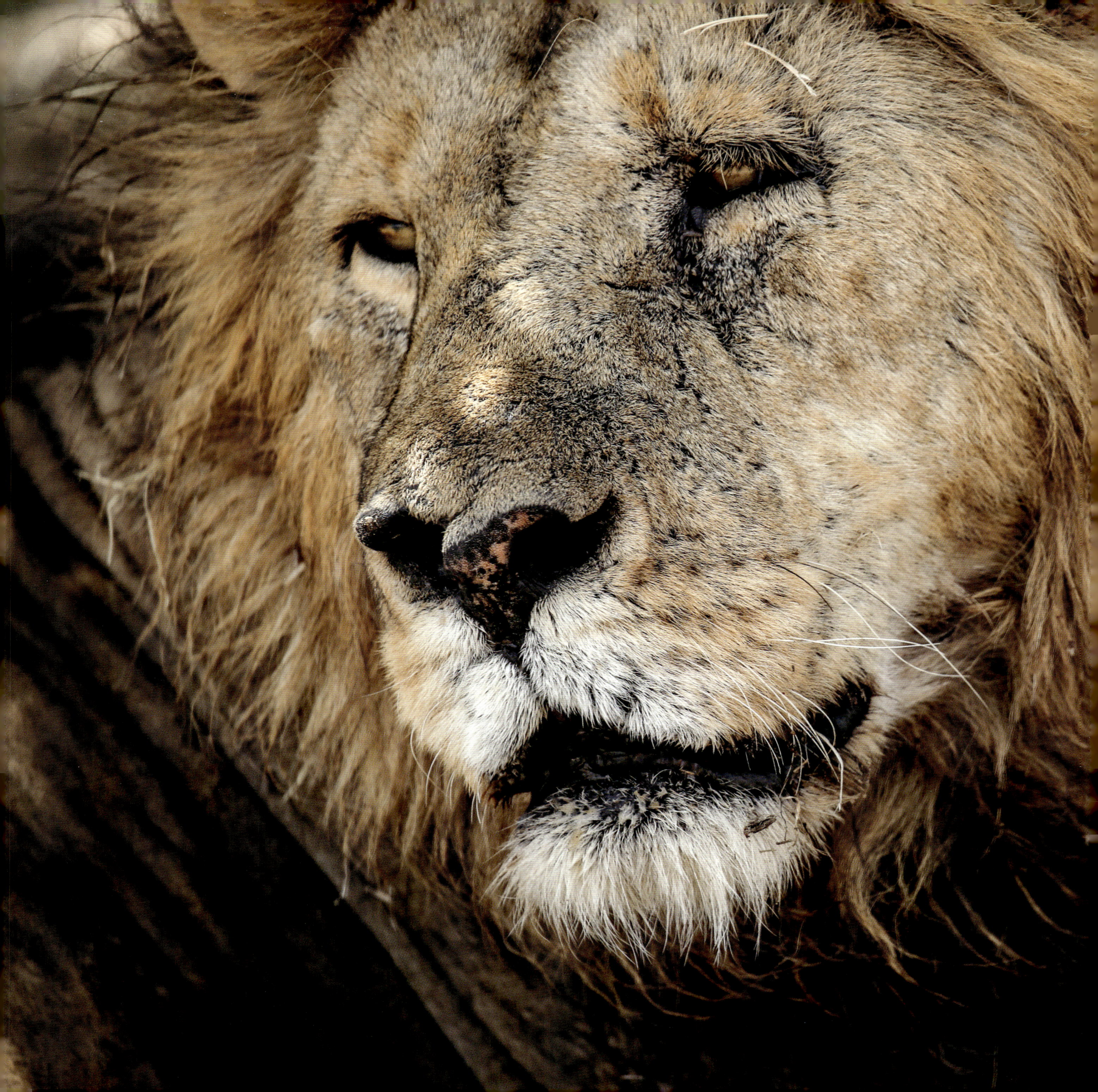

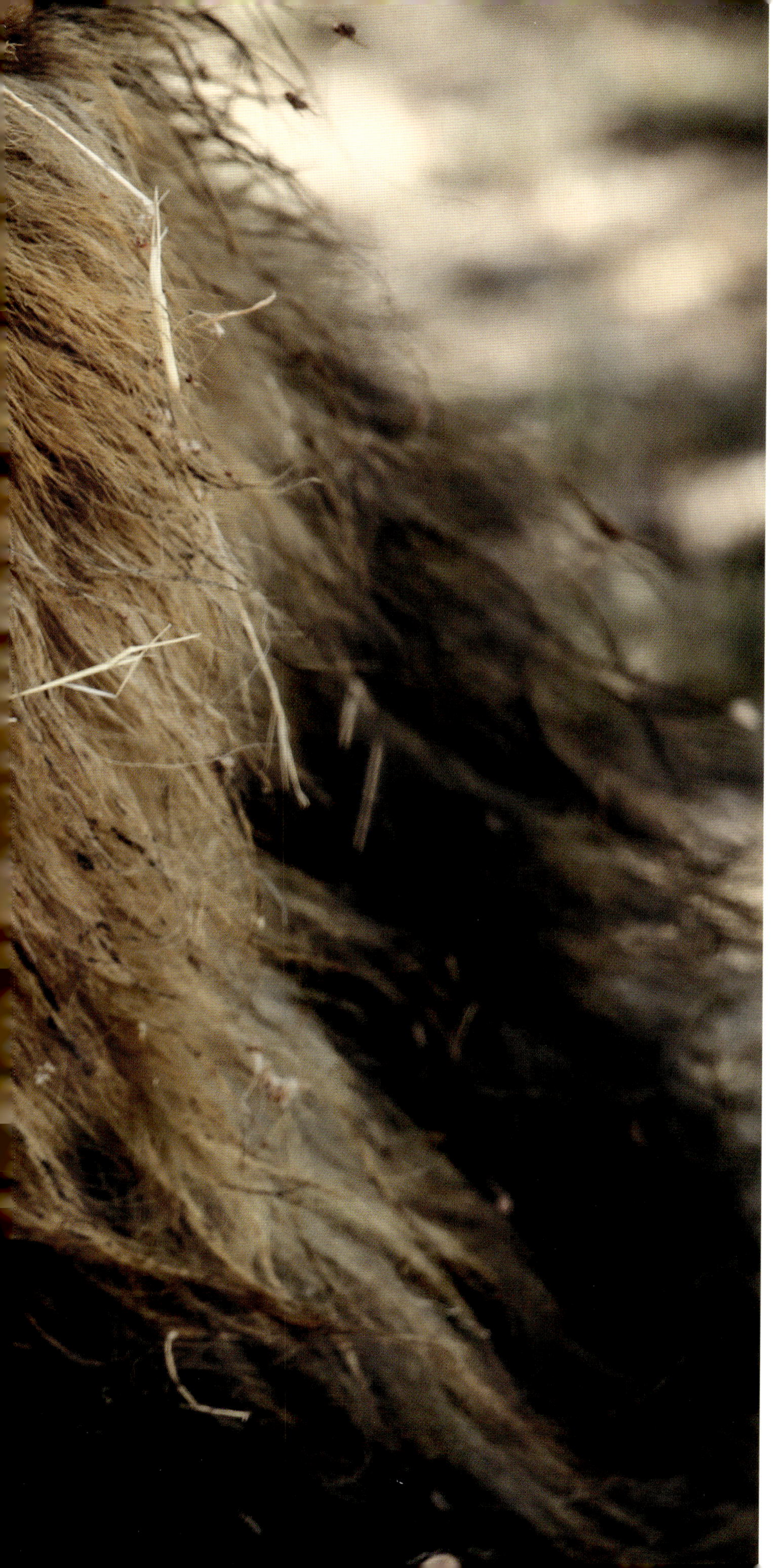

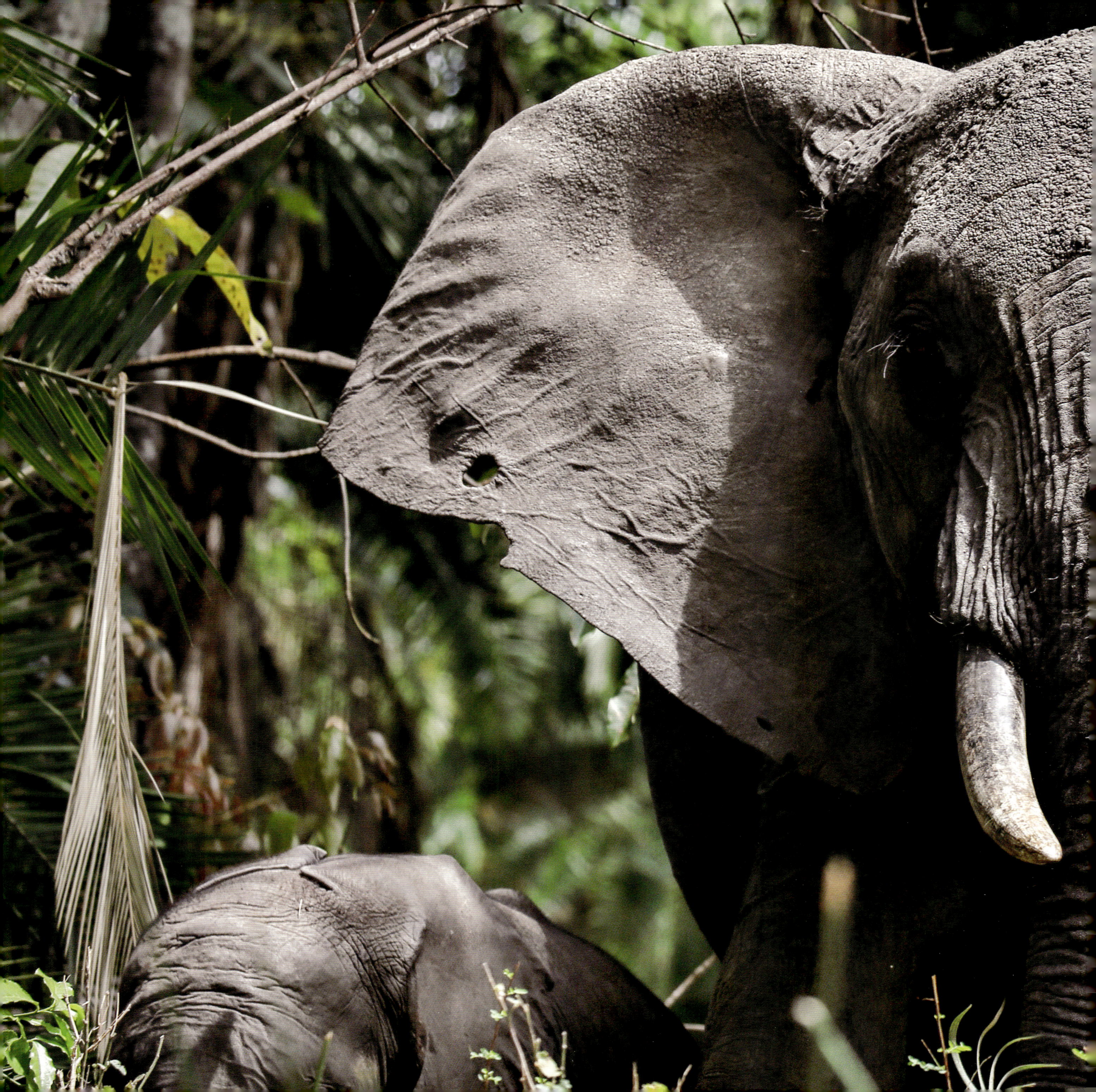

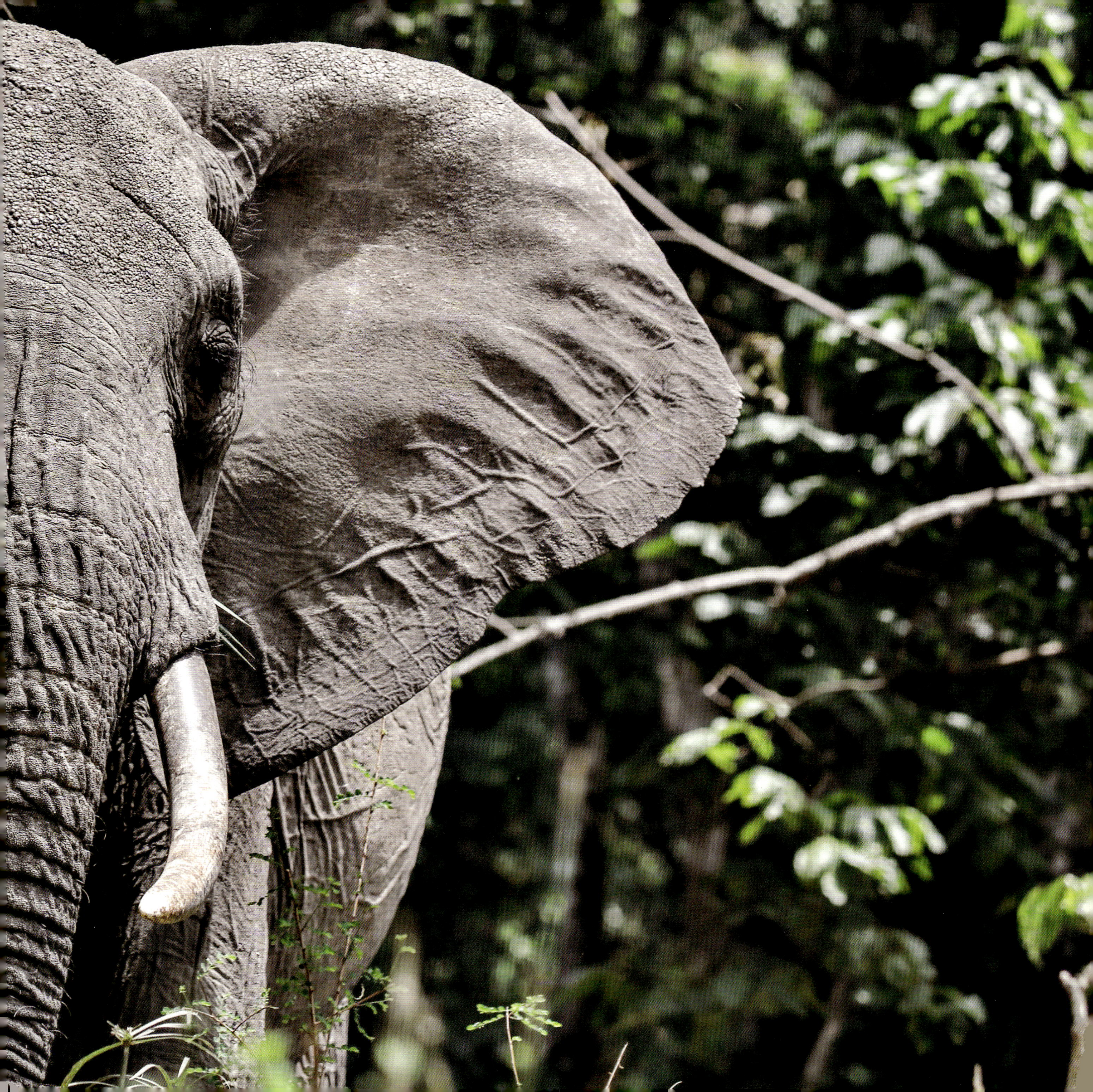

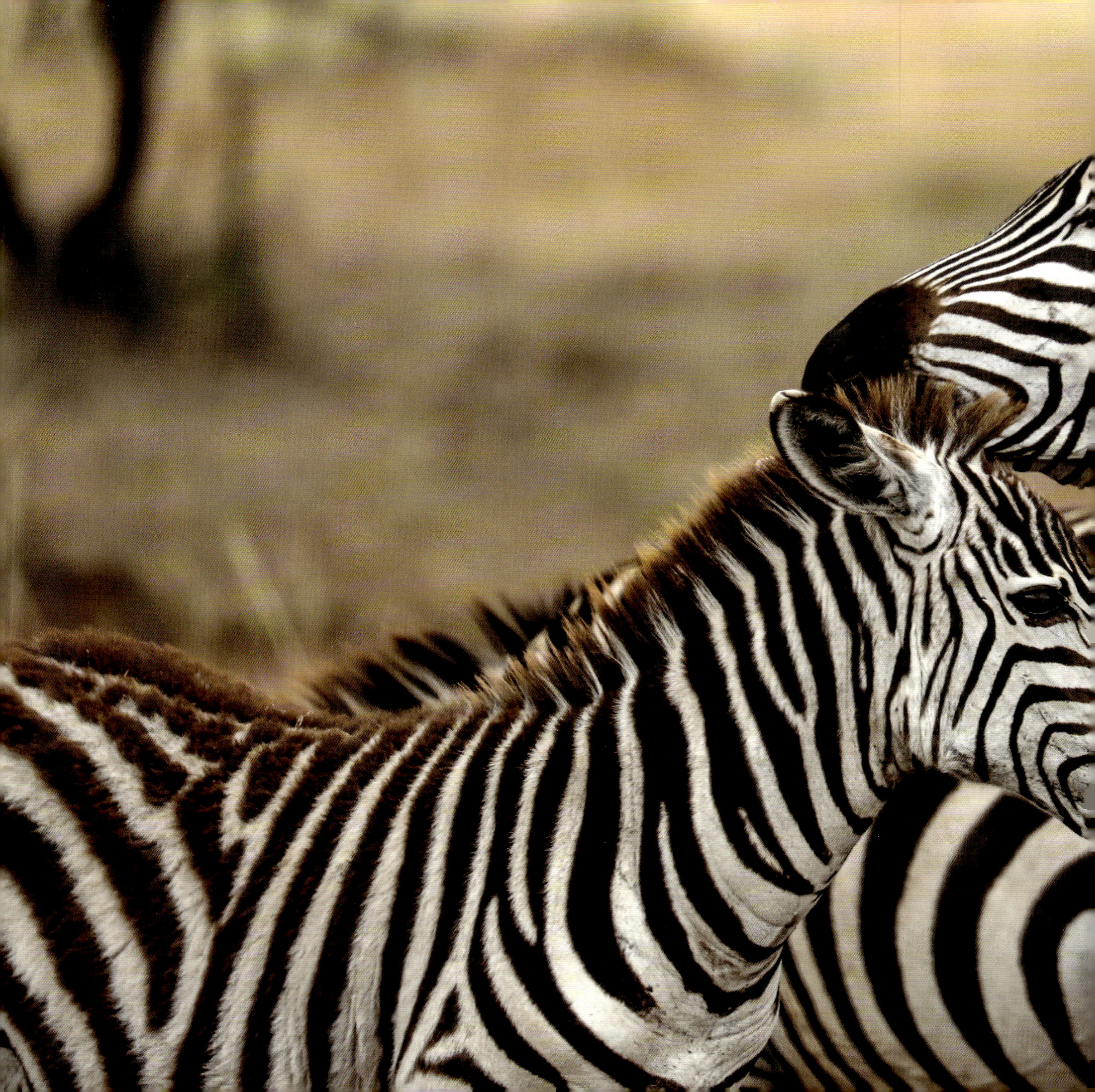

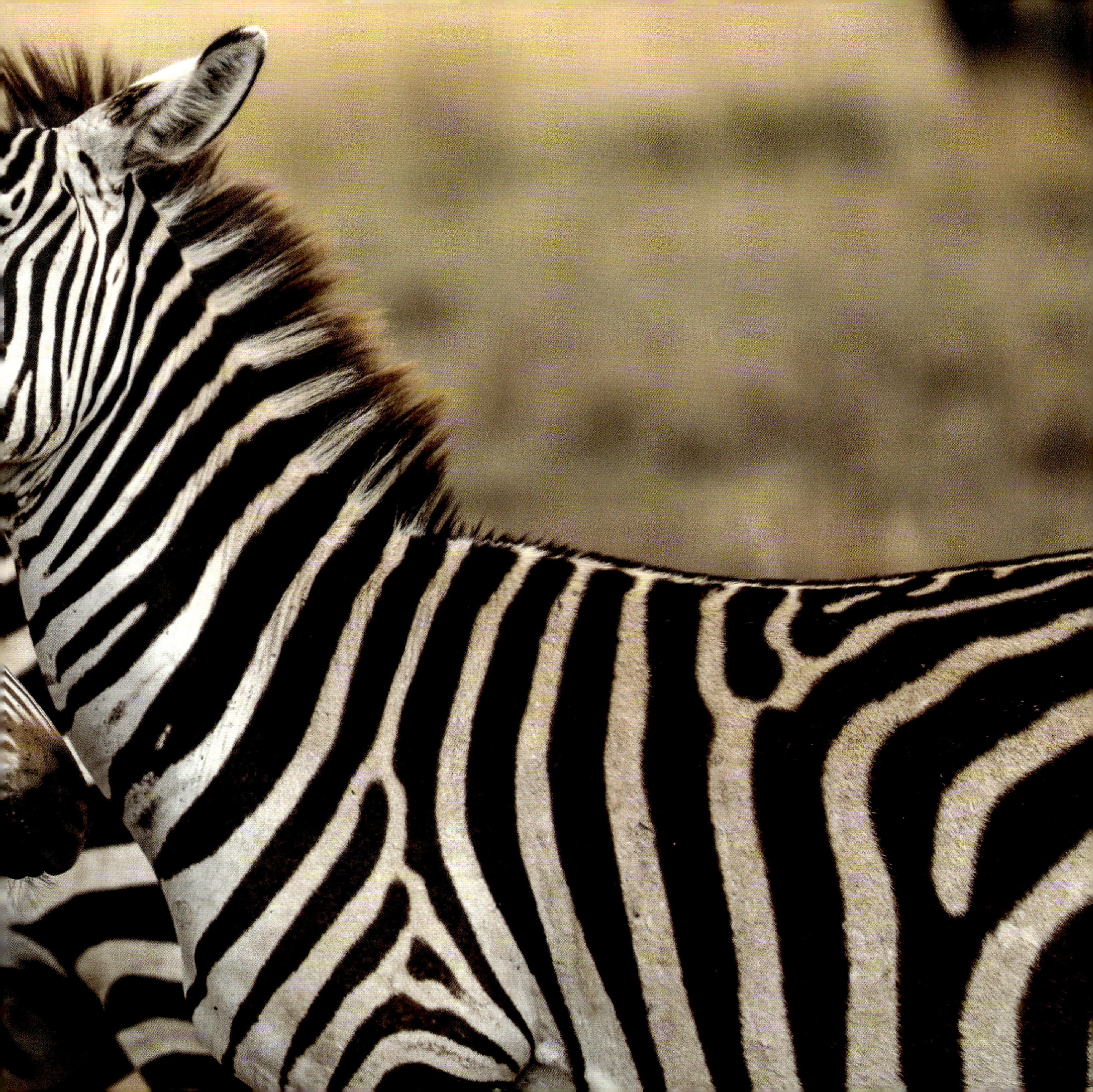

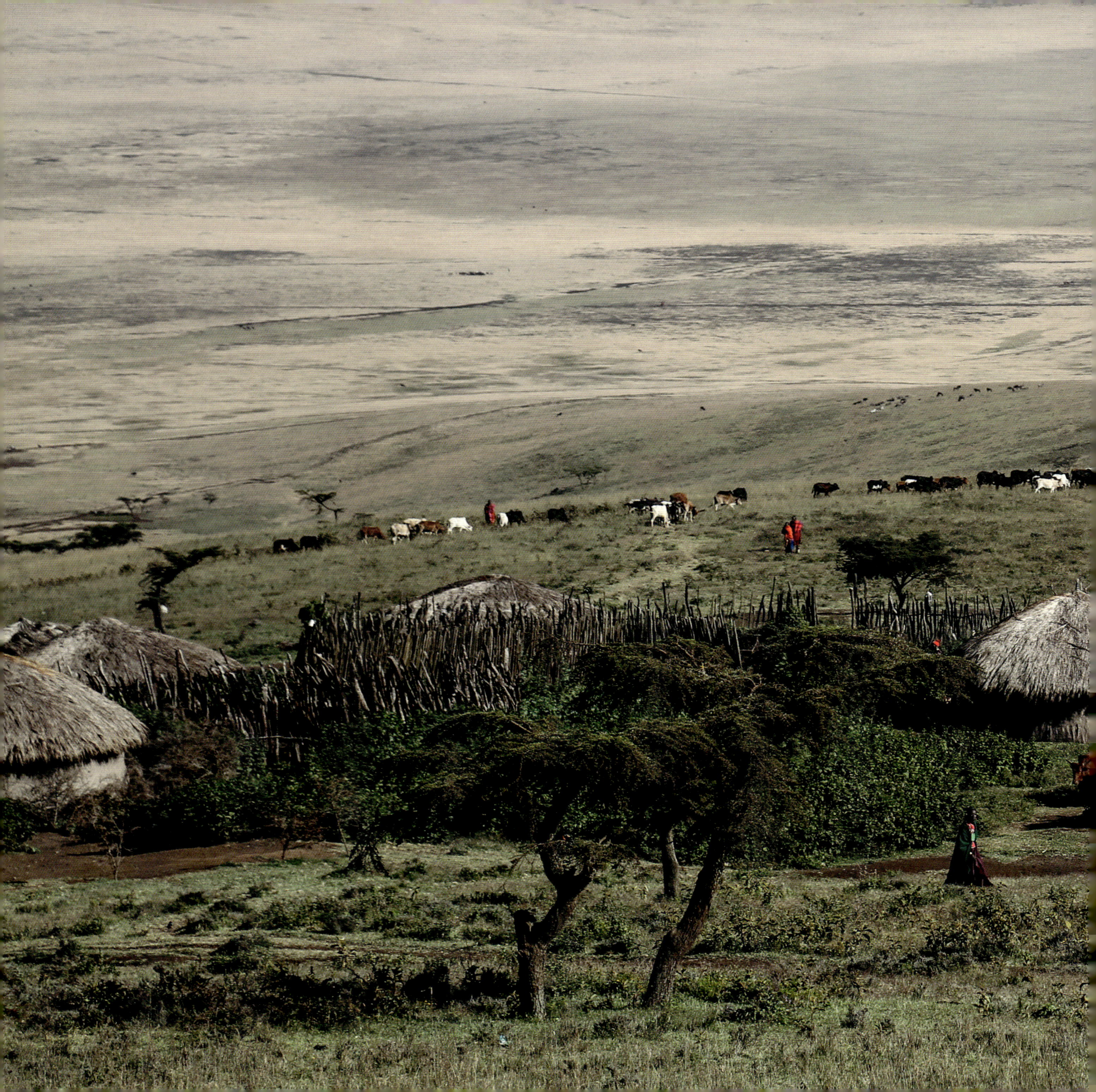

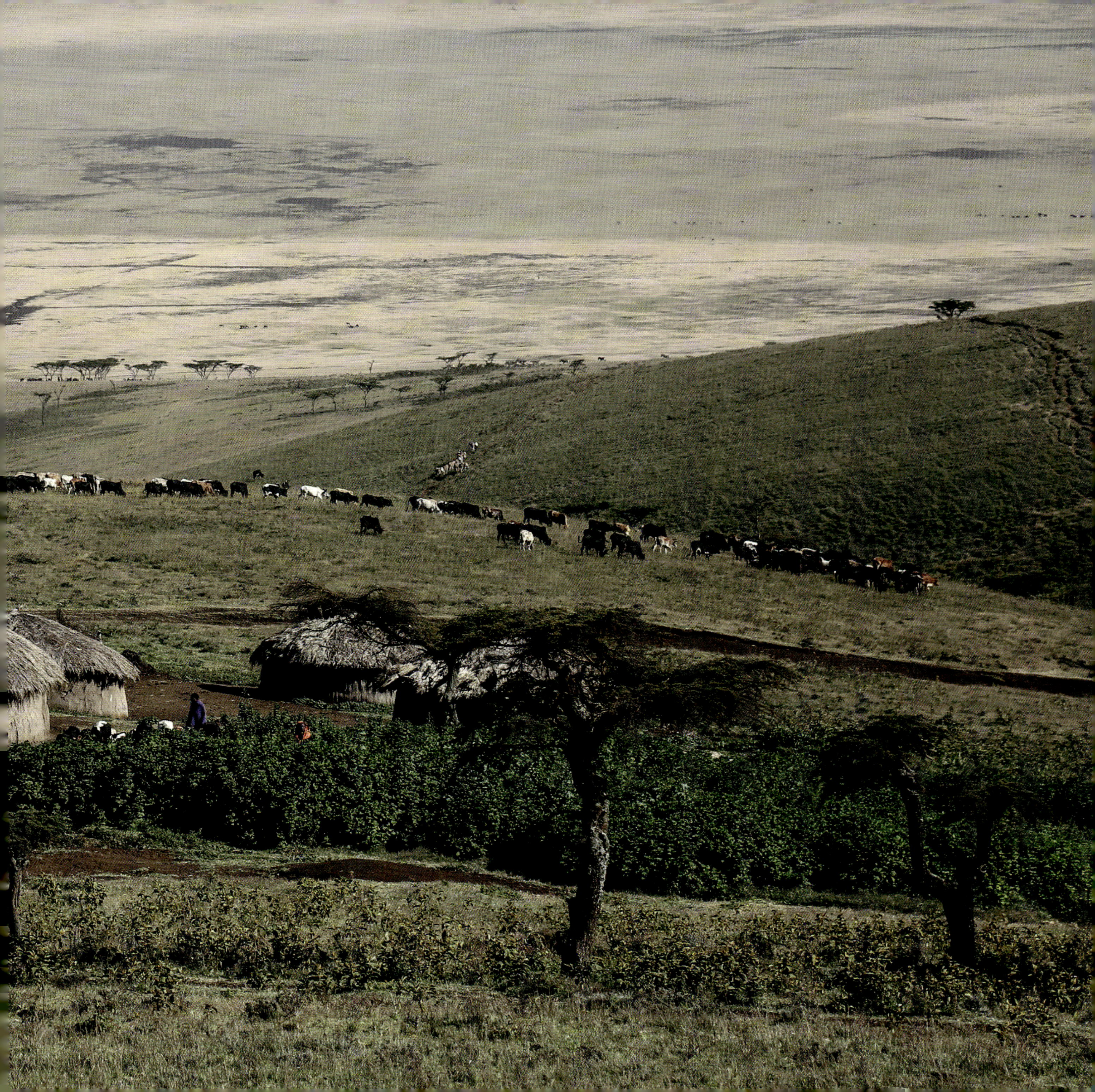

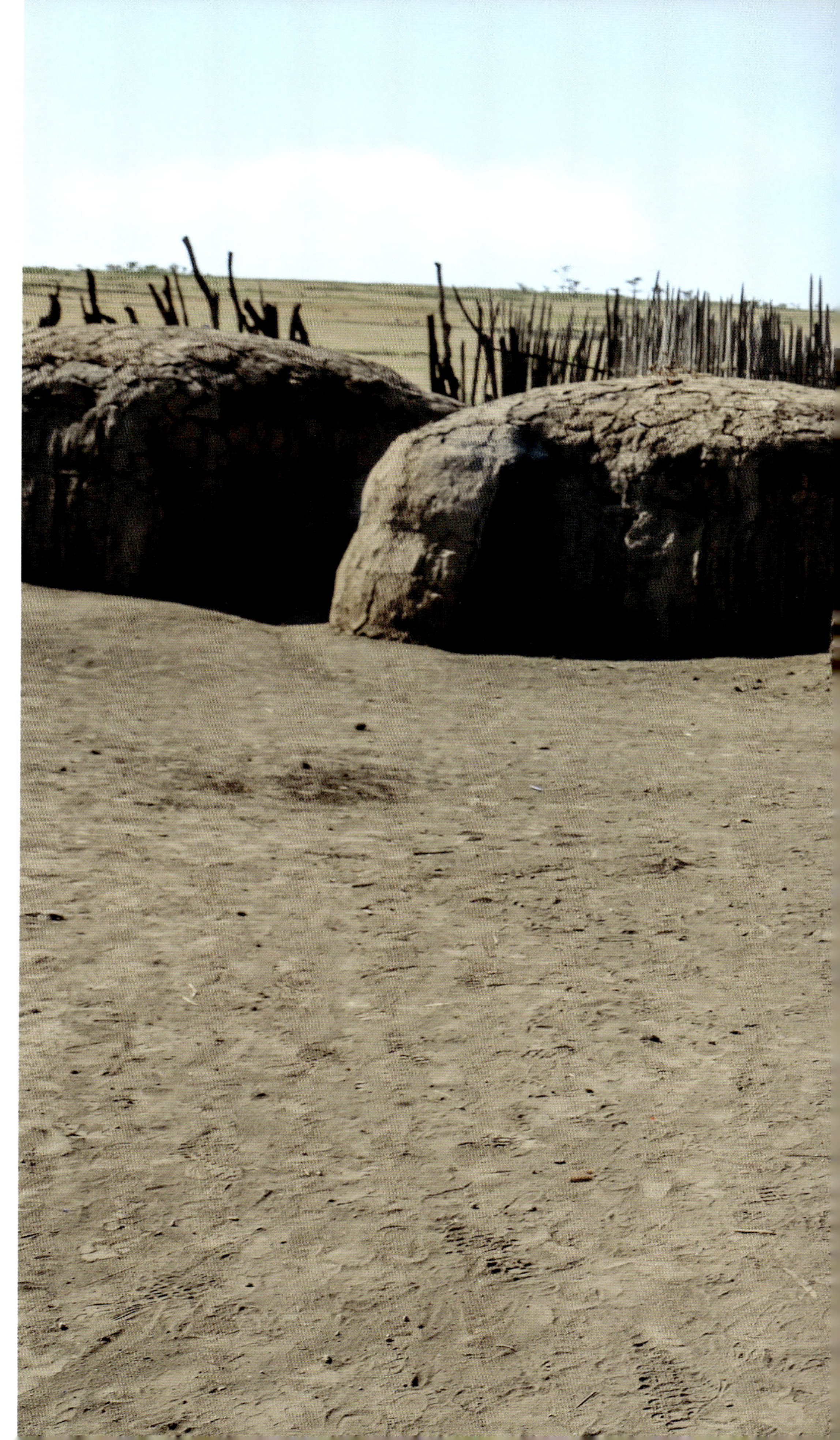

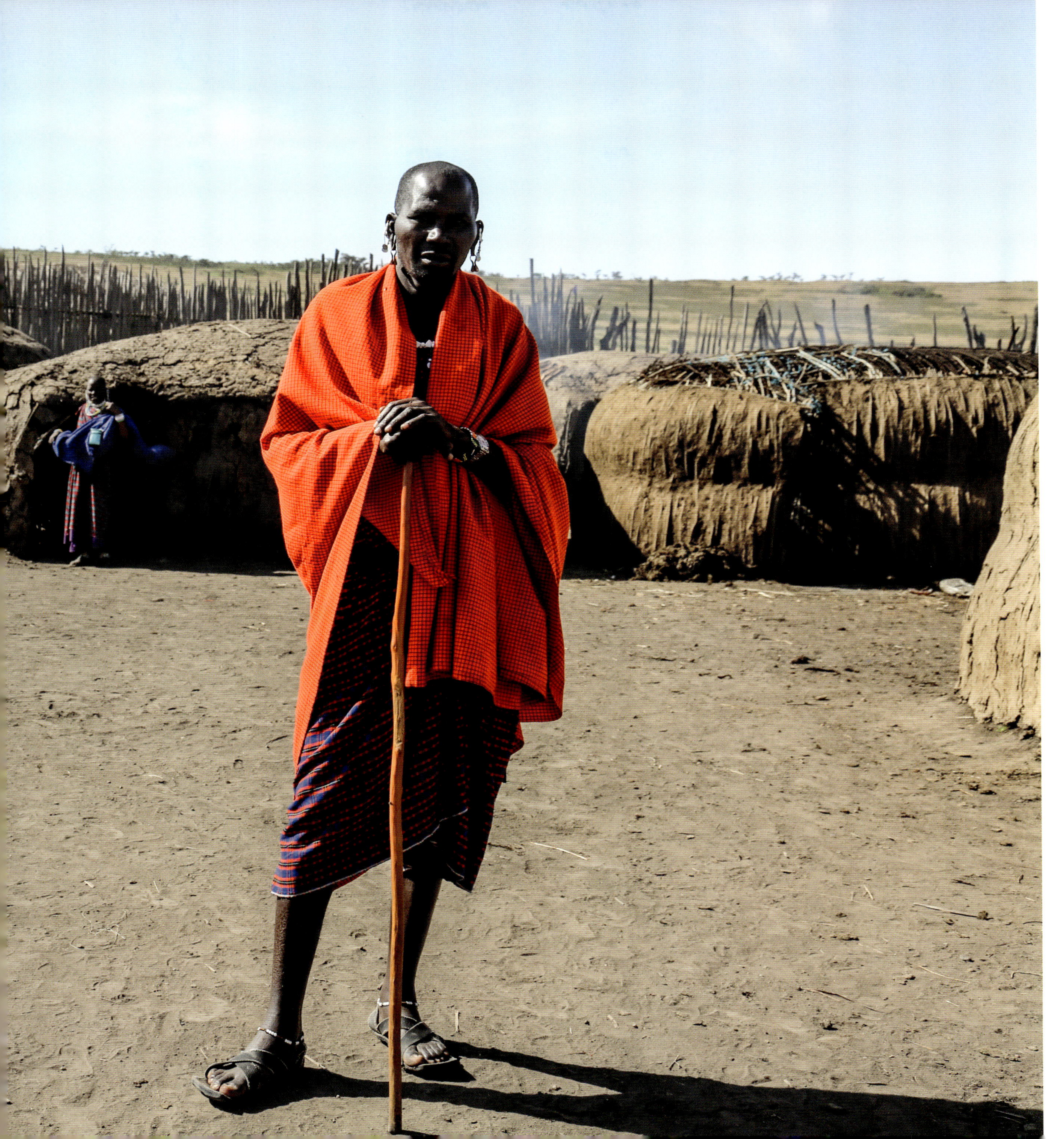

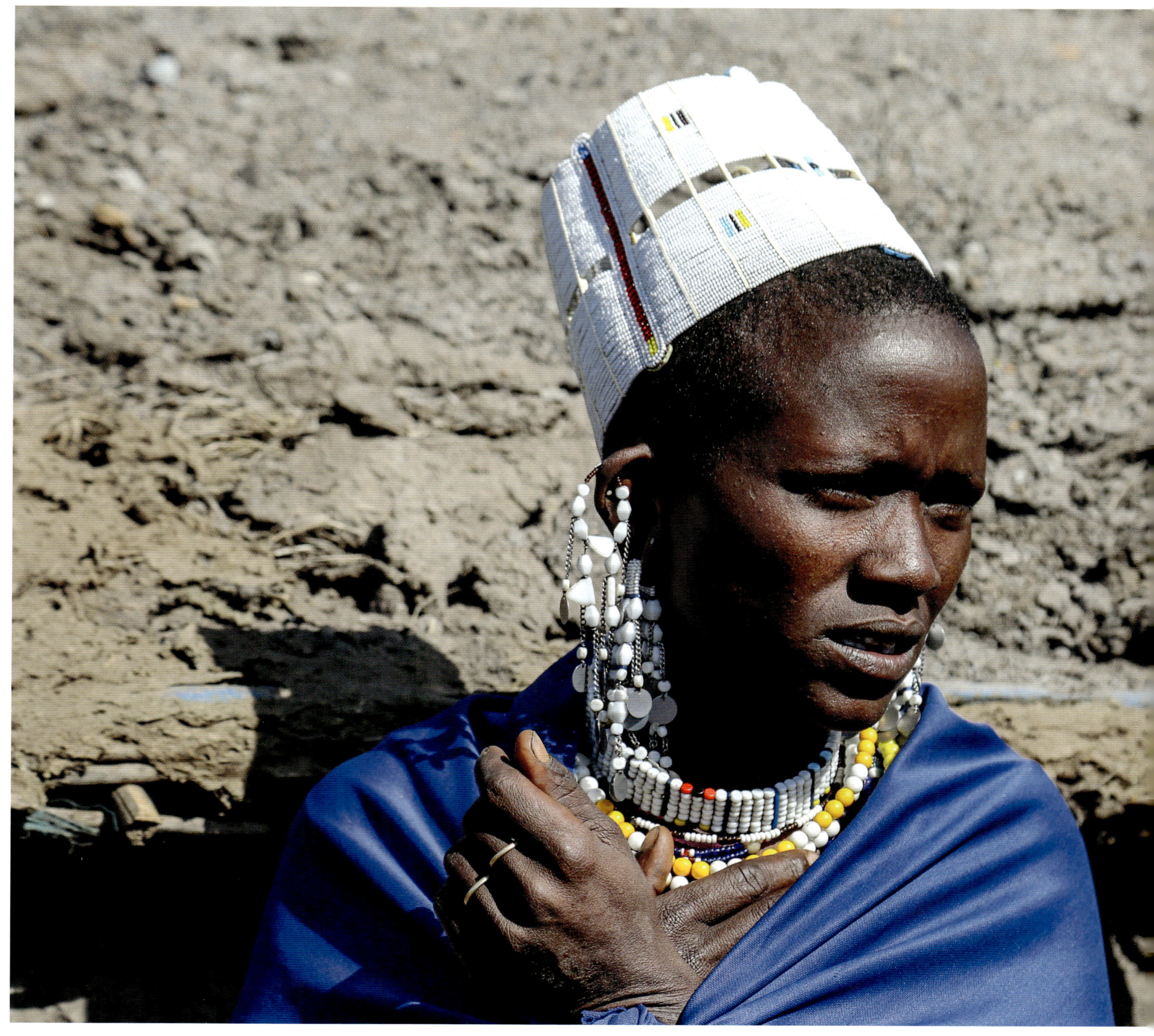

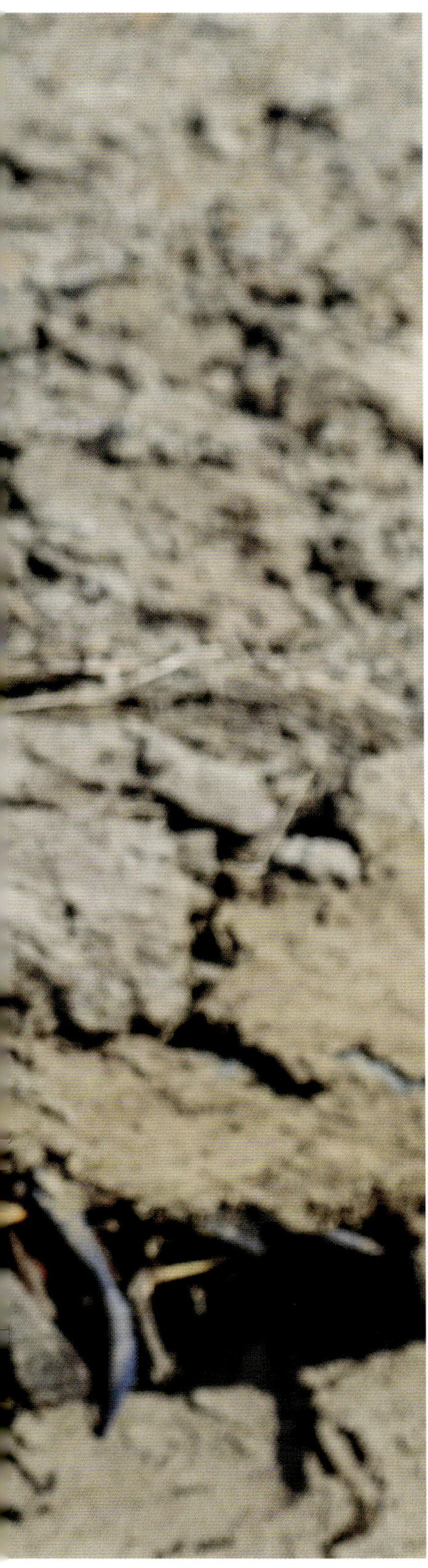

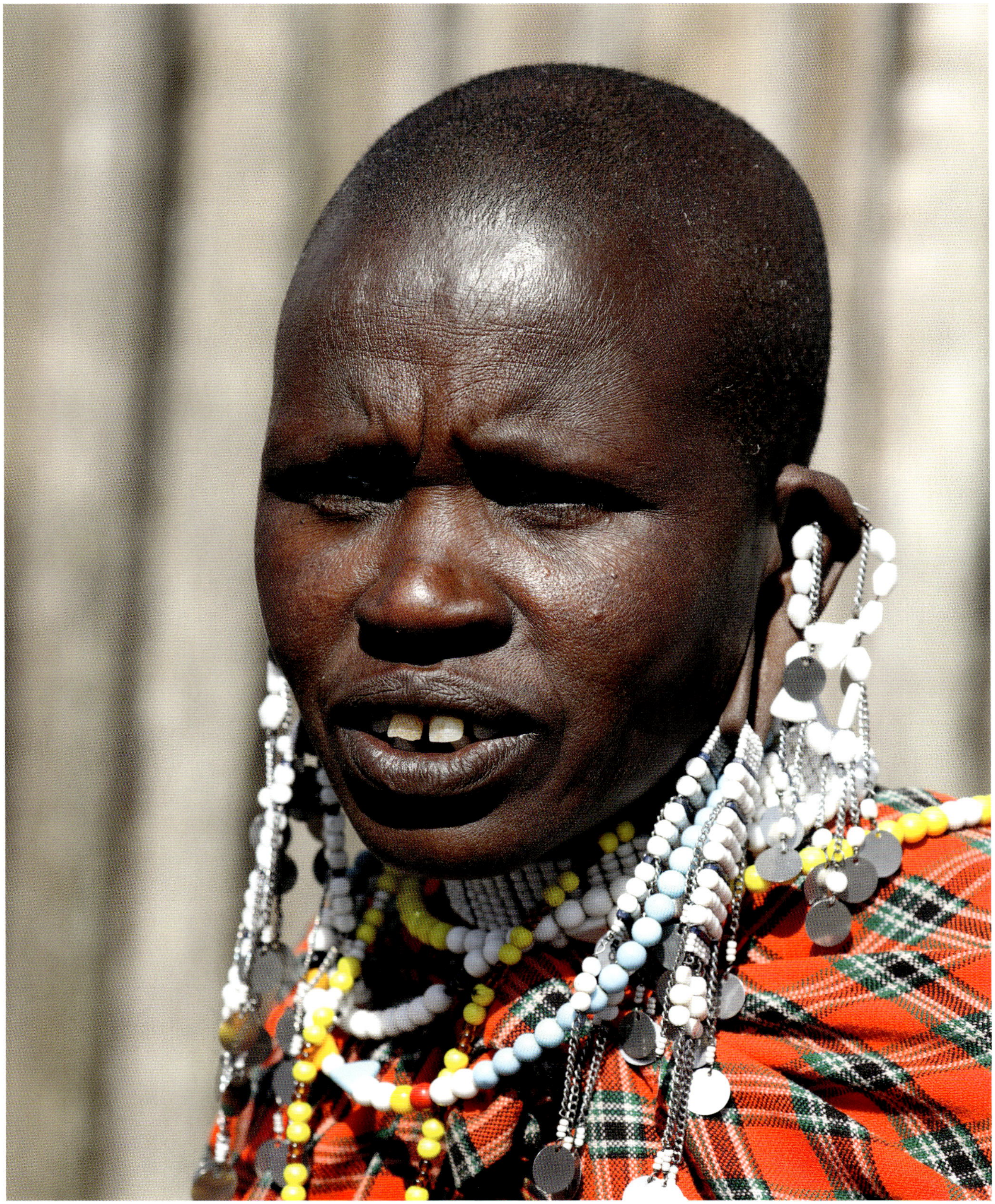

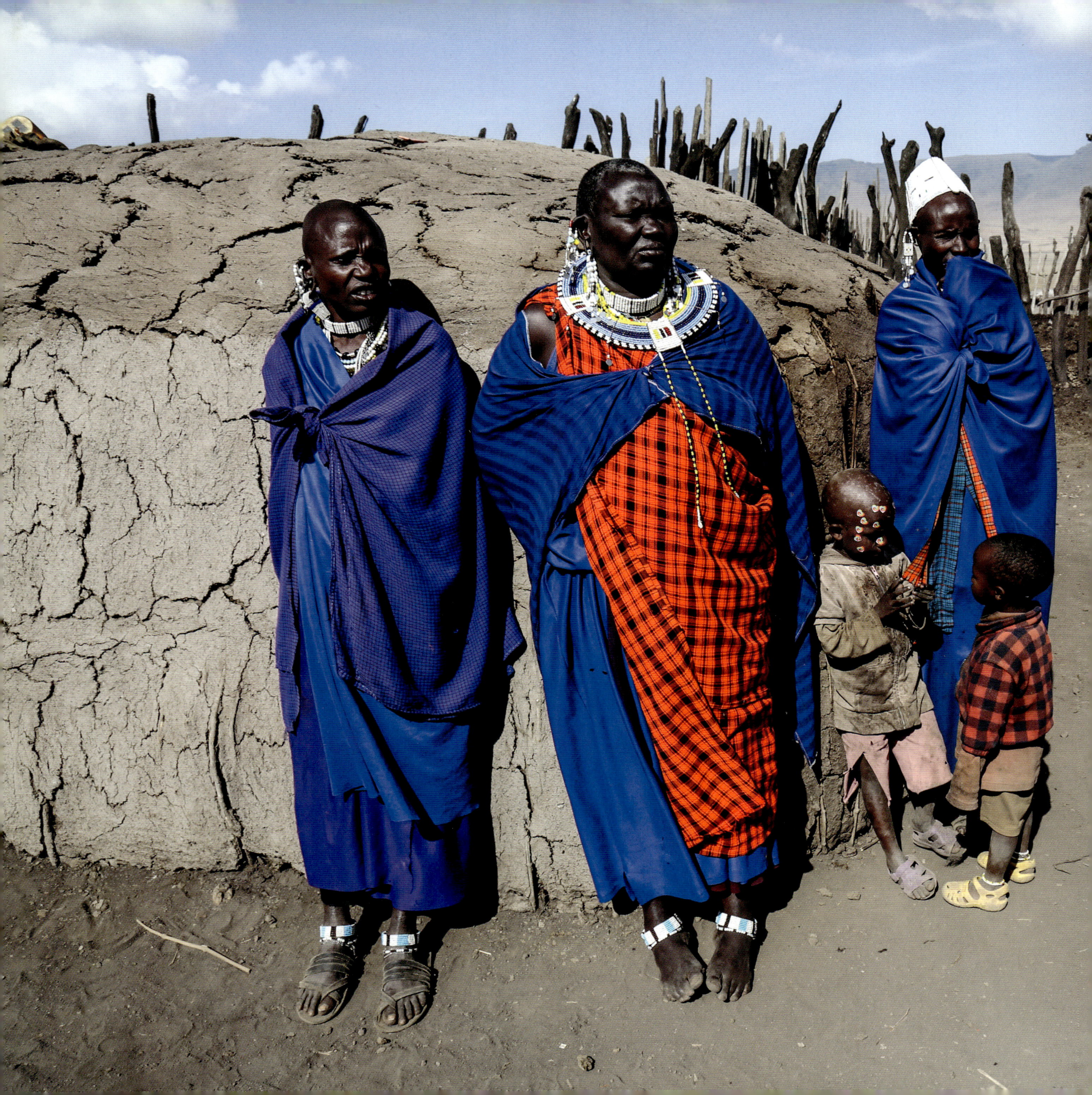

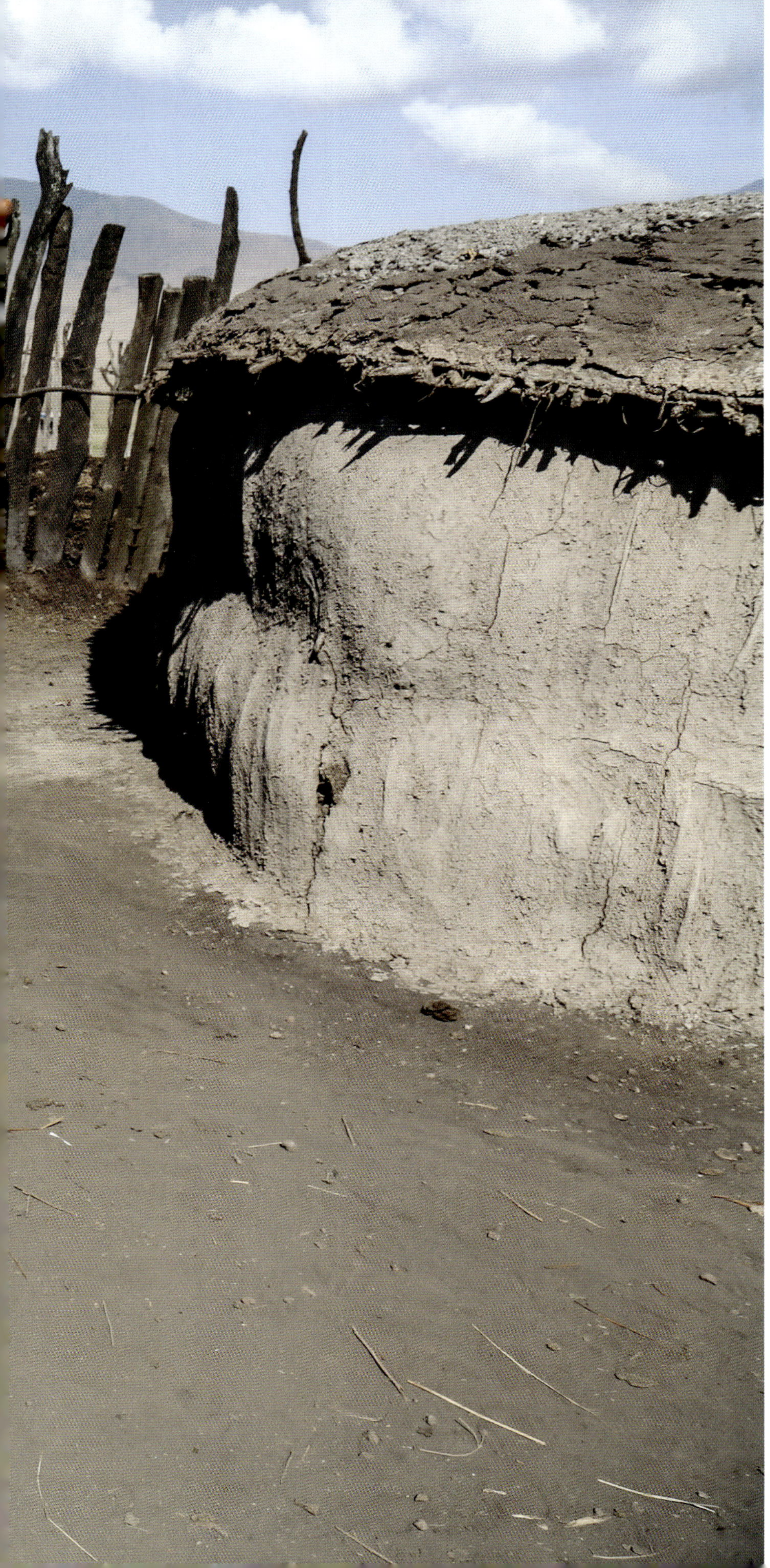

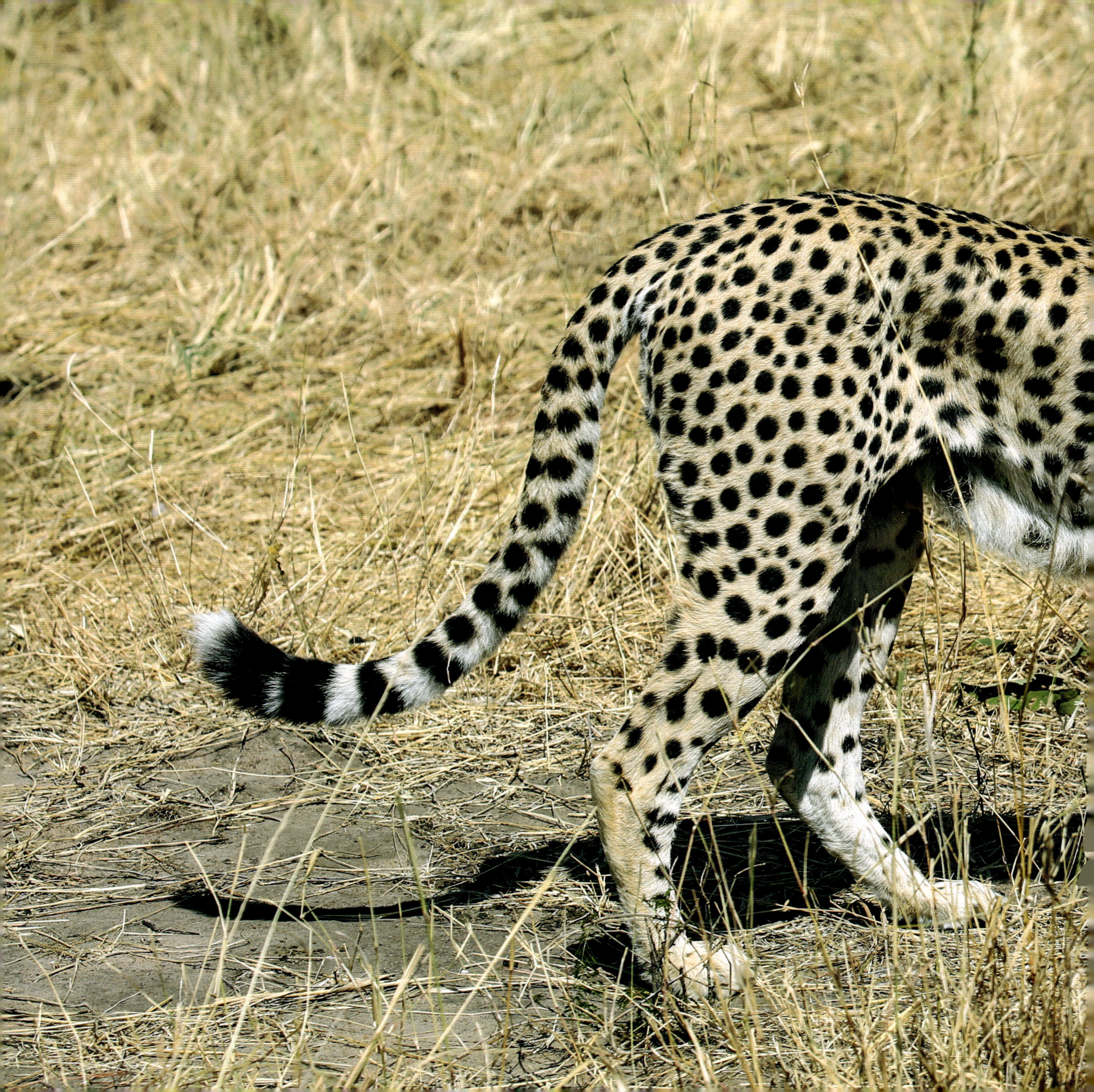

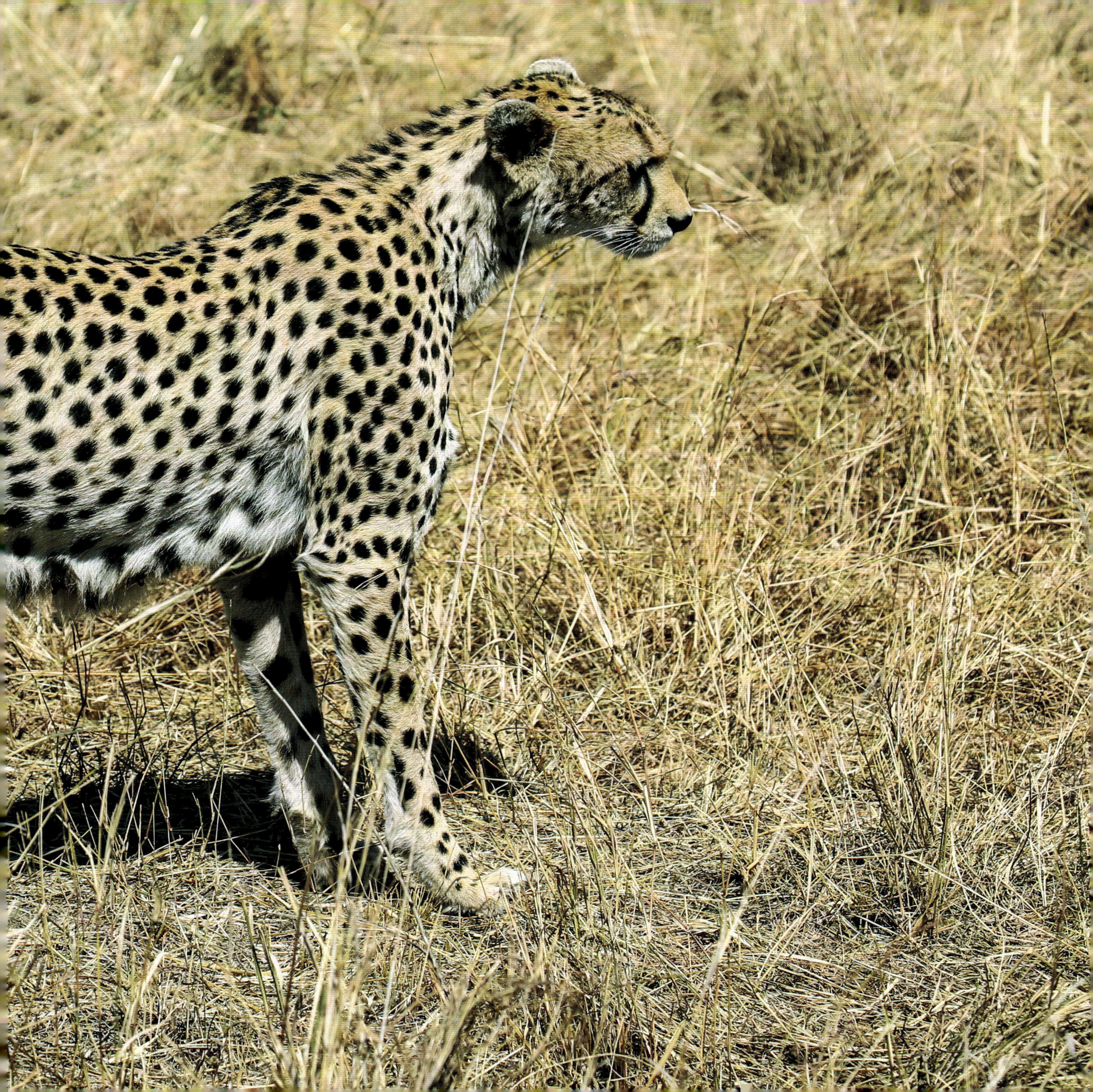

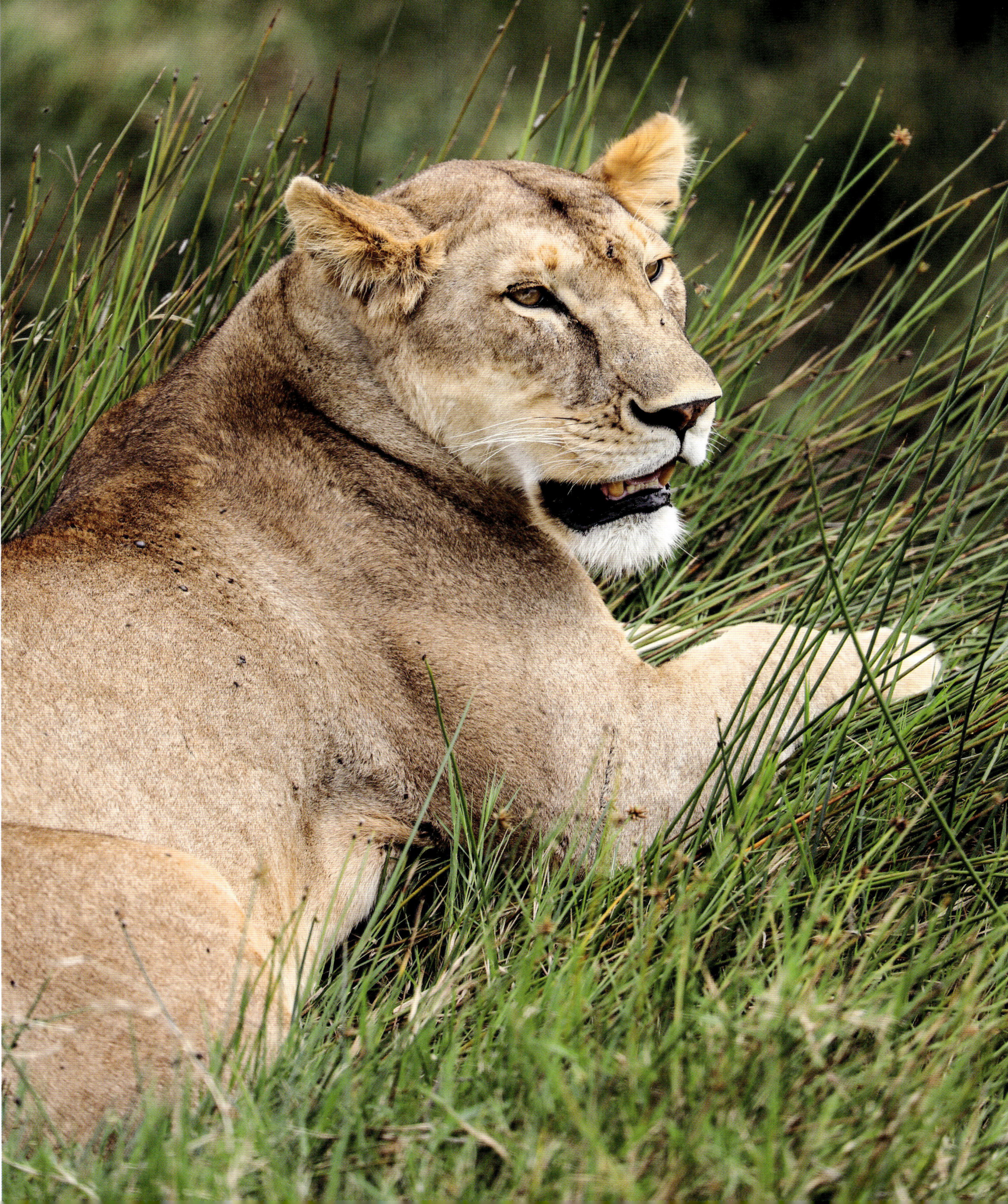

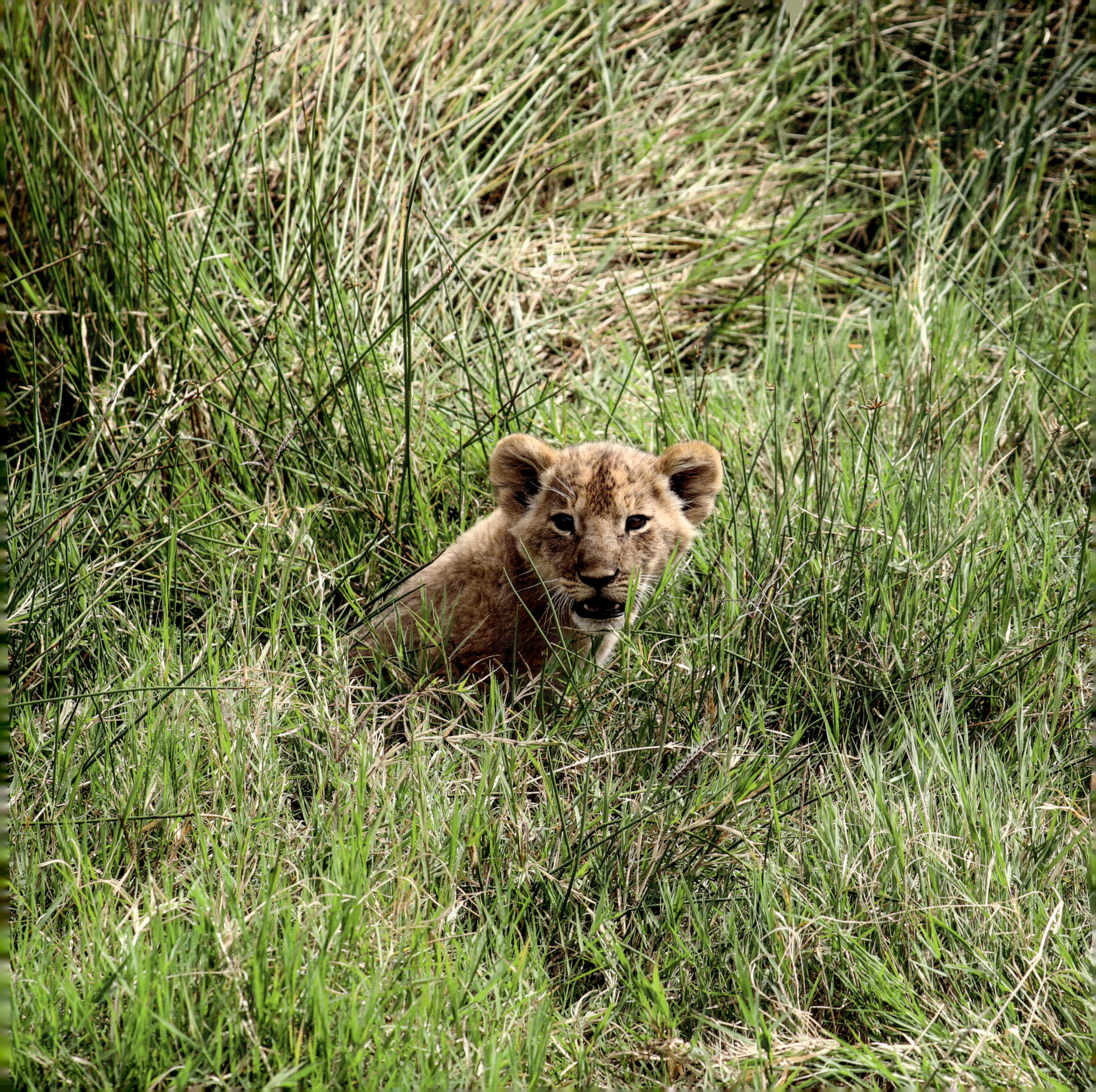

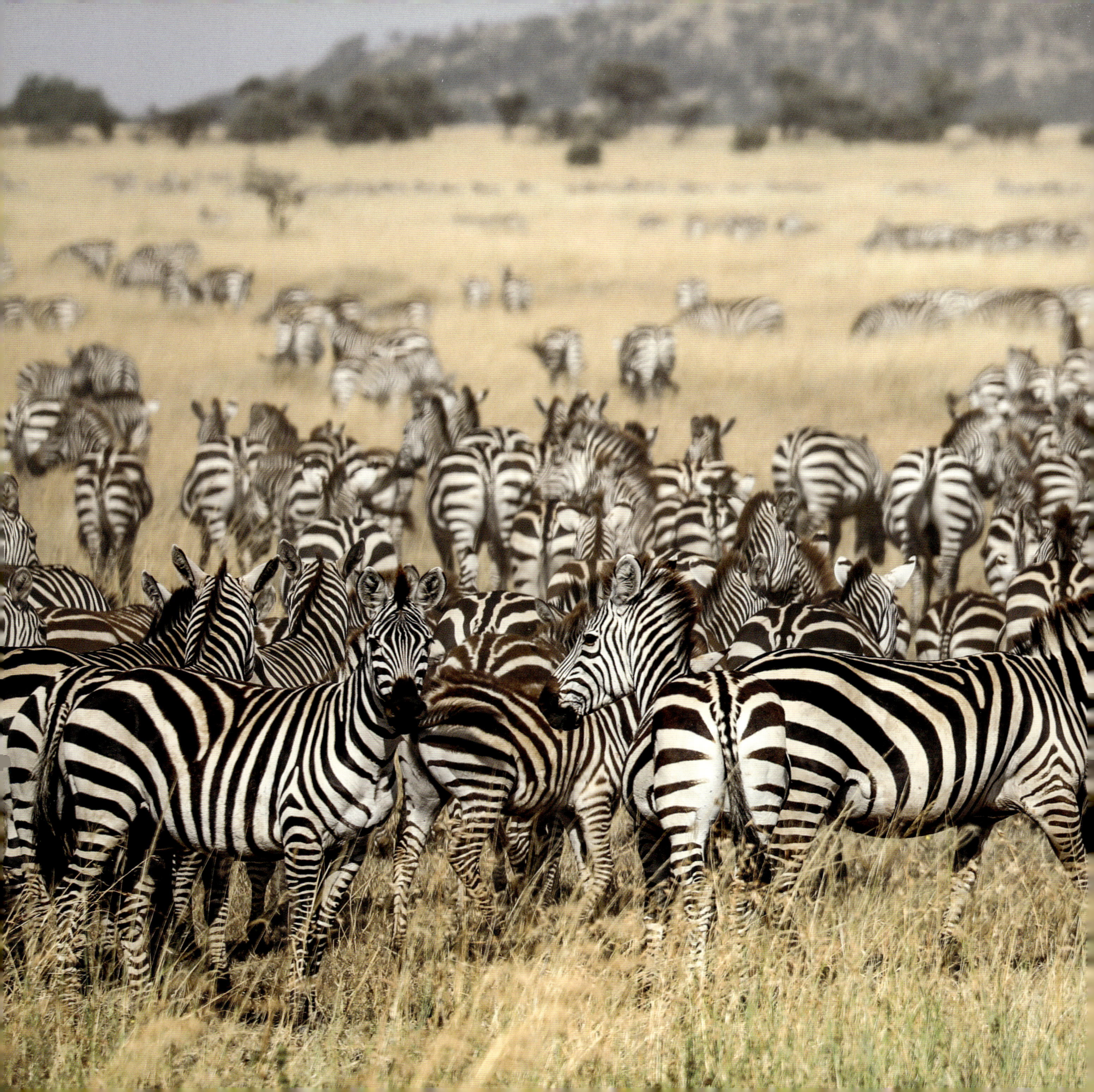

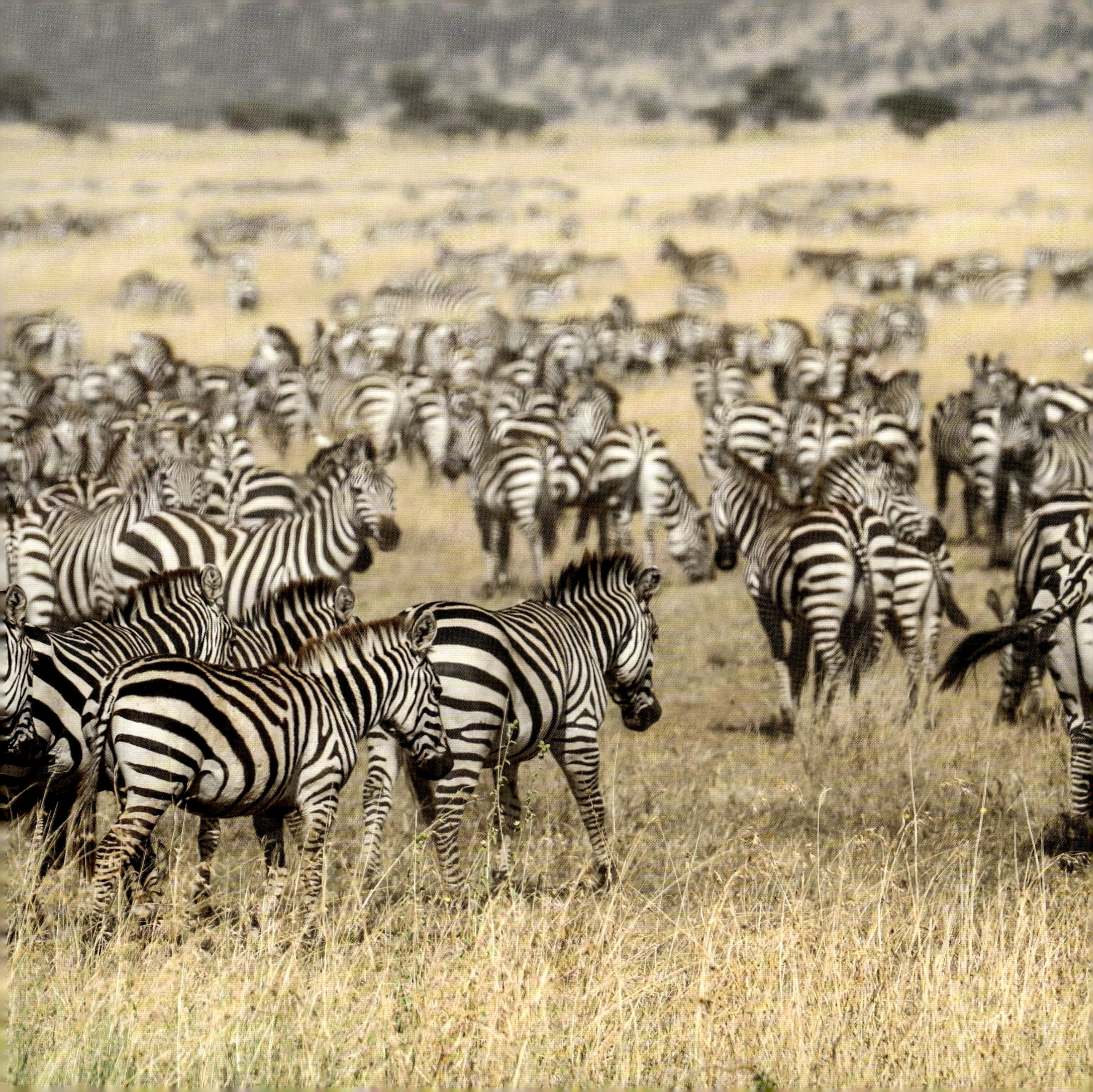

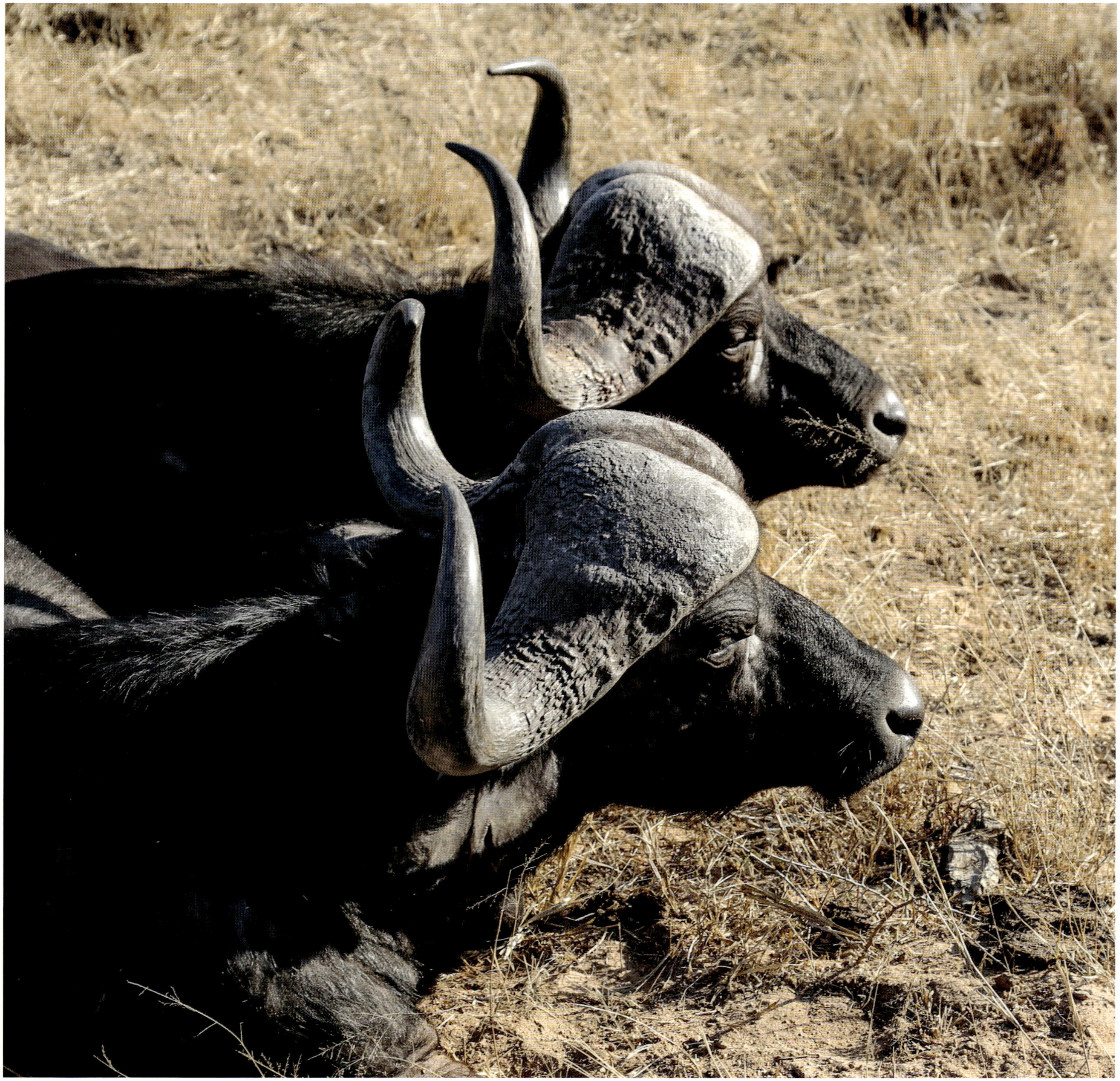

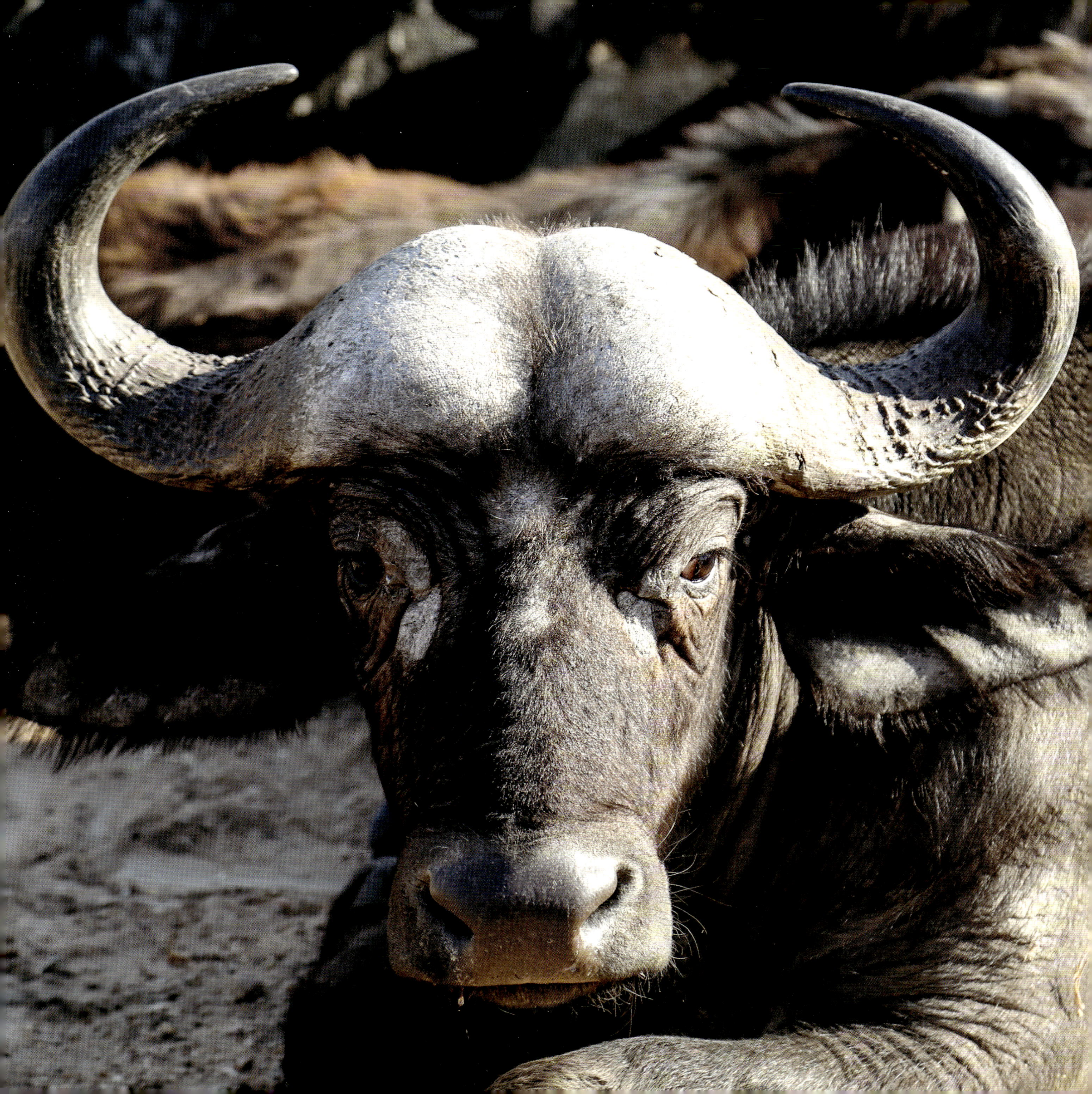

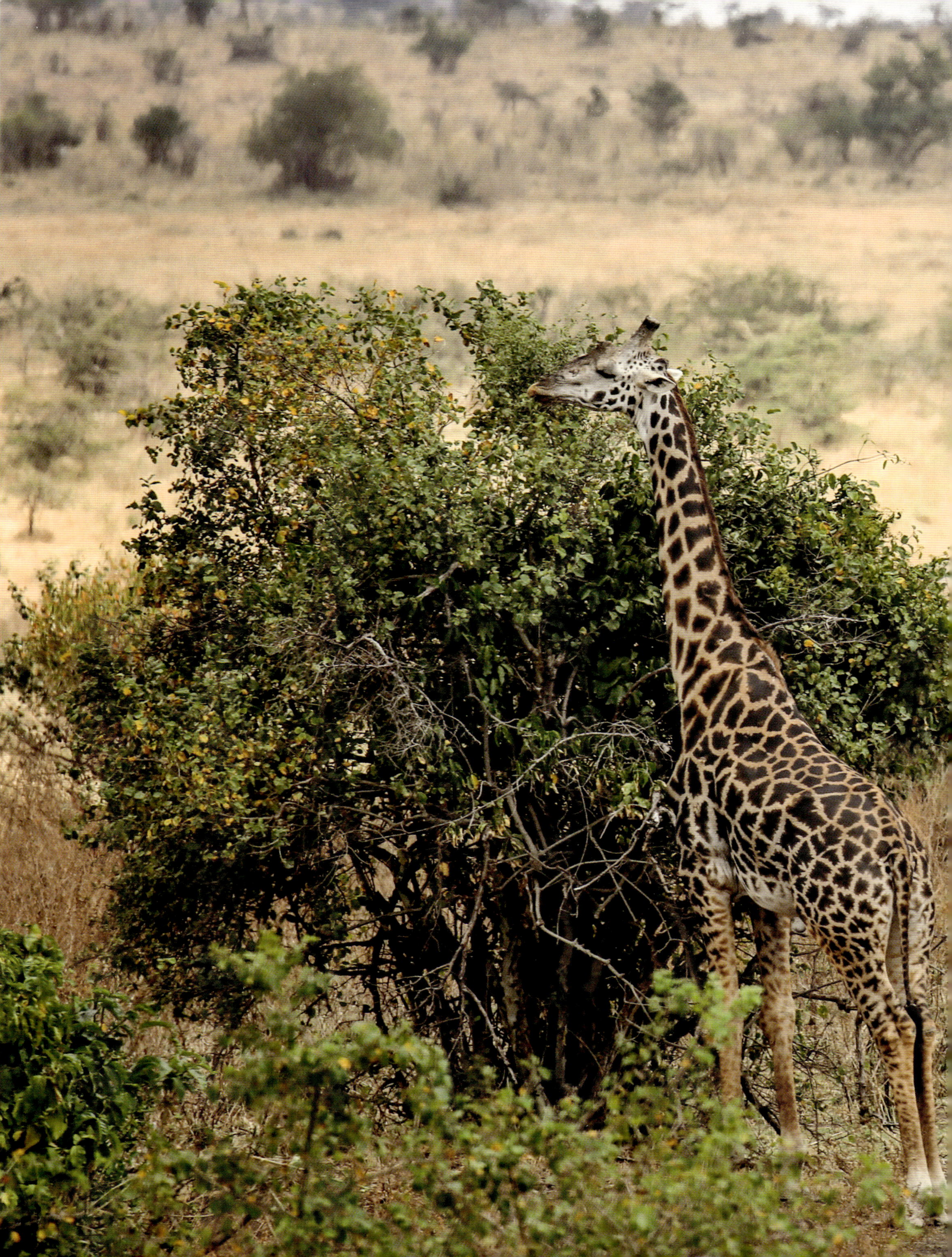

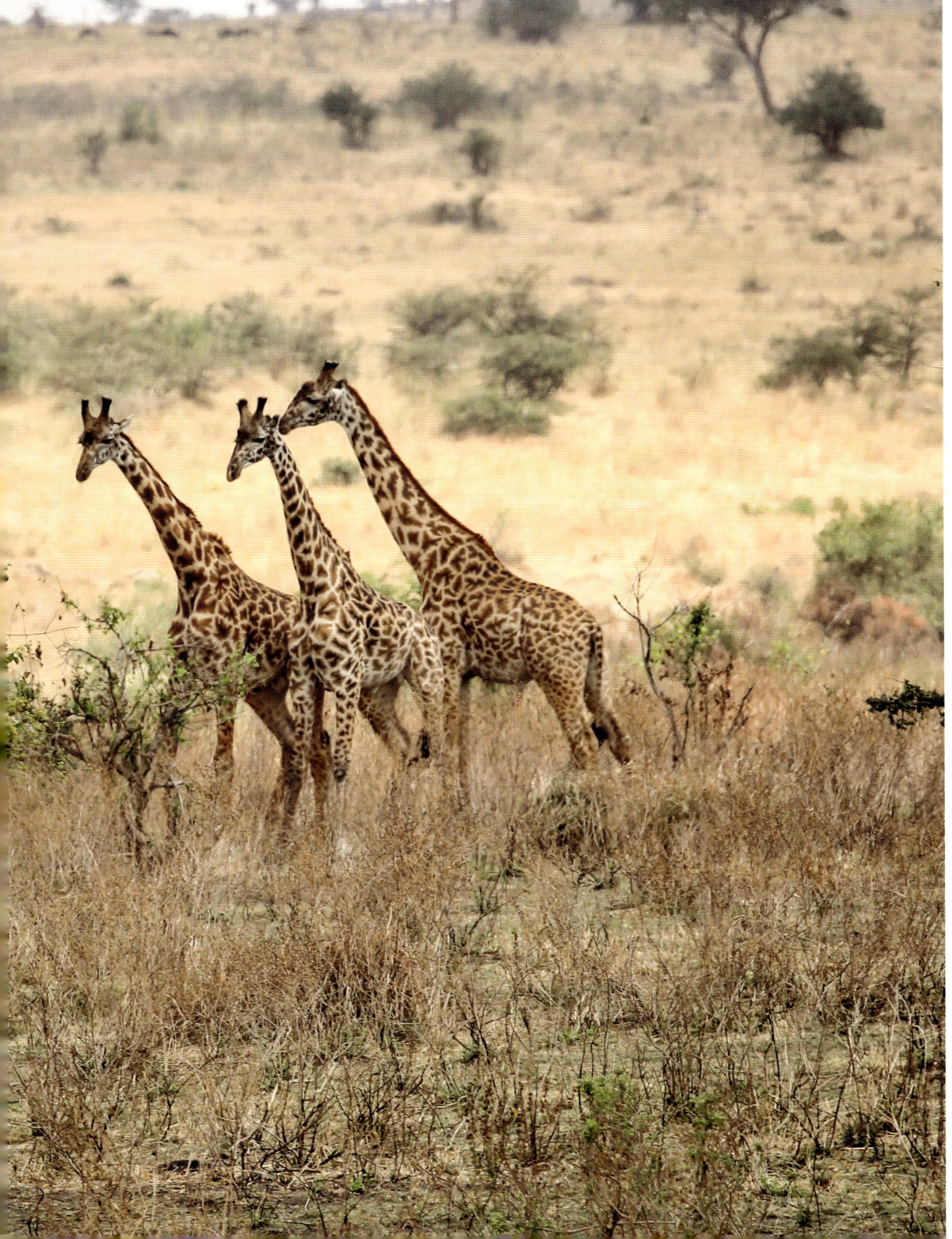

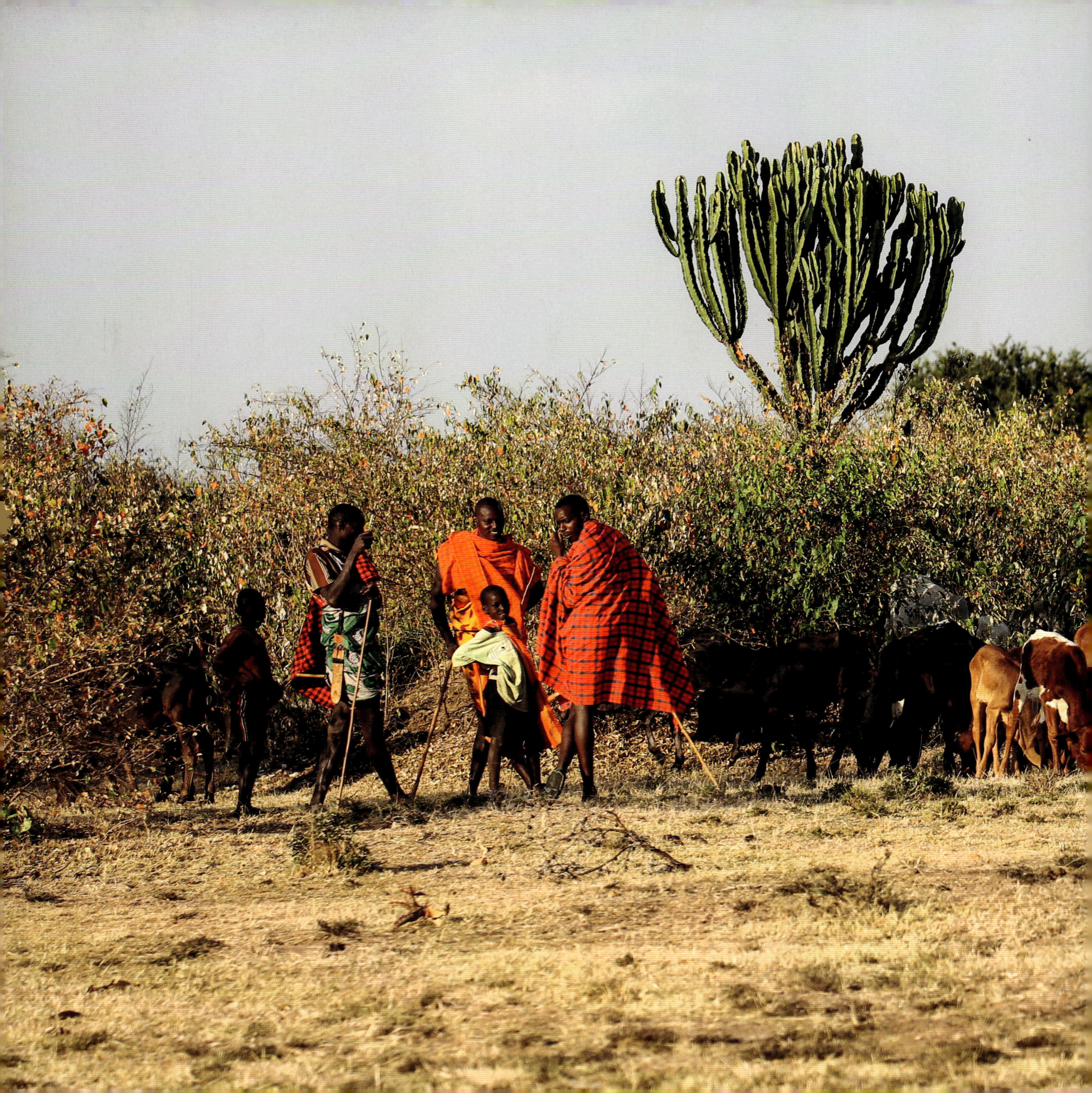

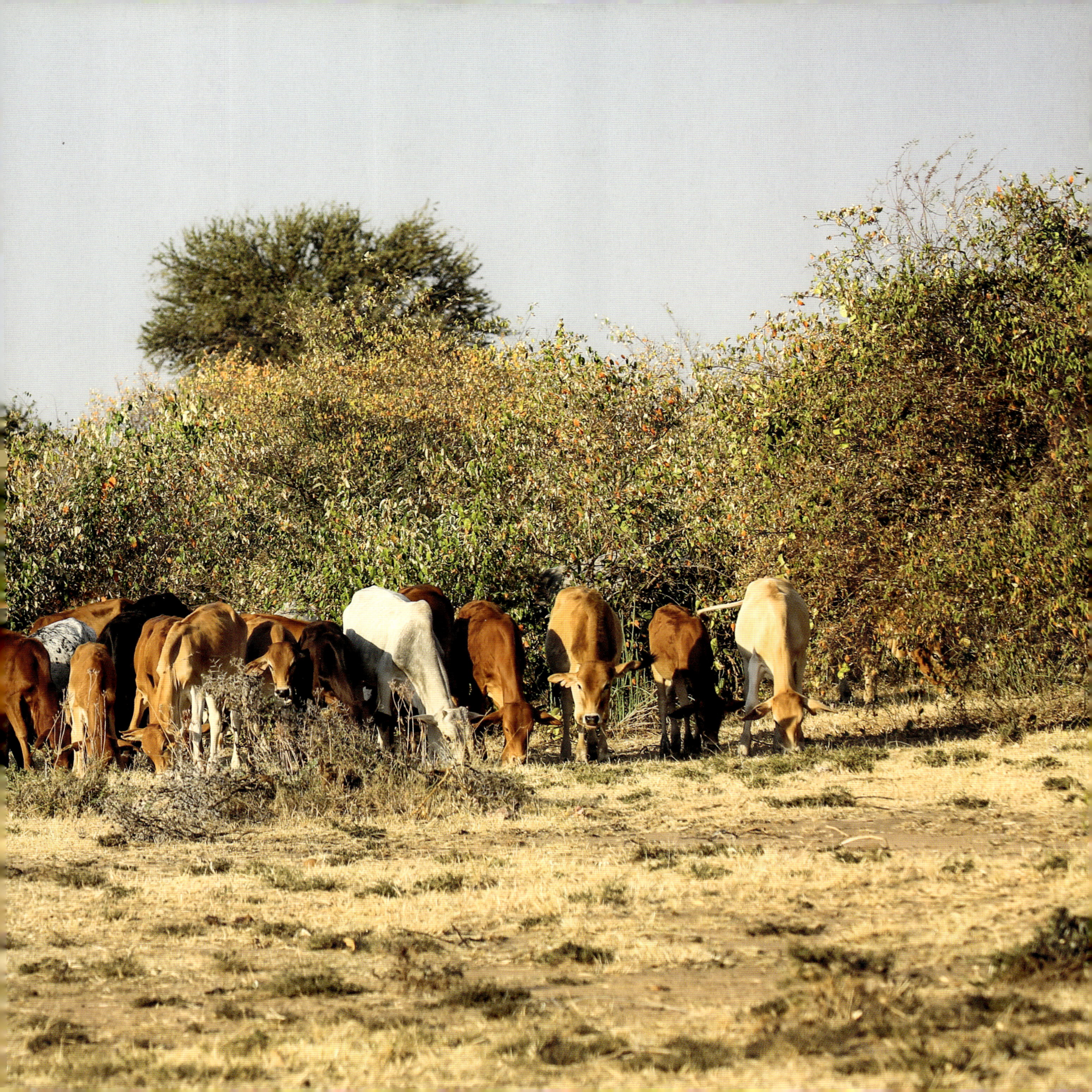

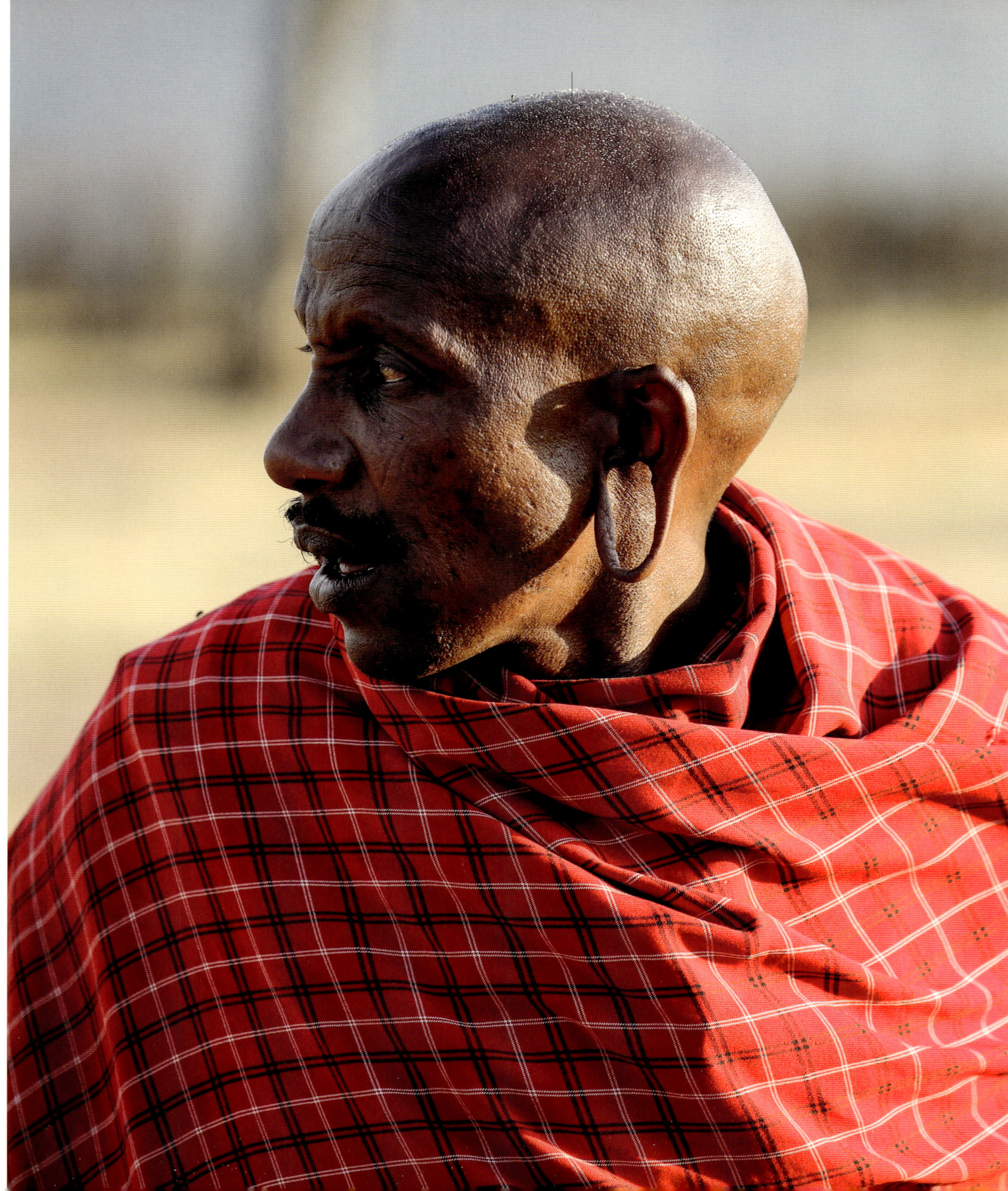

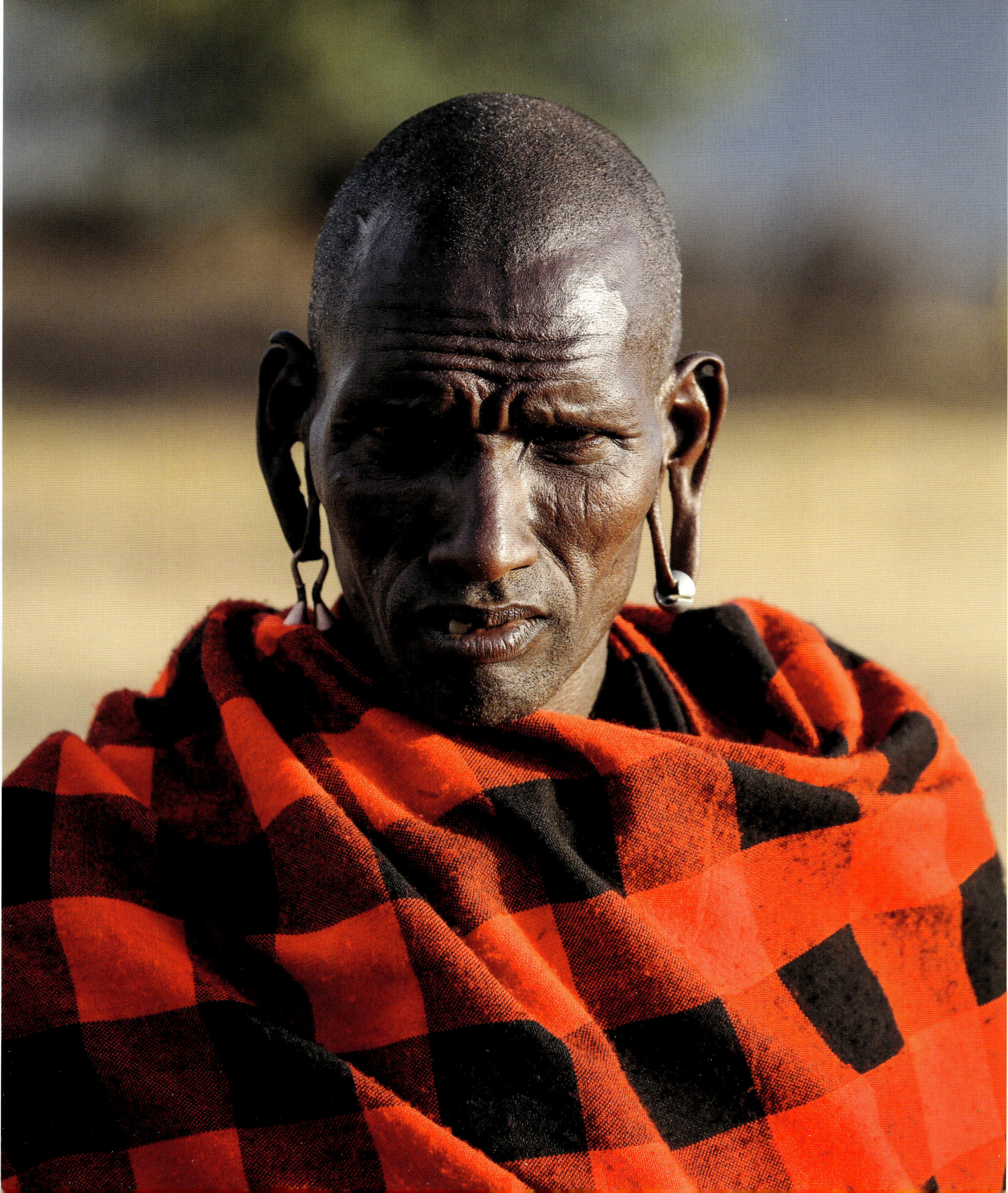

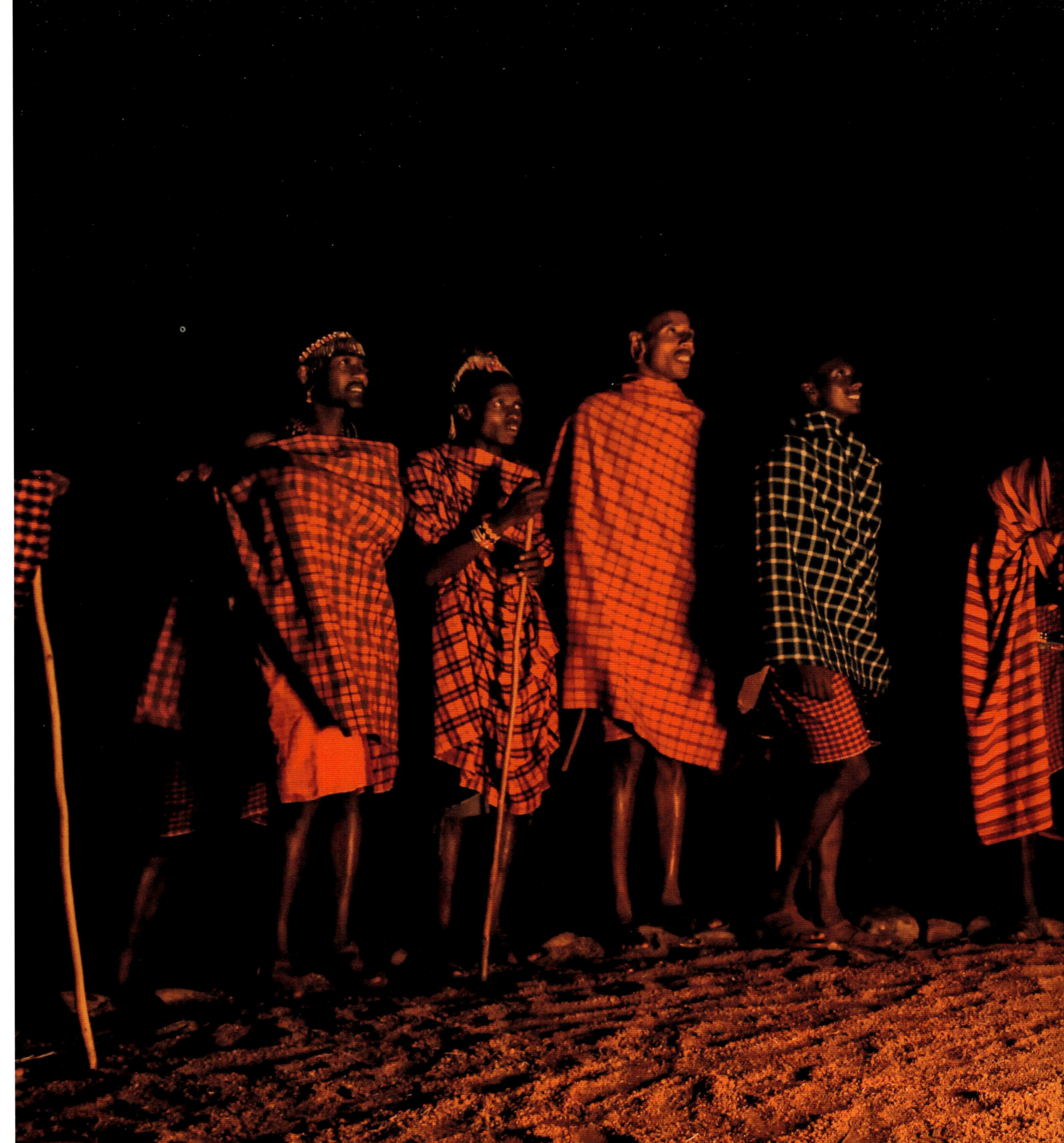

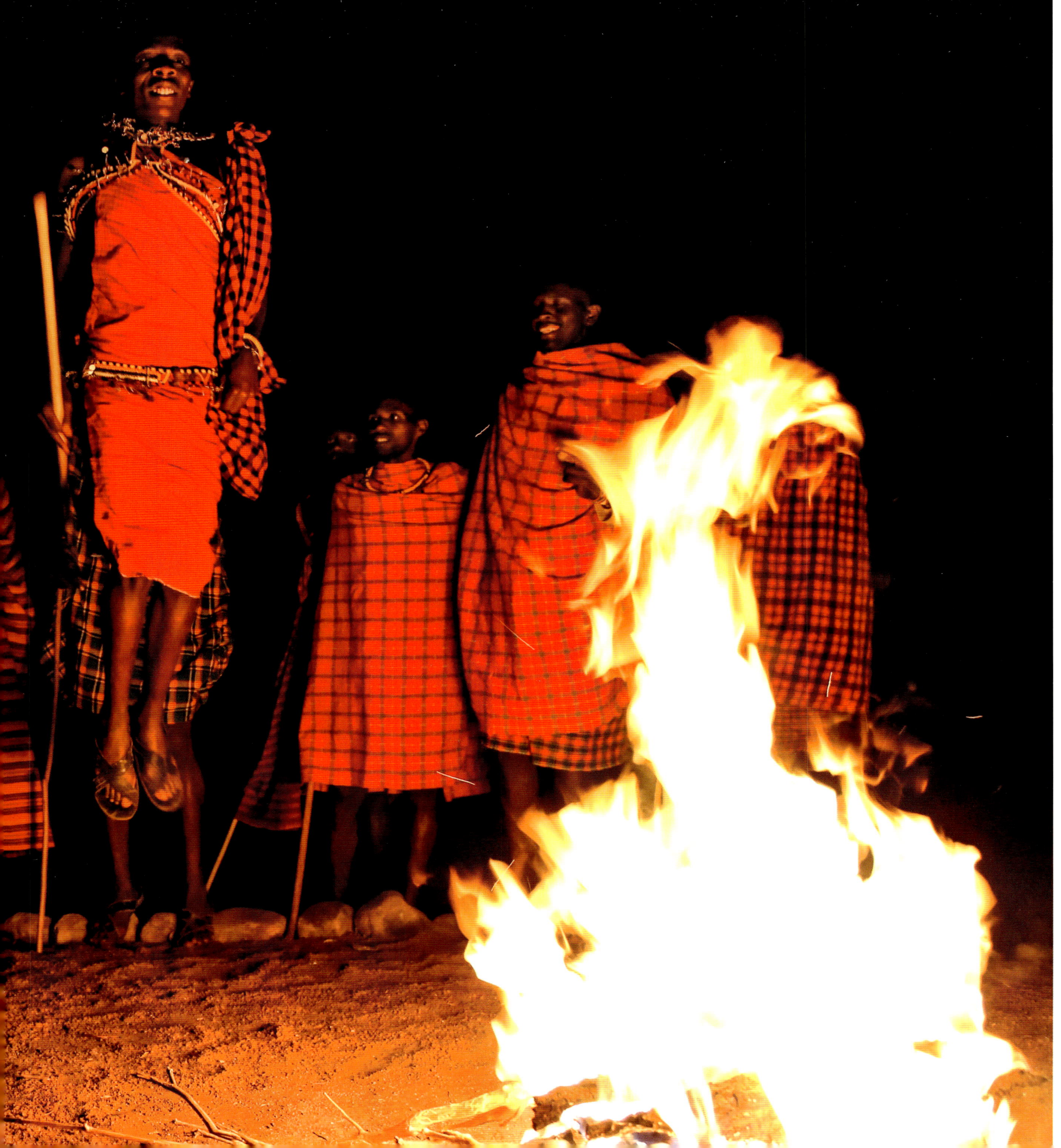

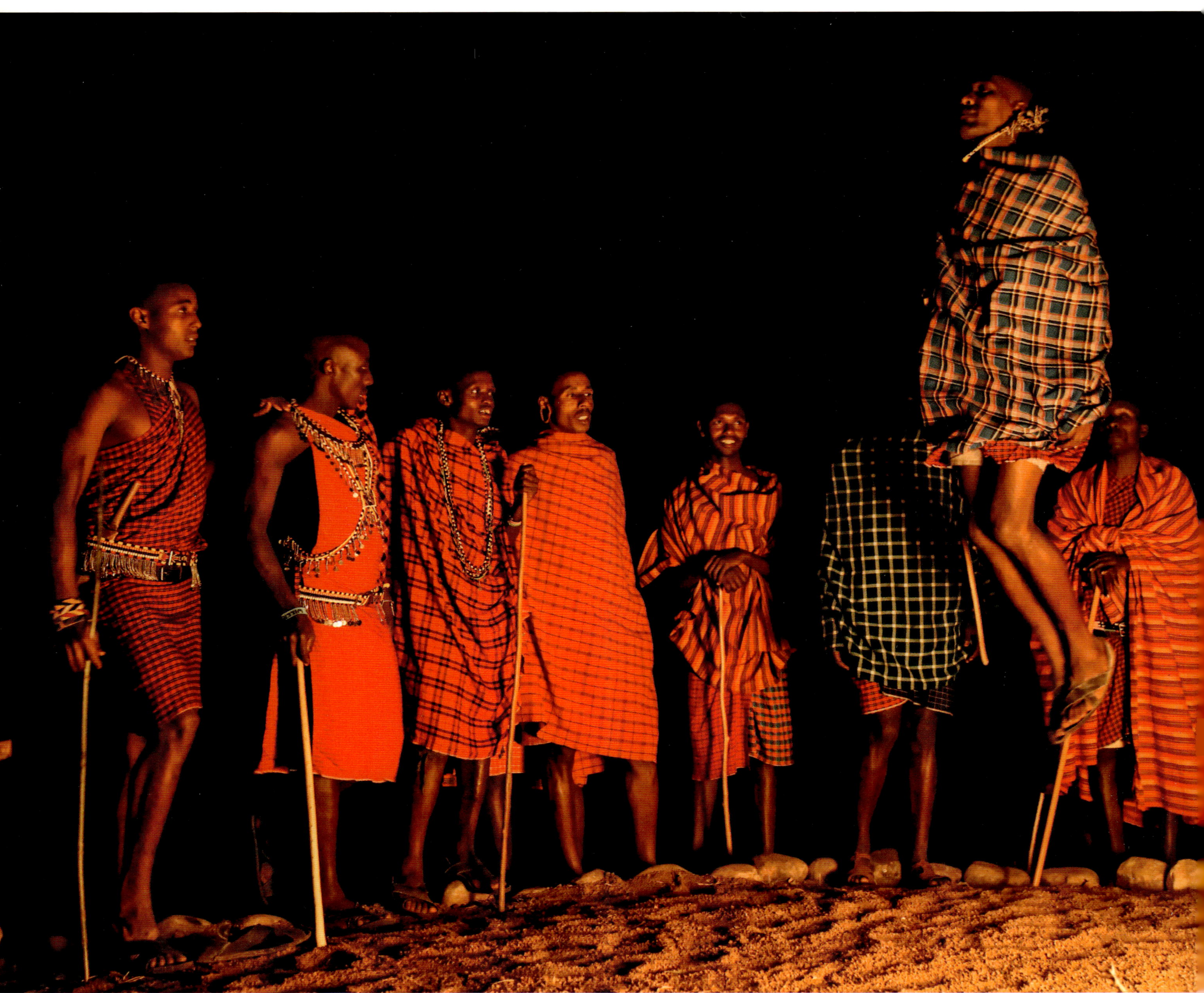

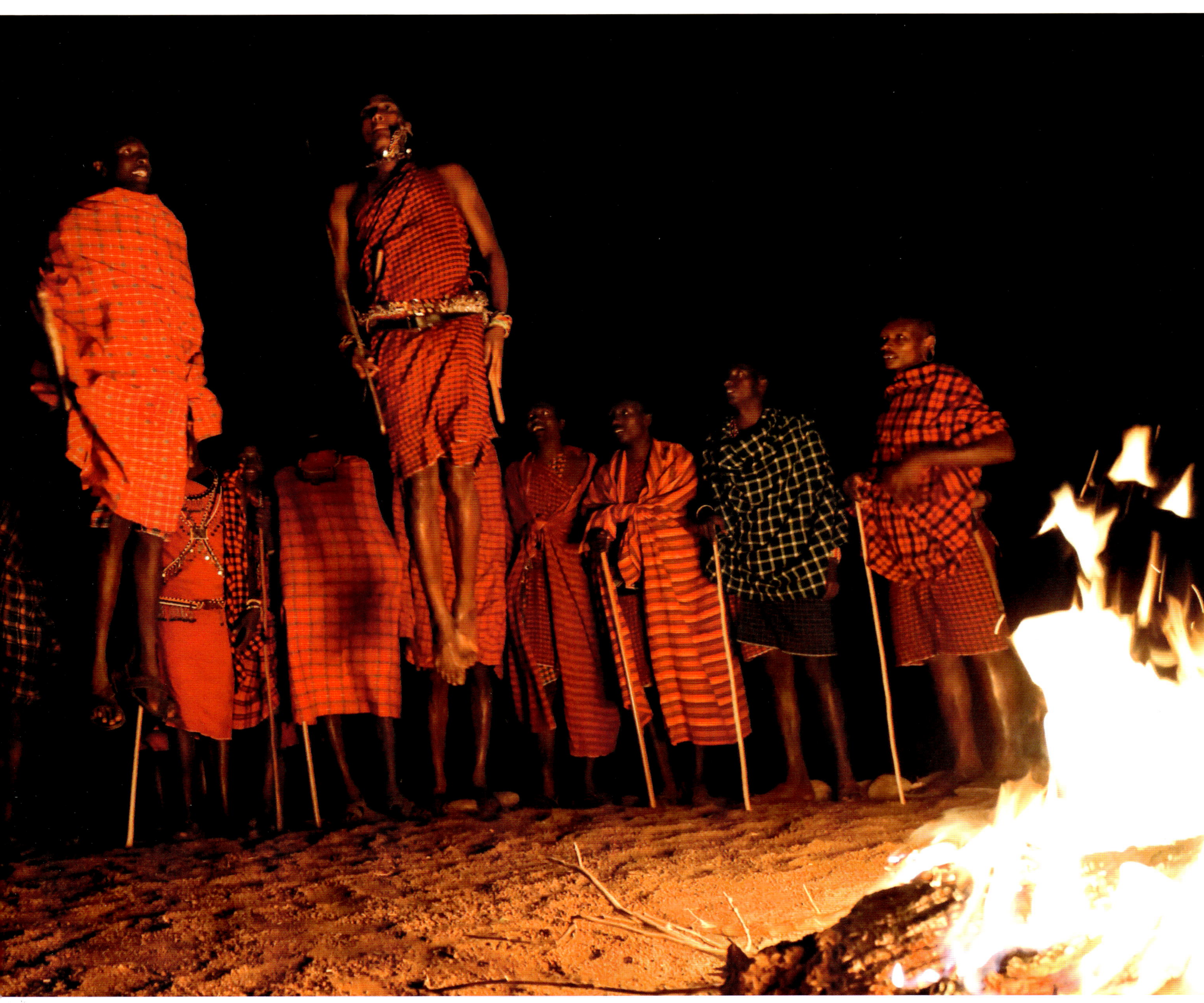

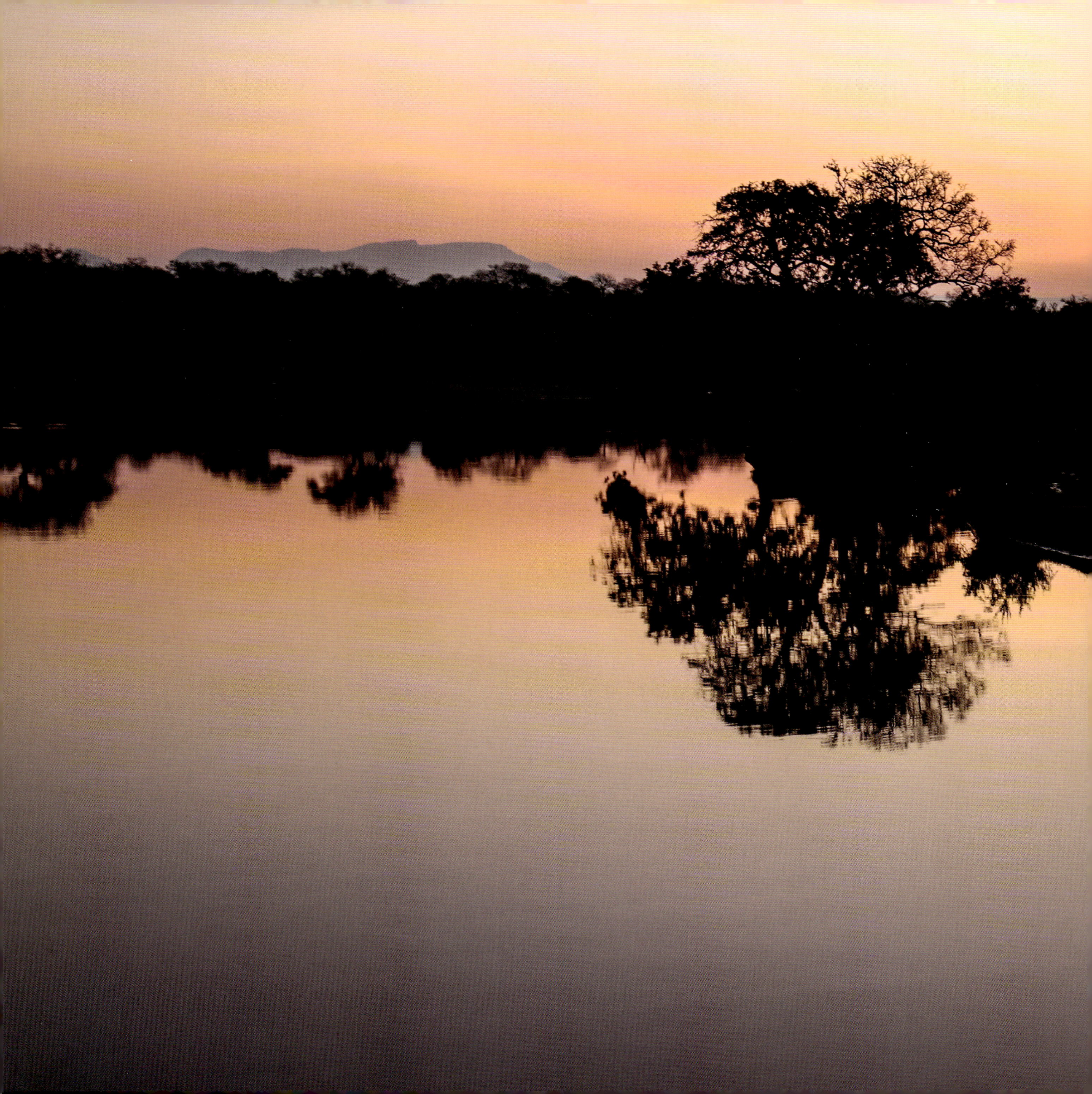

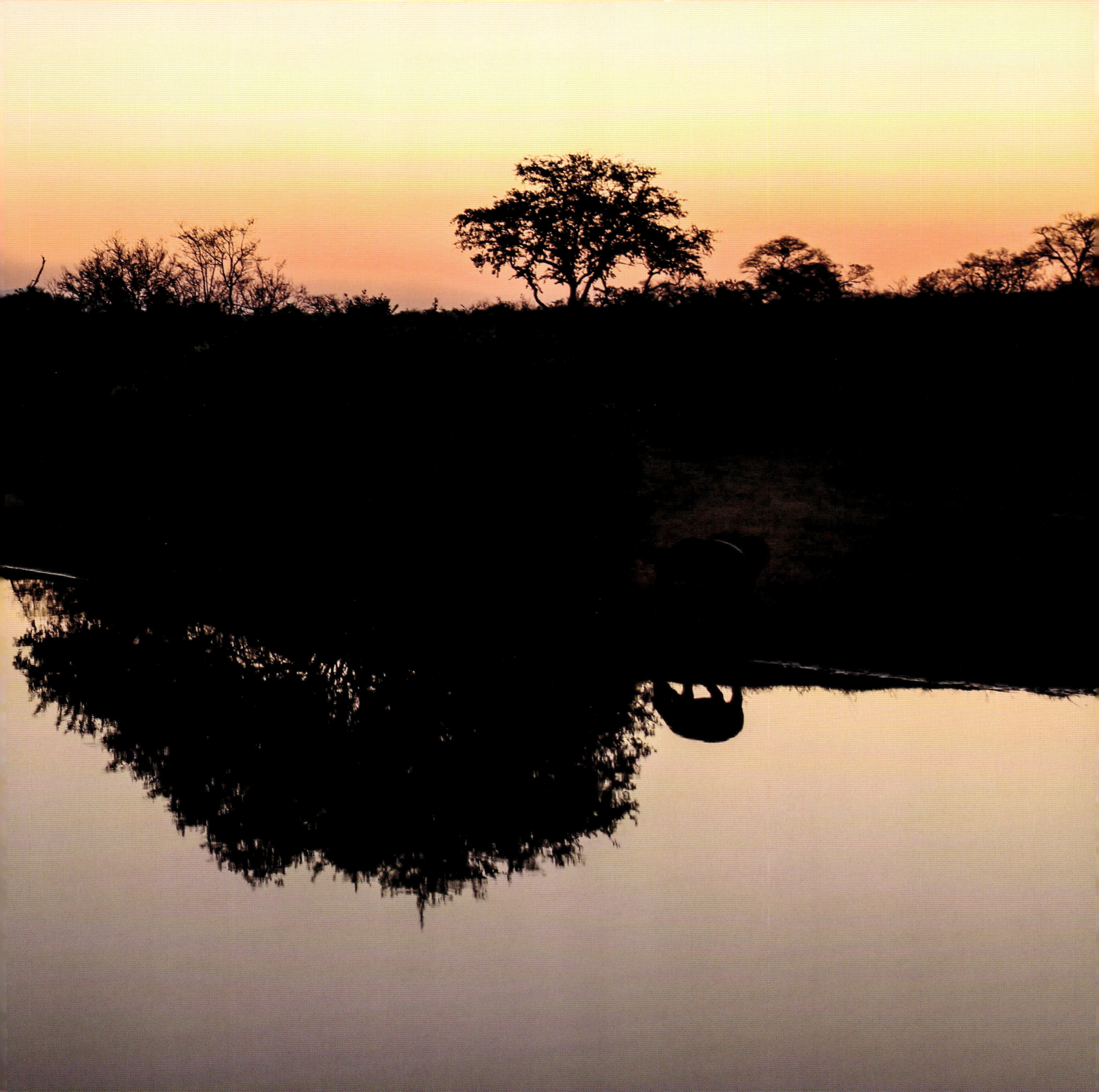

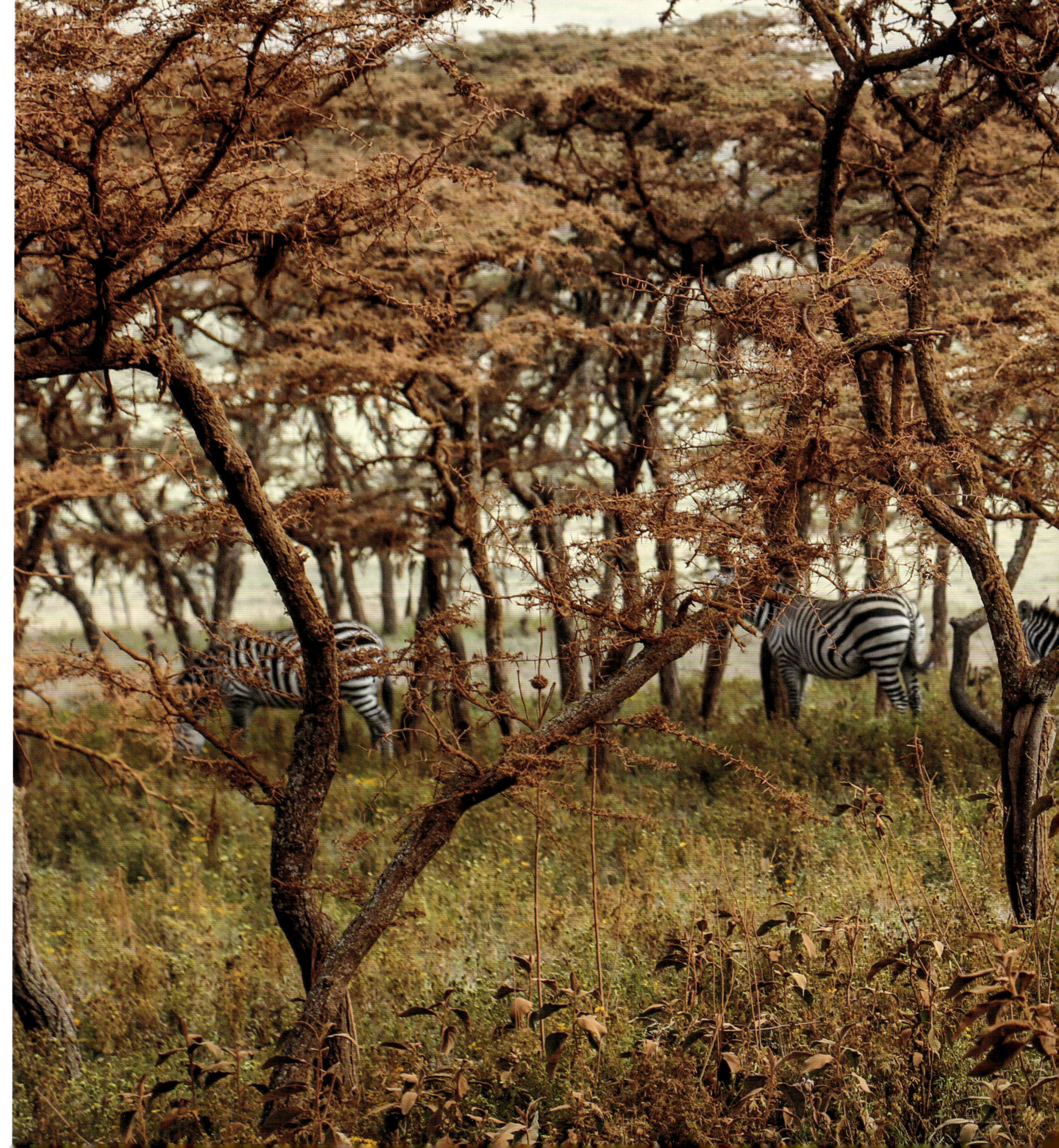

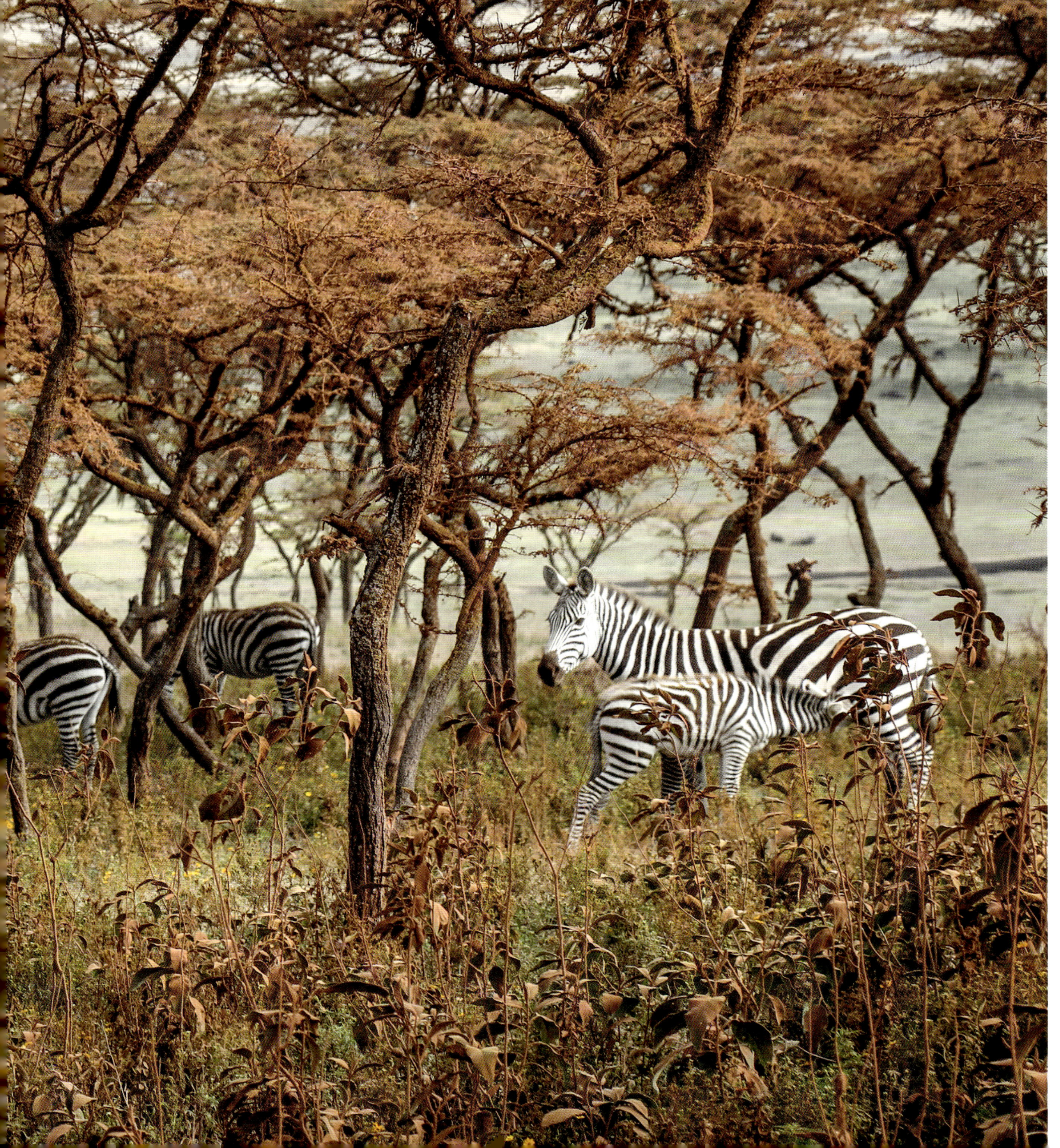

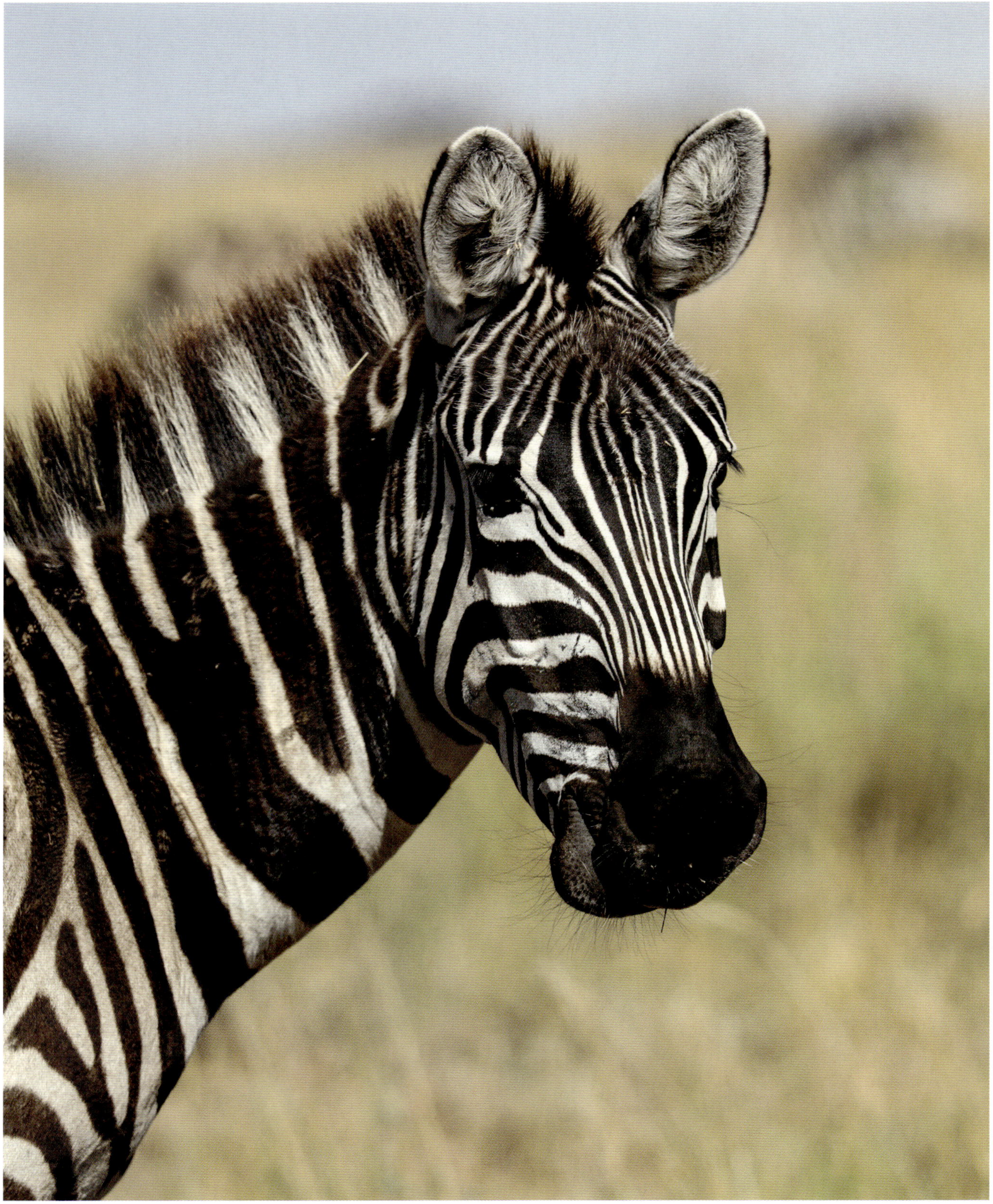

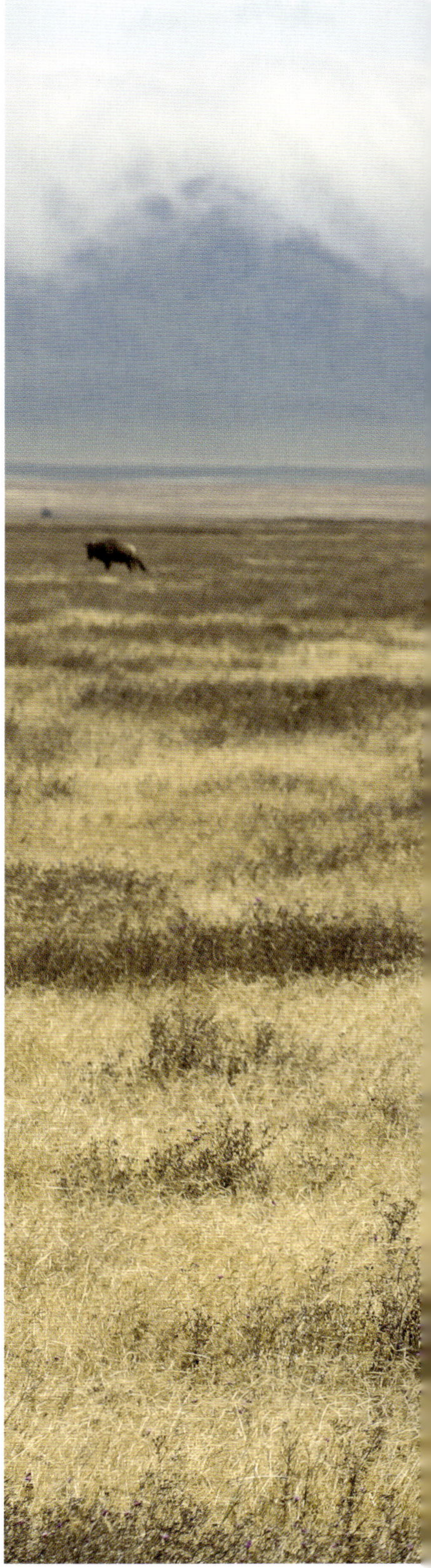

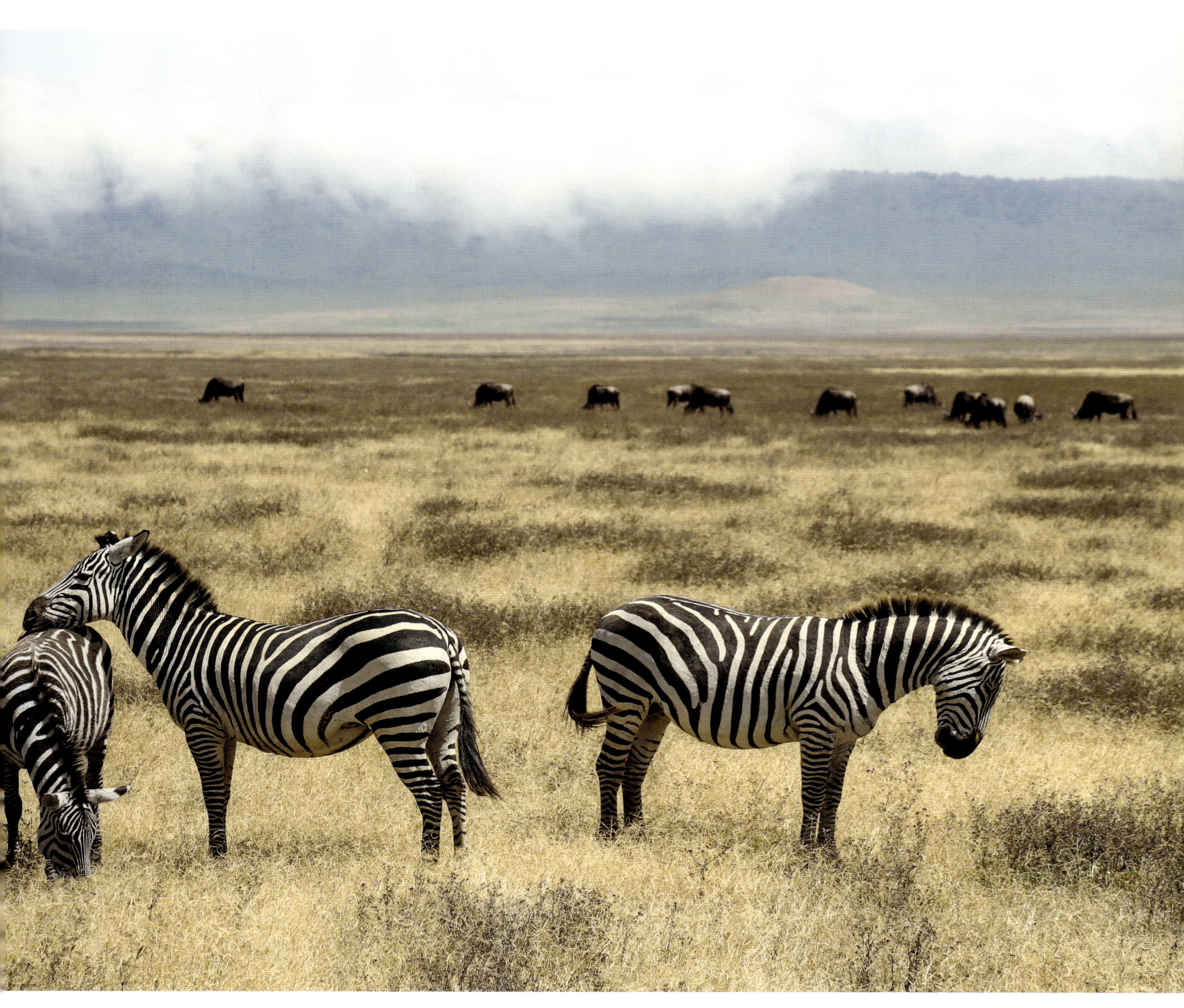

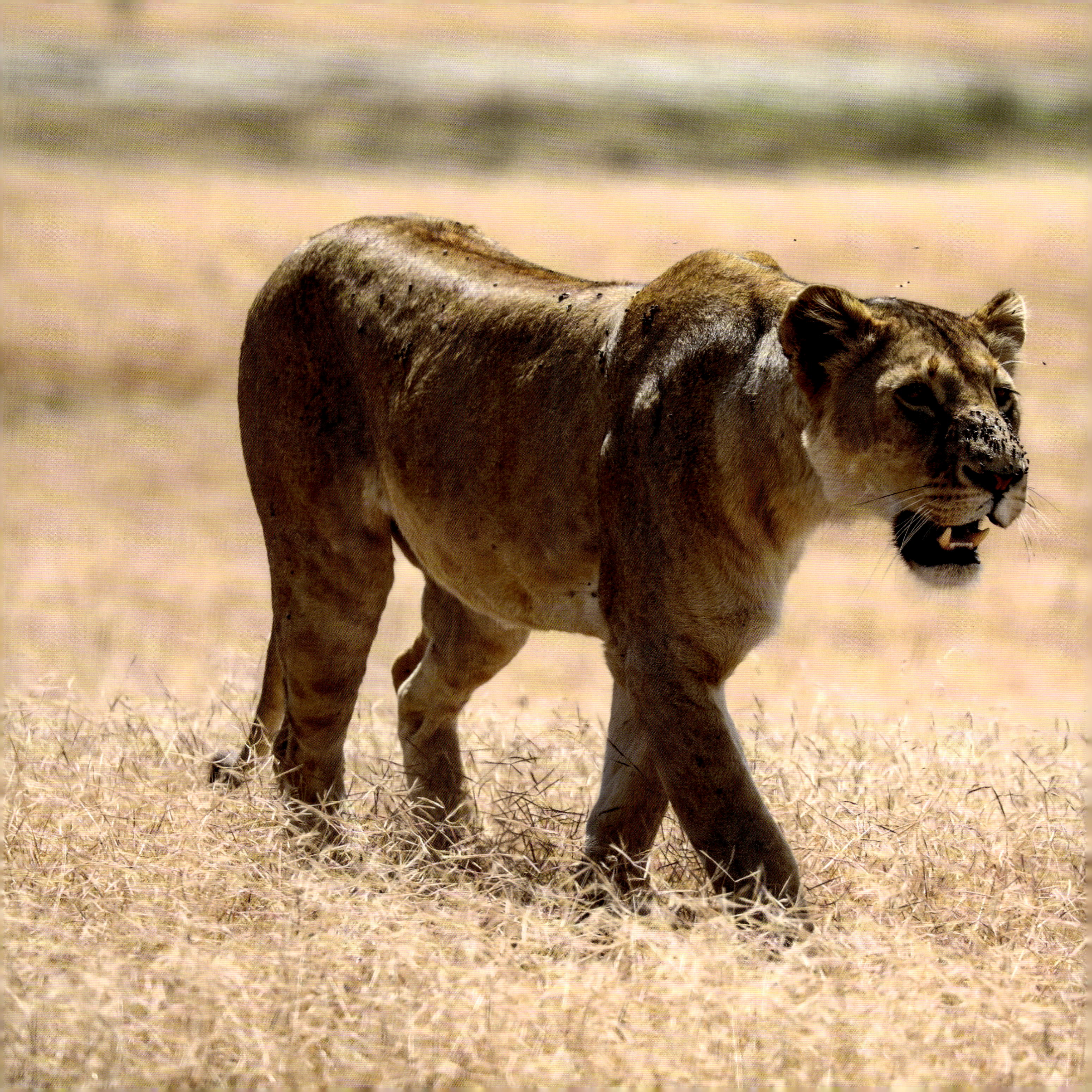

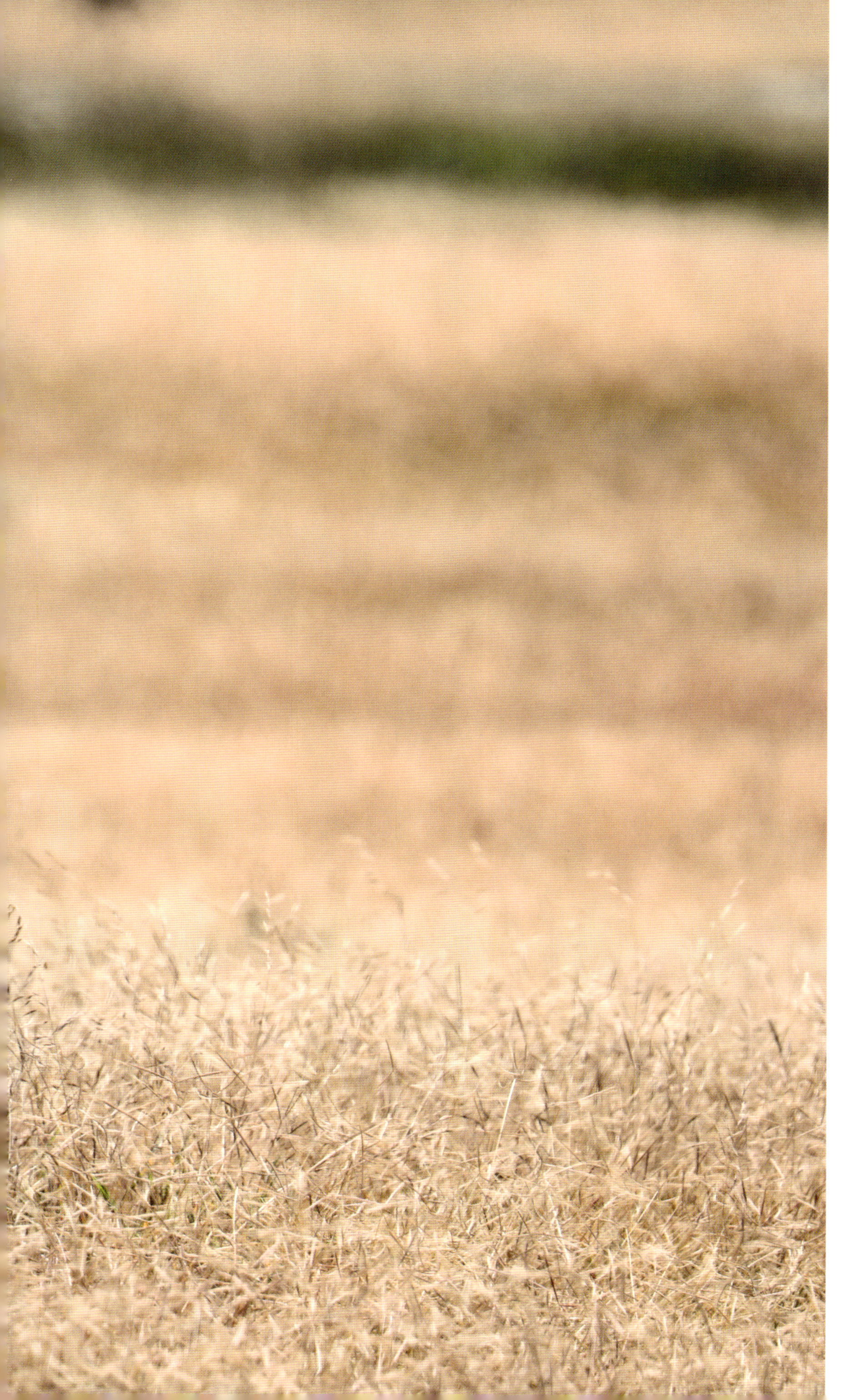

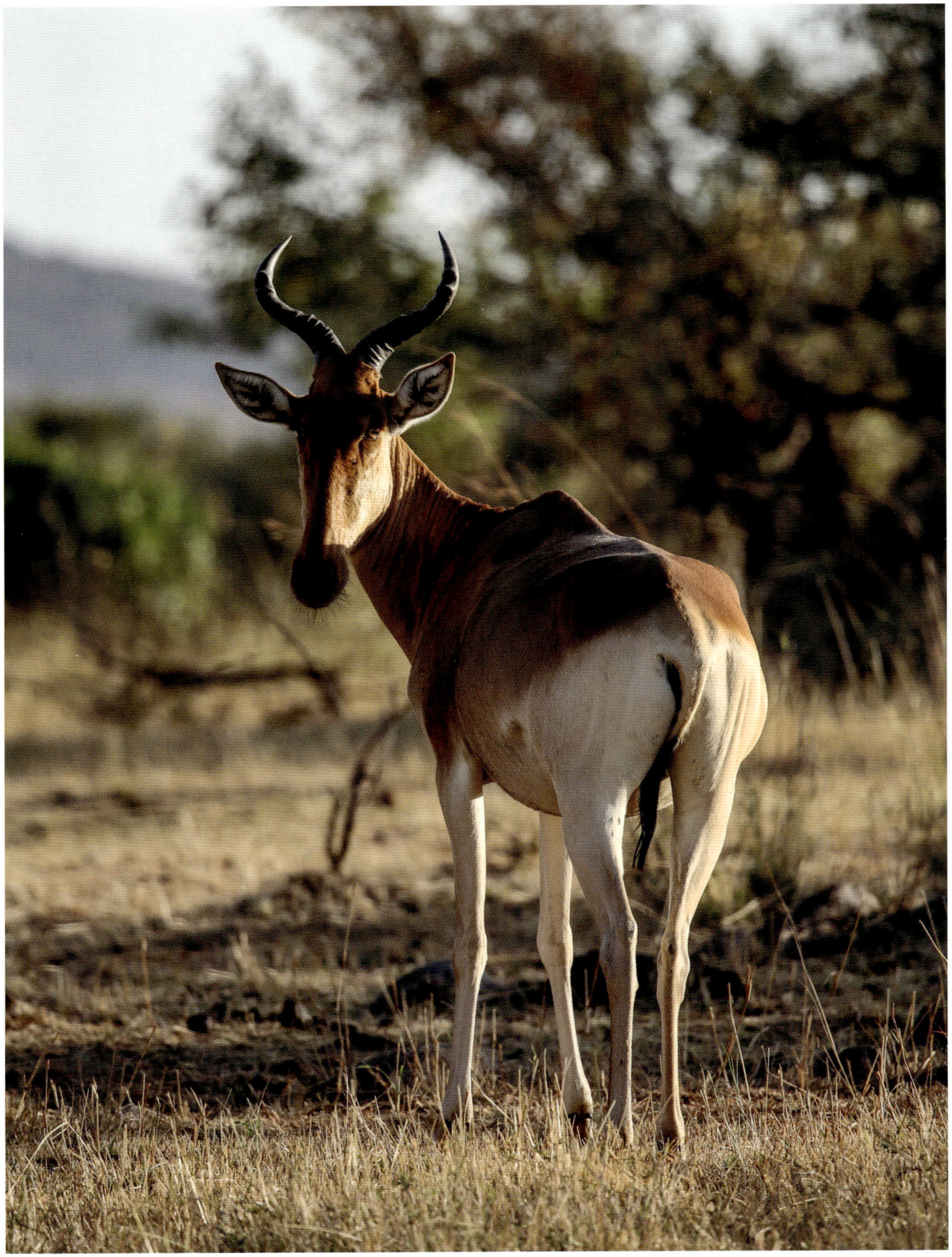

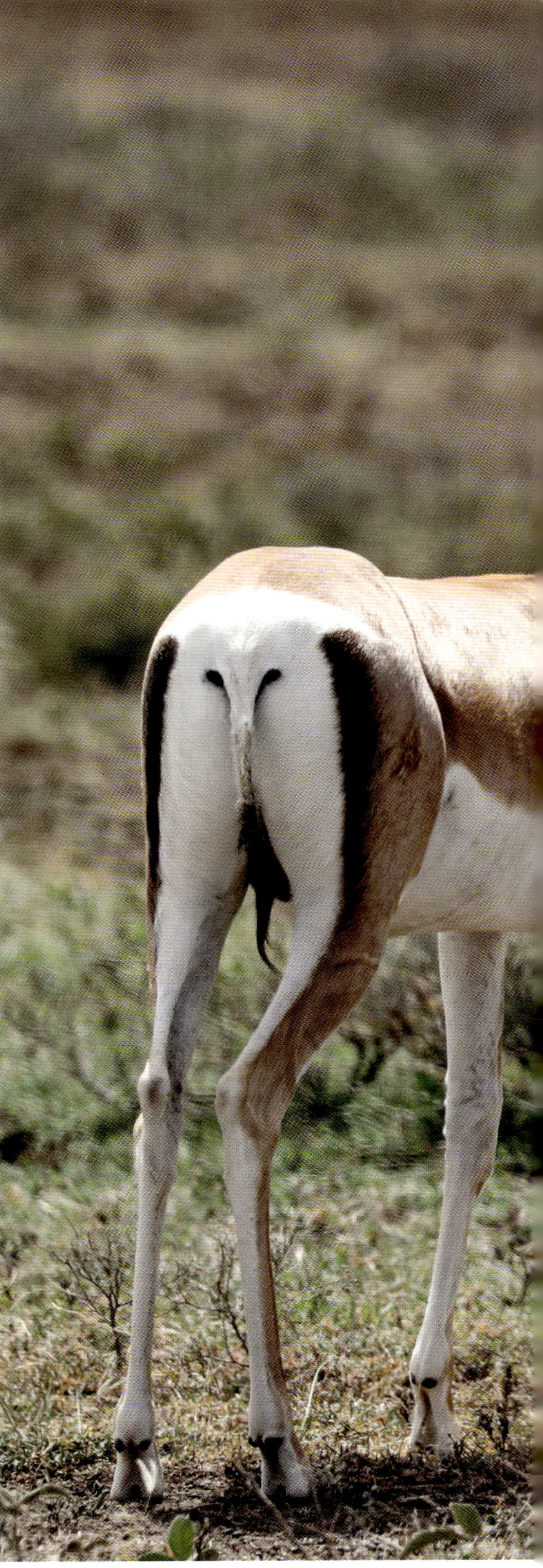

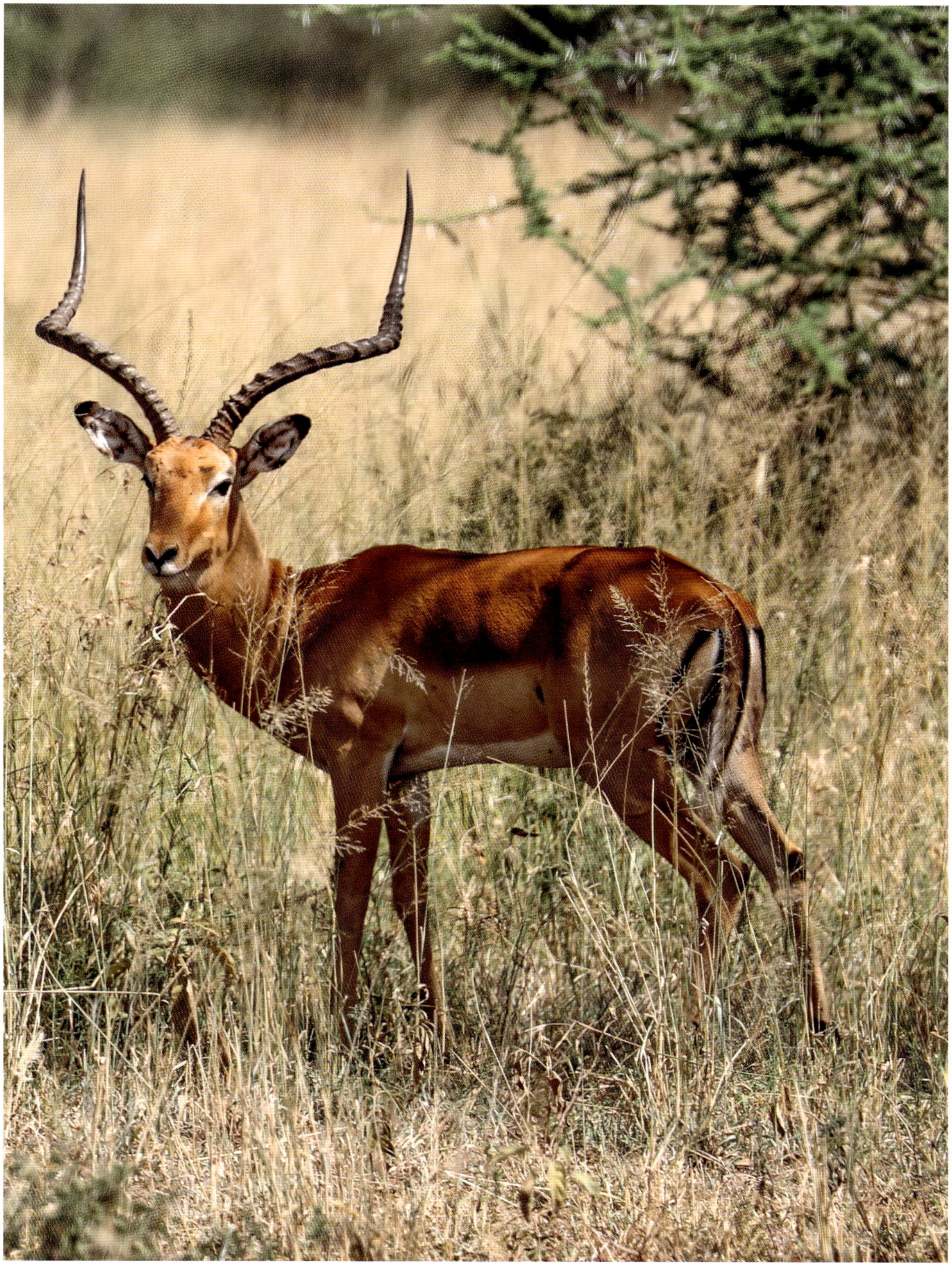

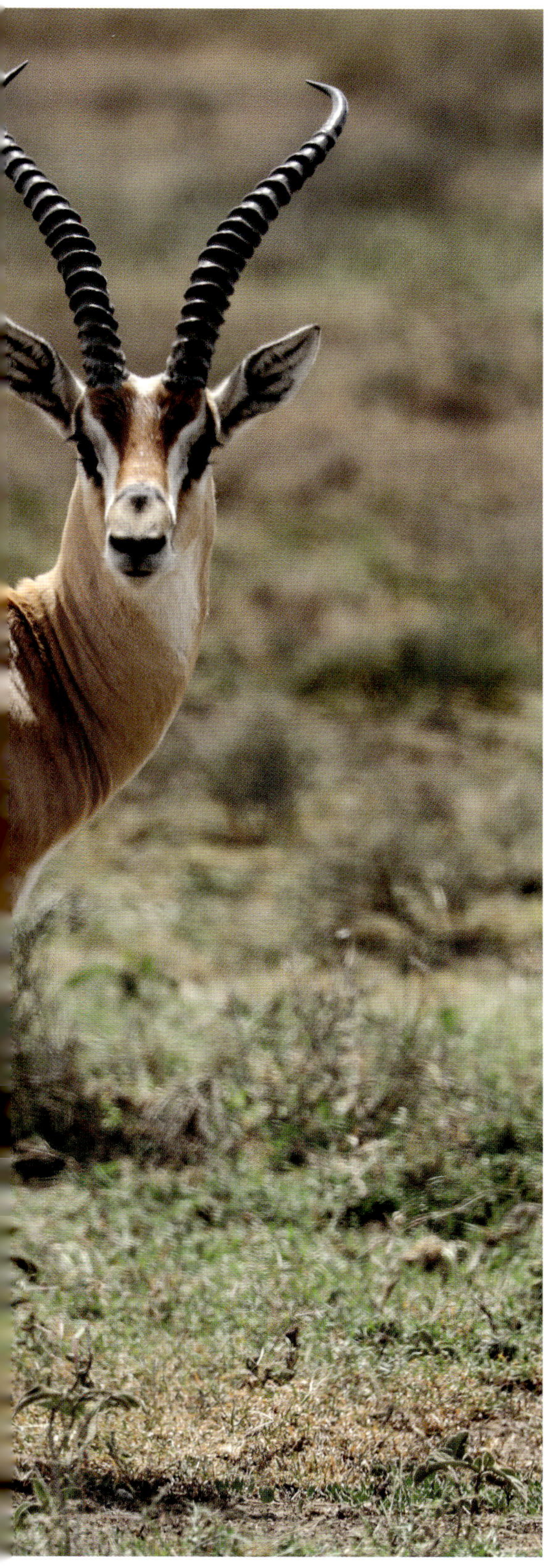

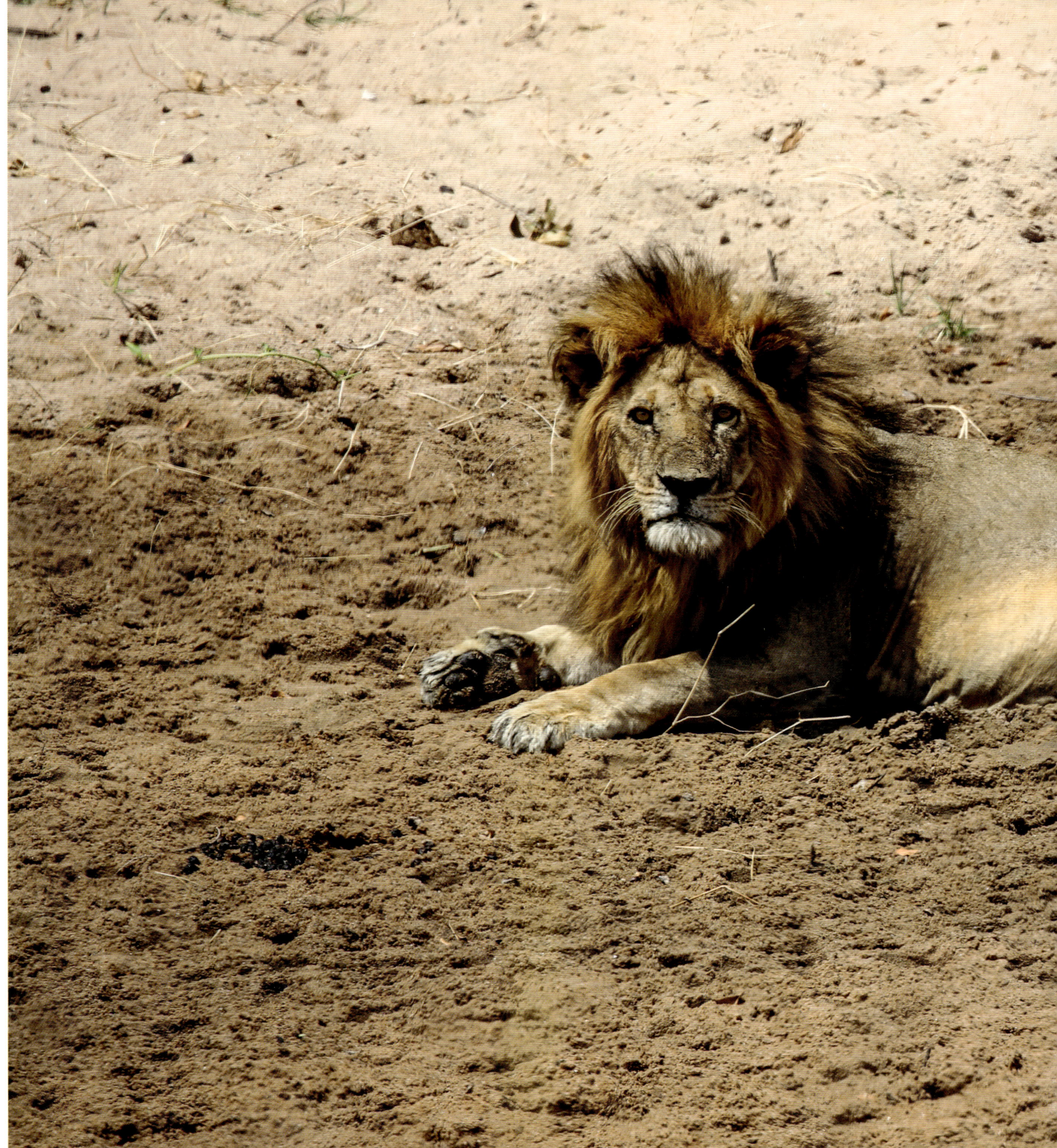

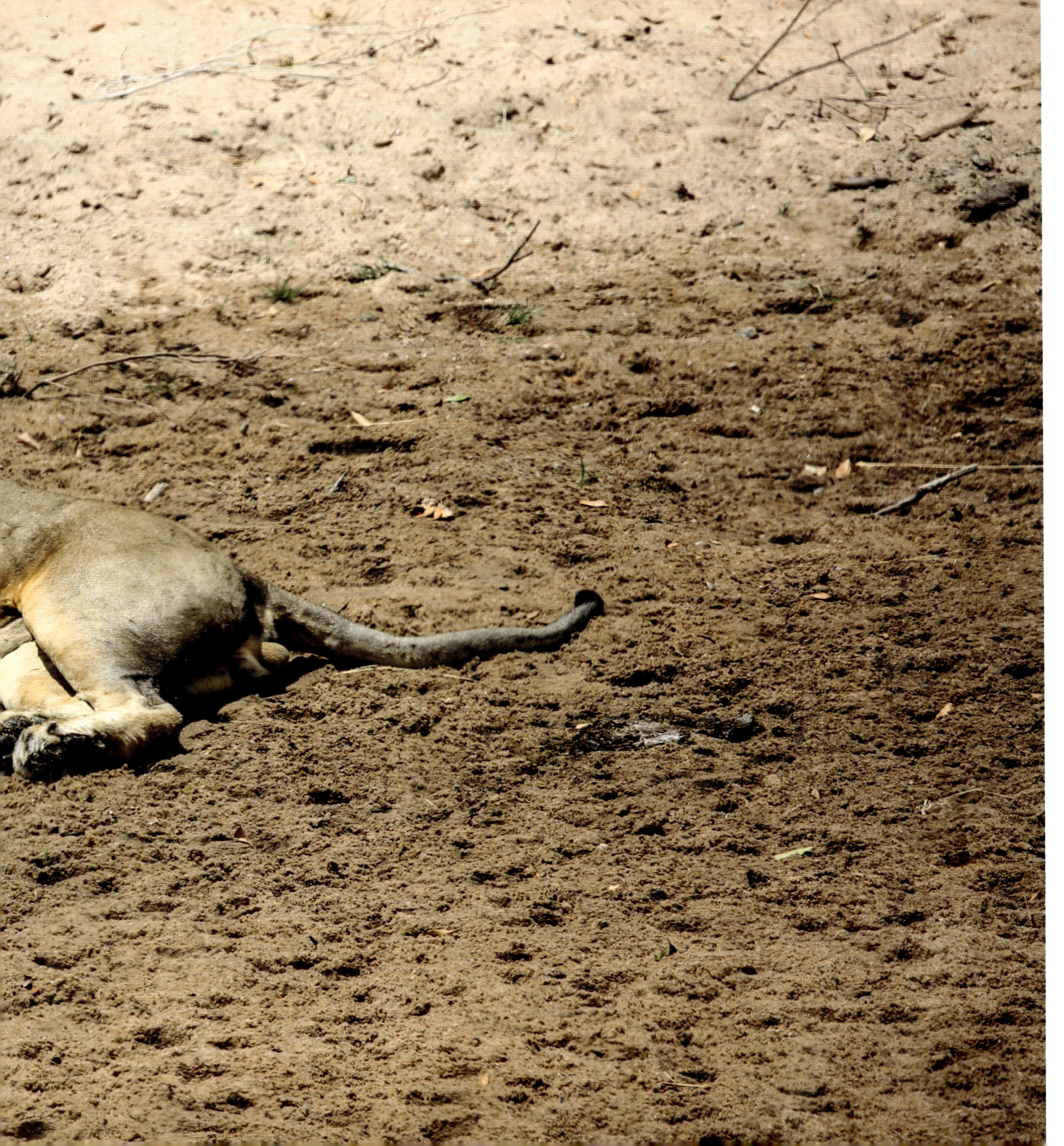

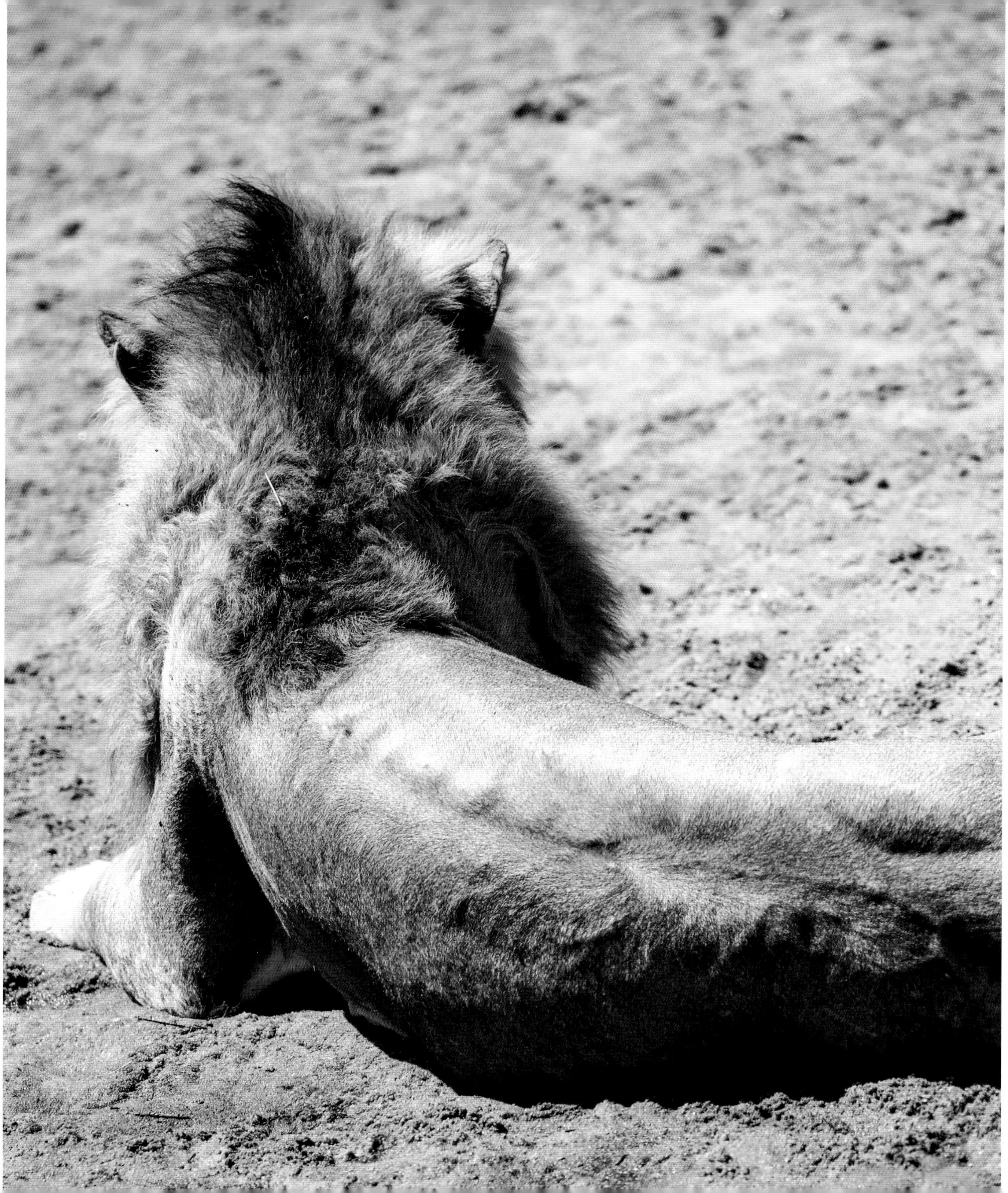

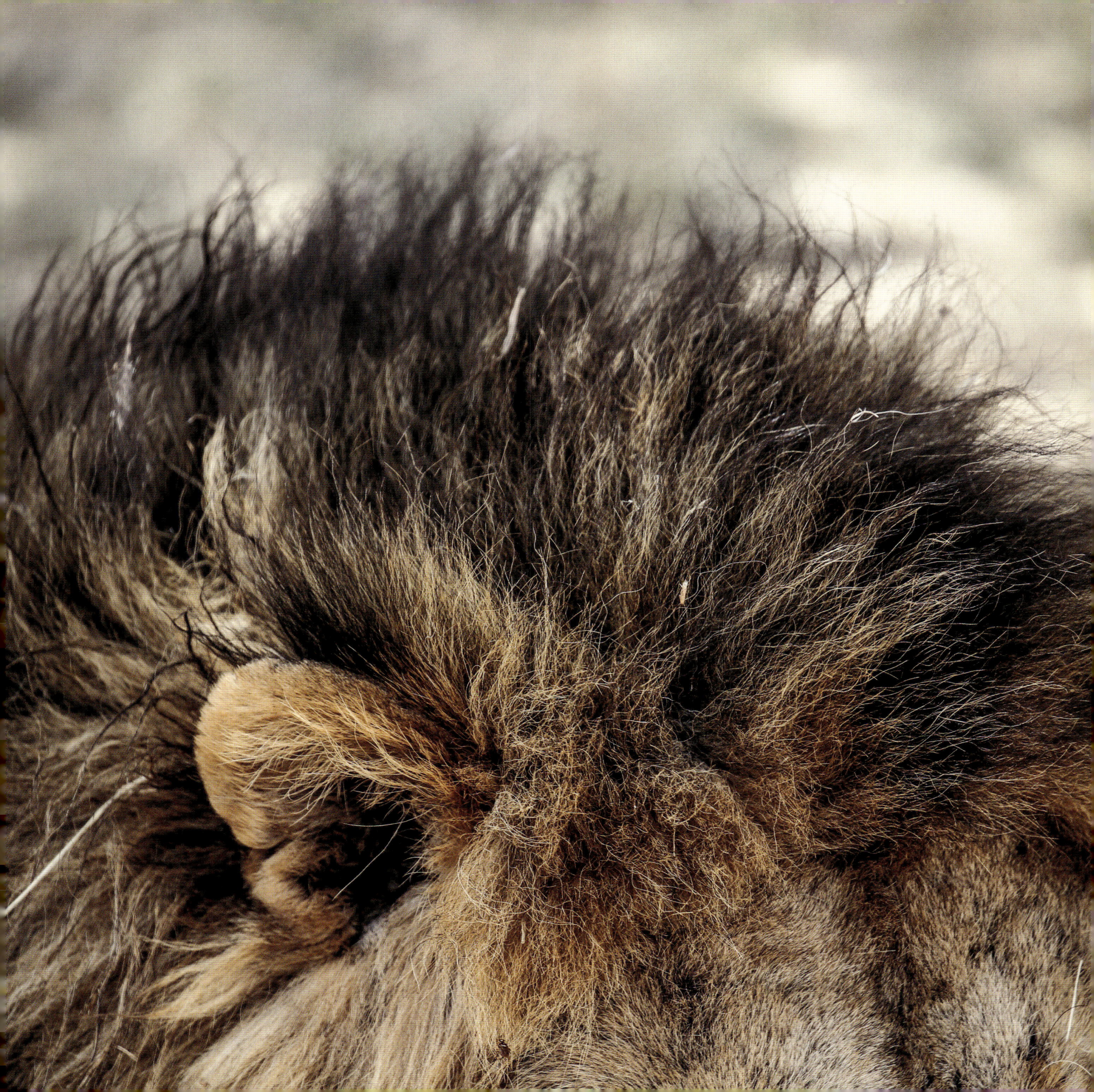

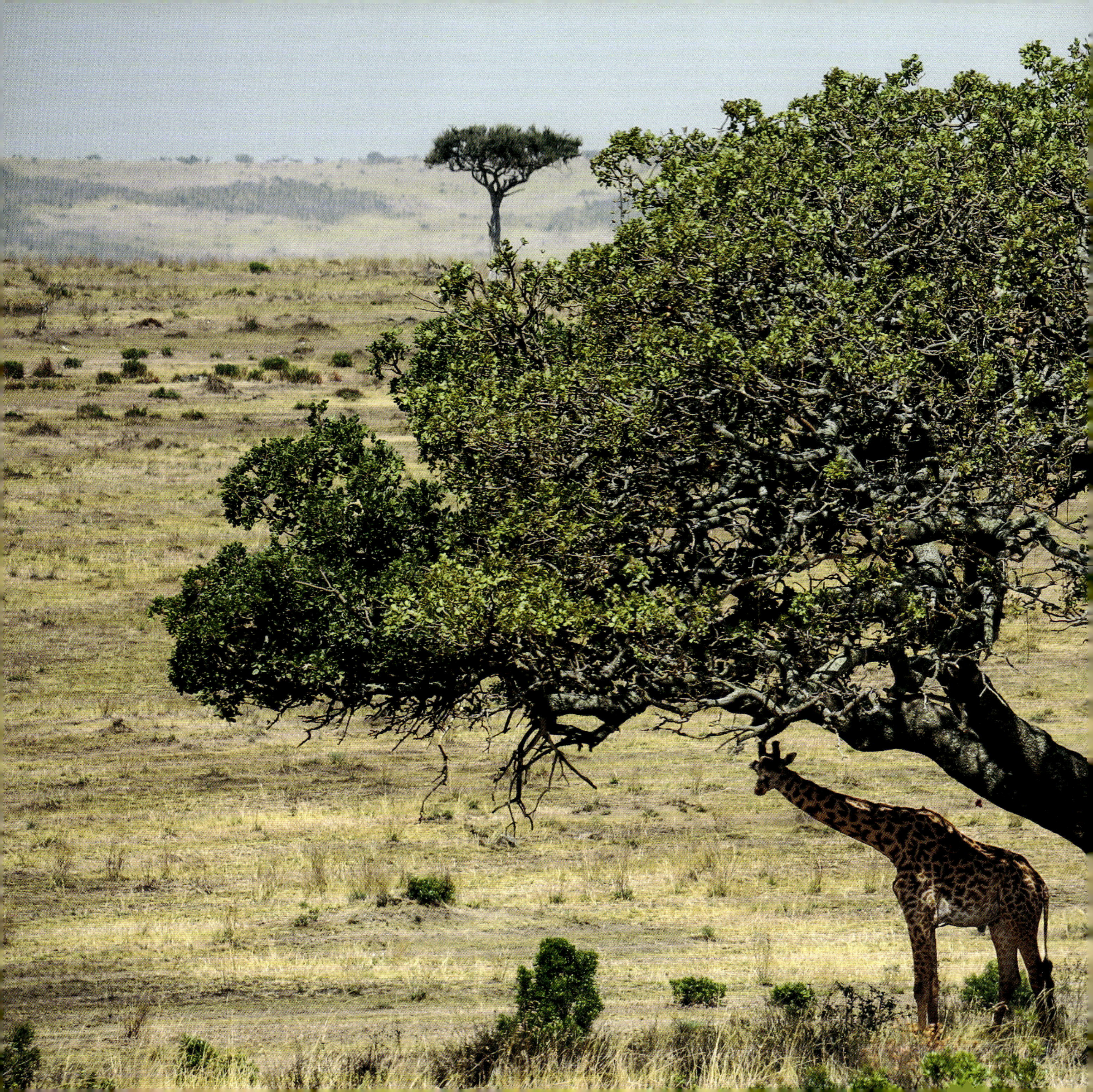

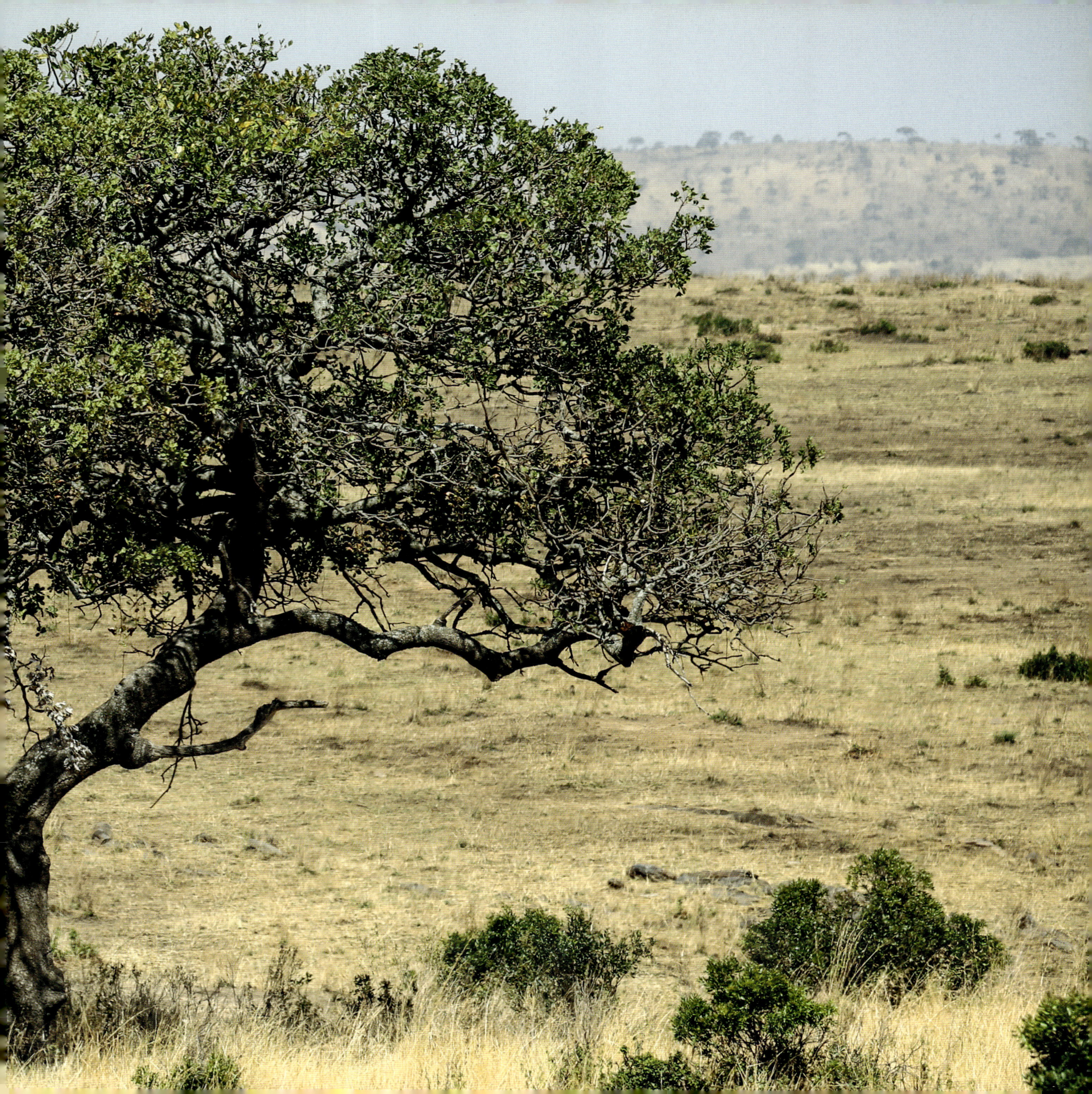

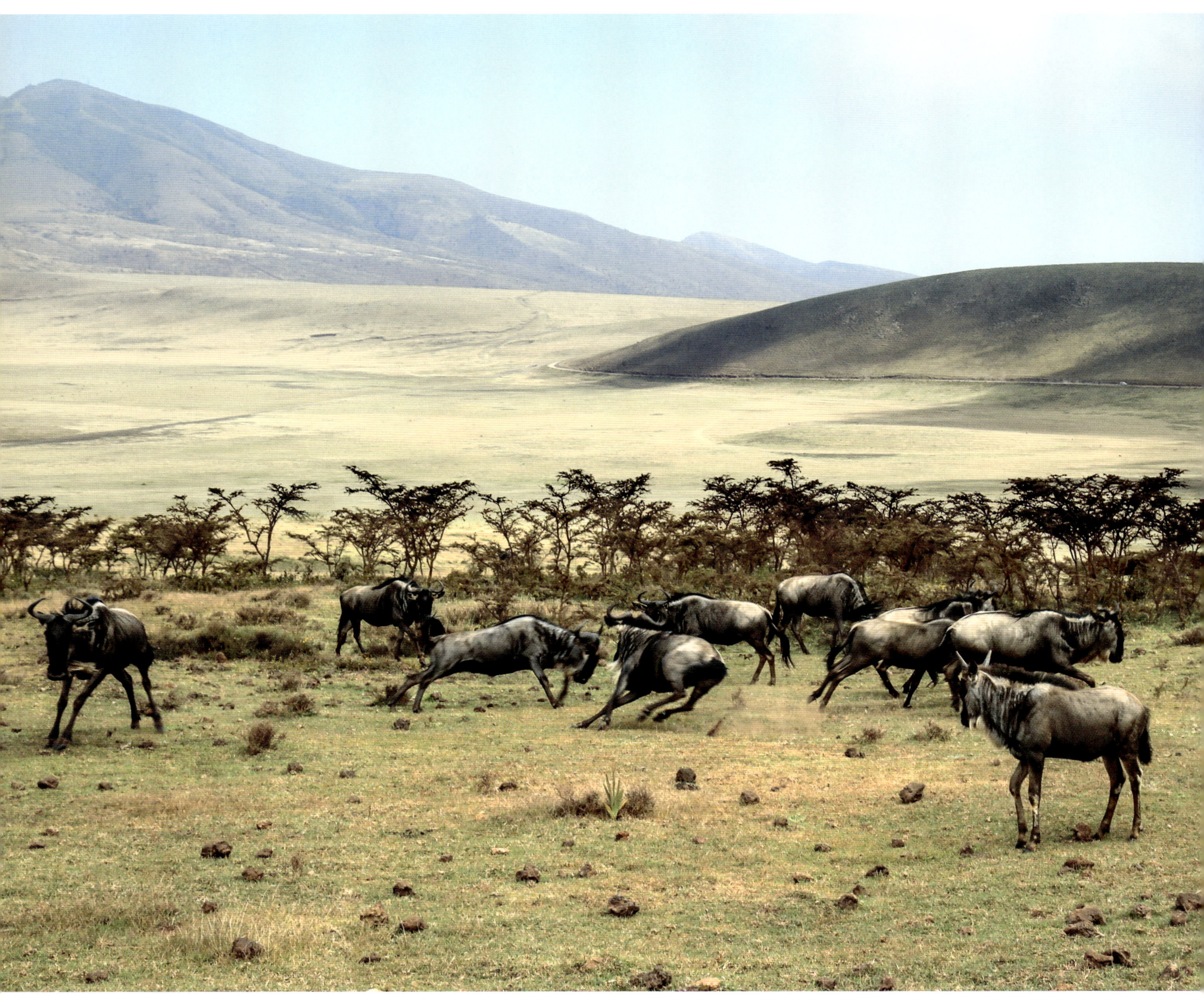

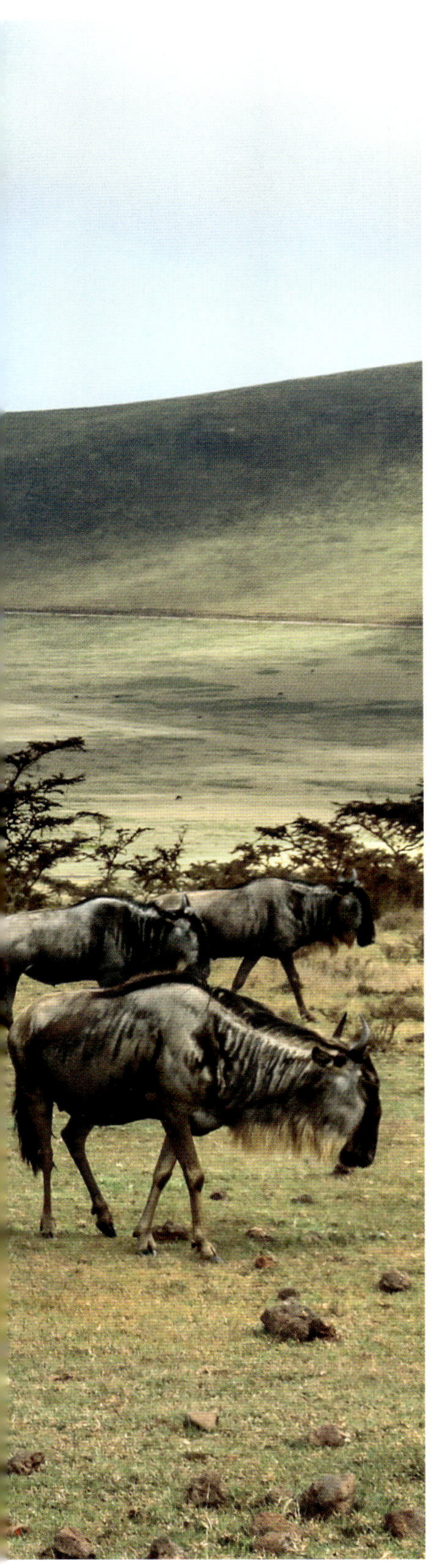

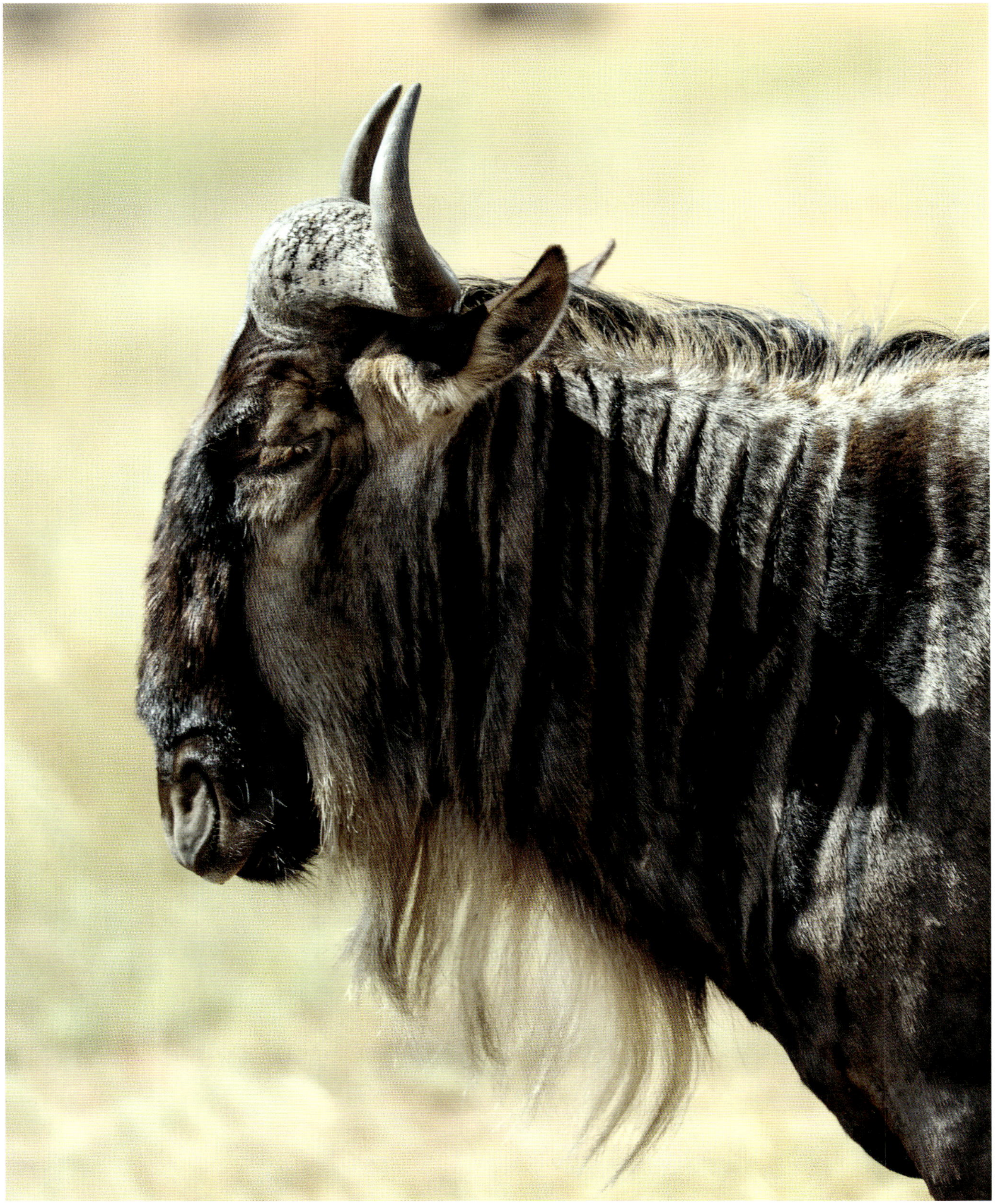

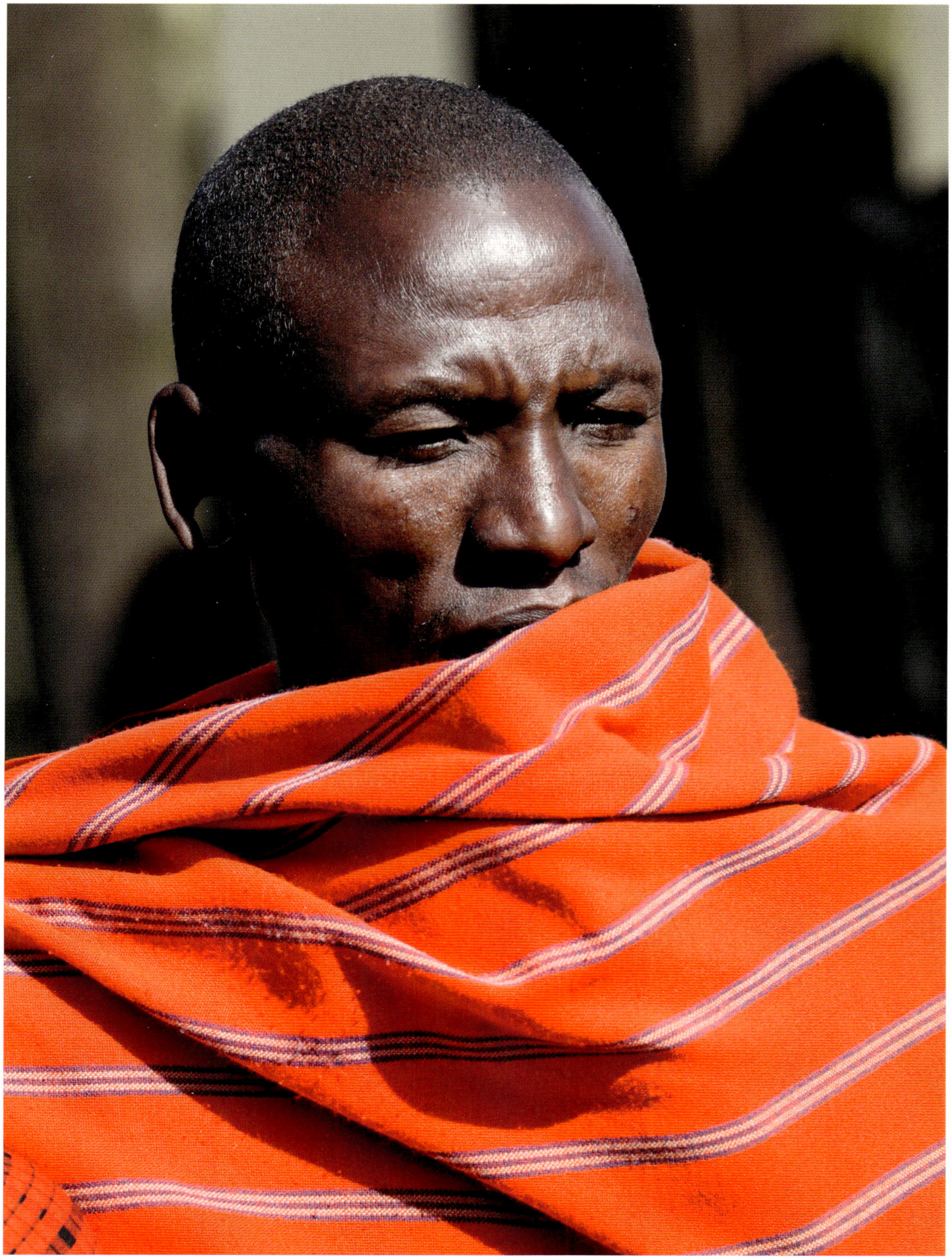

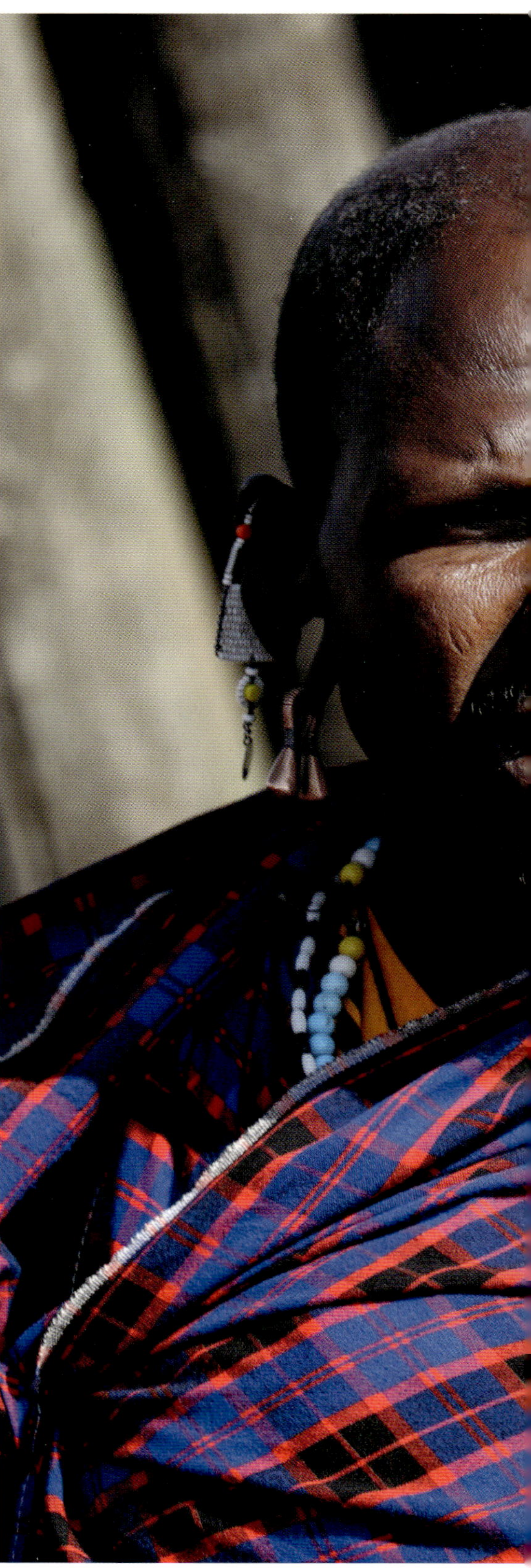

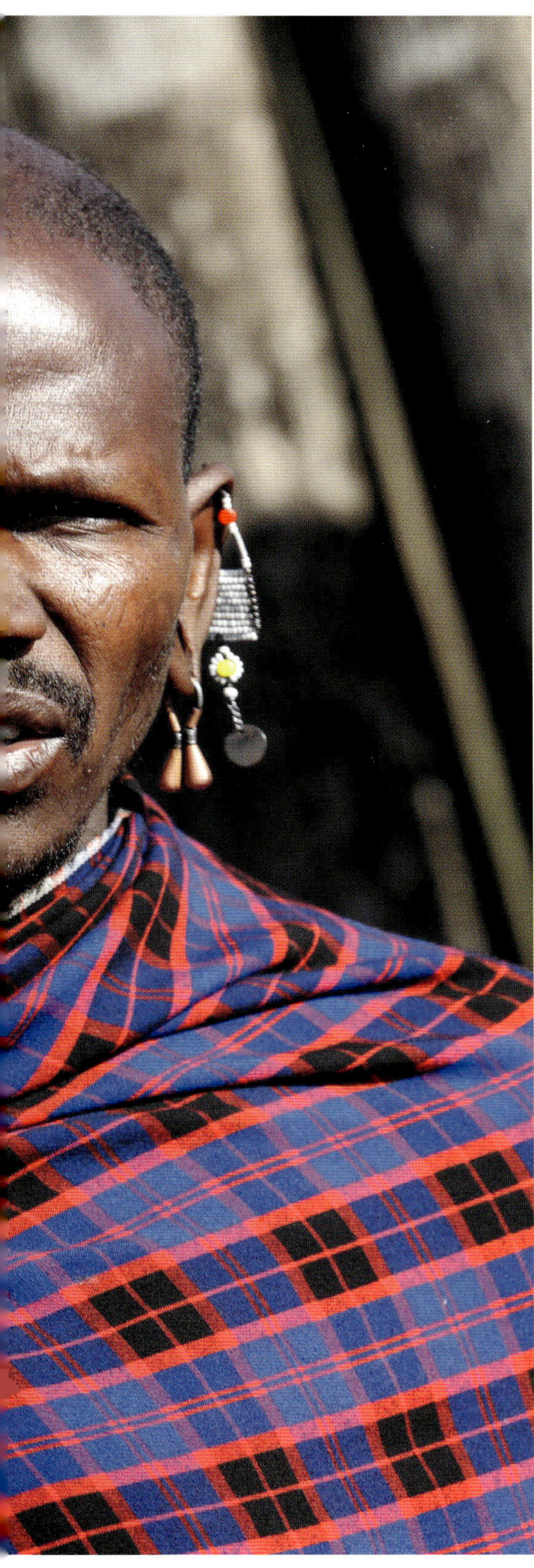

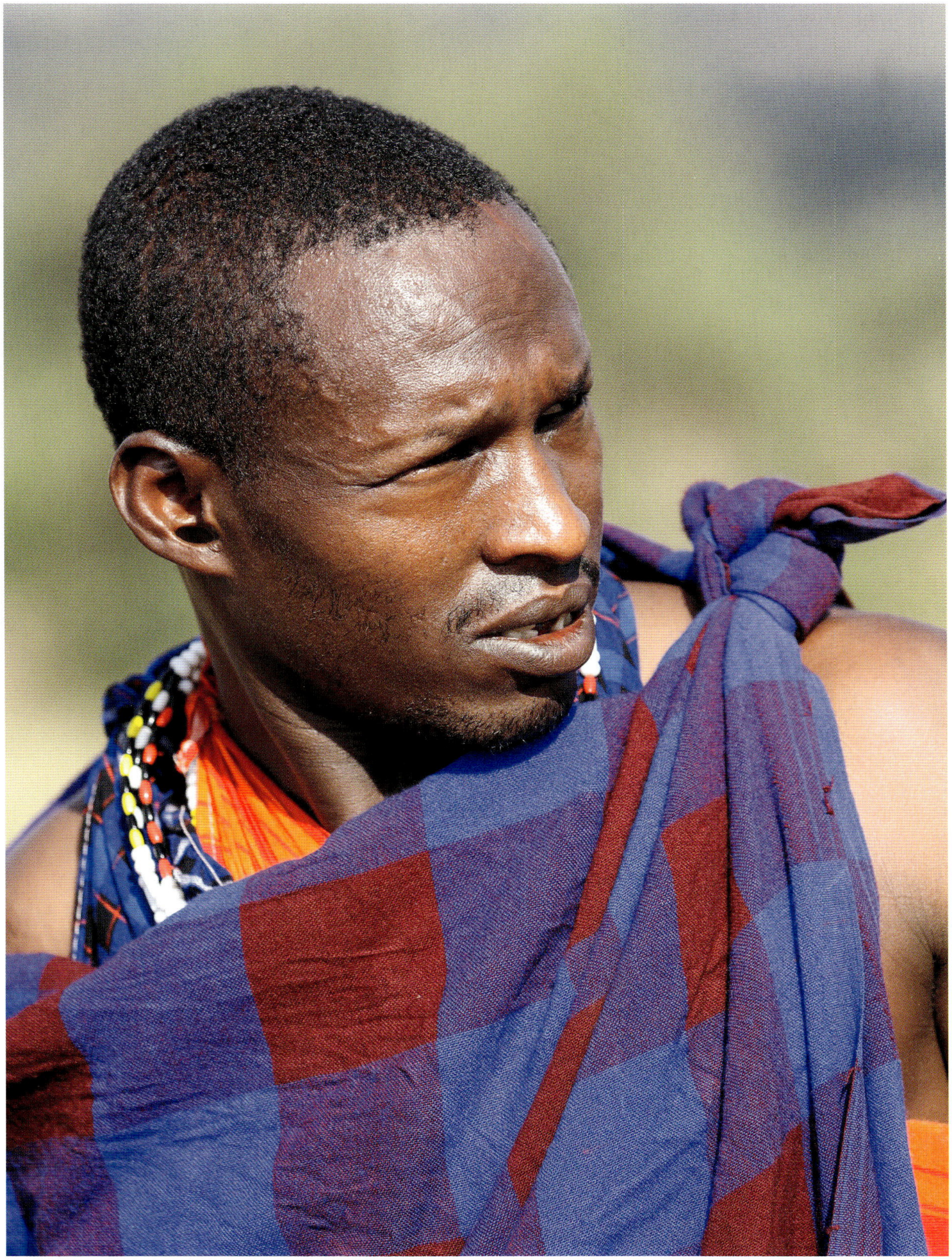

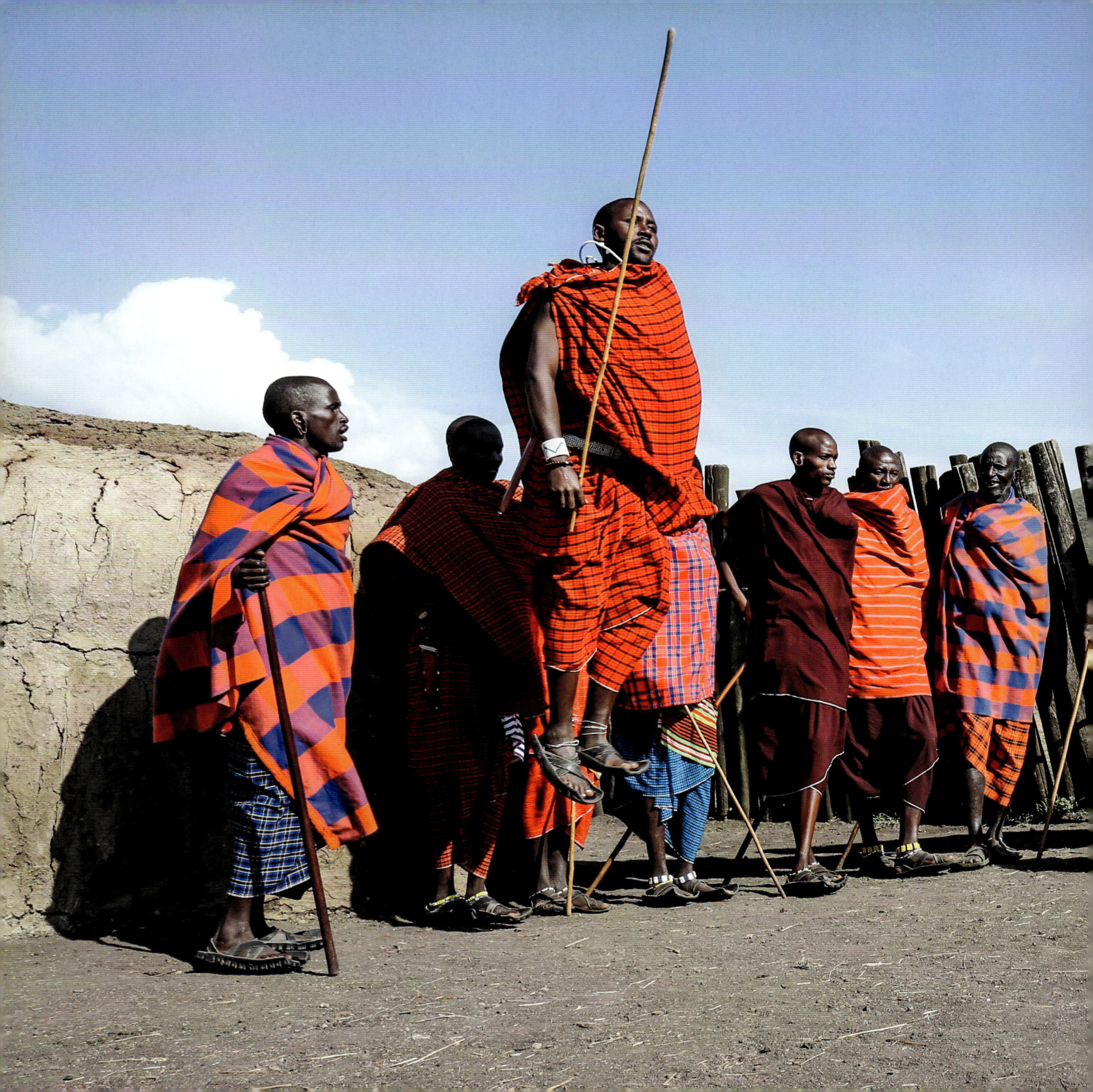

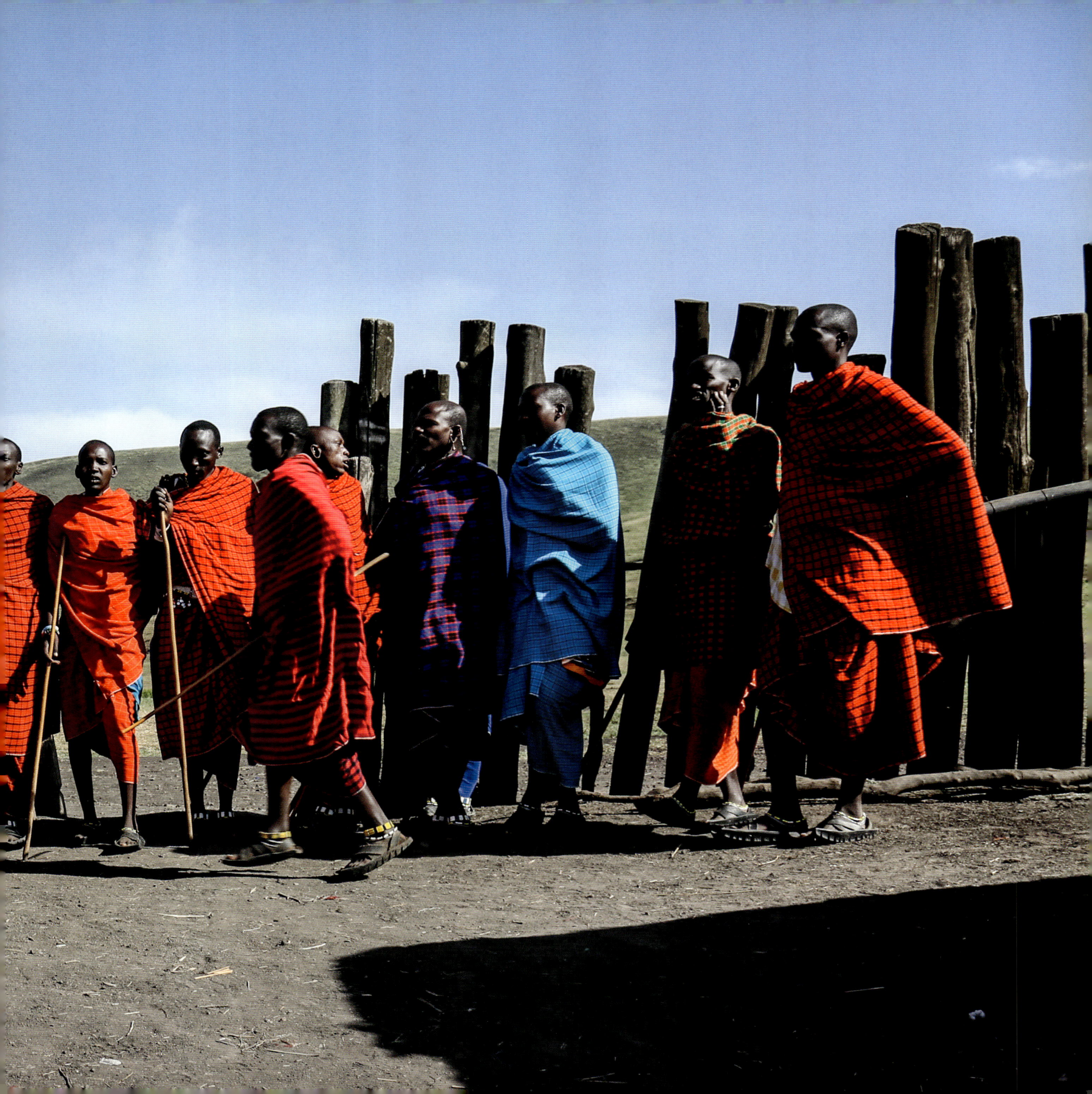

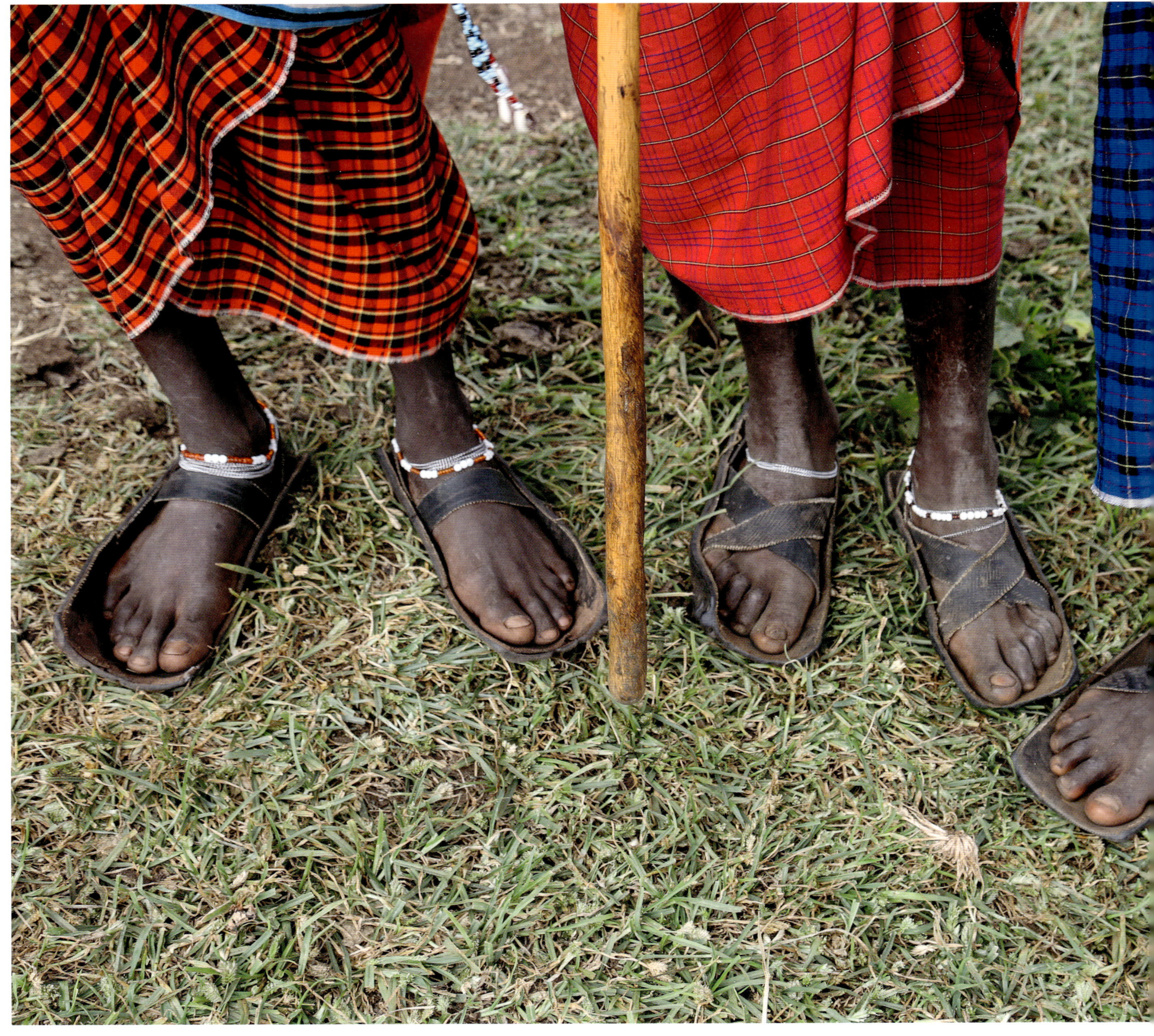

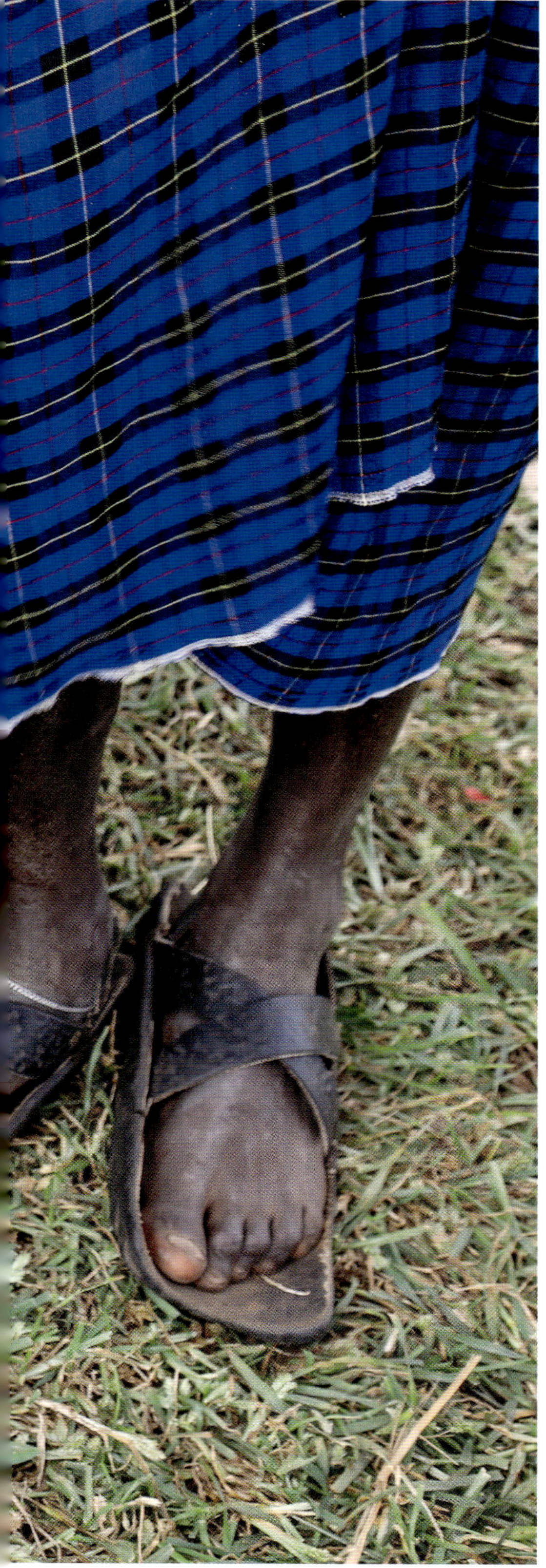

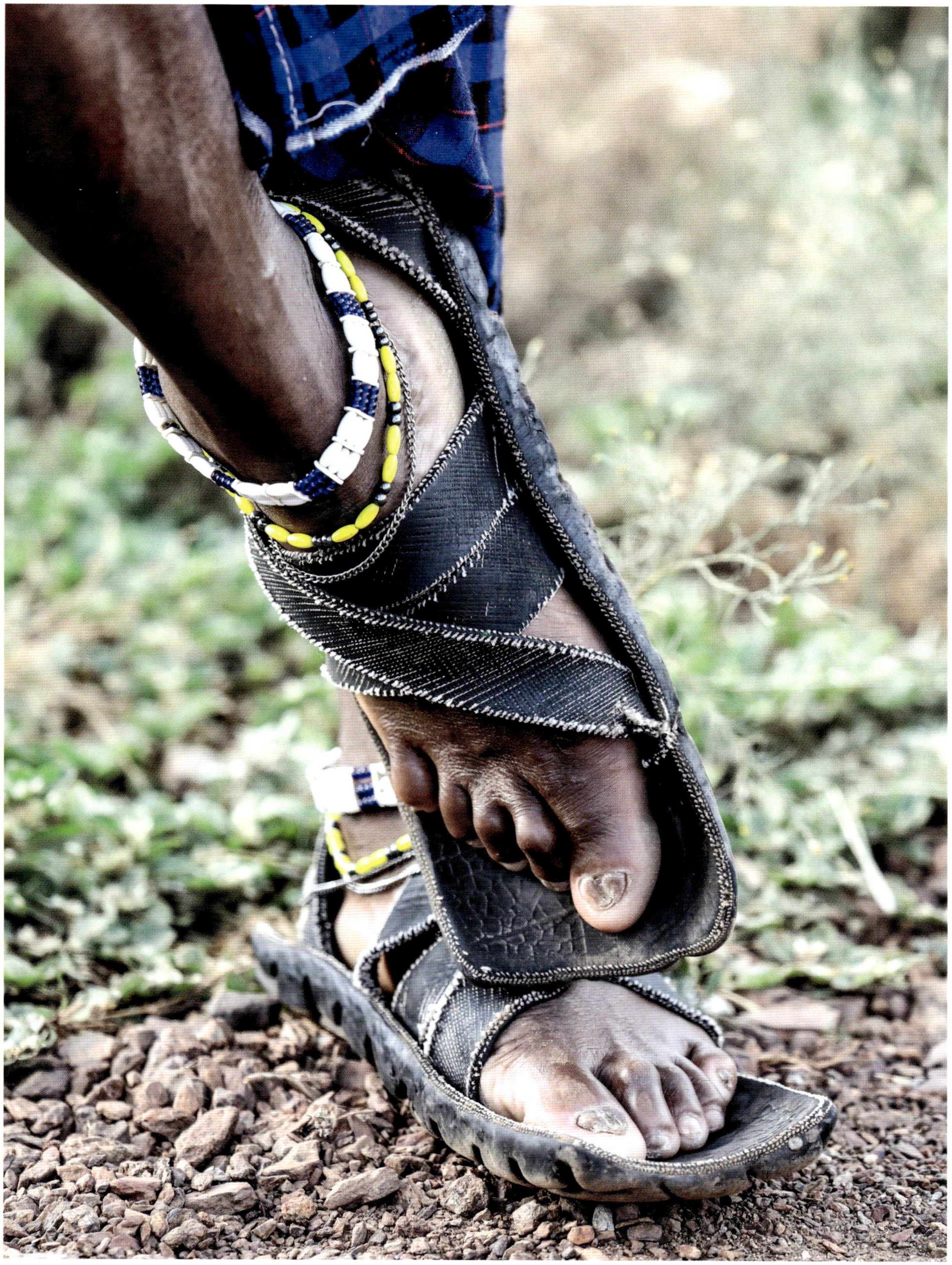

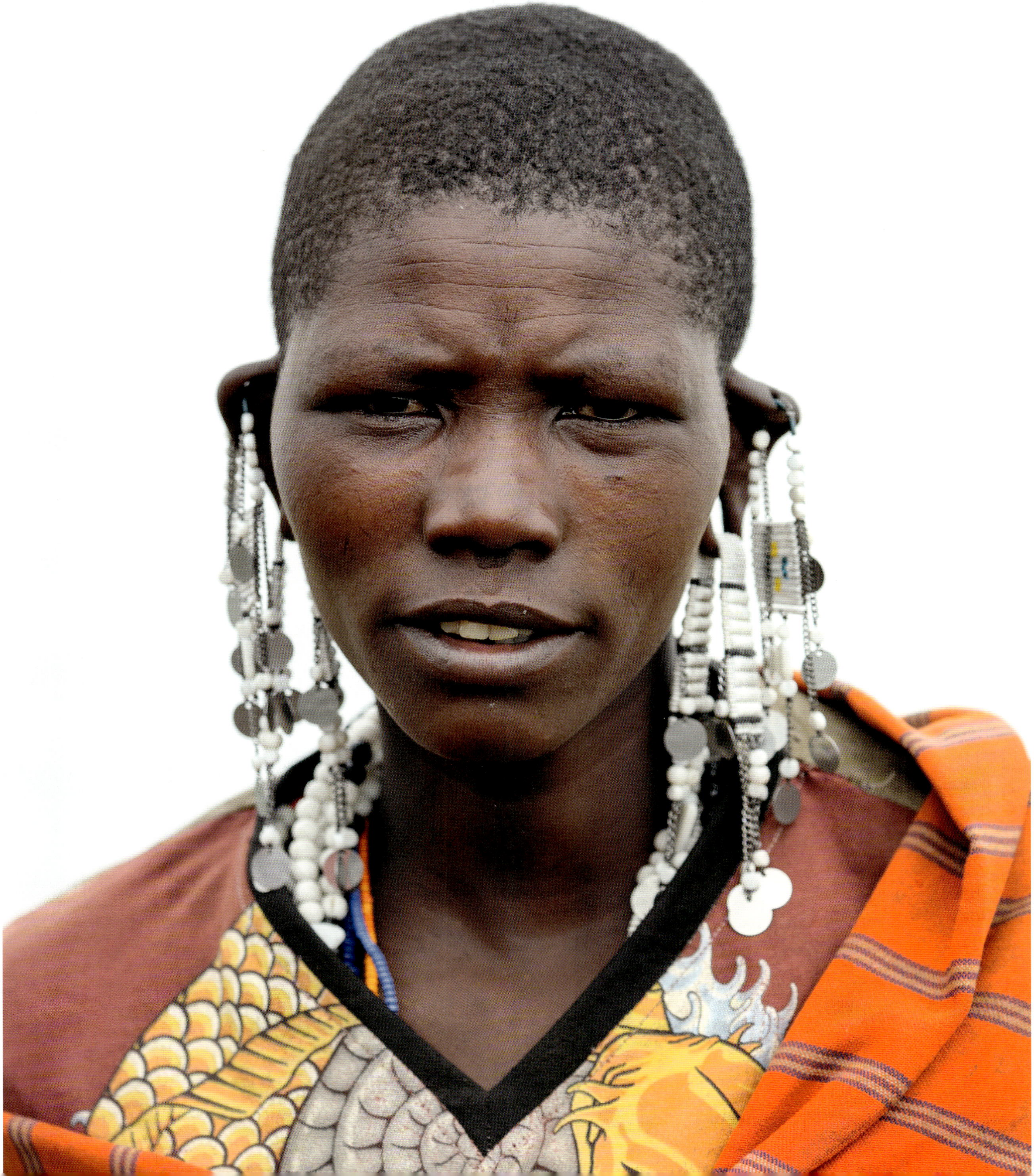

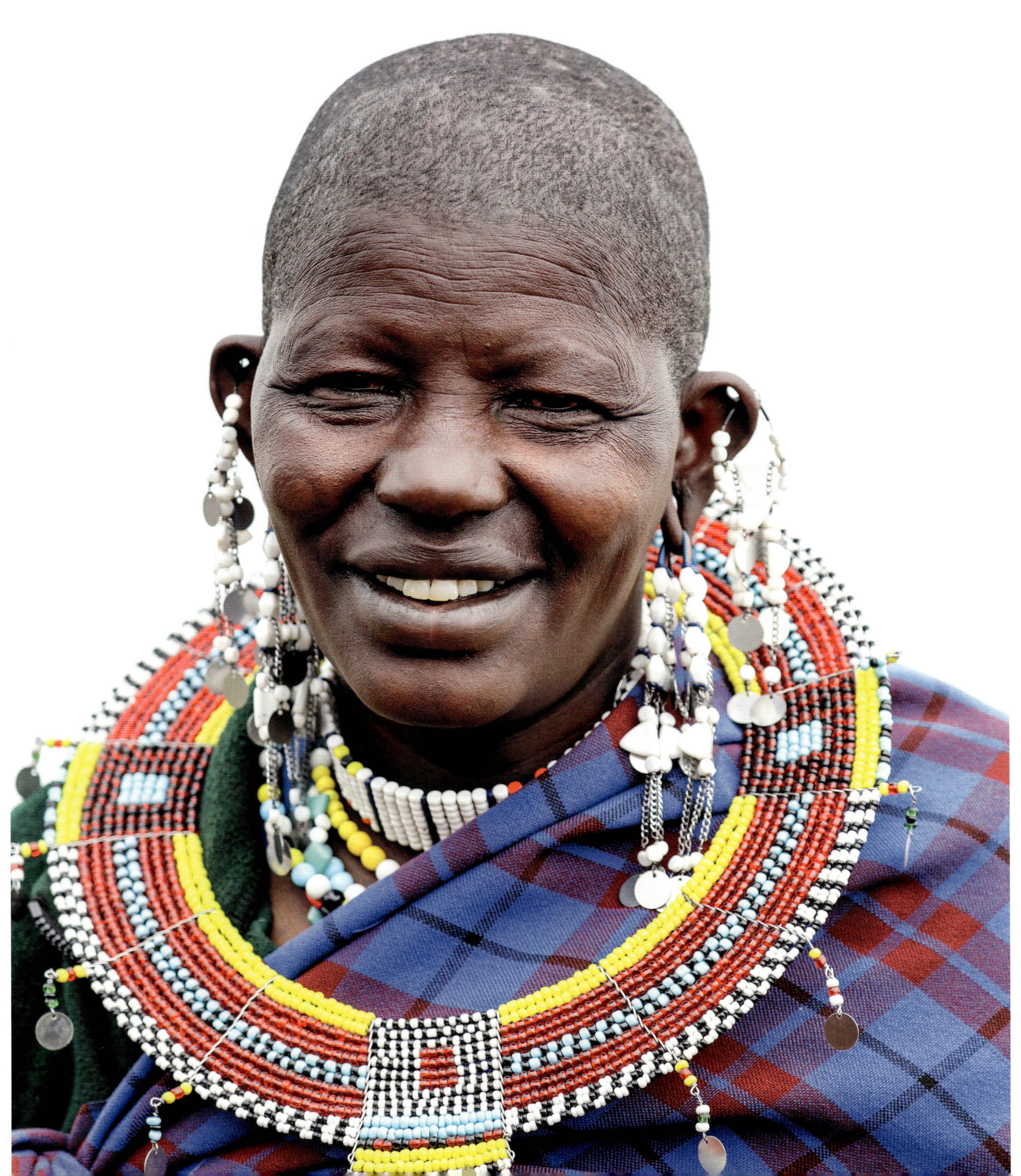

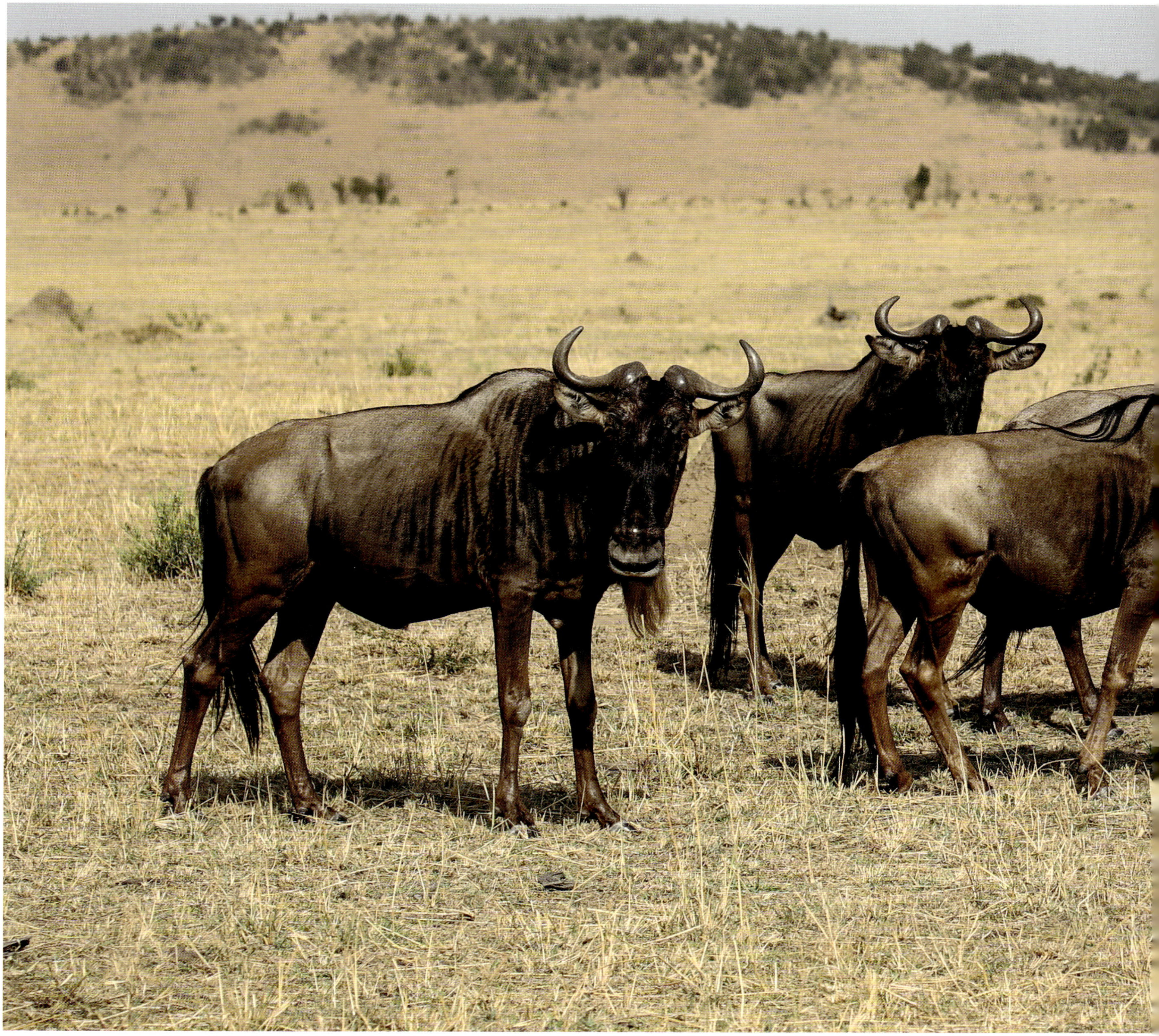

114

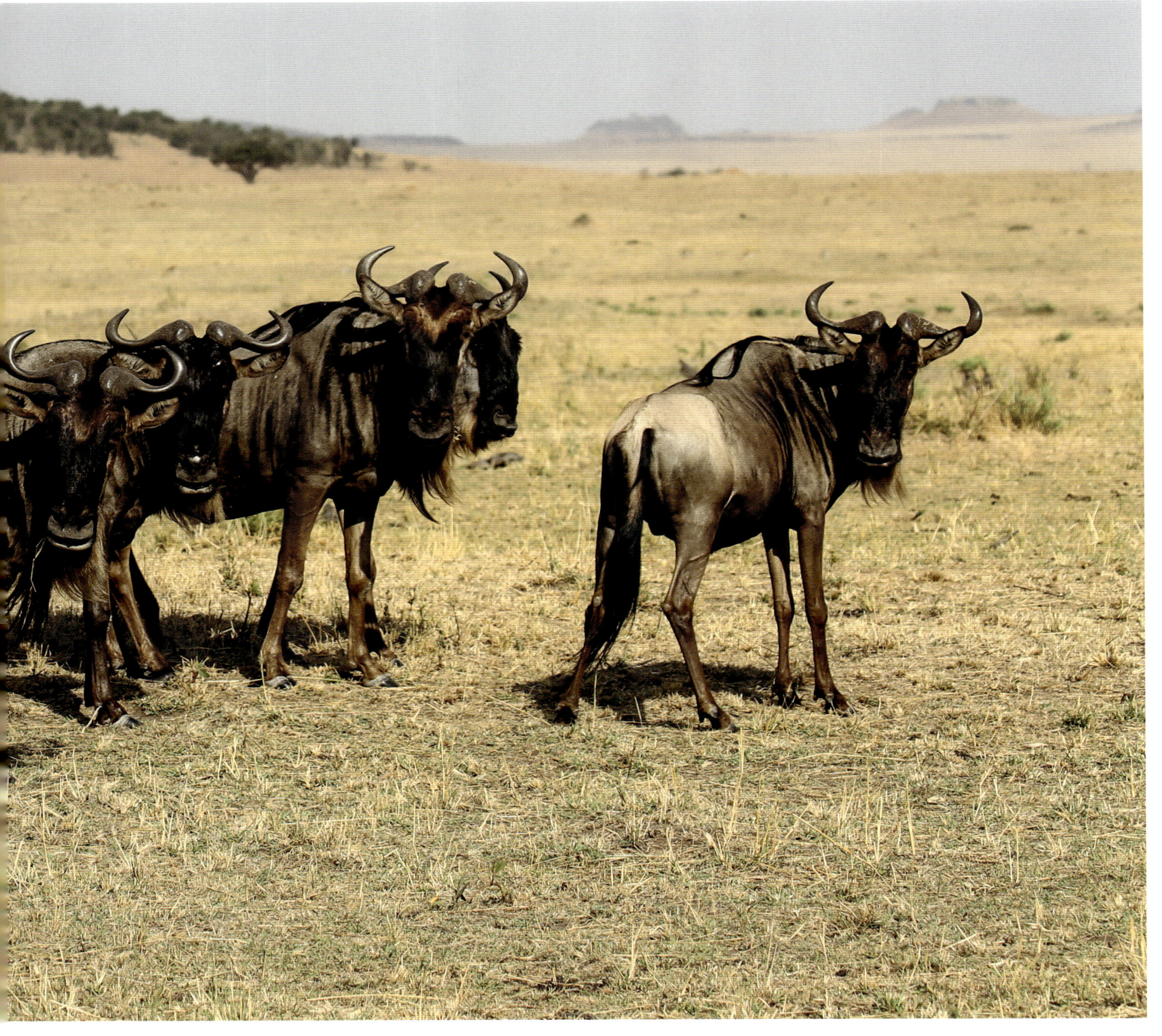

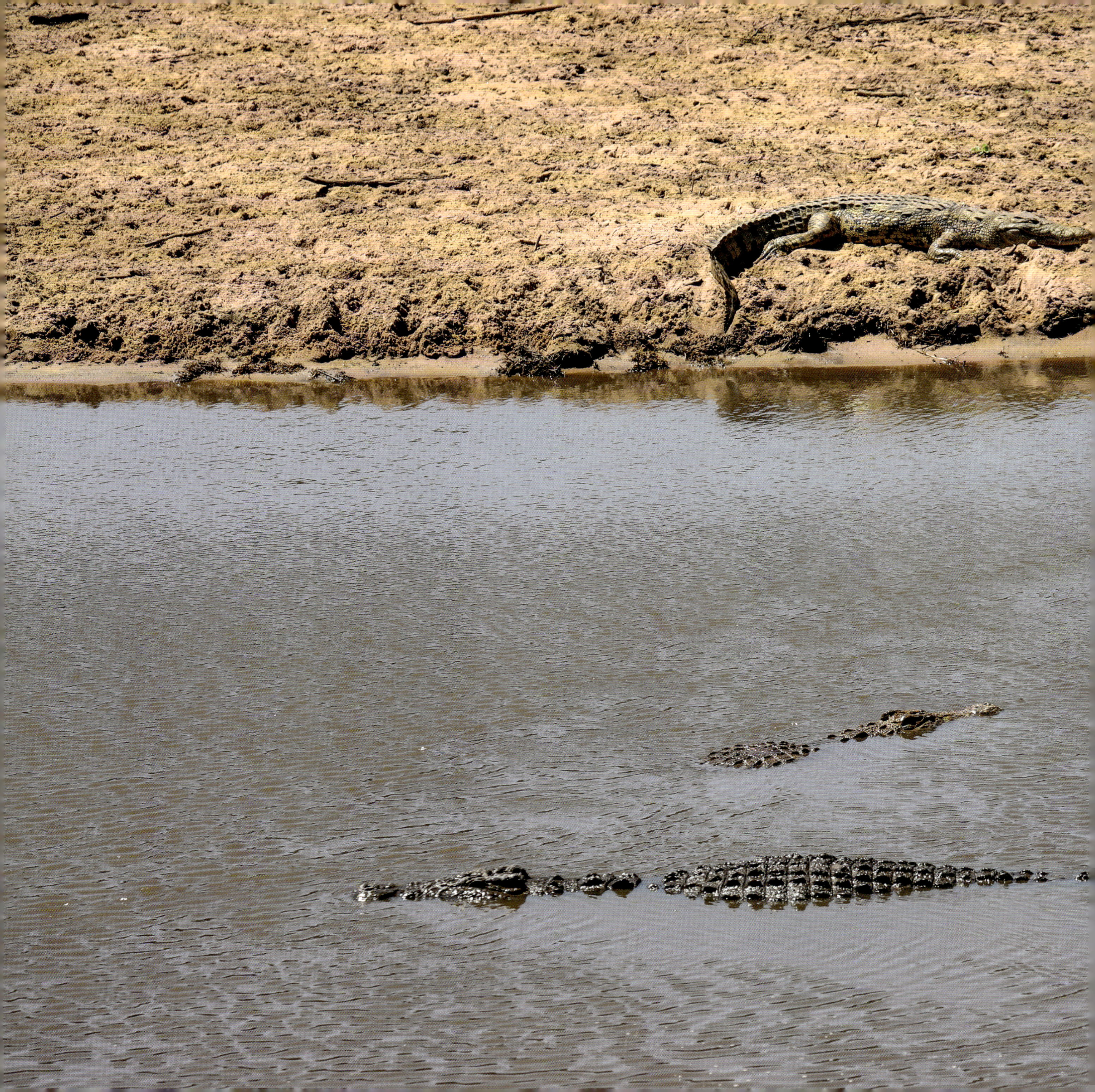

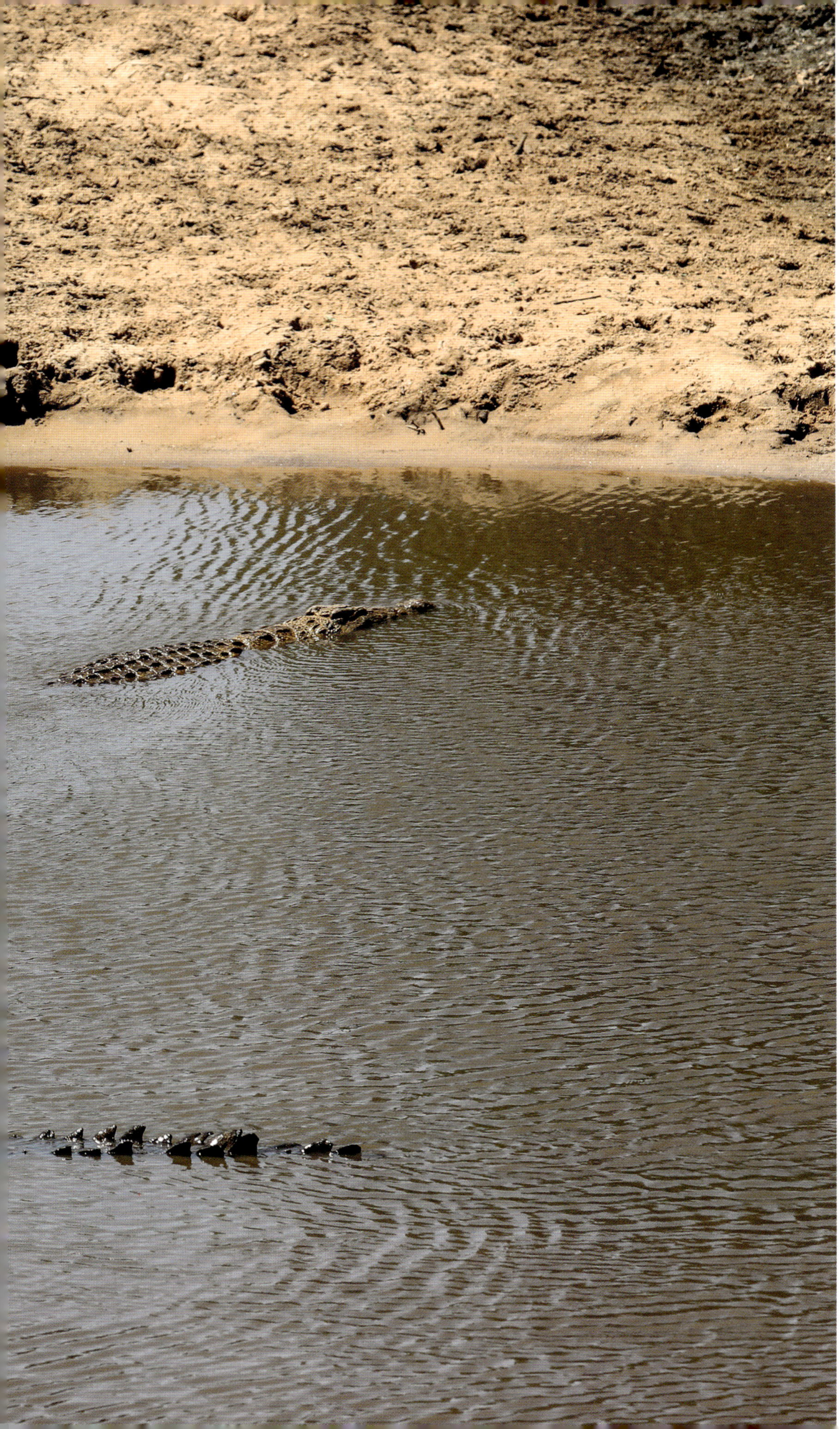

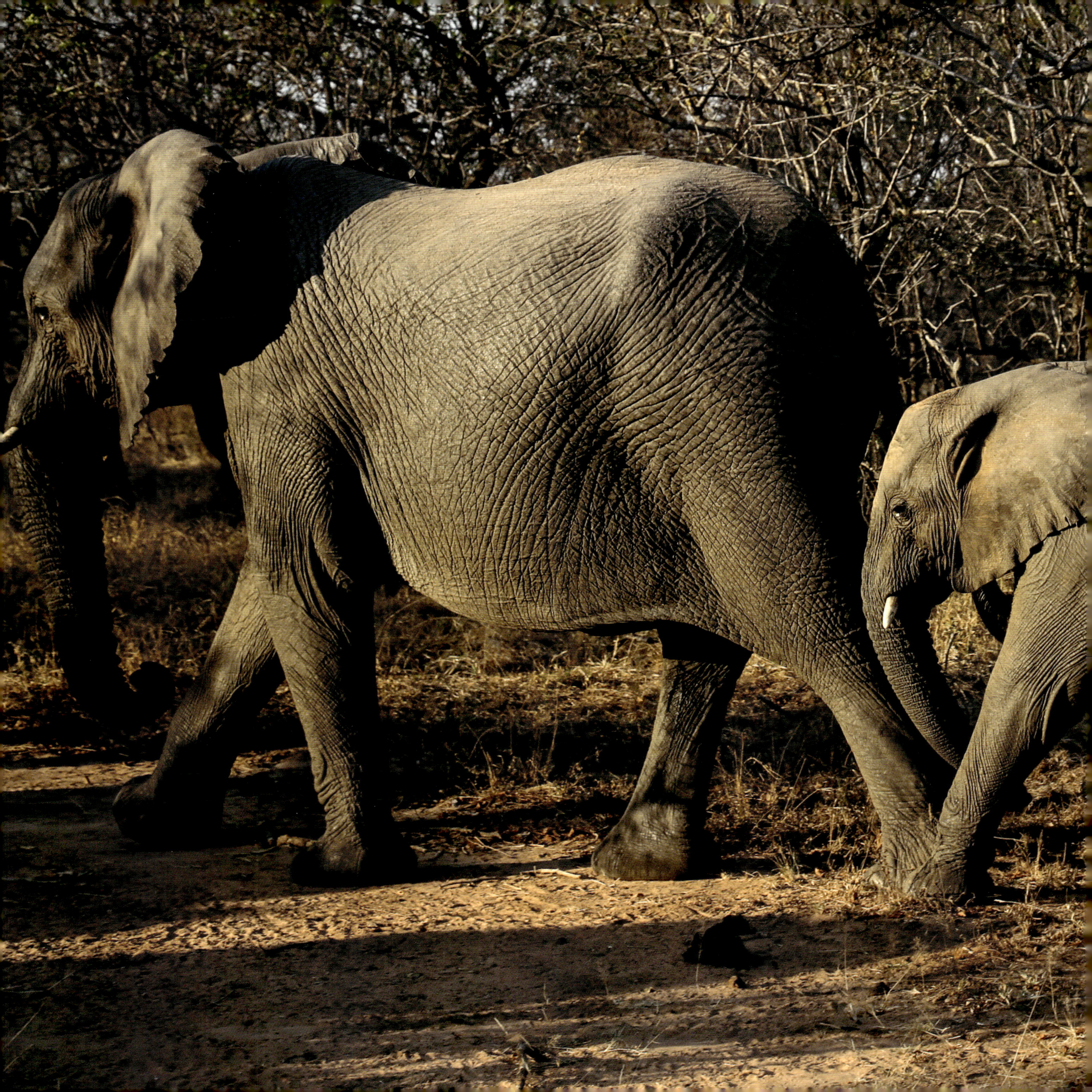

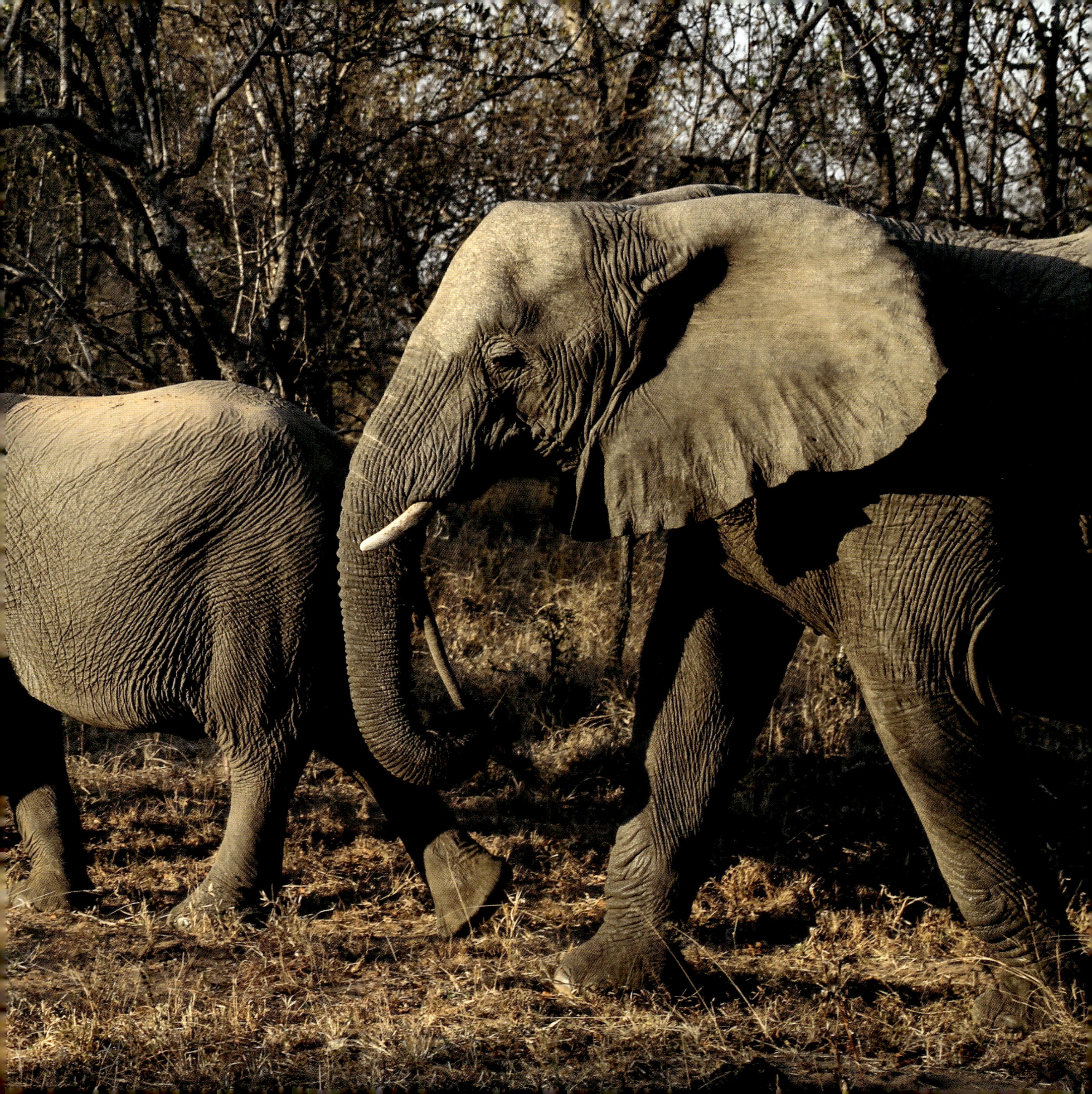

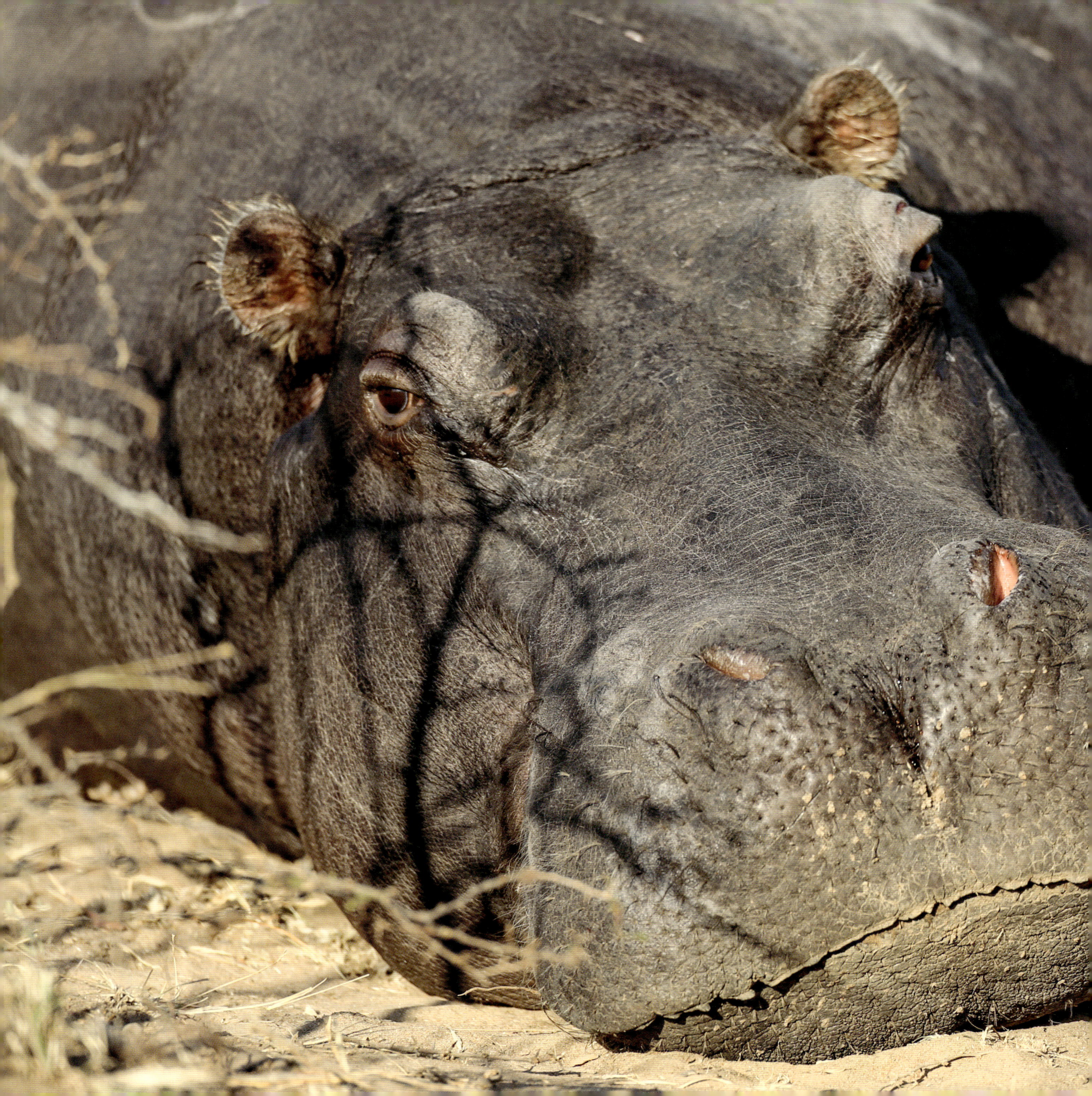

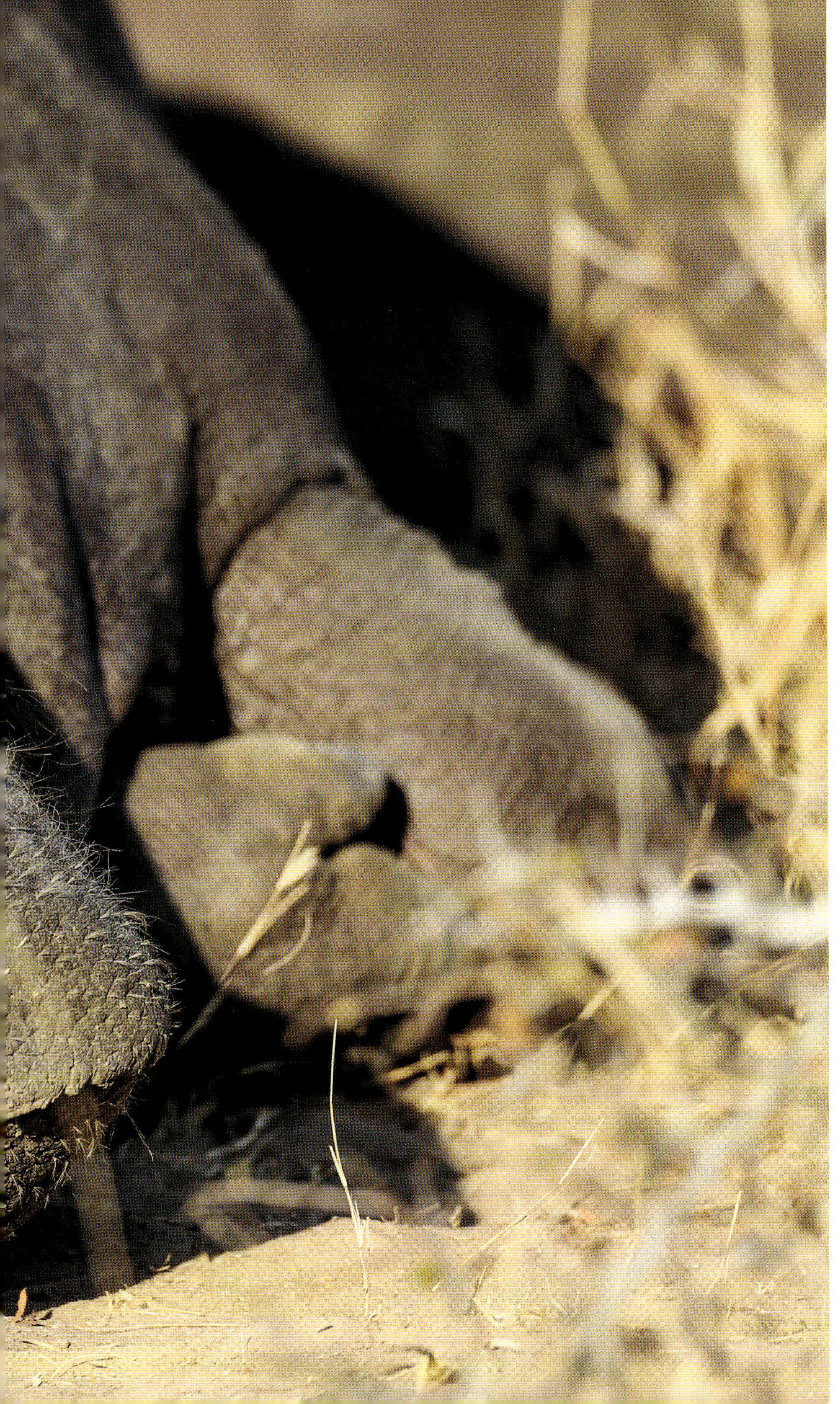

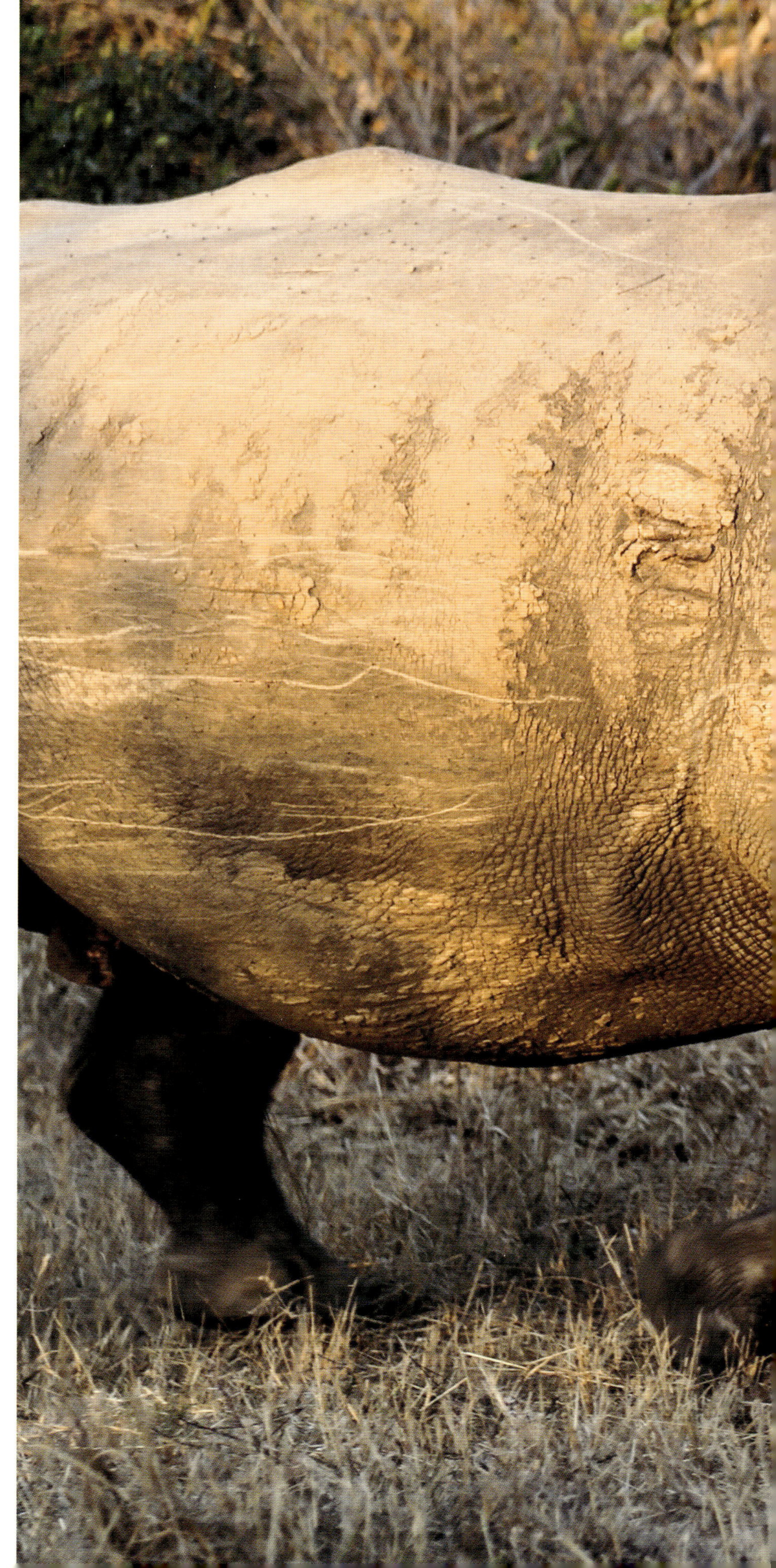

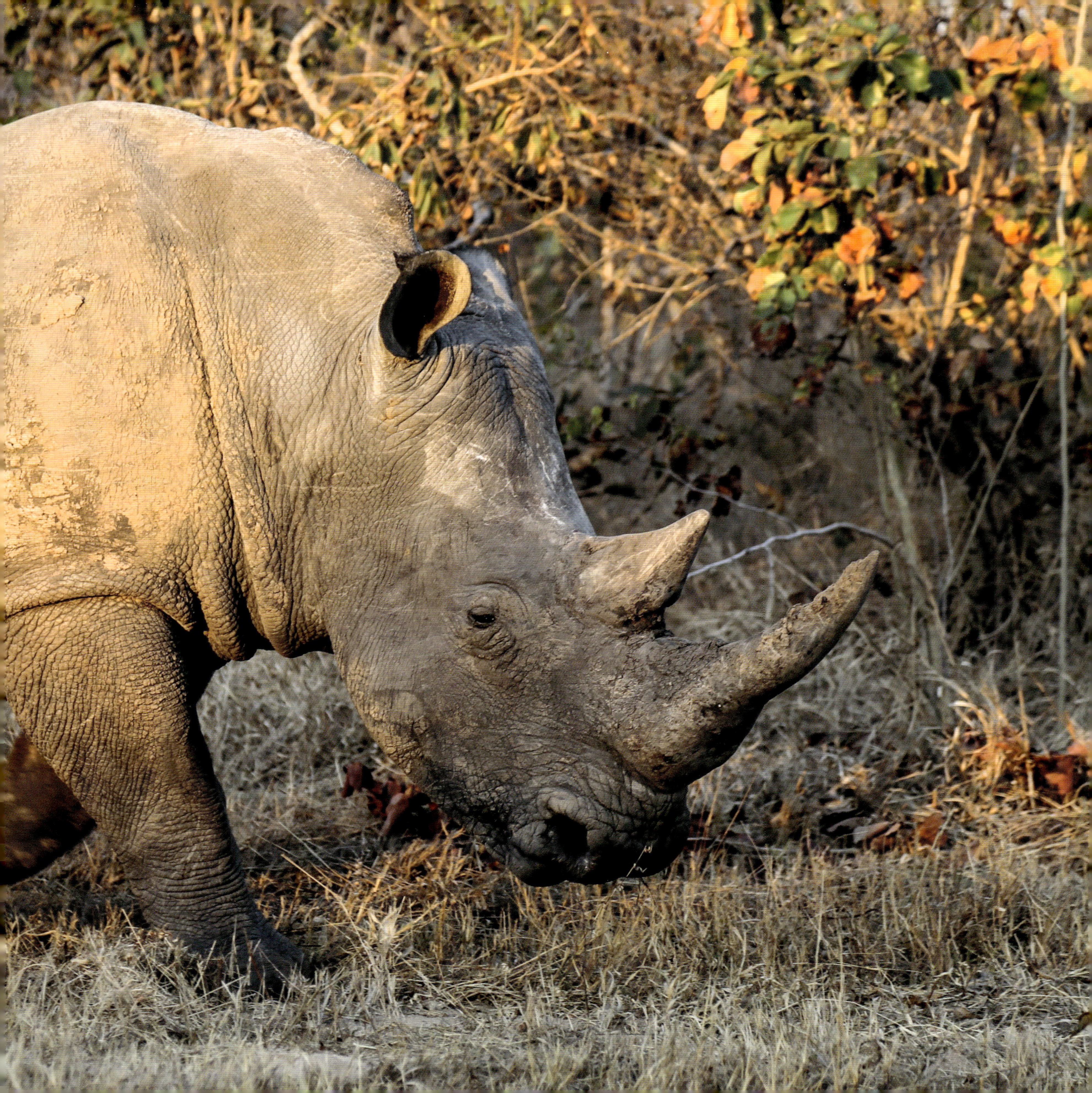

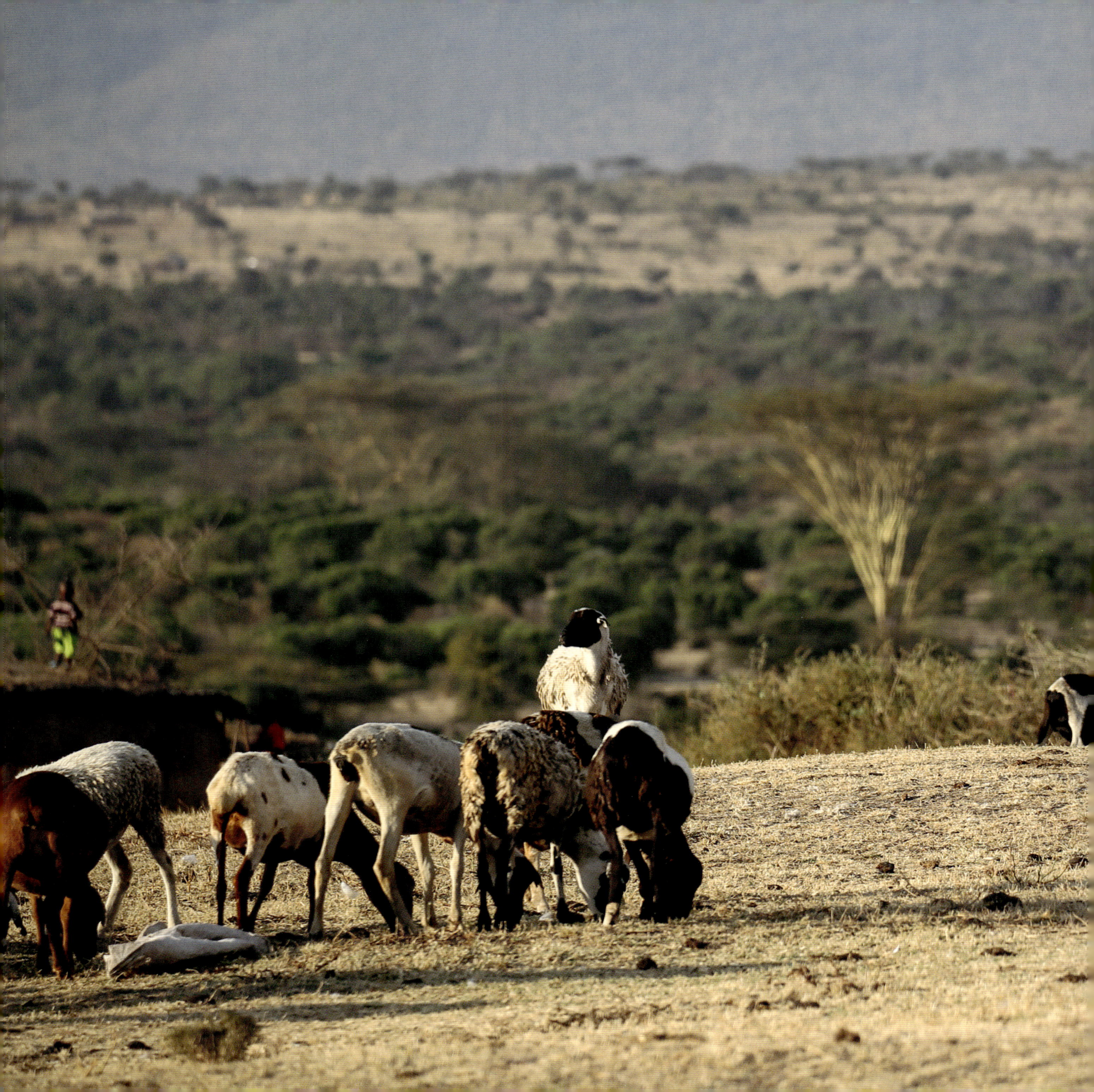

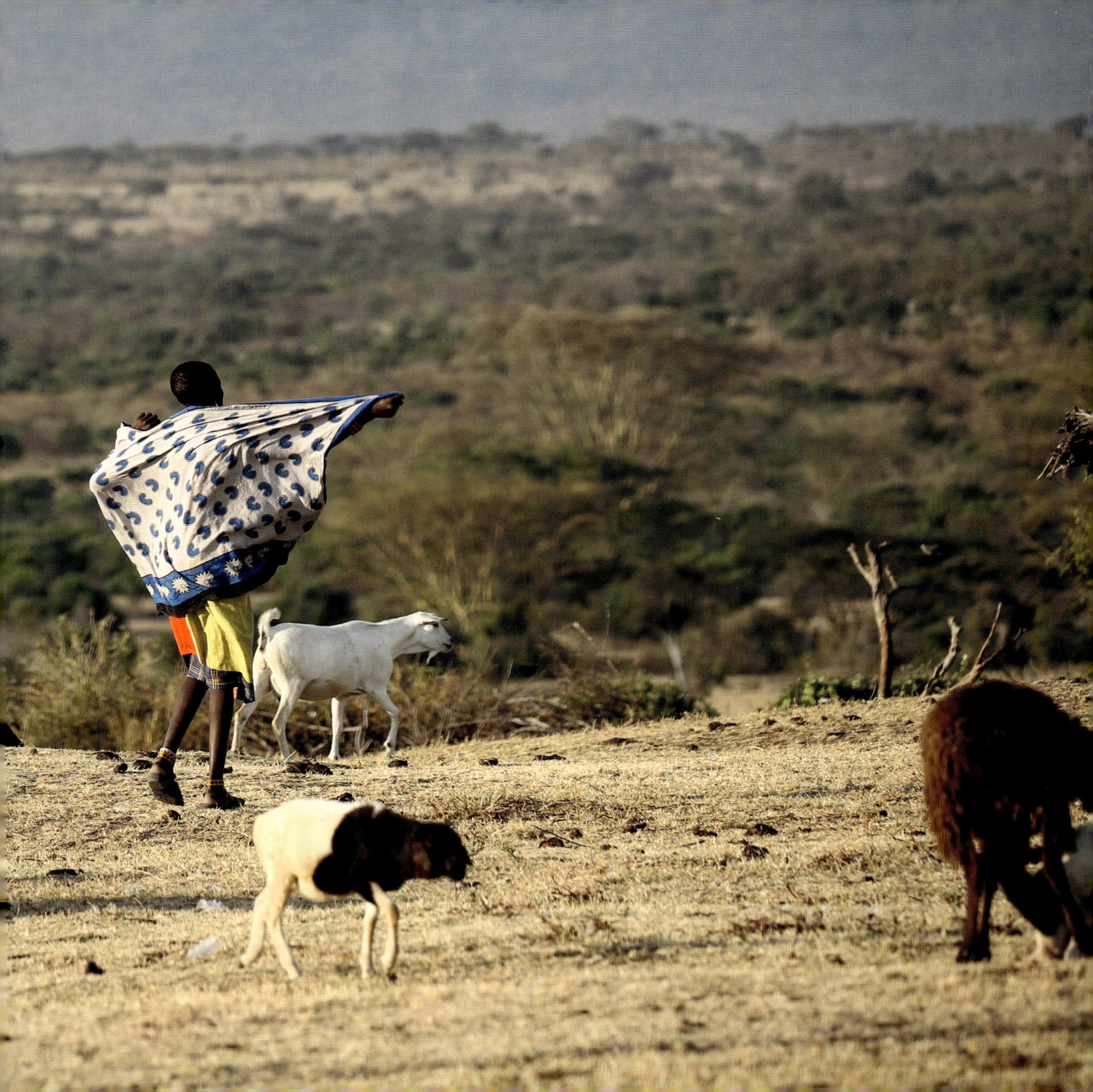

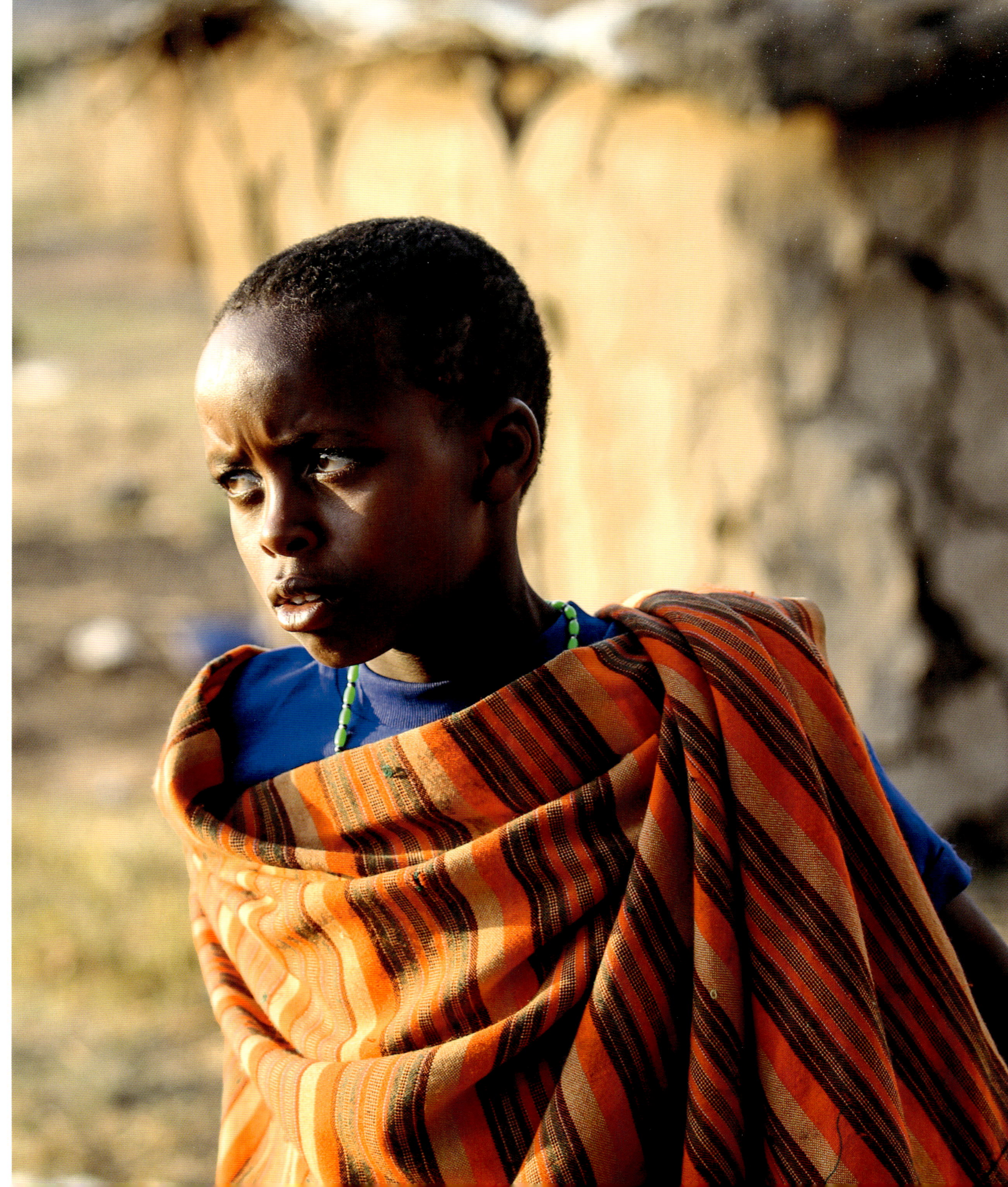

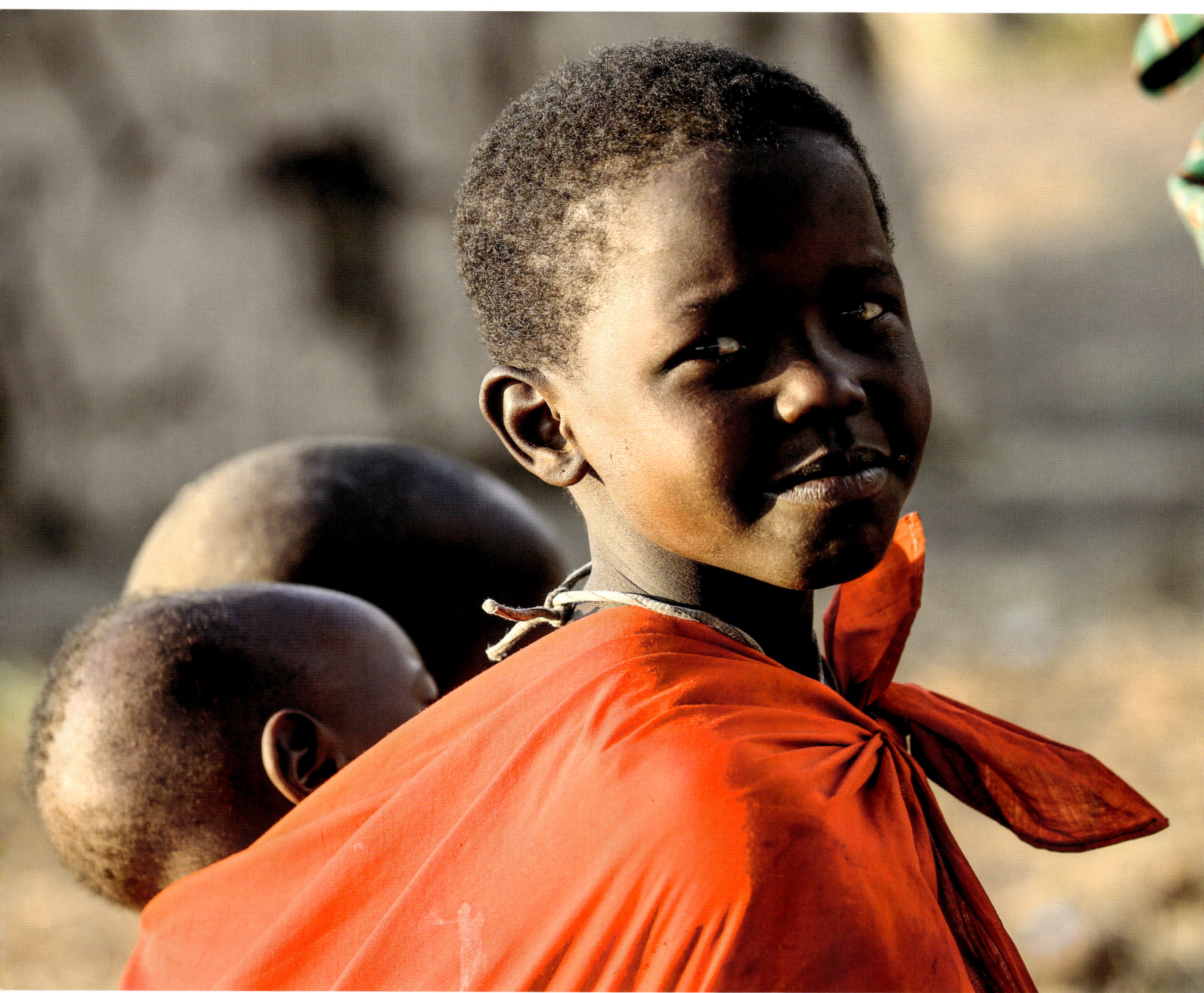

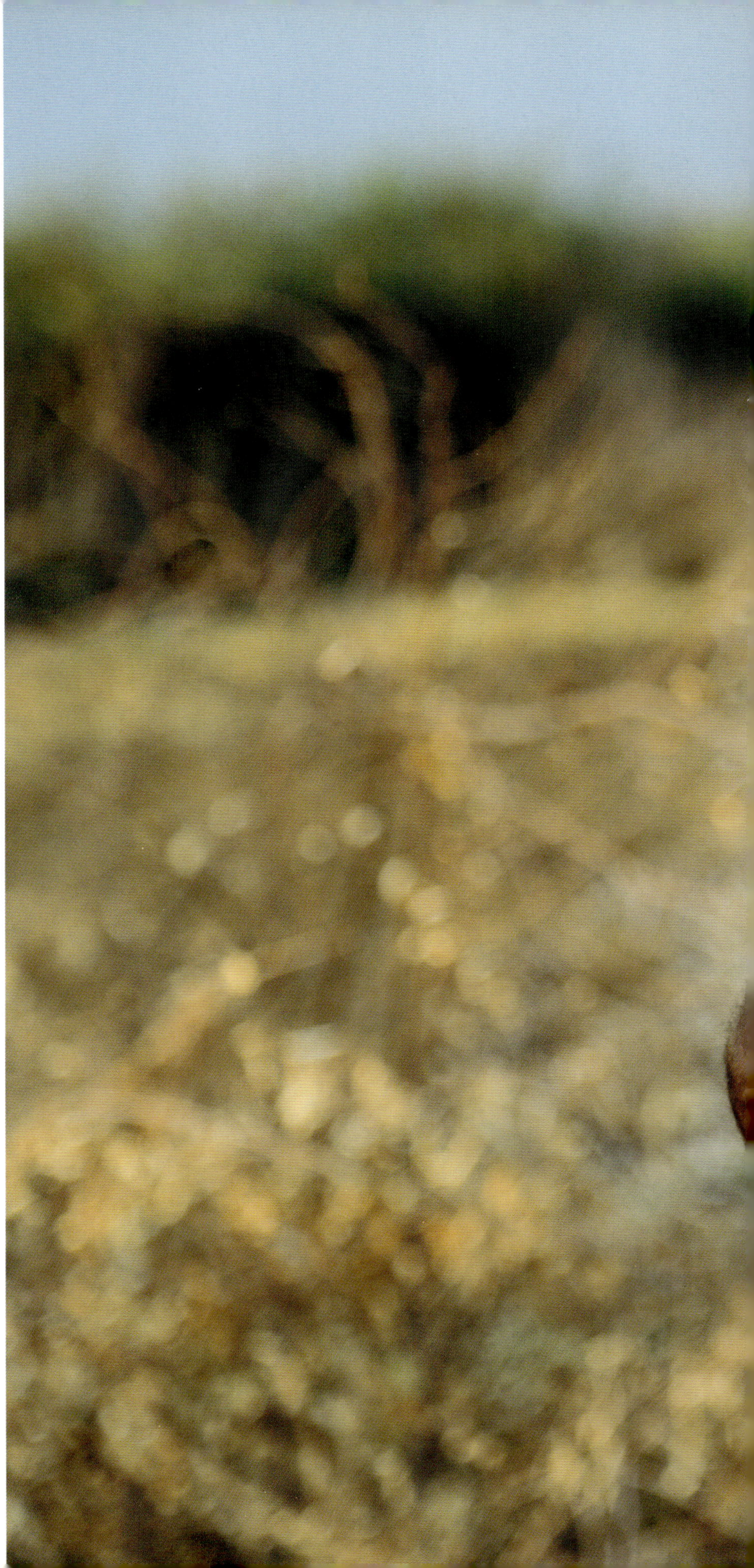

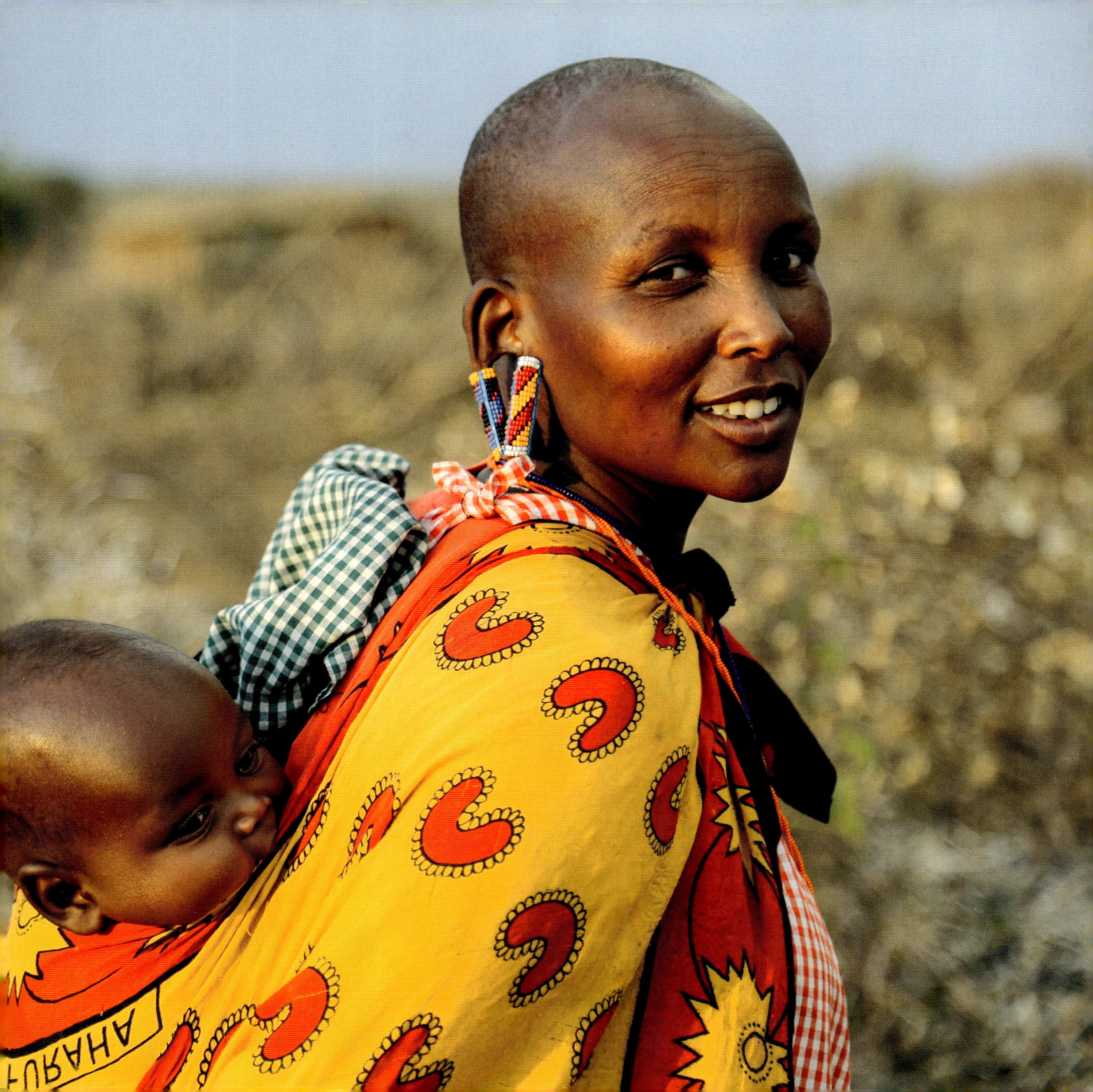

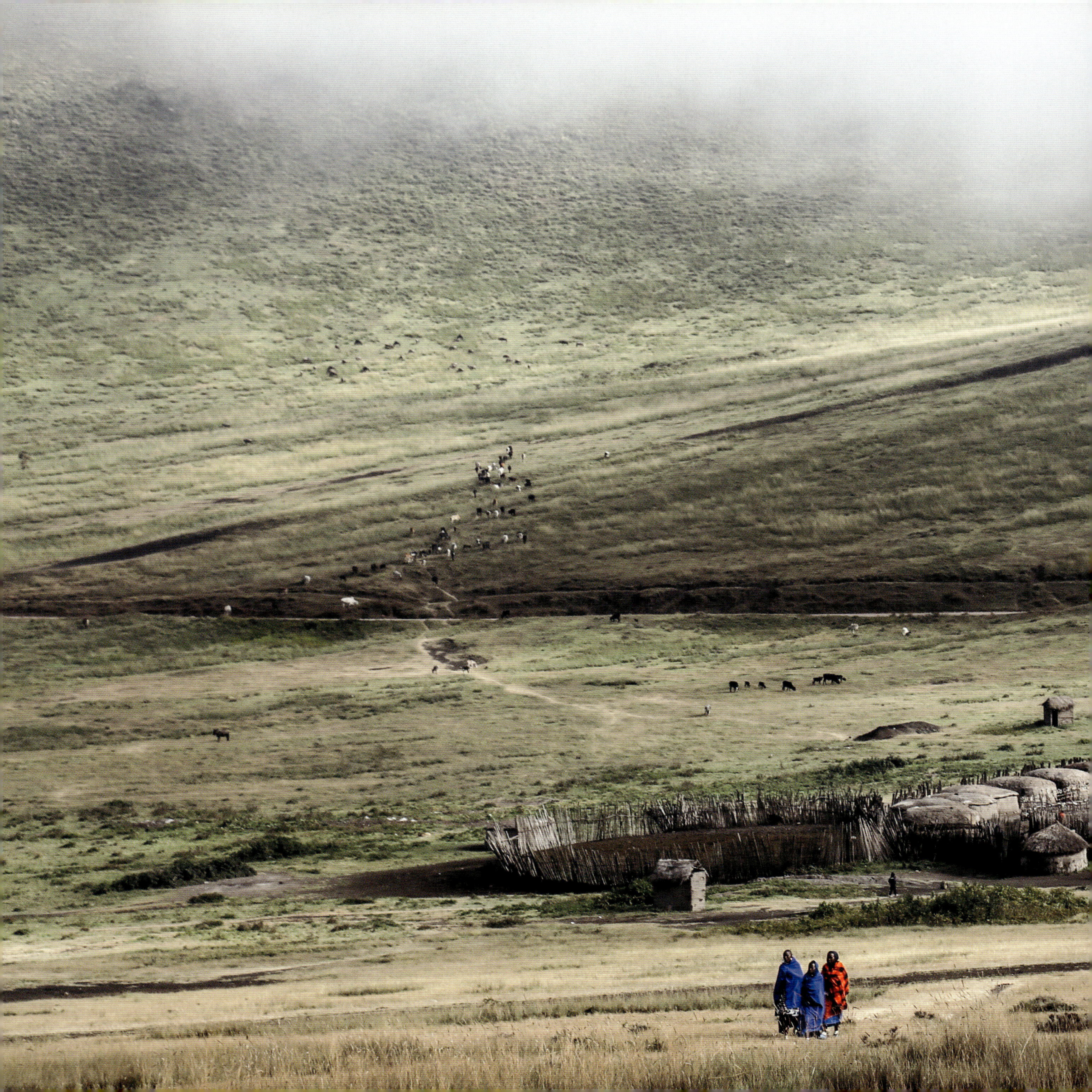

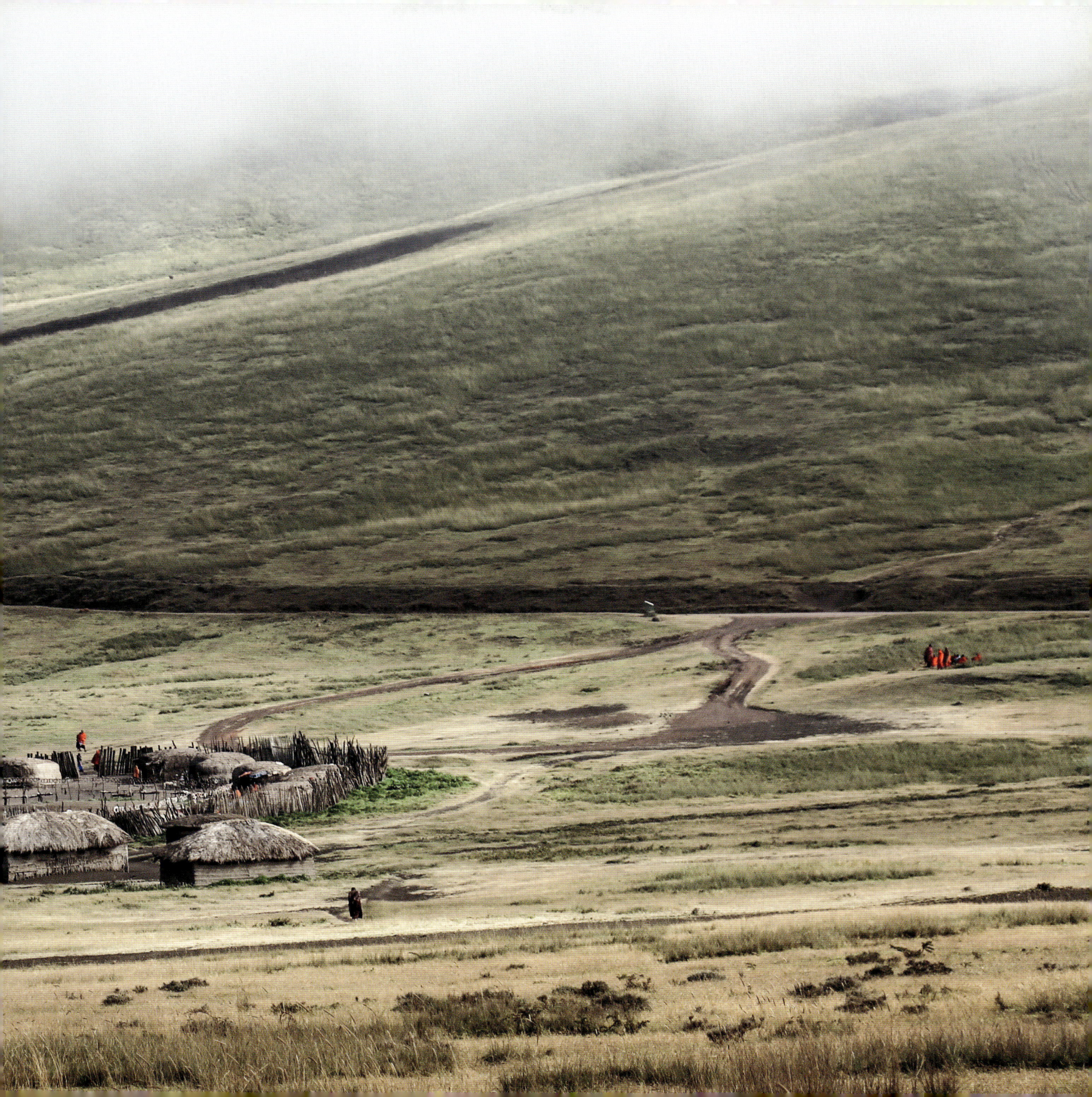

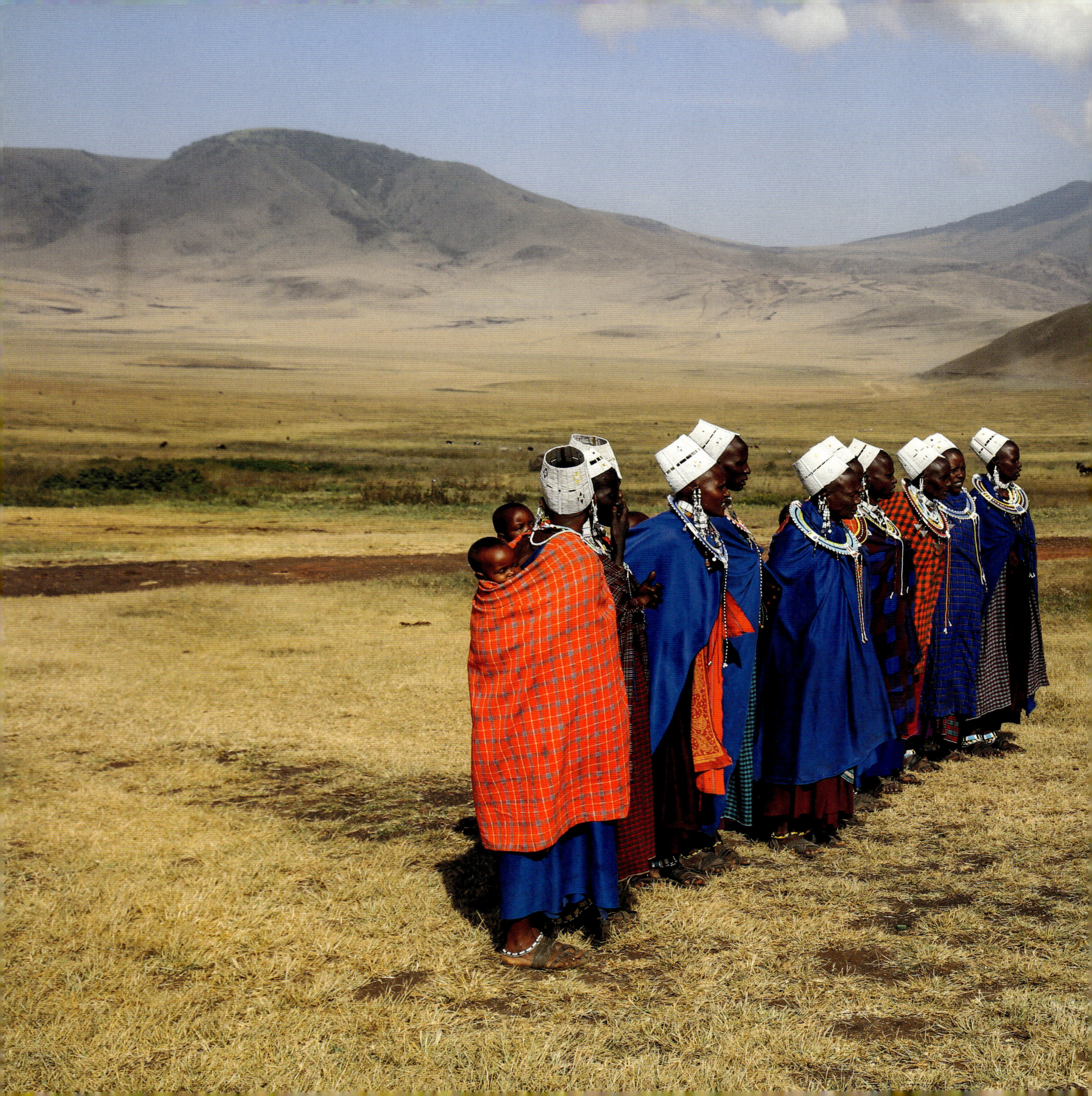

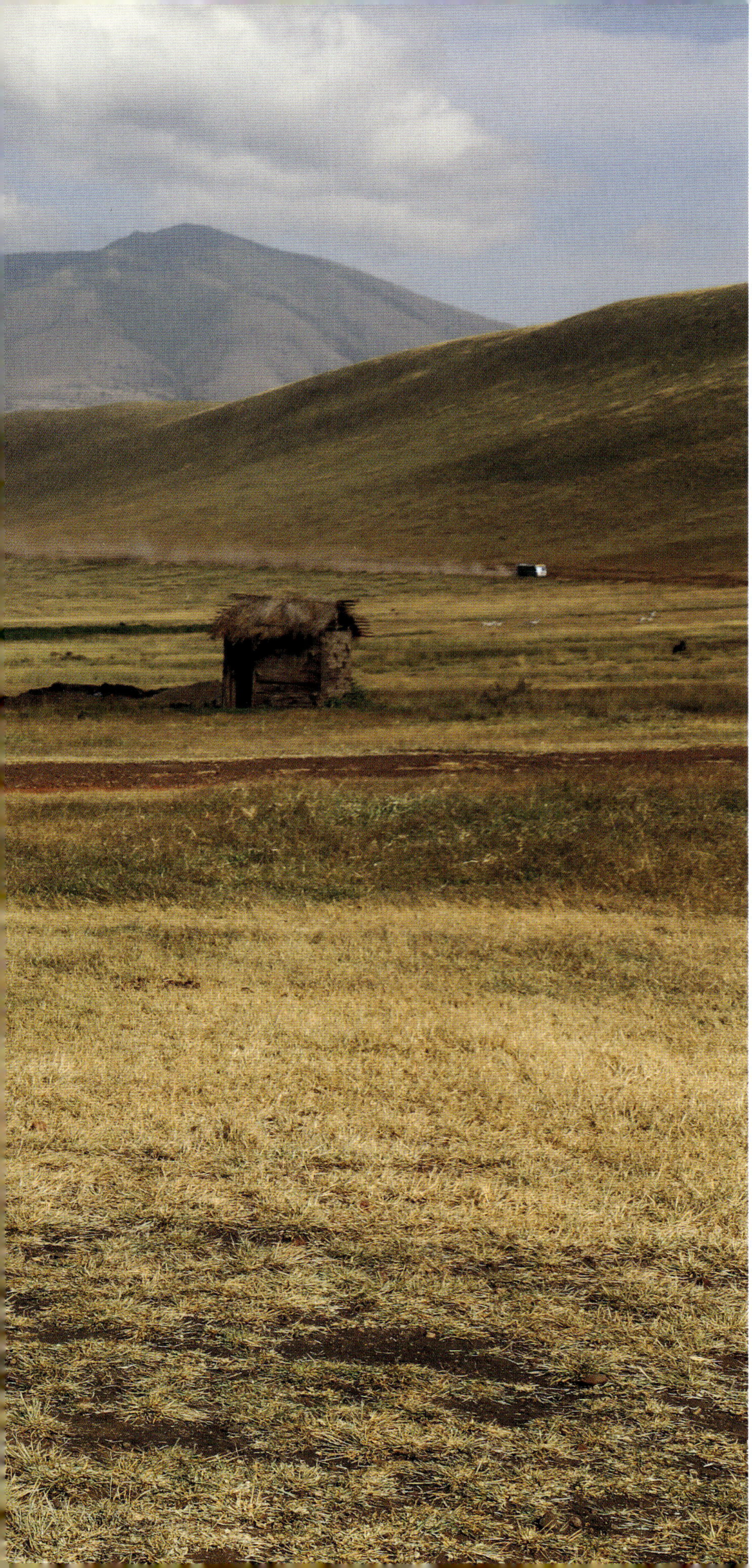

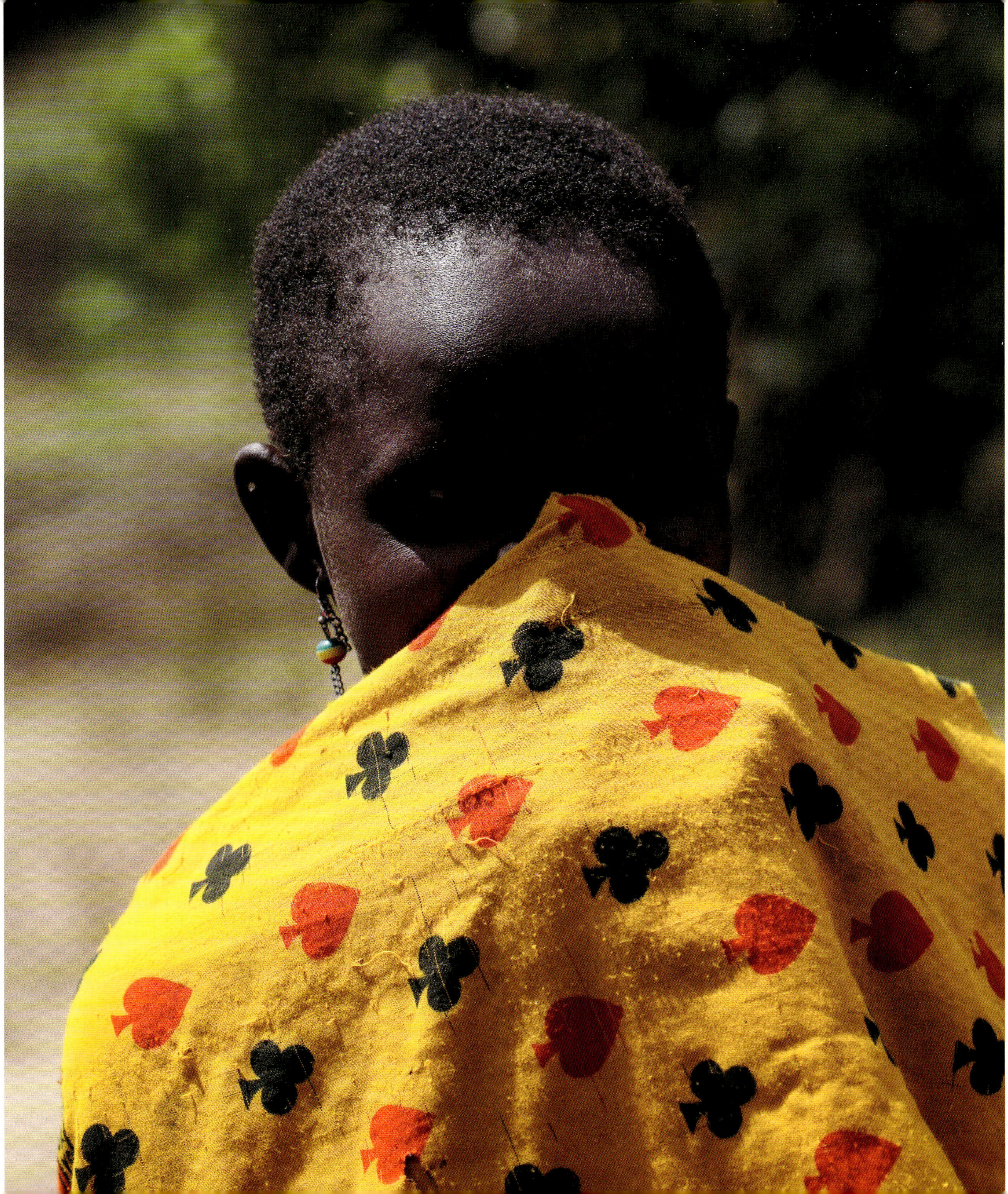

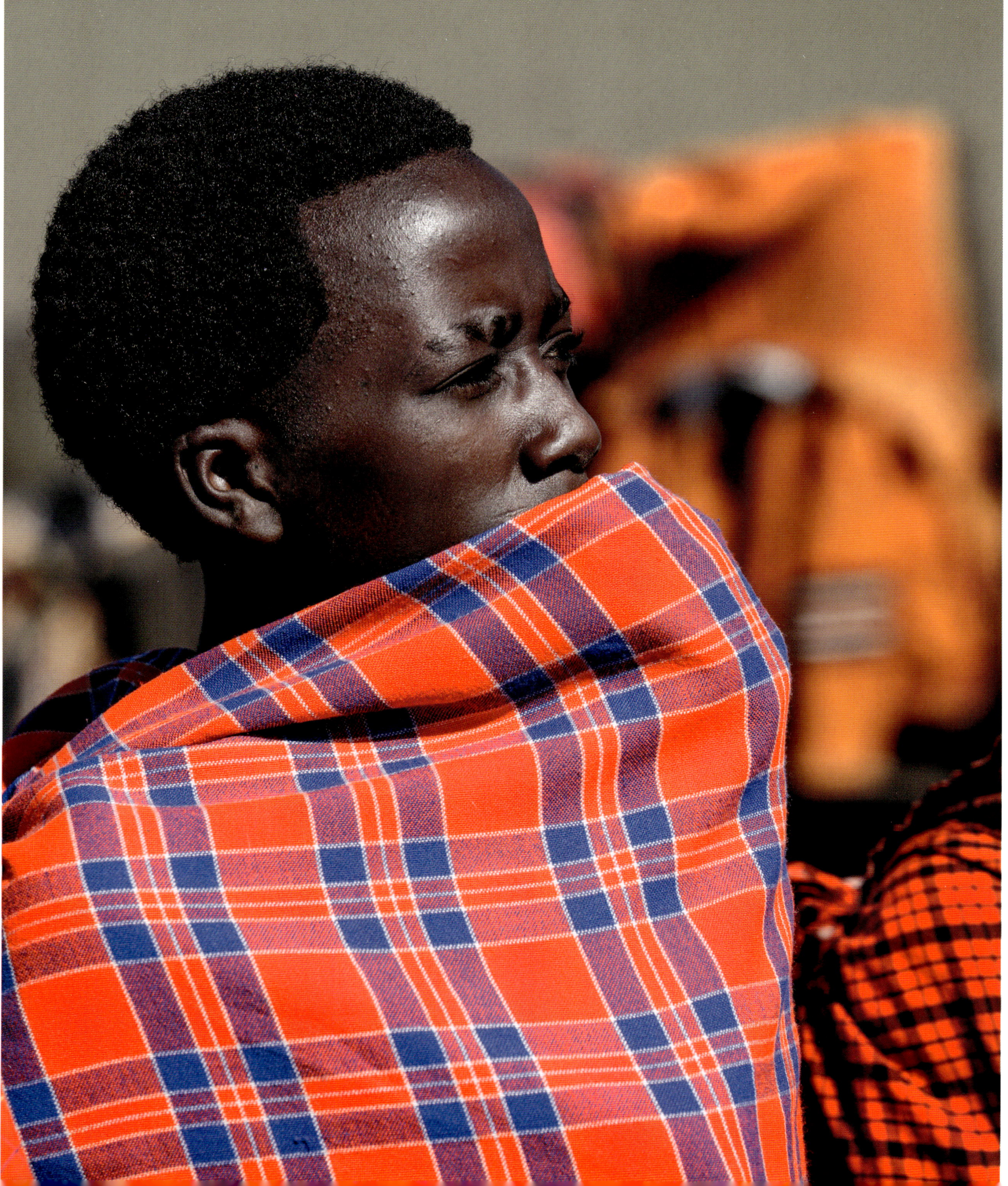

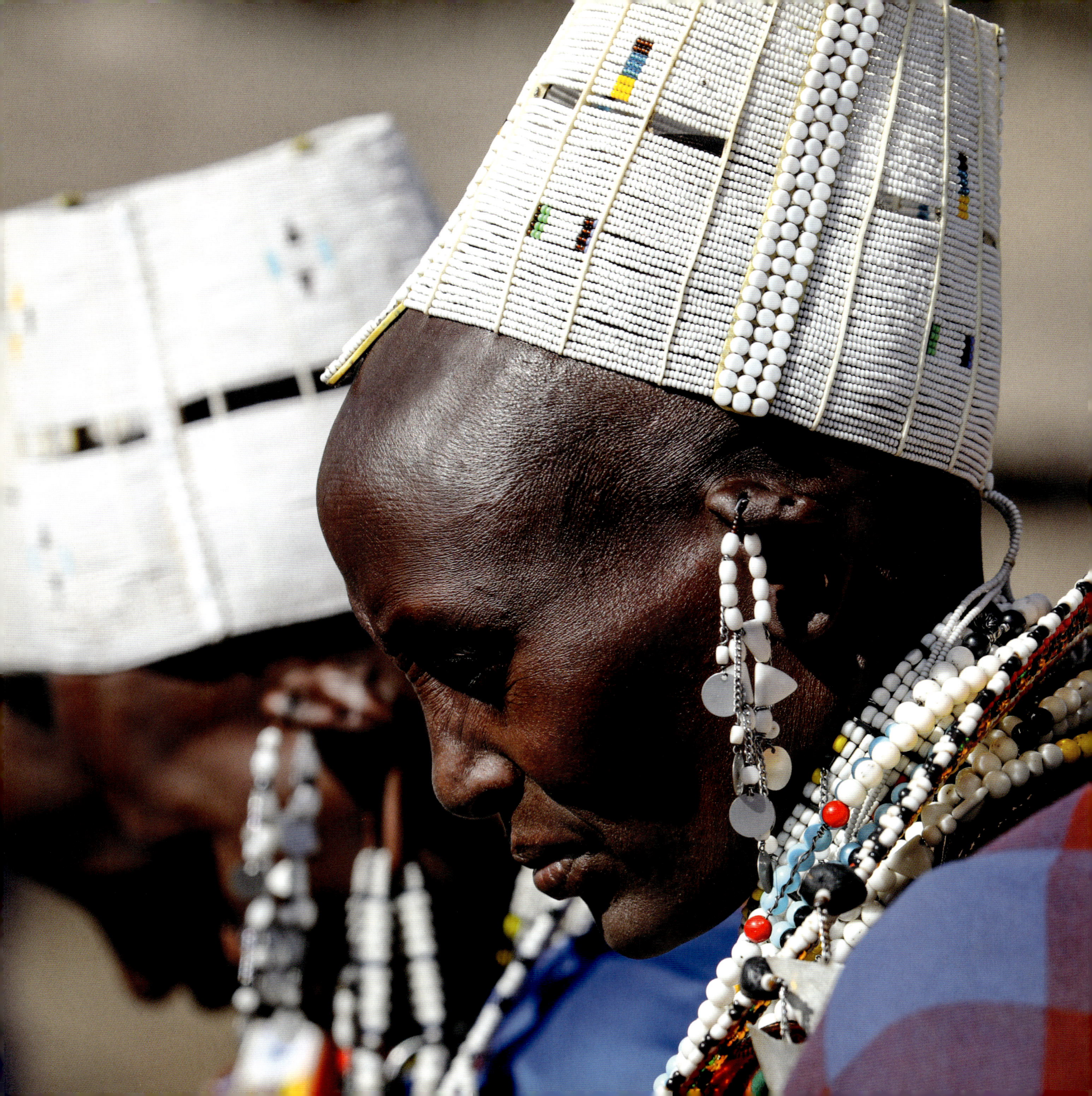

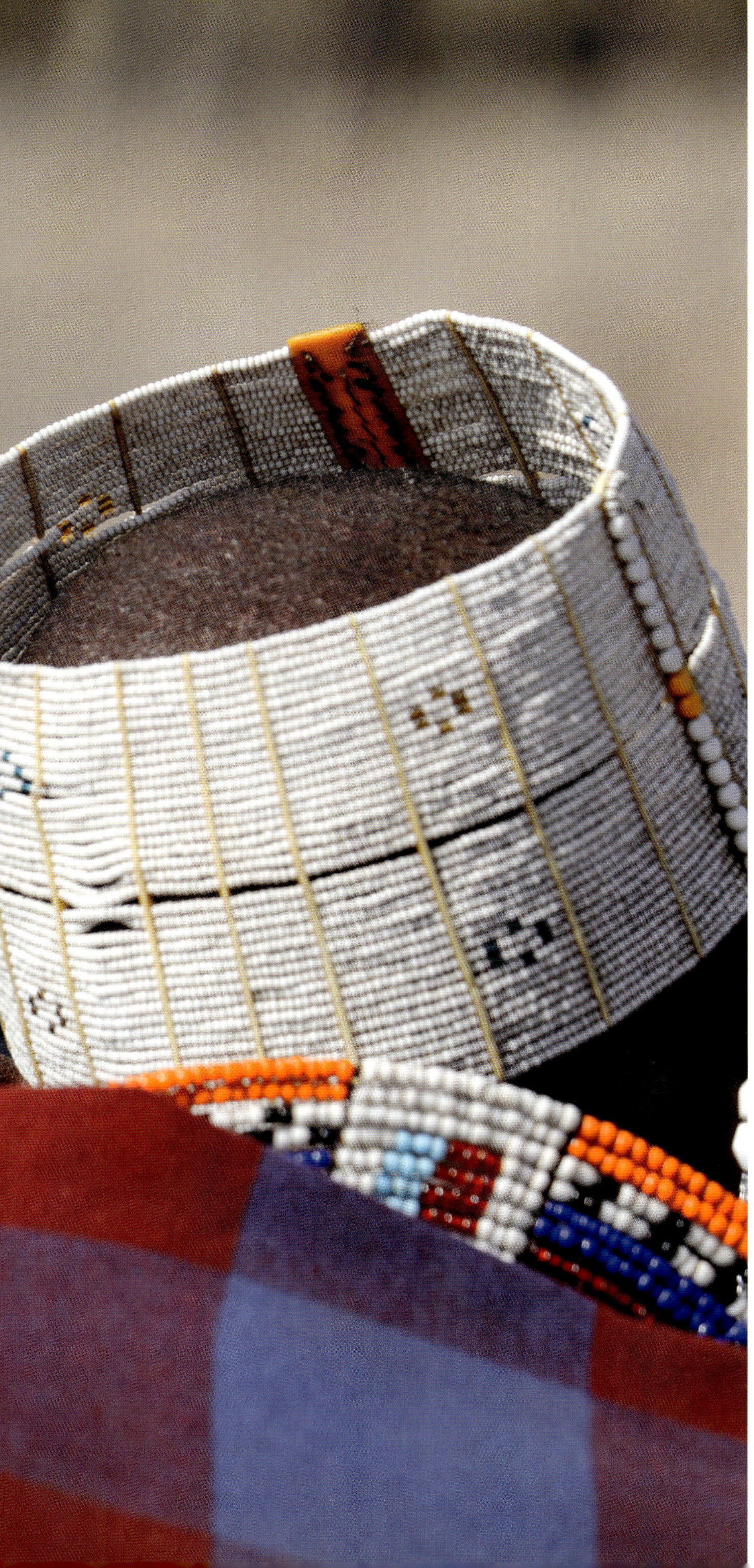

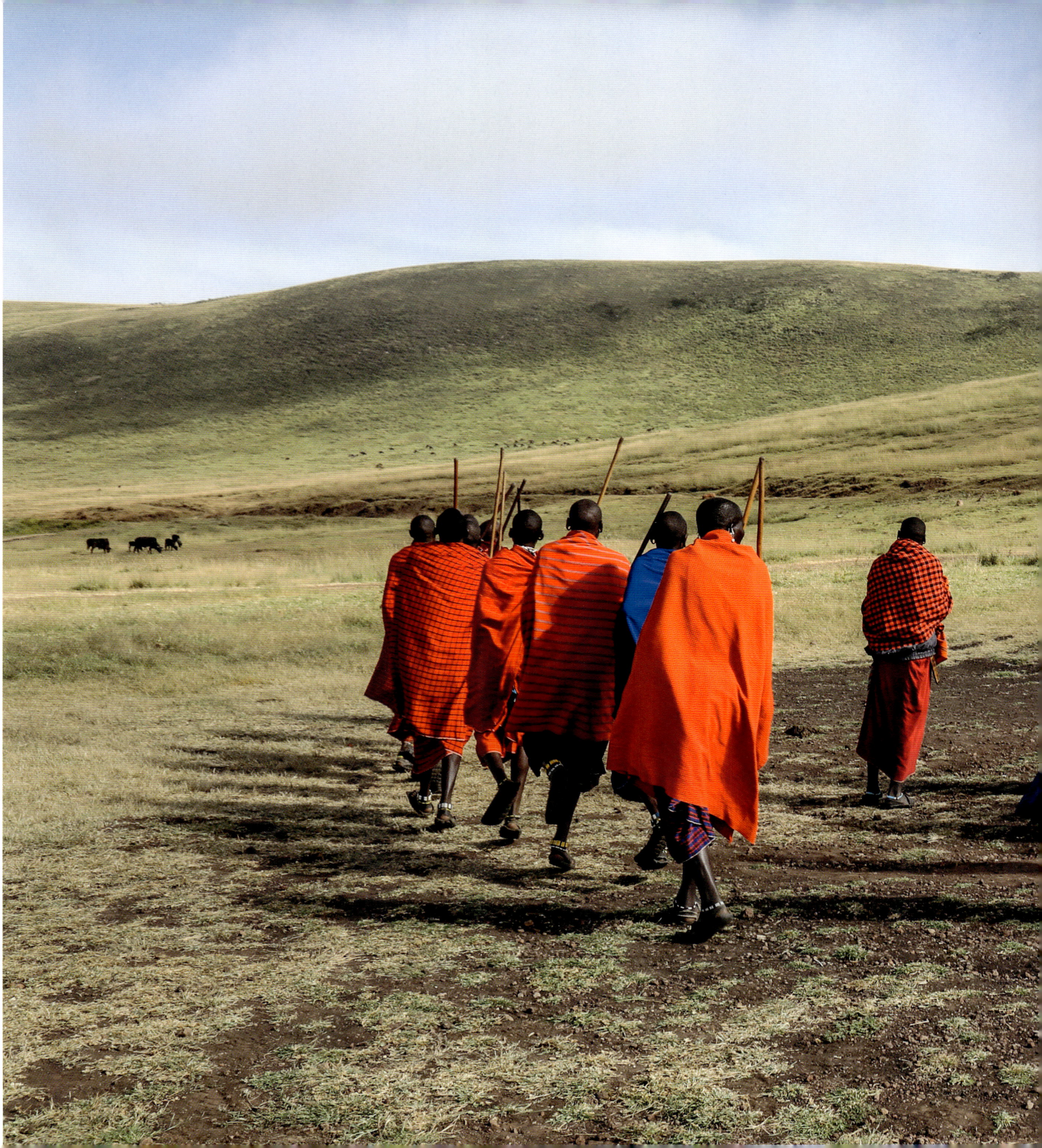

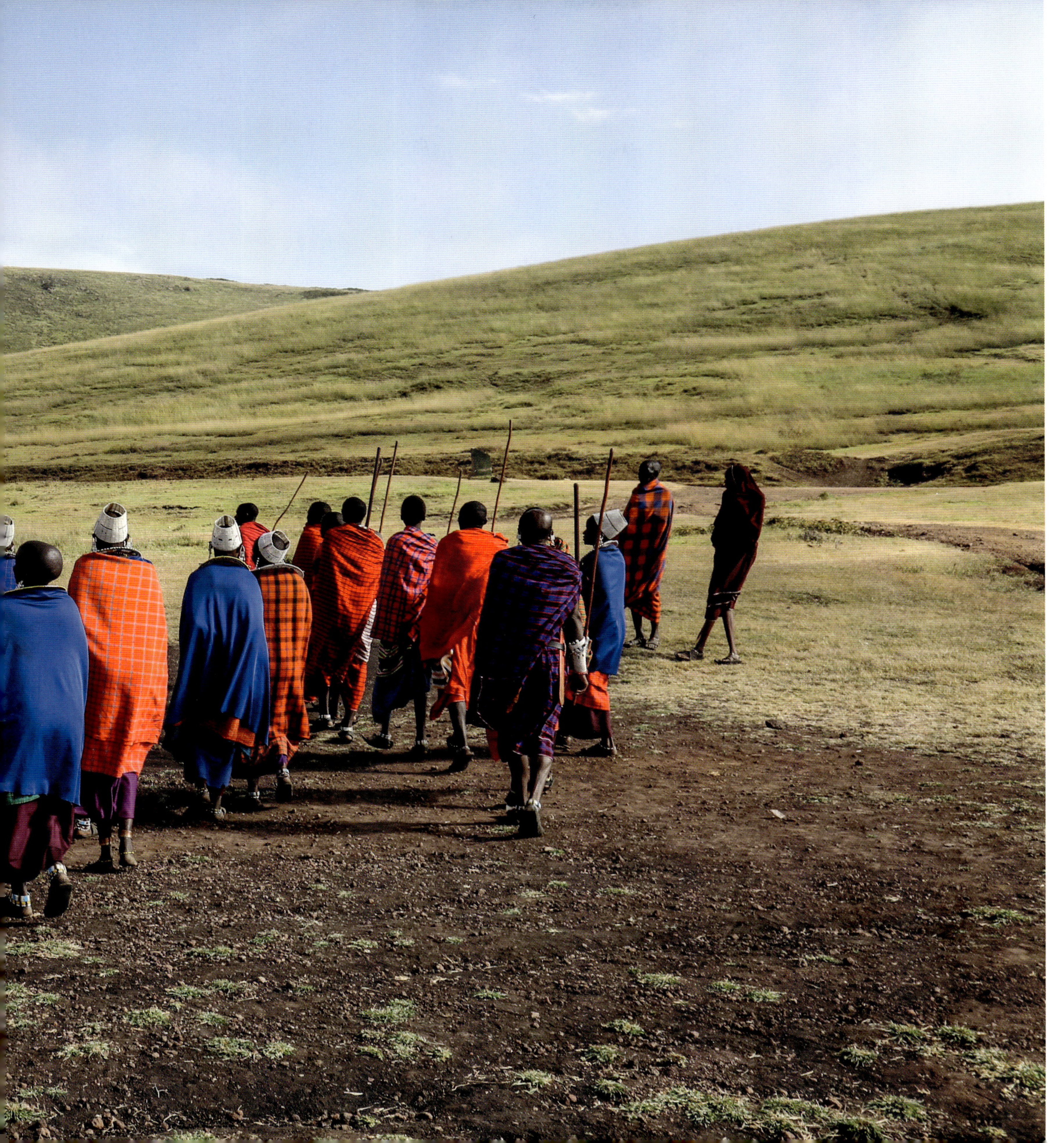

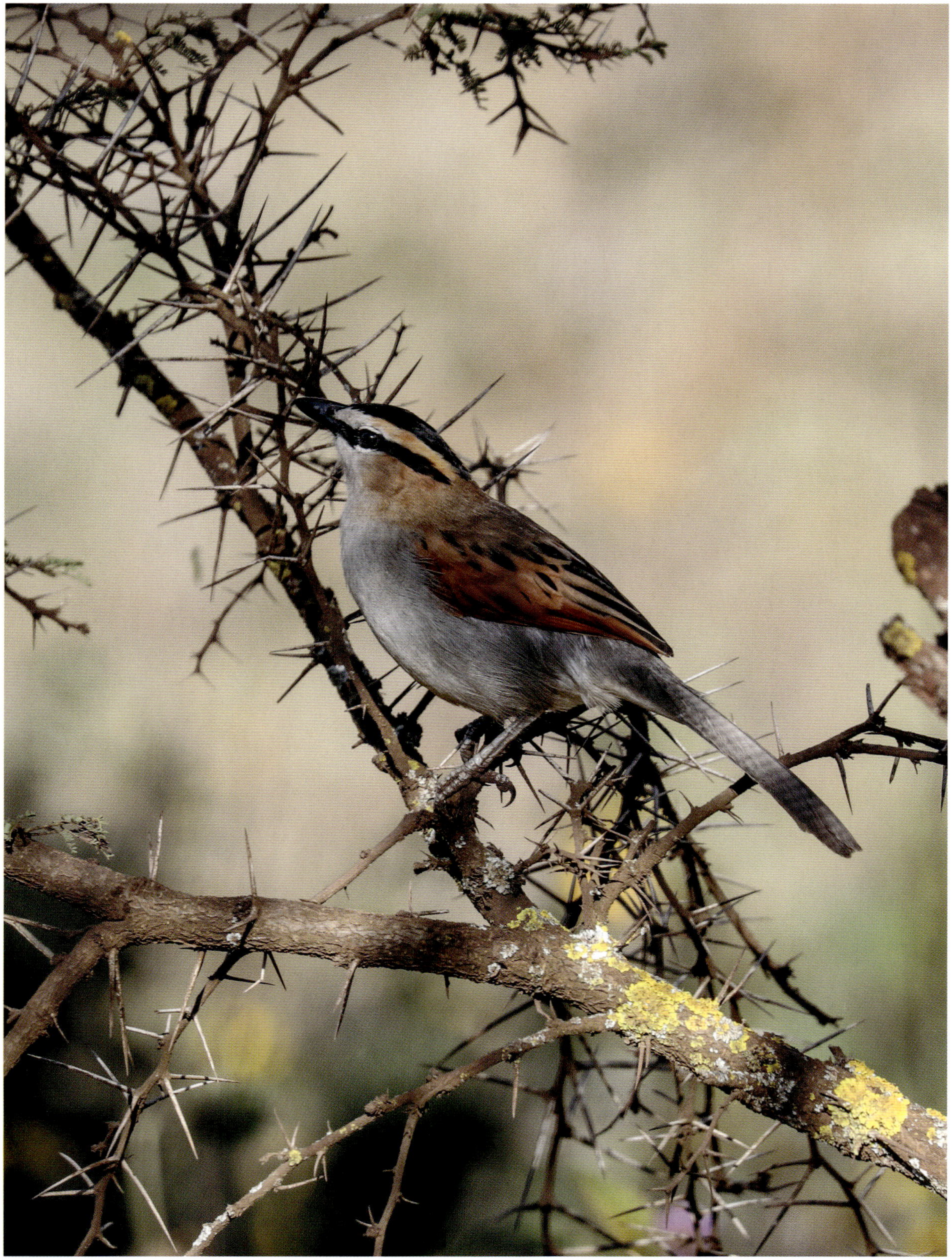

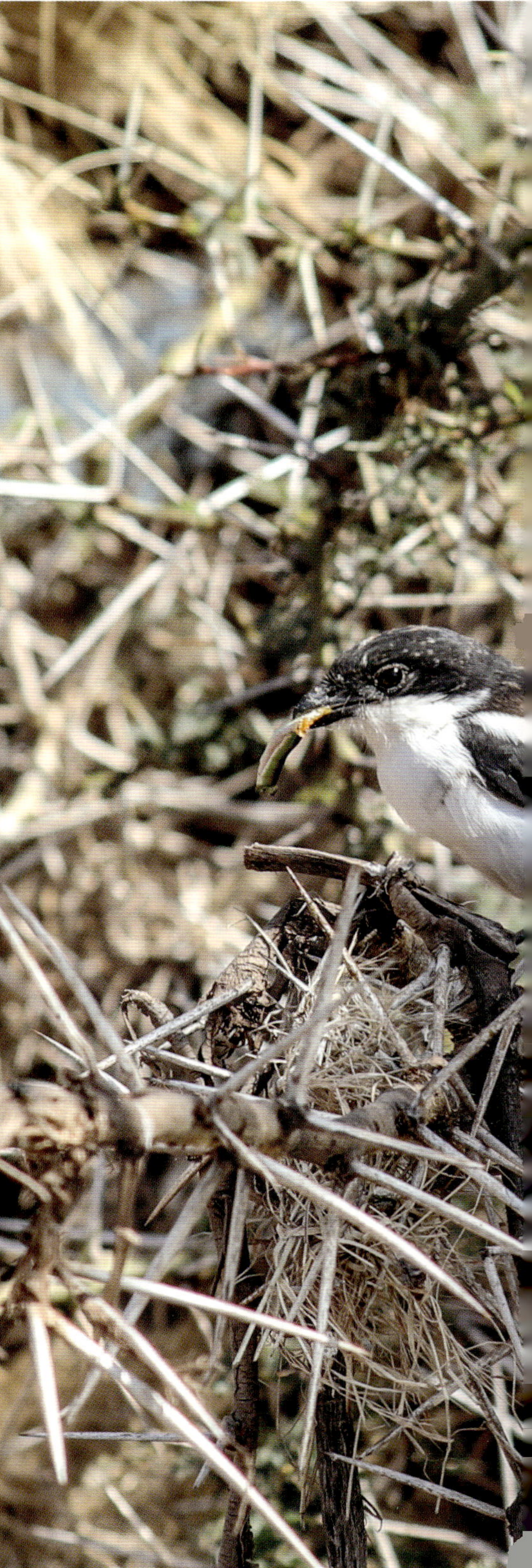

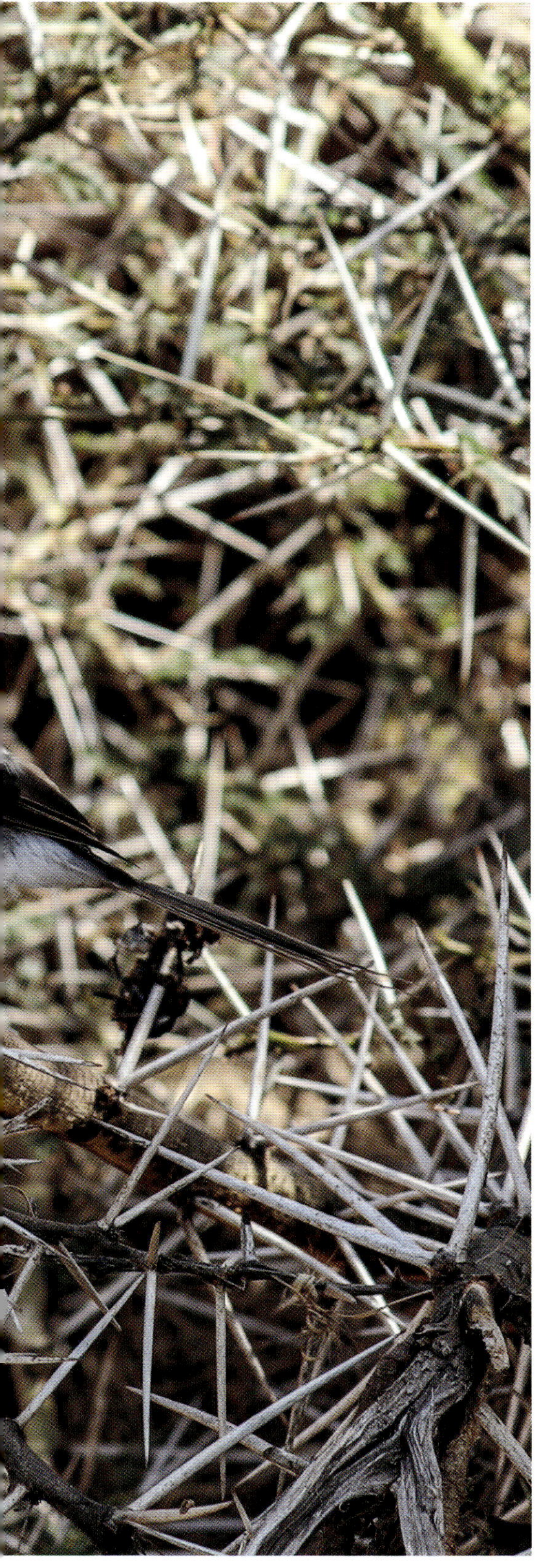

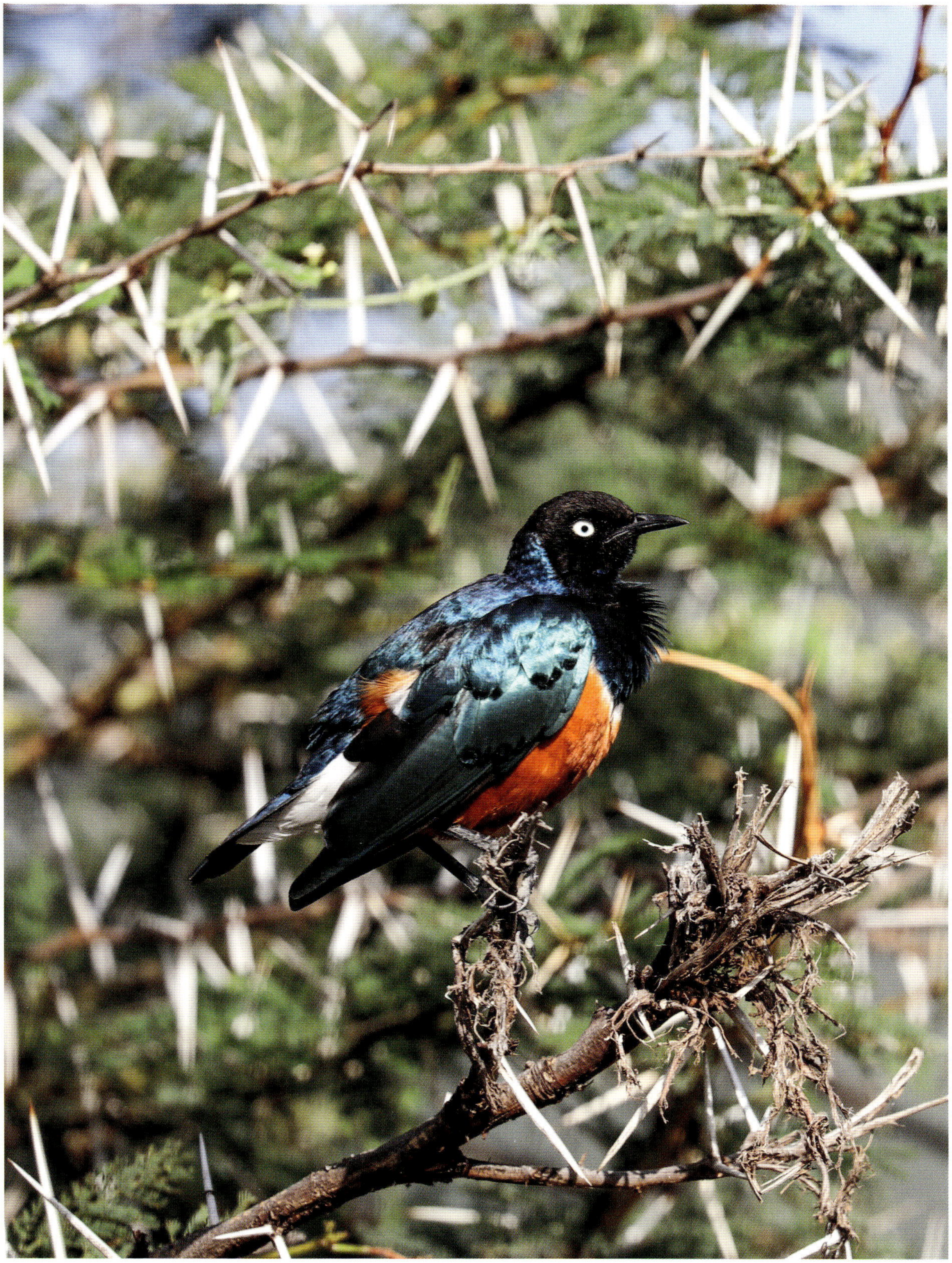

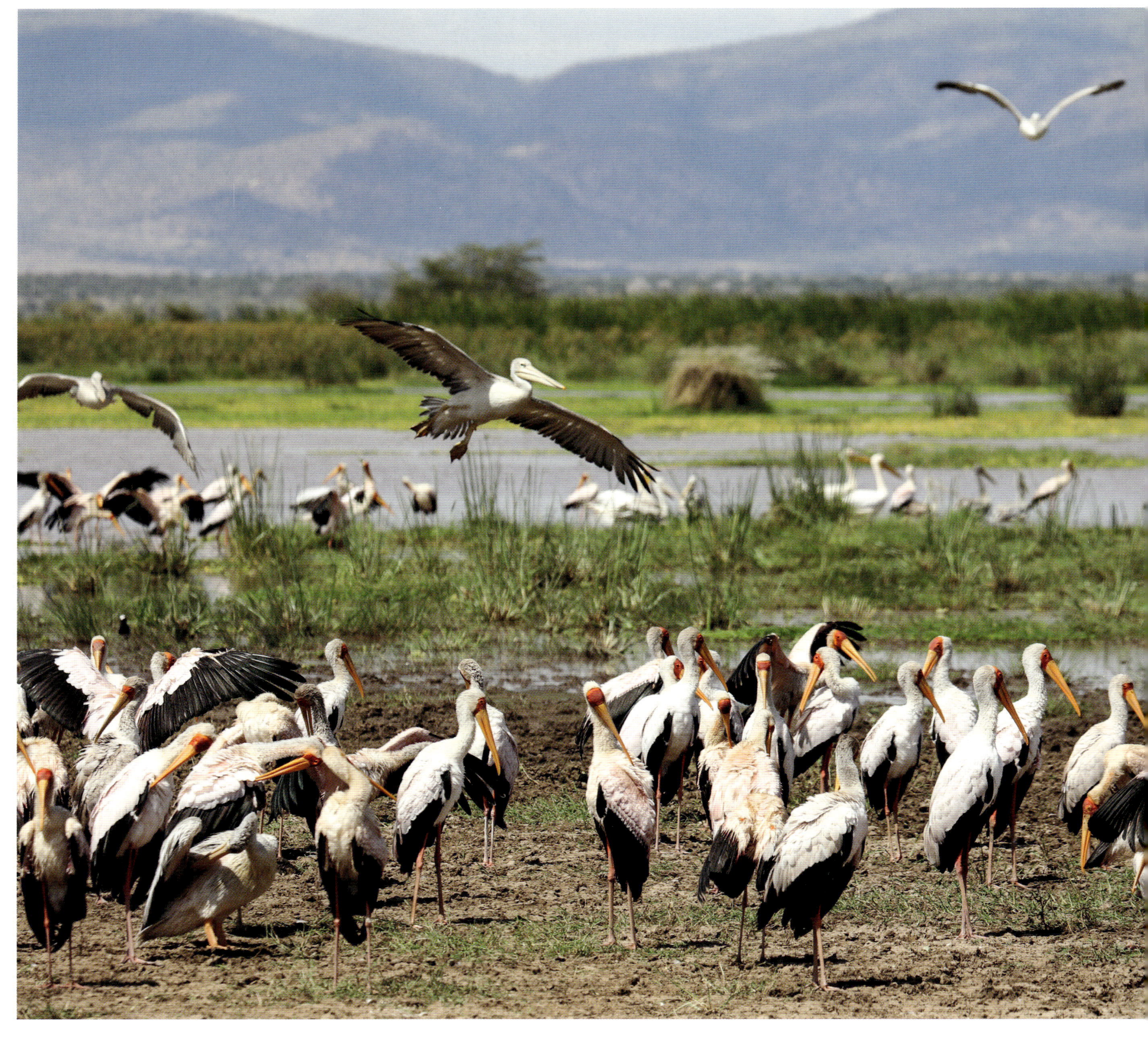

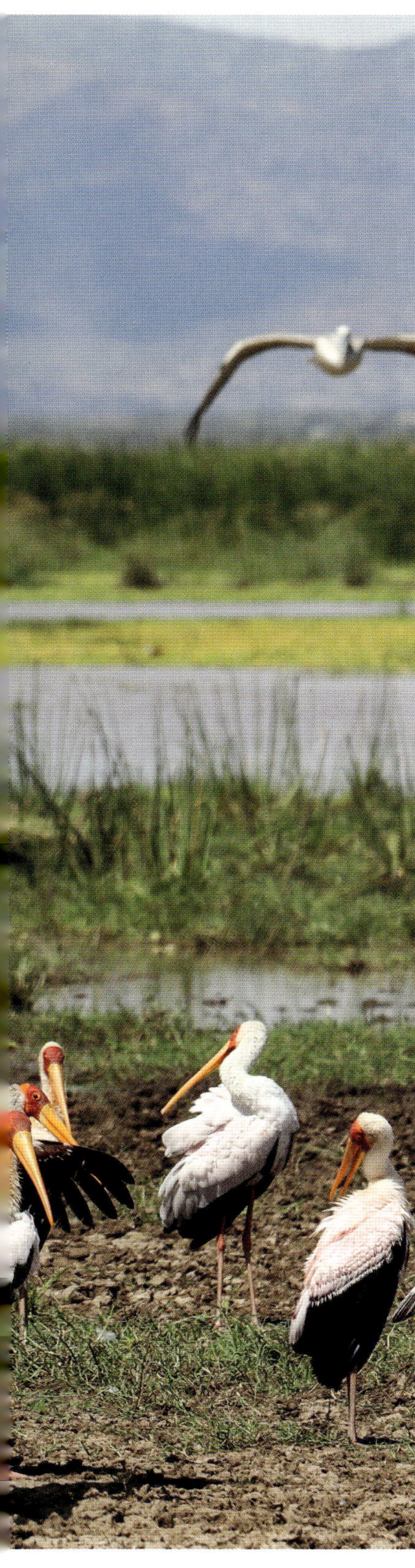

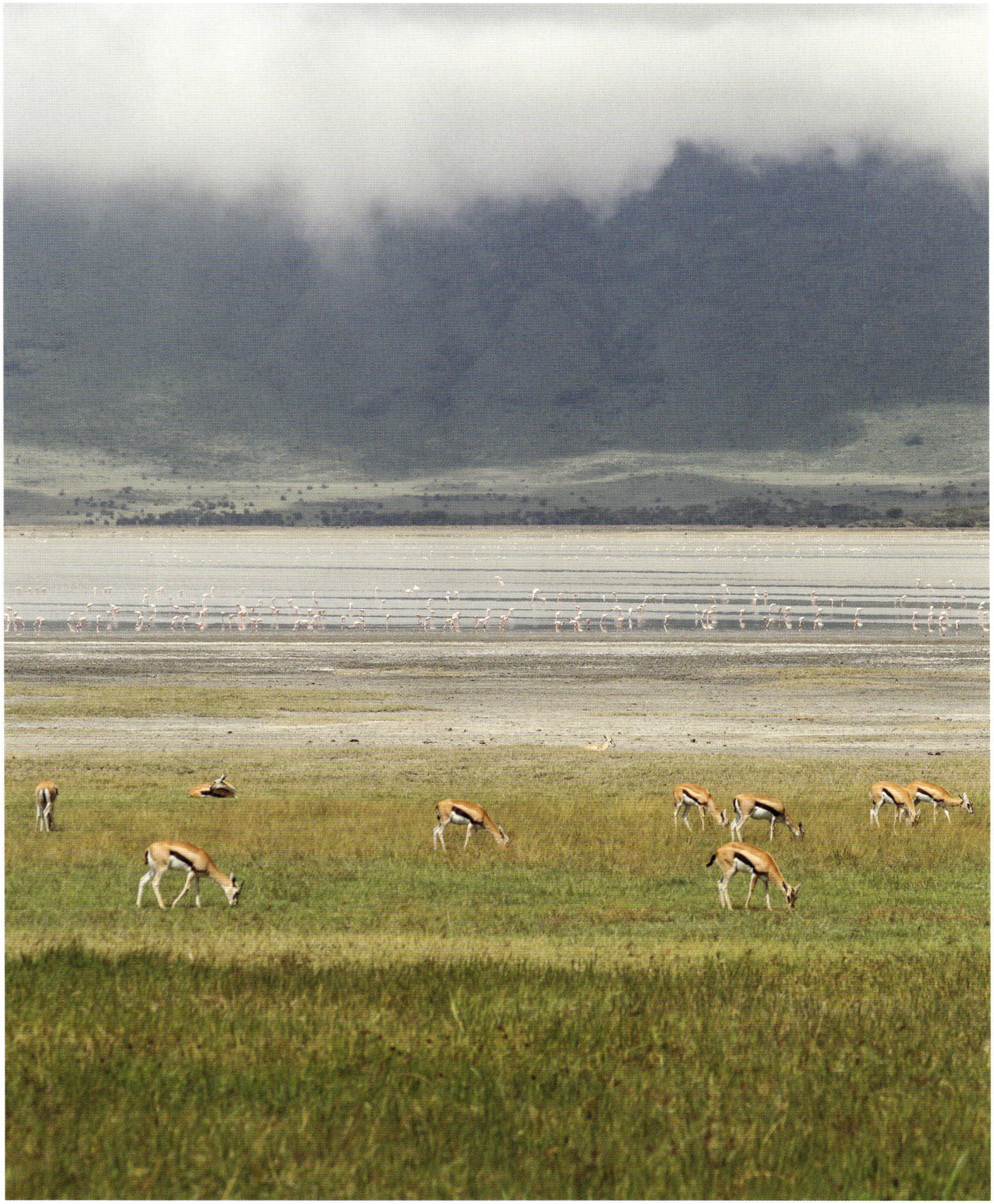

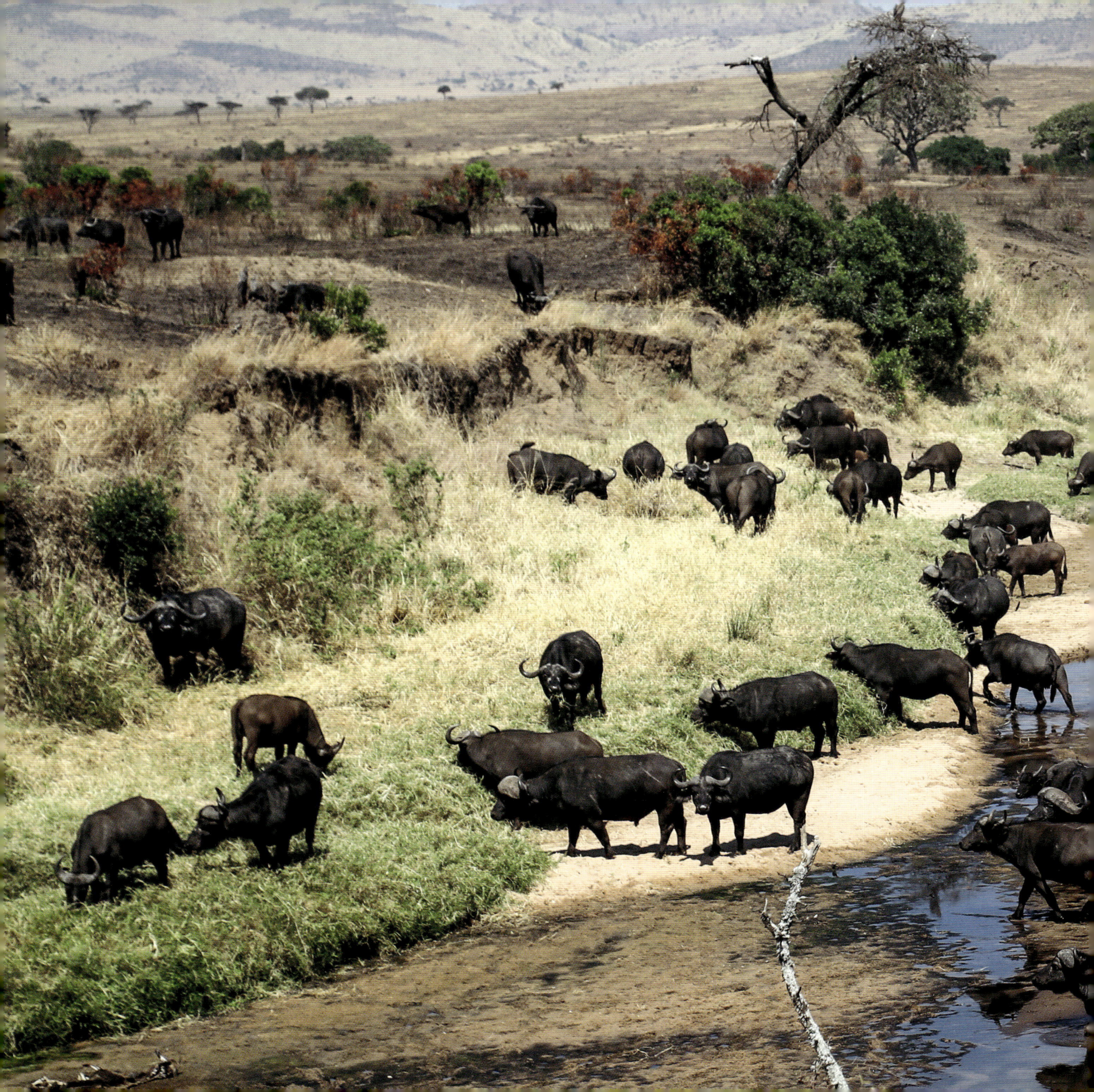

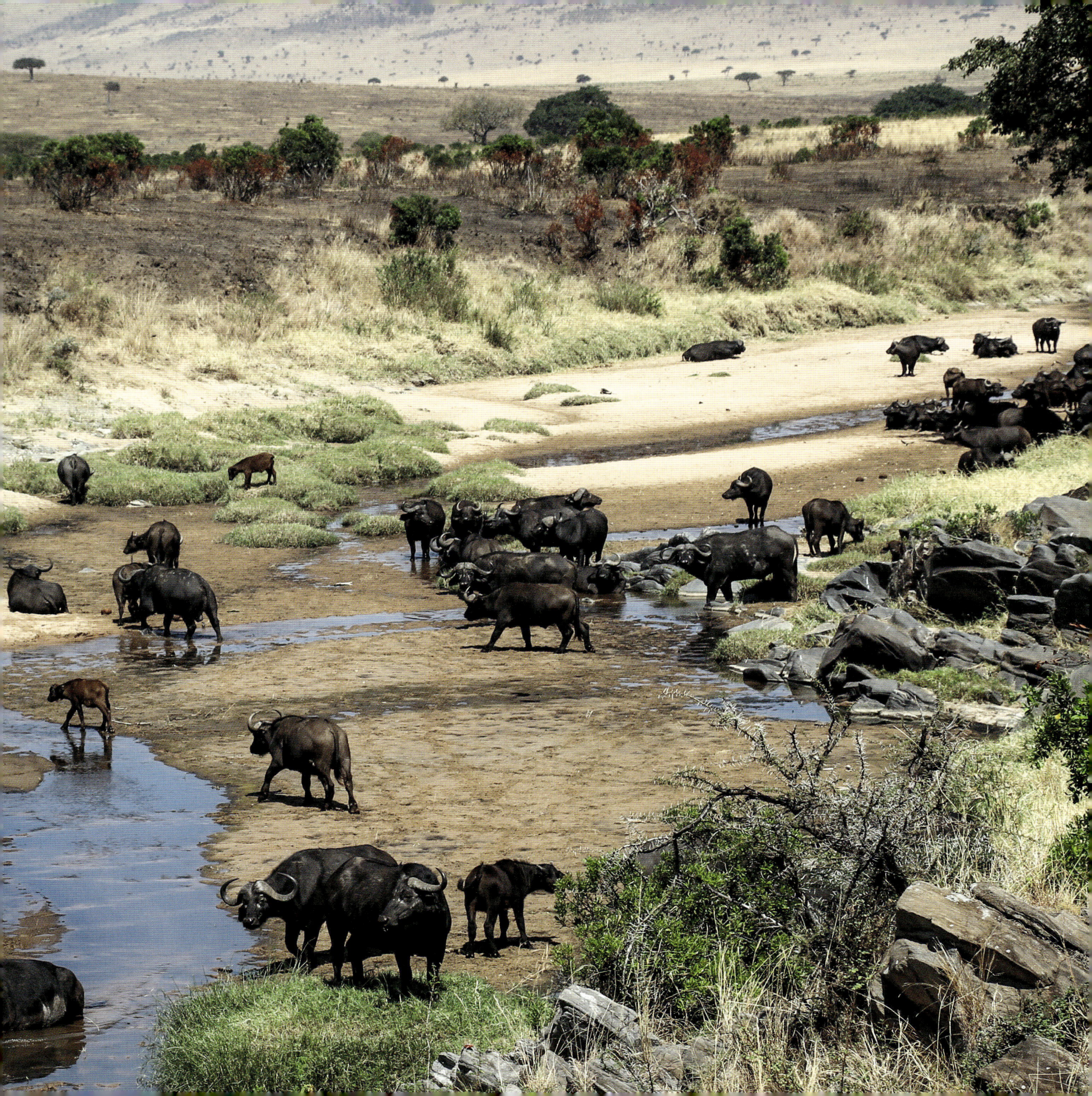

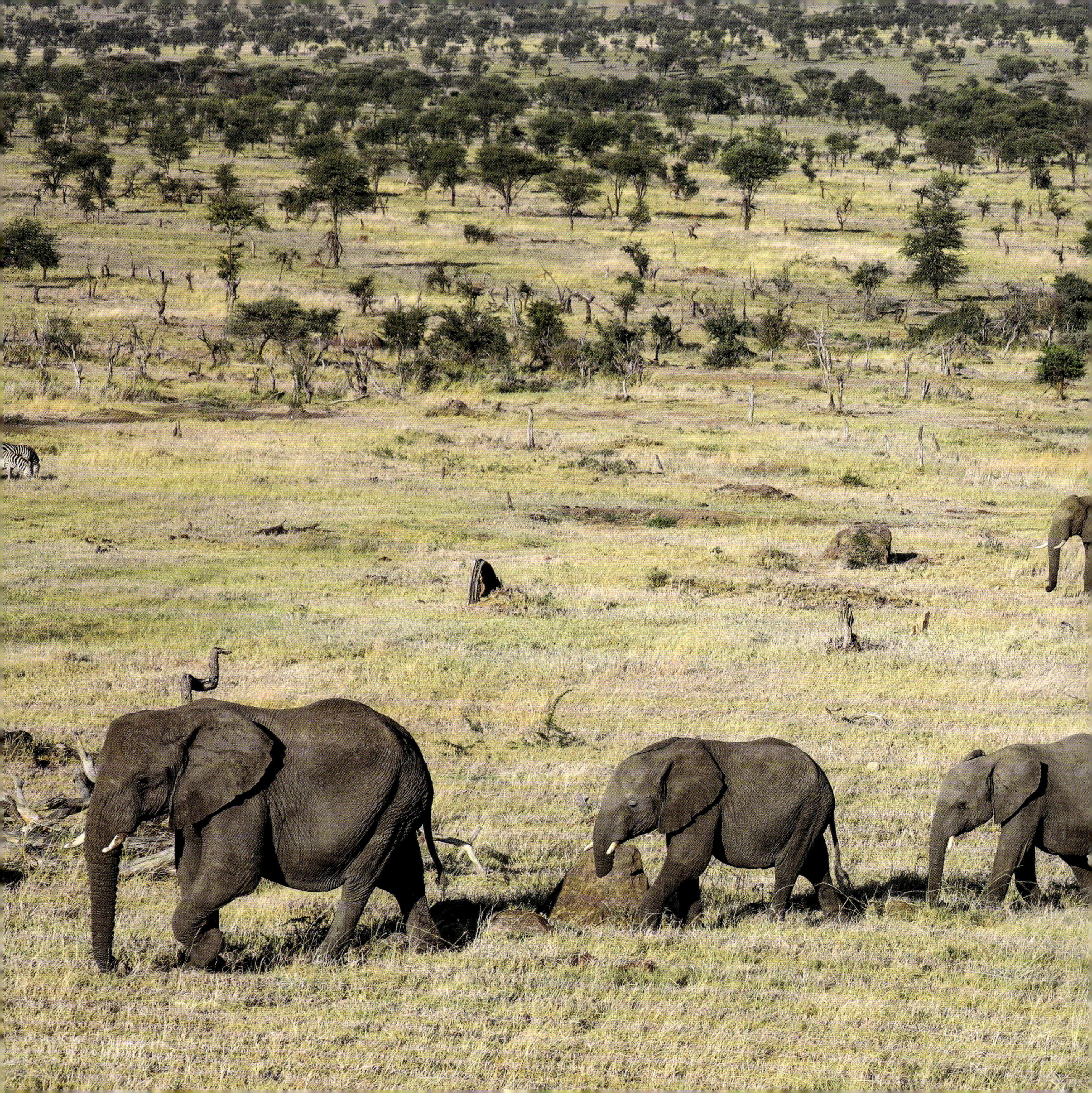

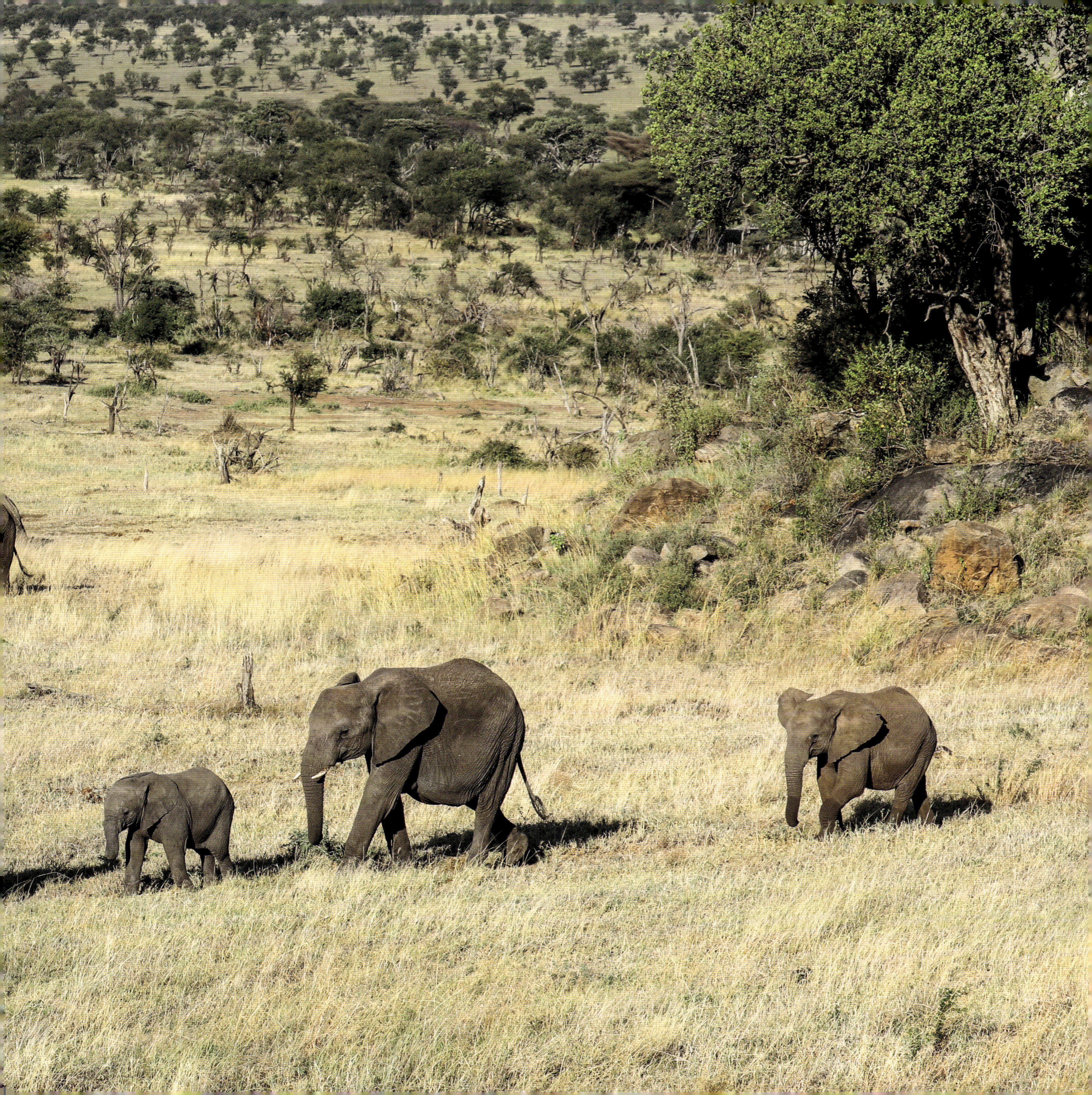

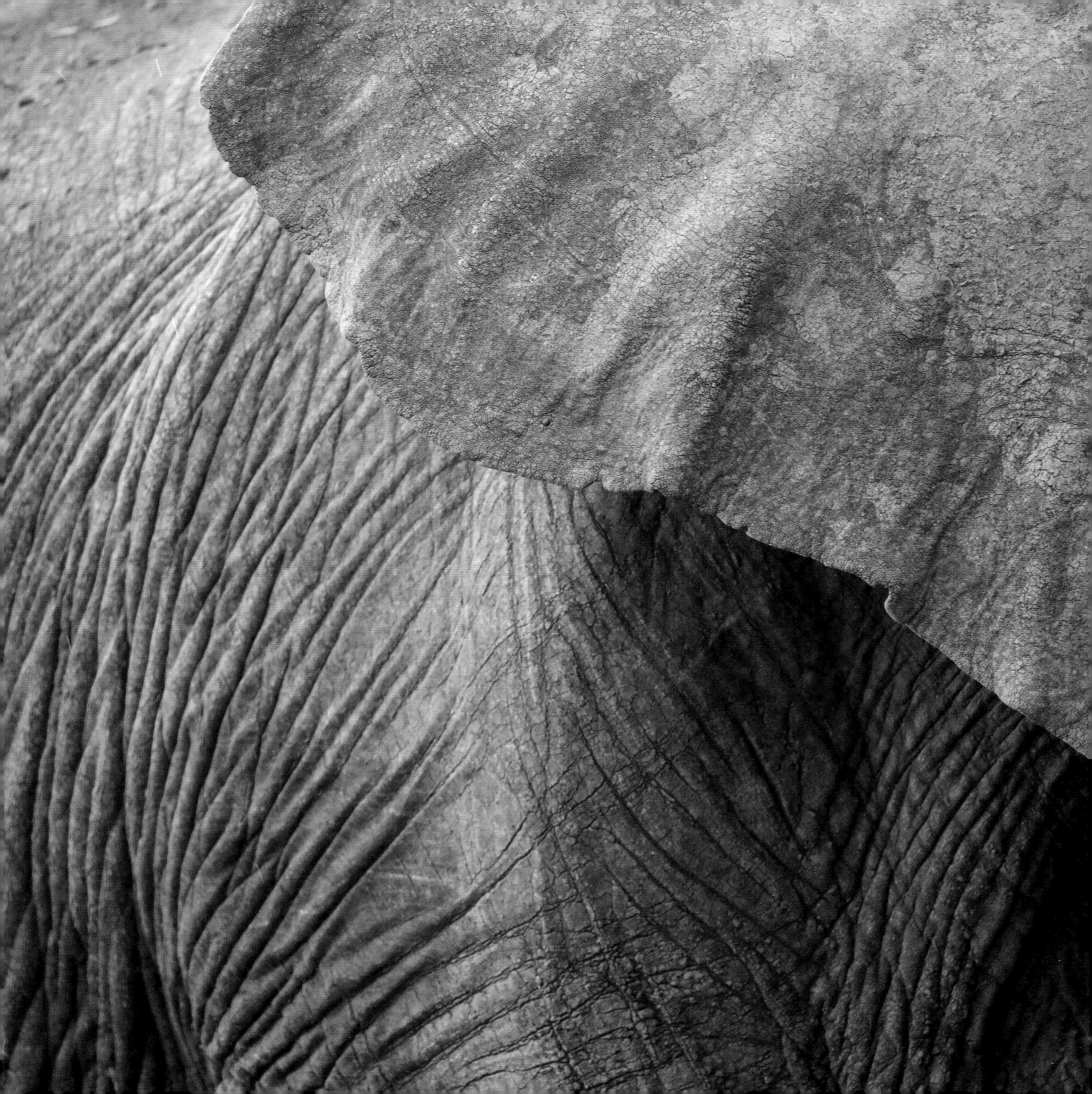

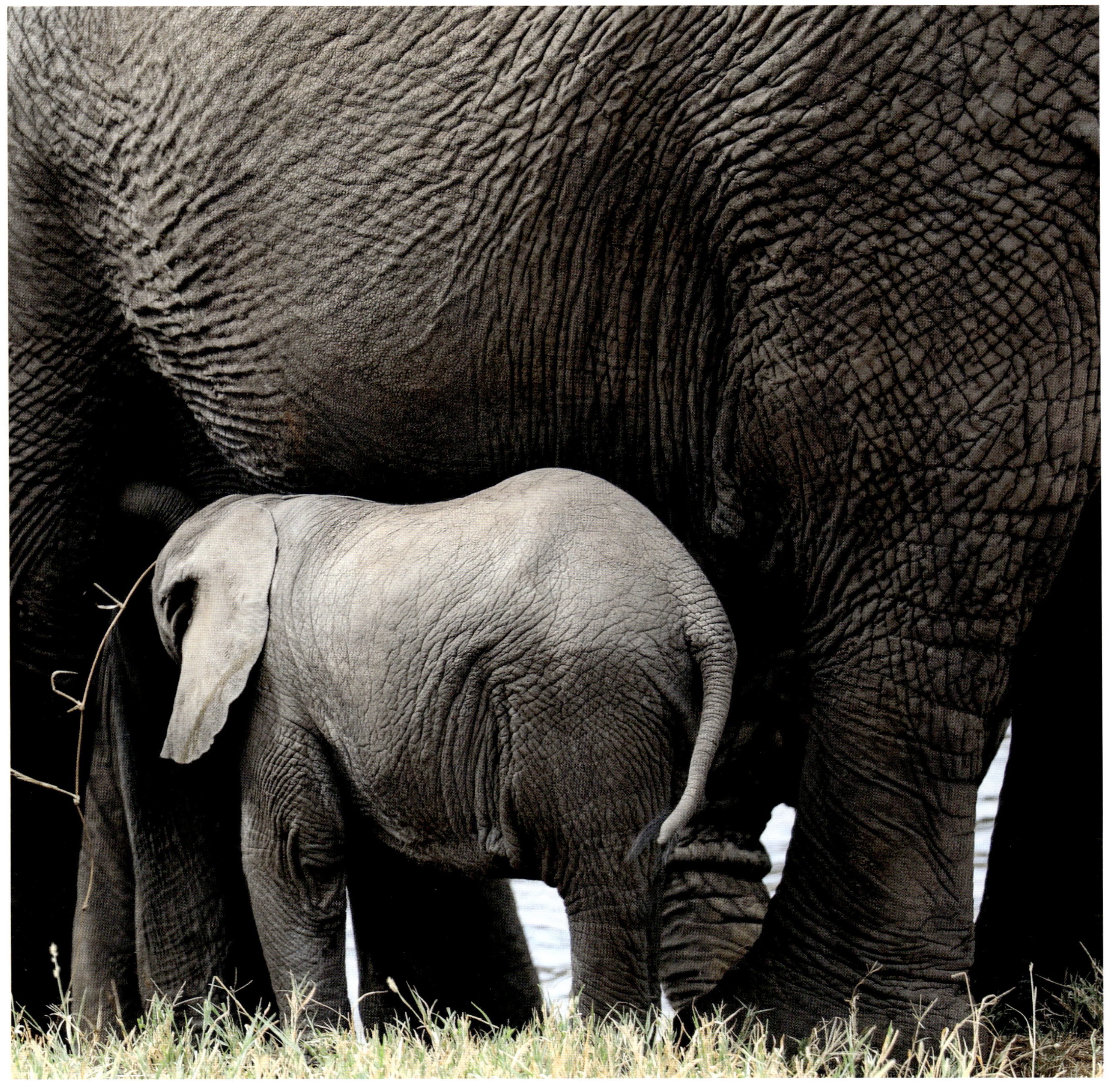

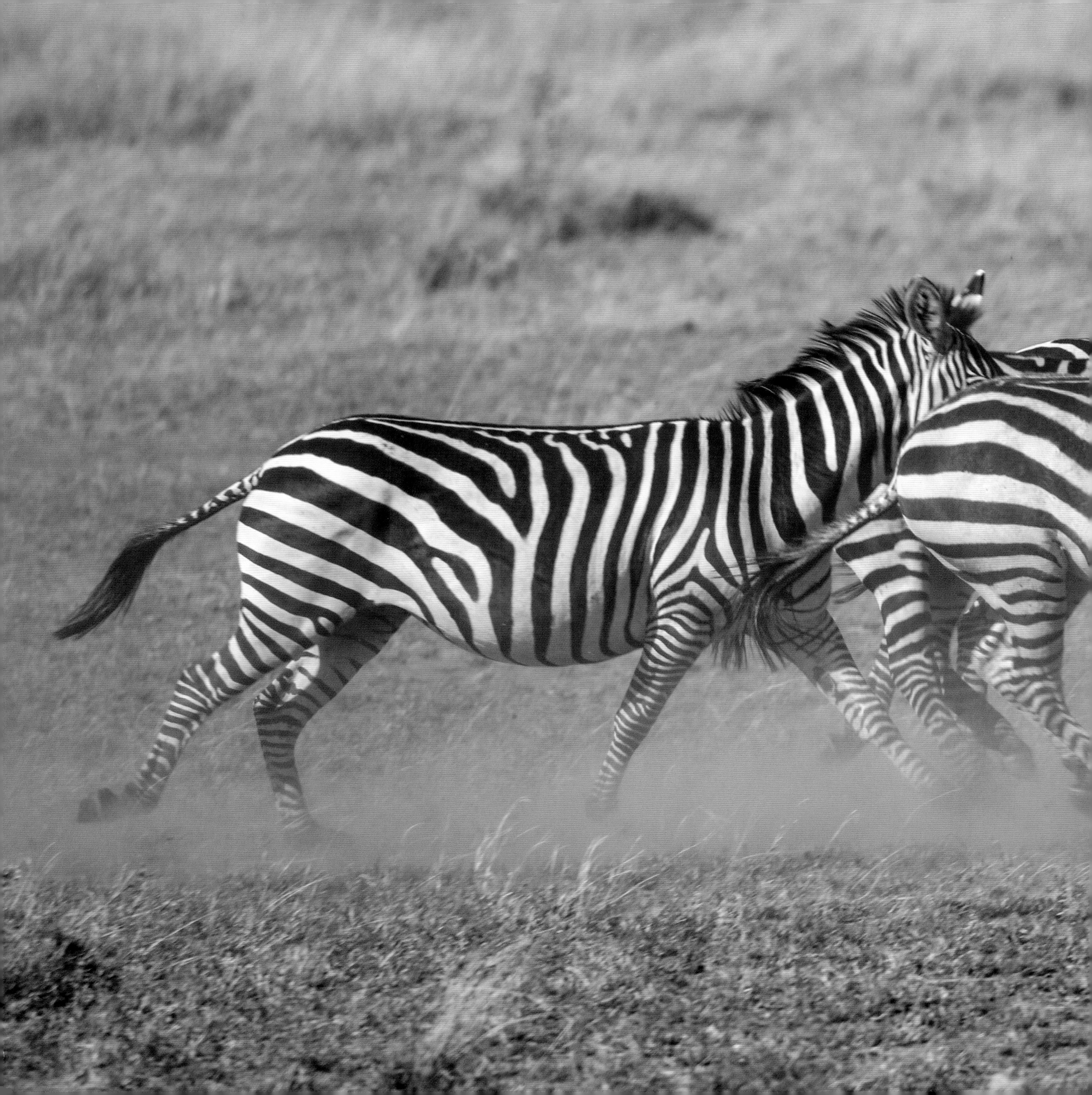

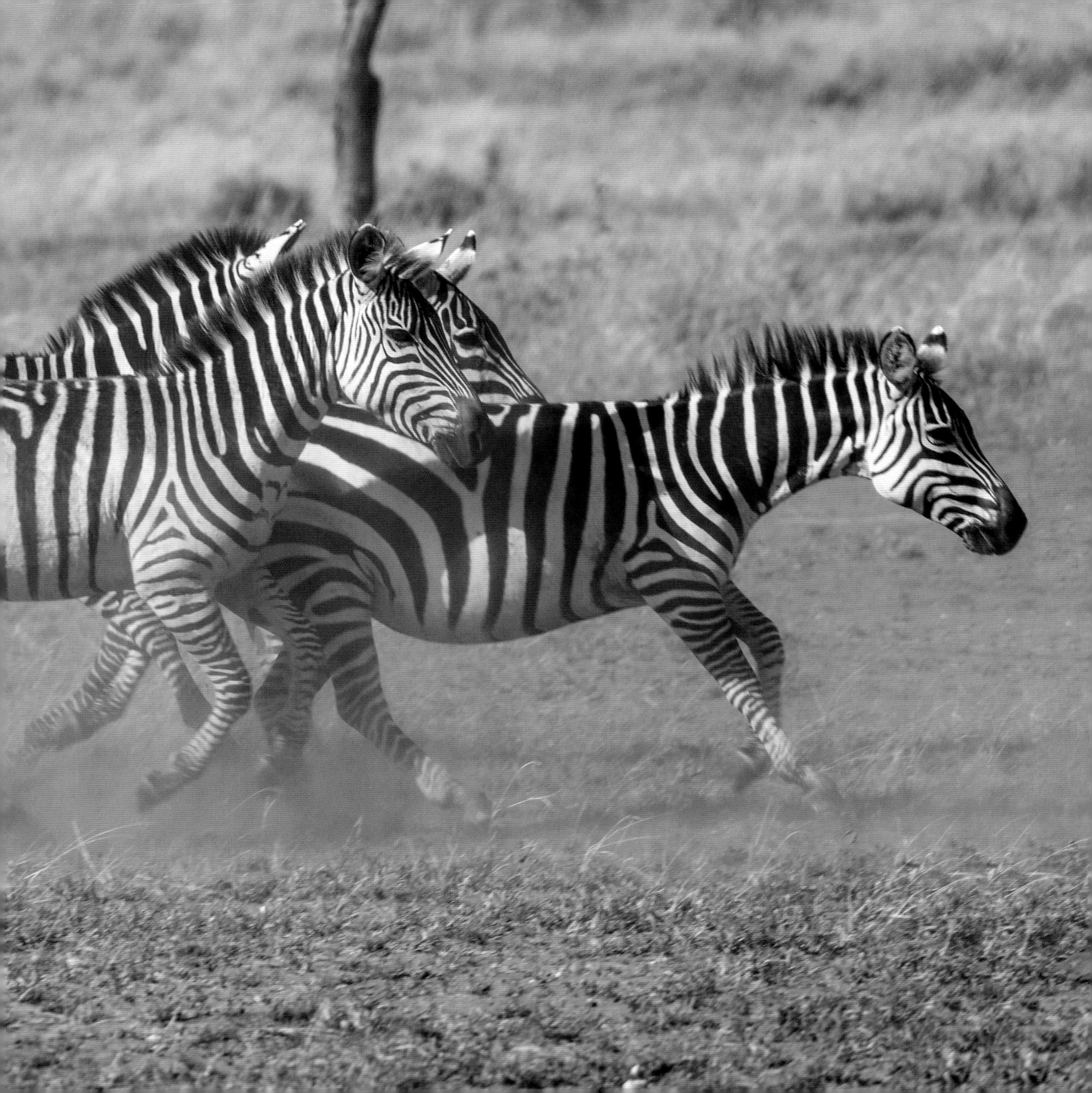

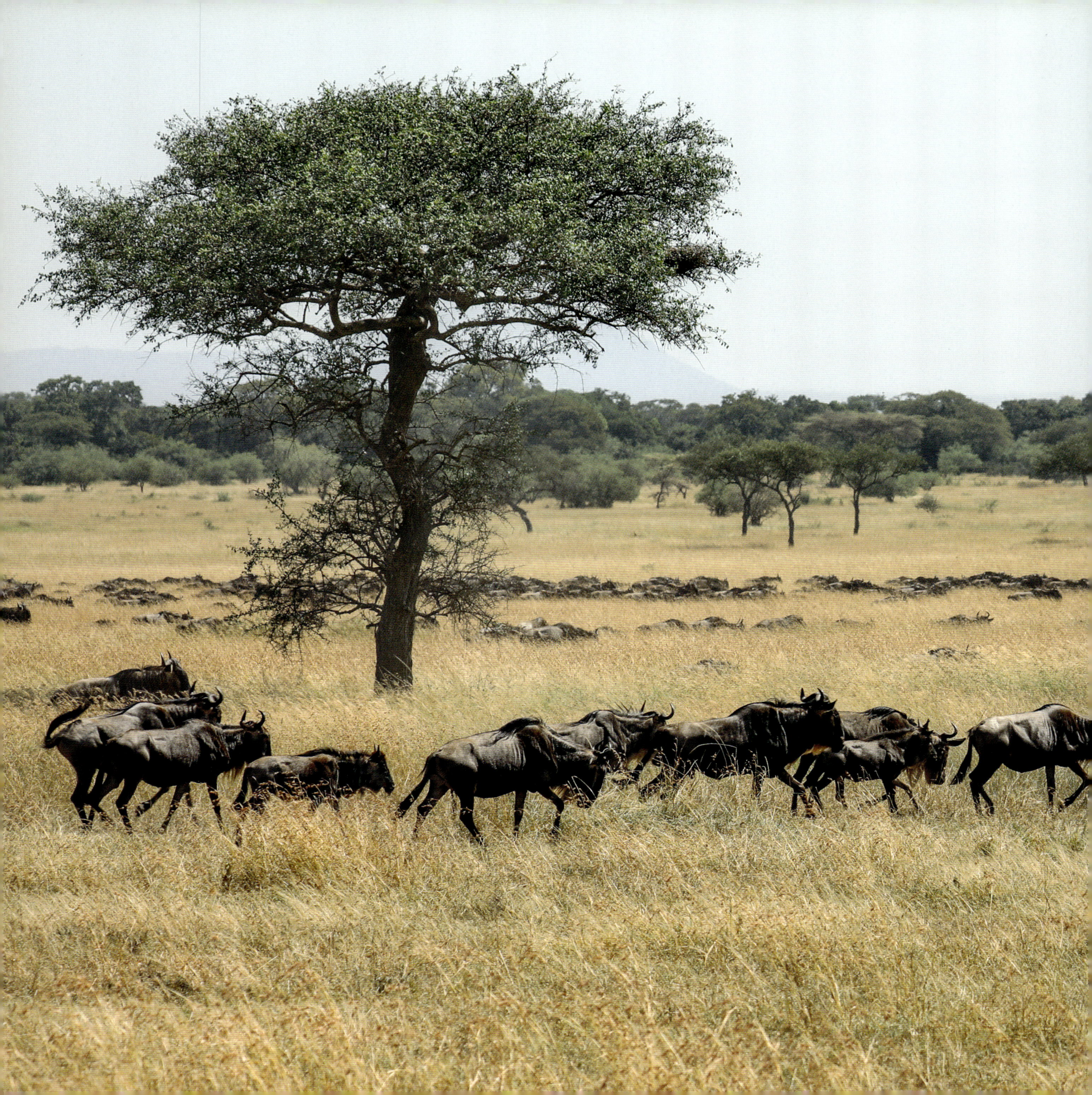

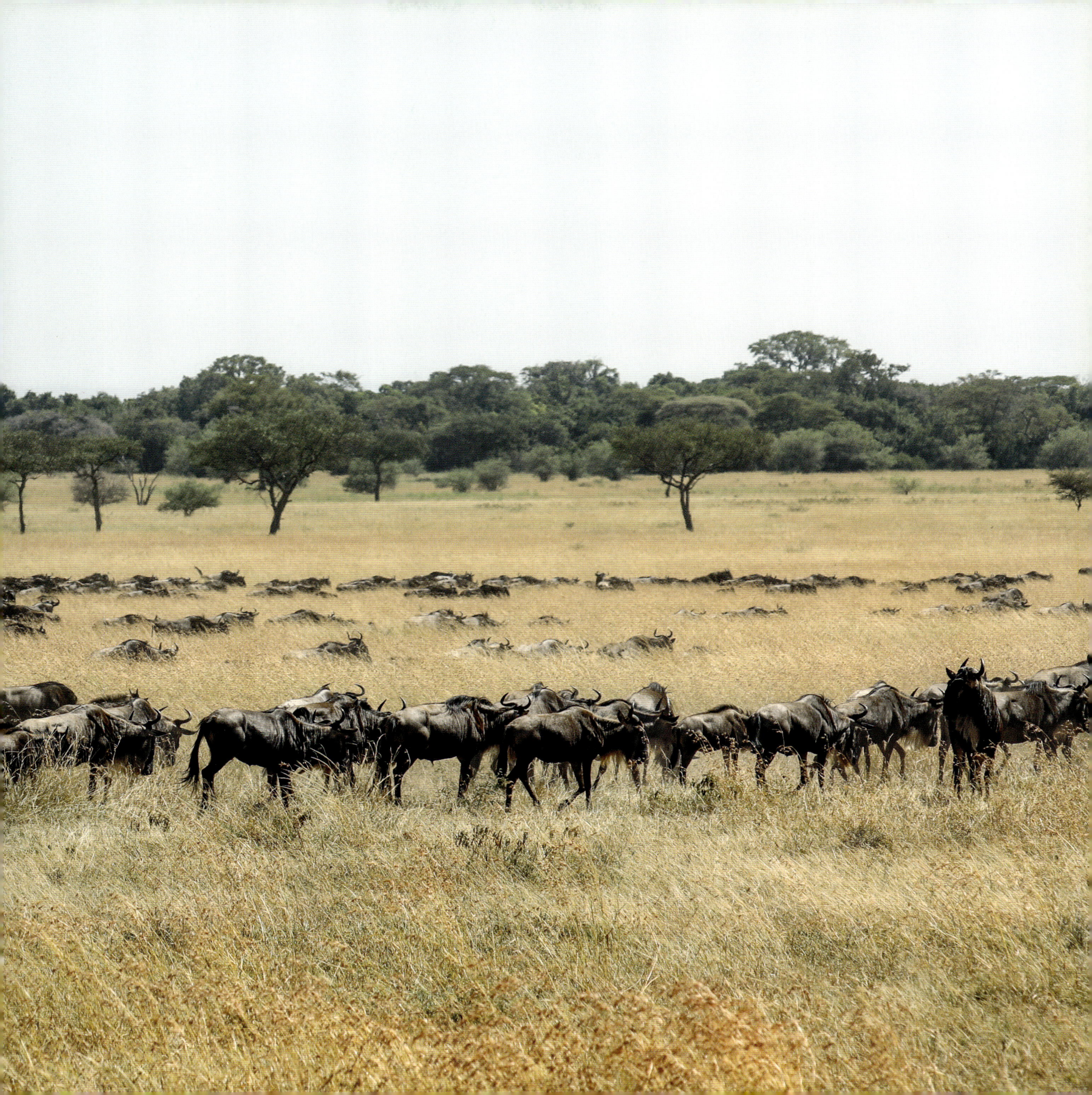

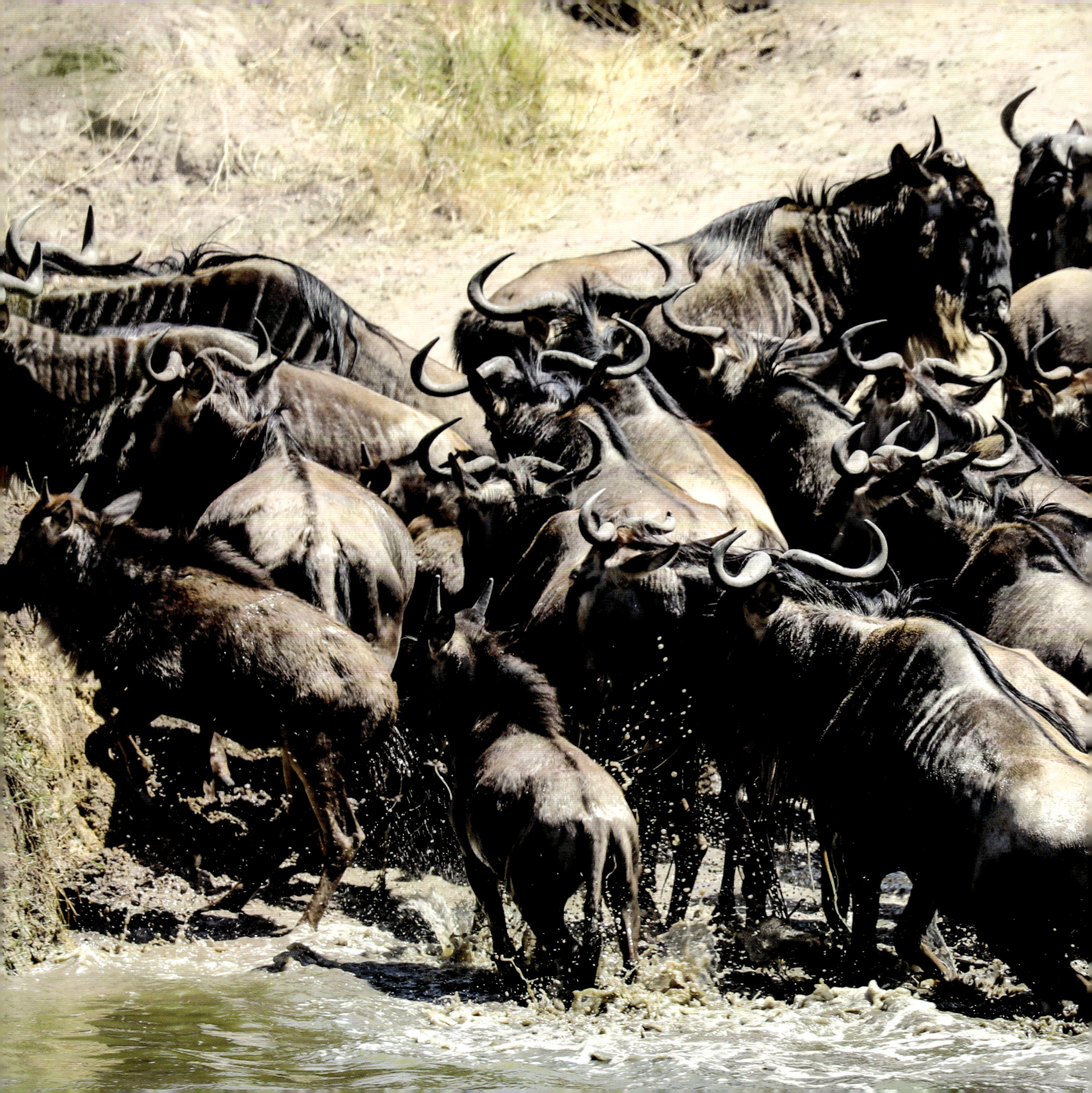

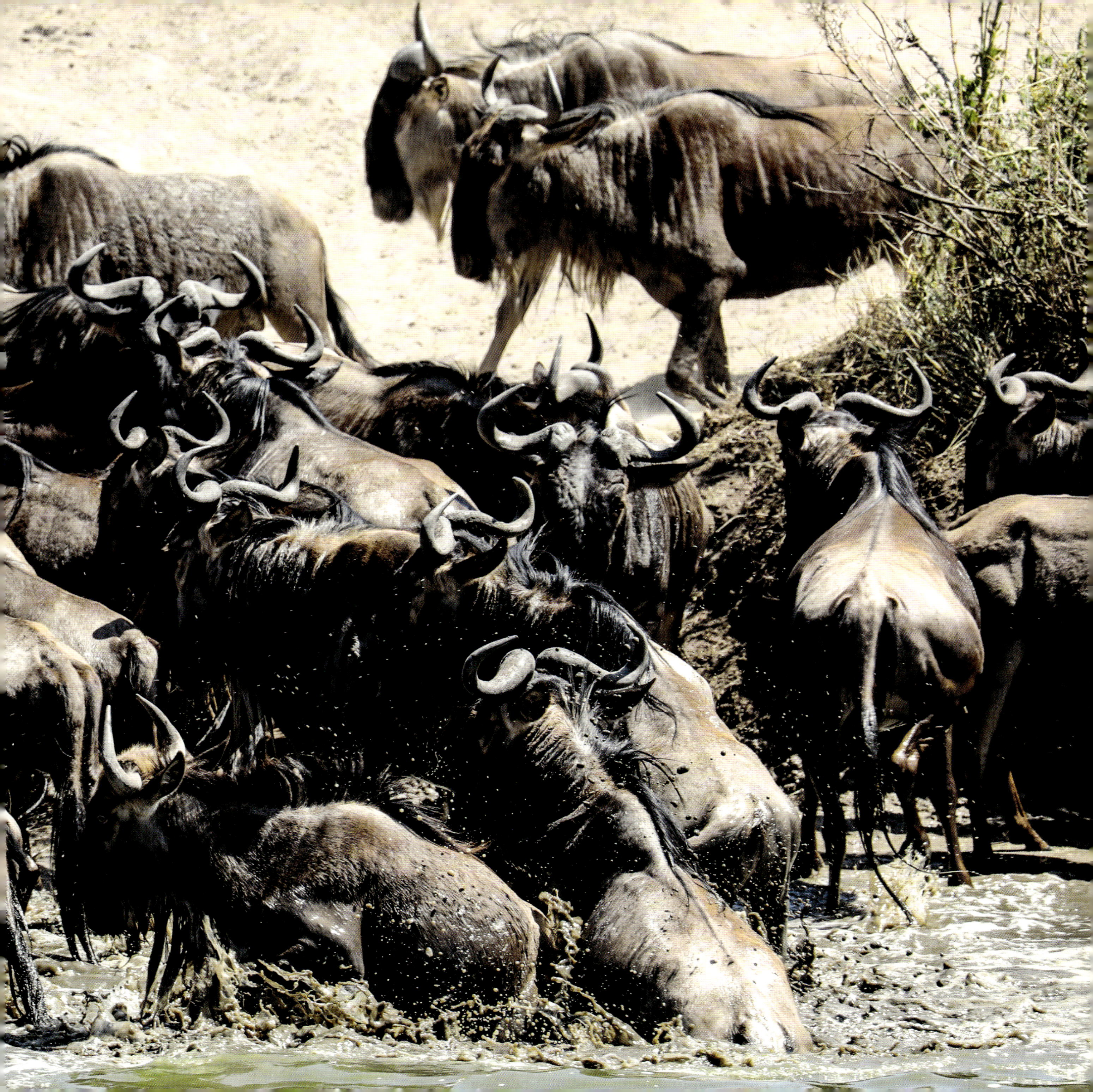

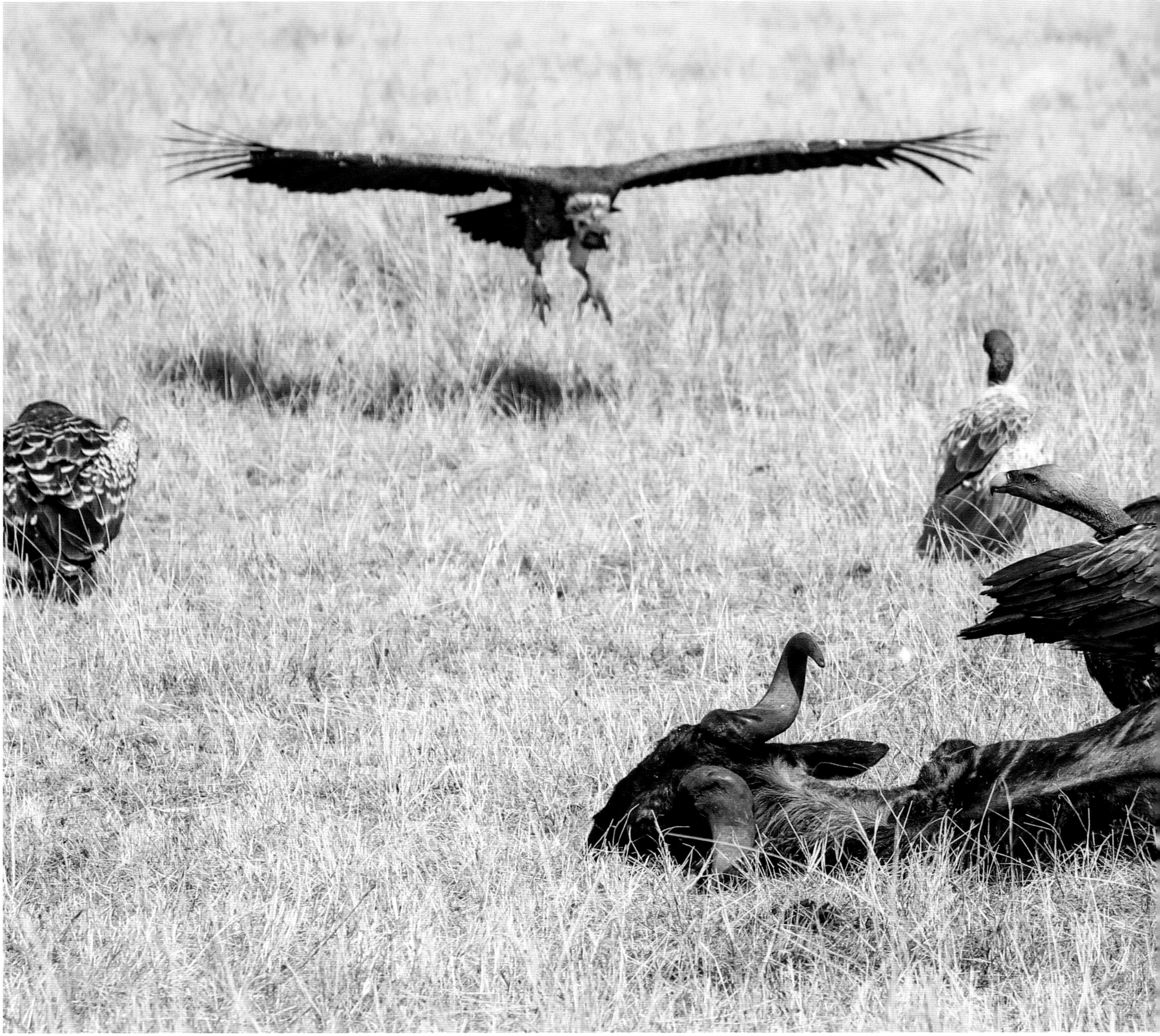

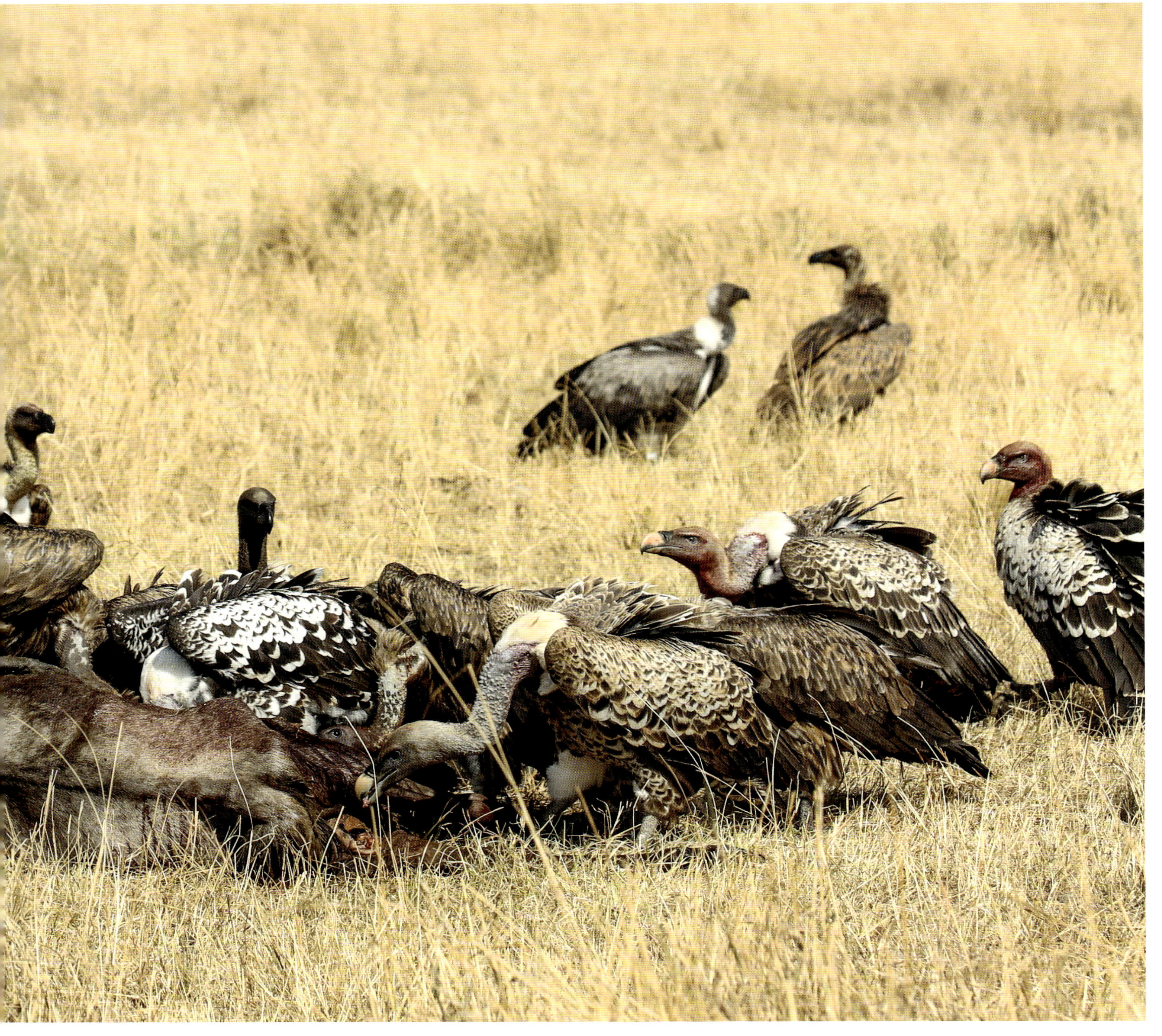

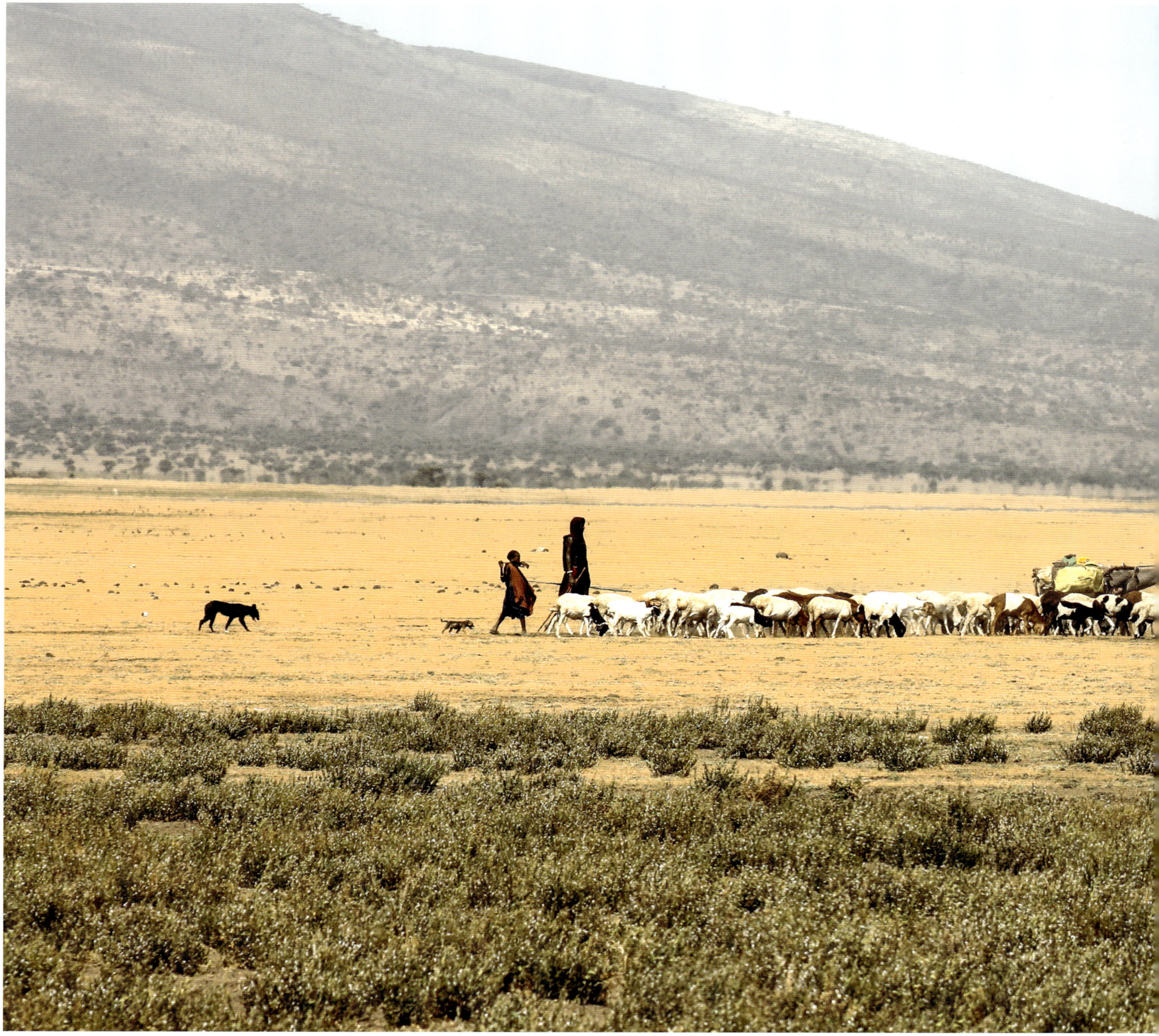

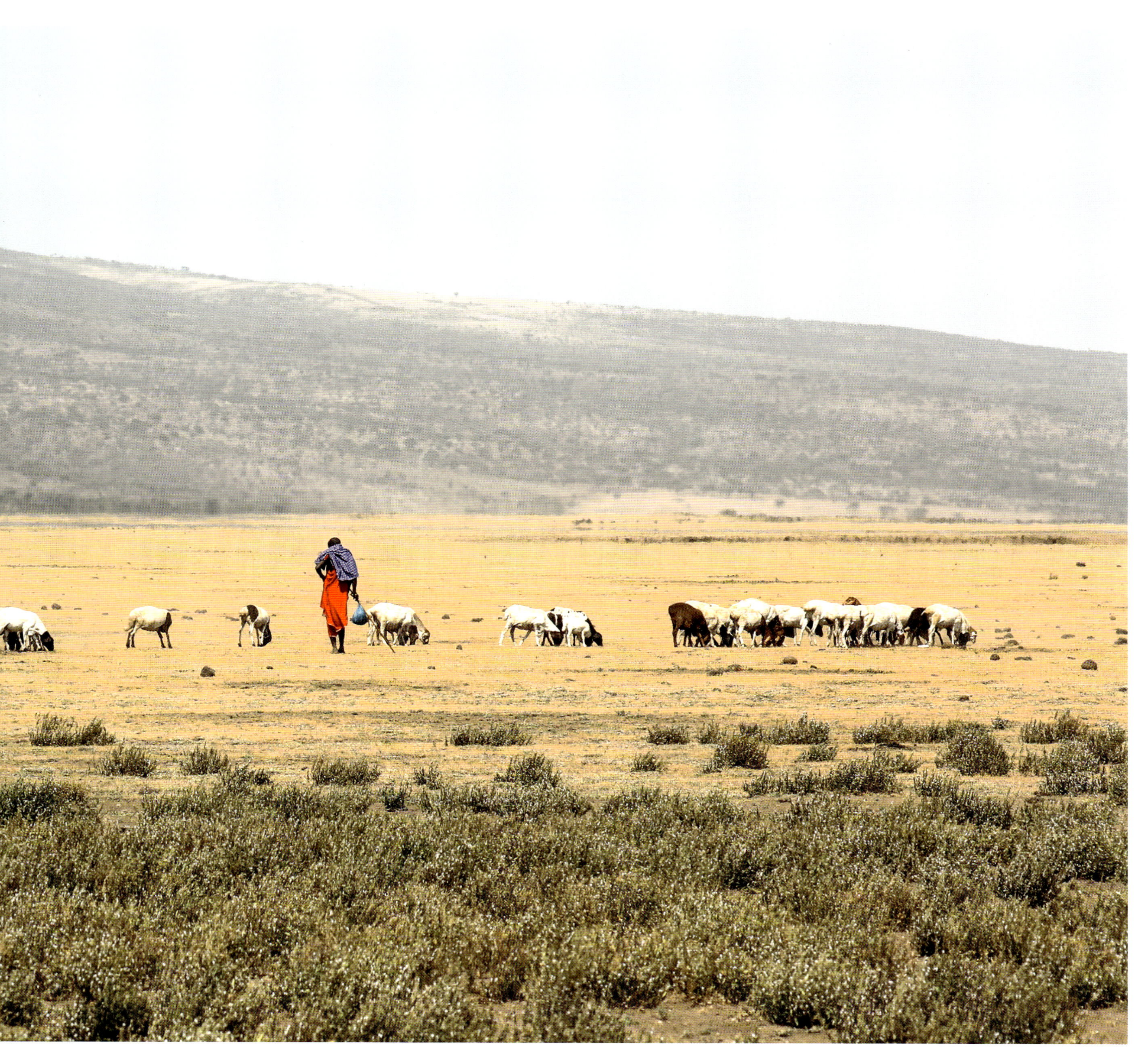

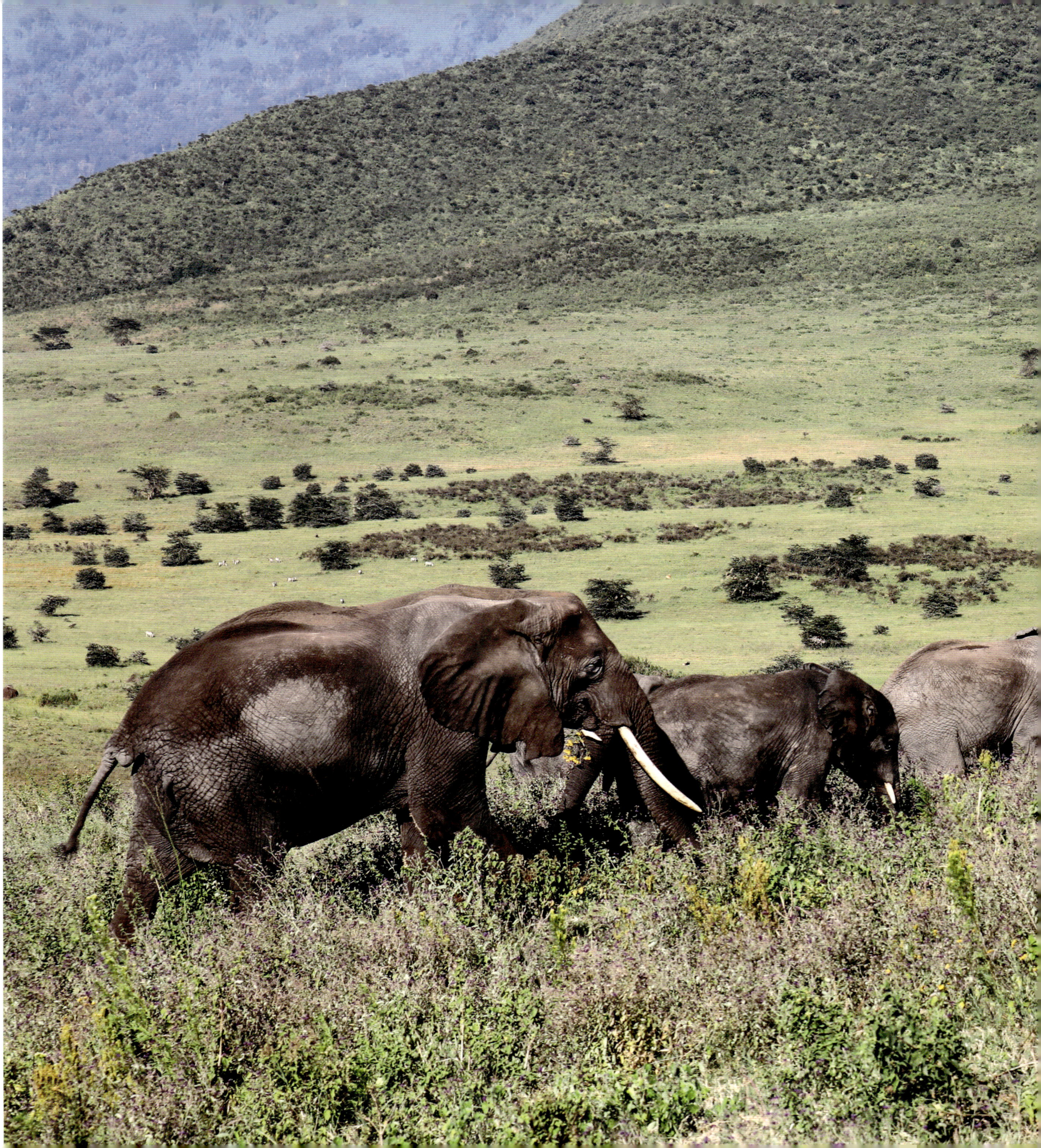

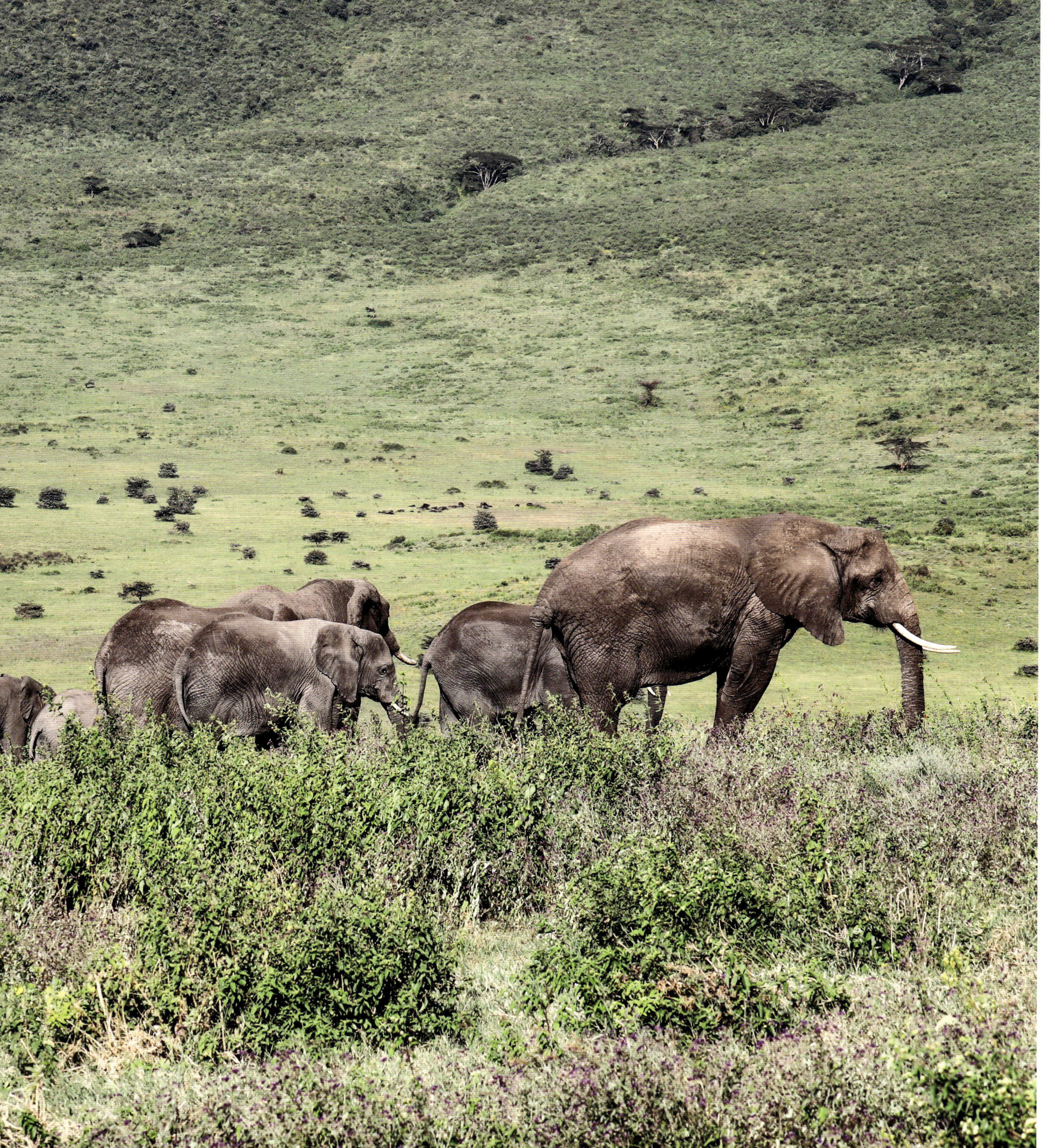

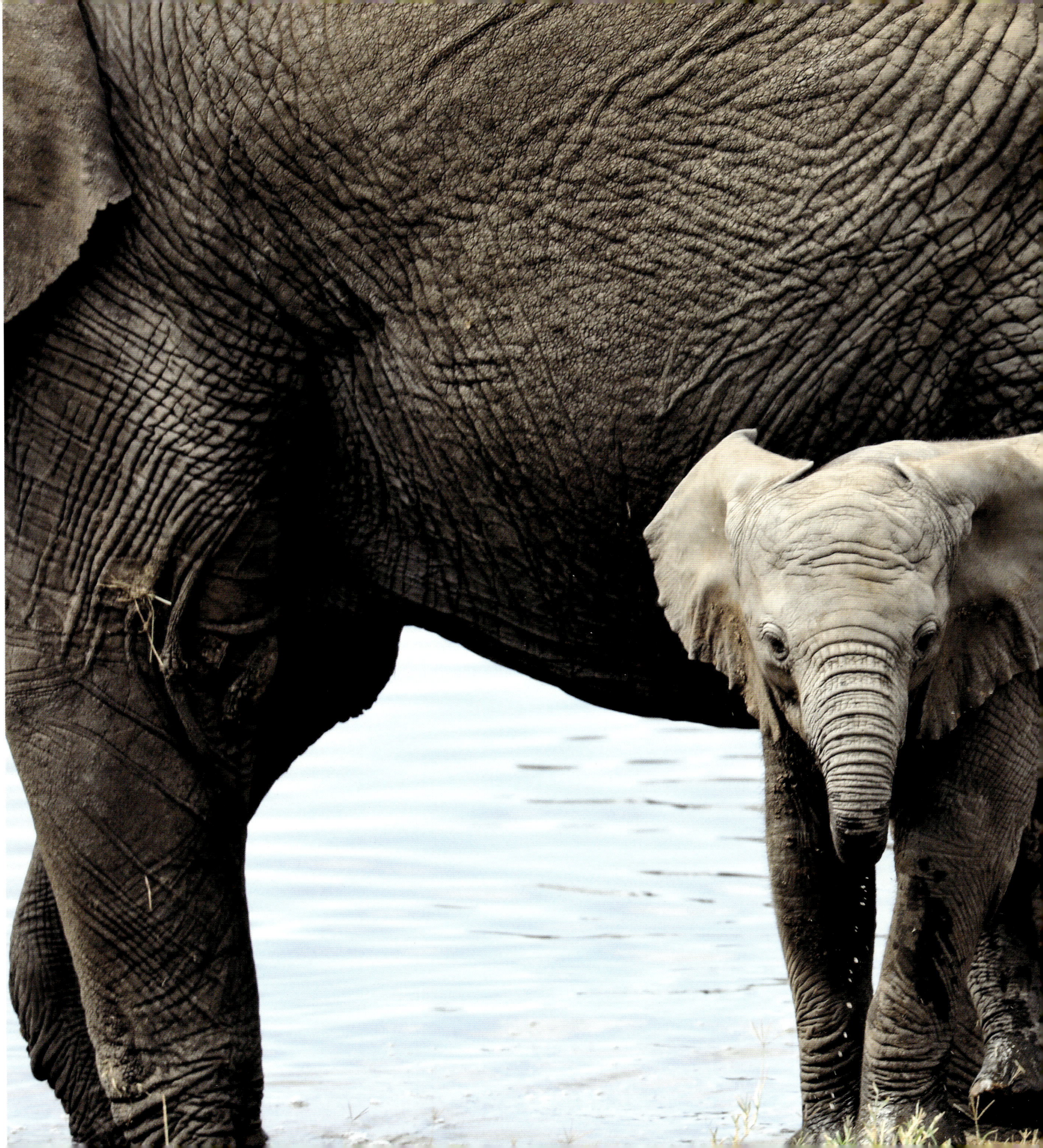

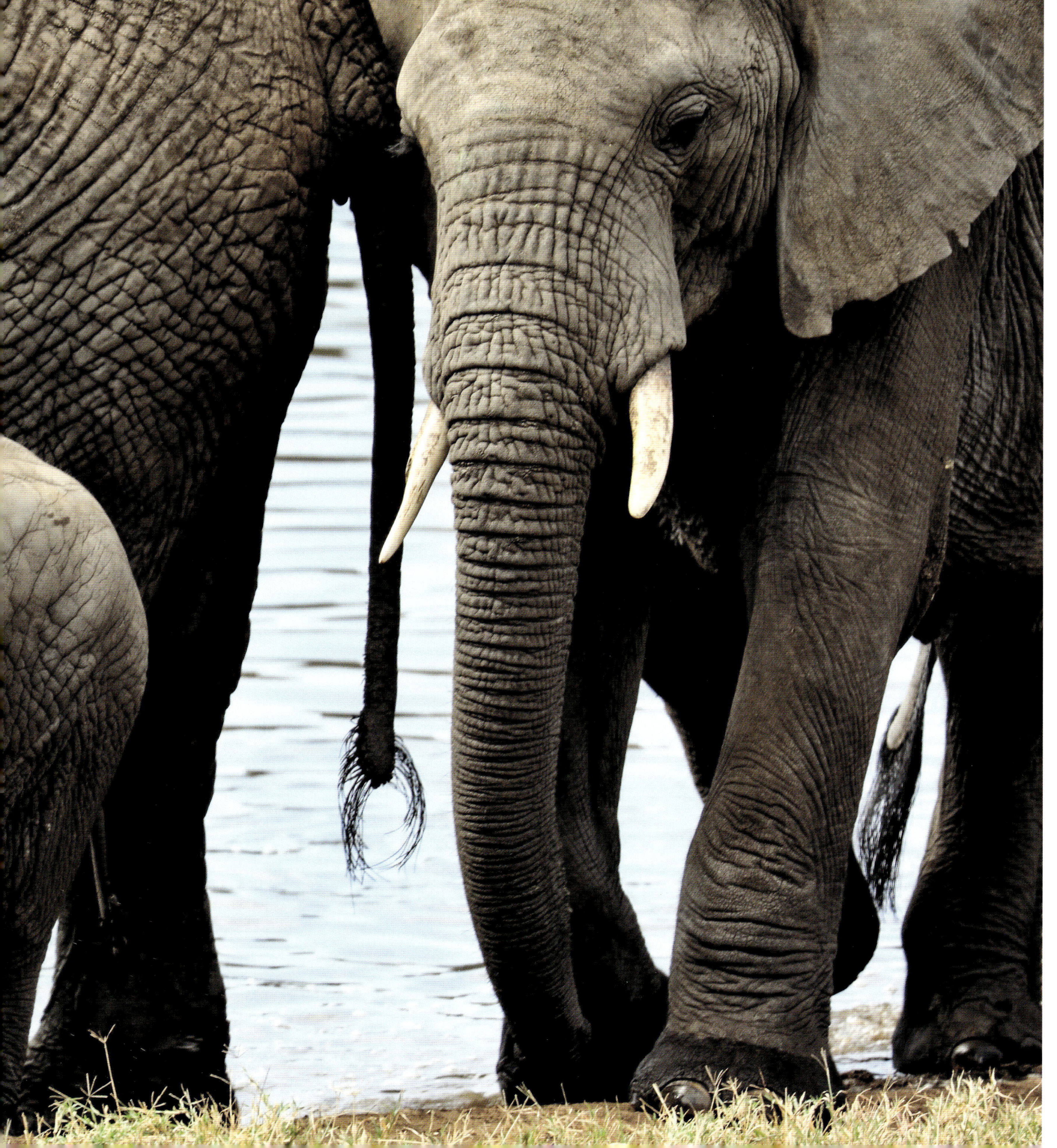

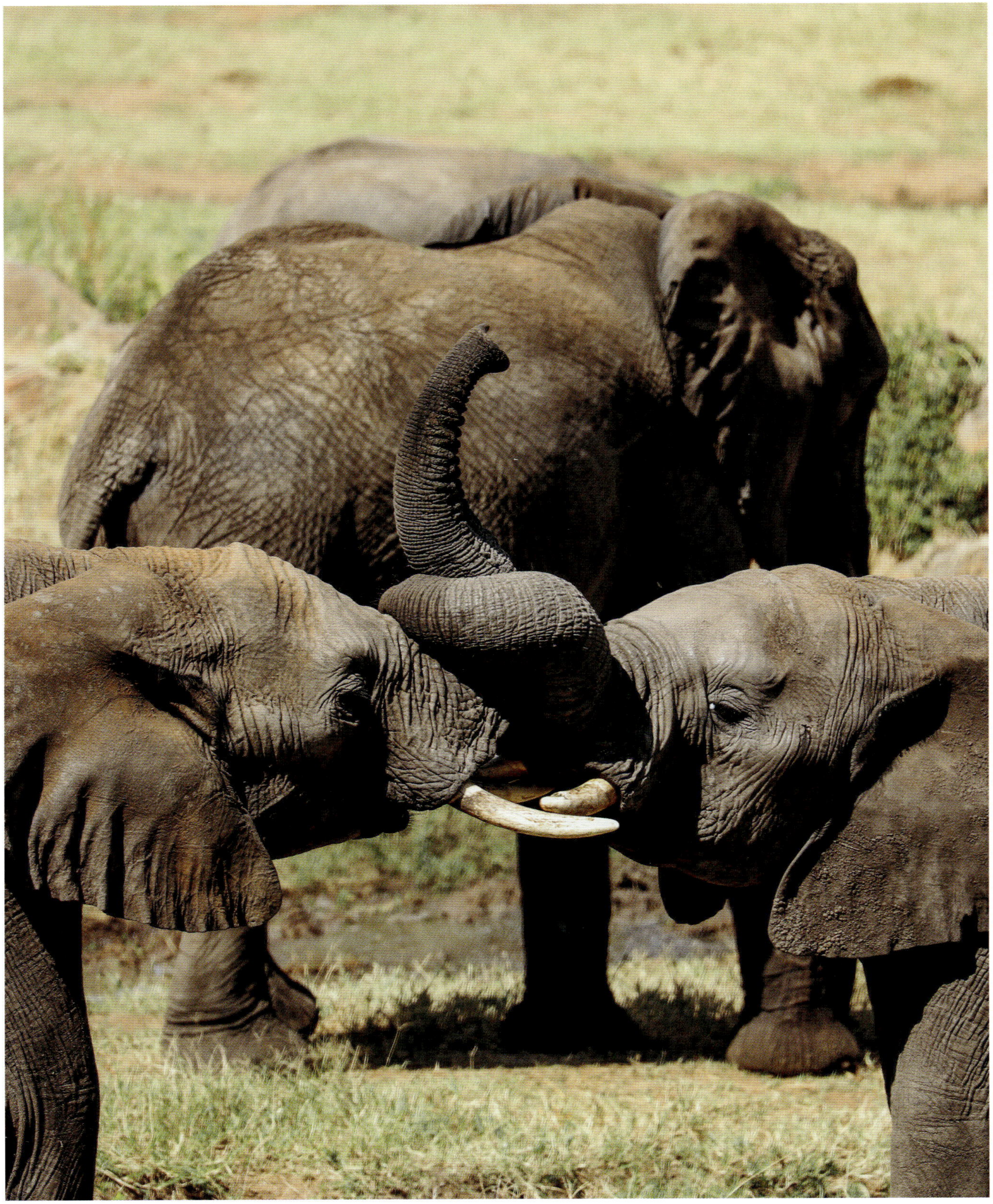

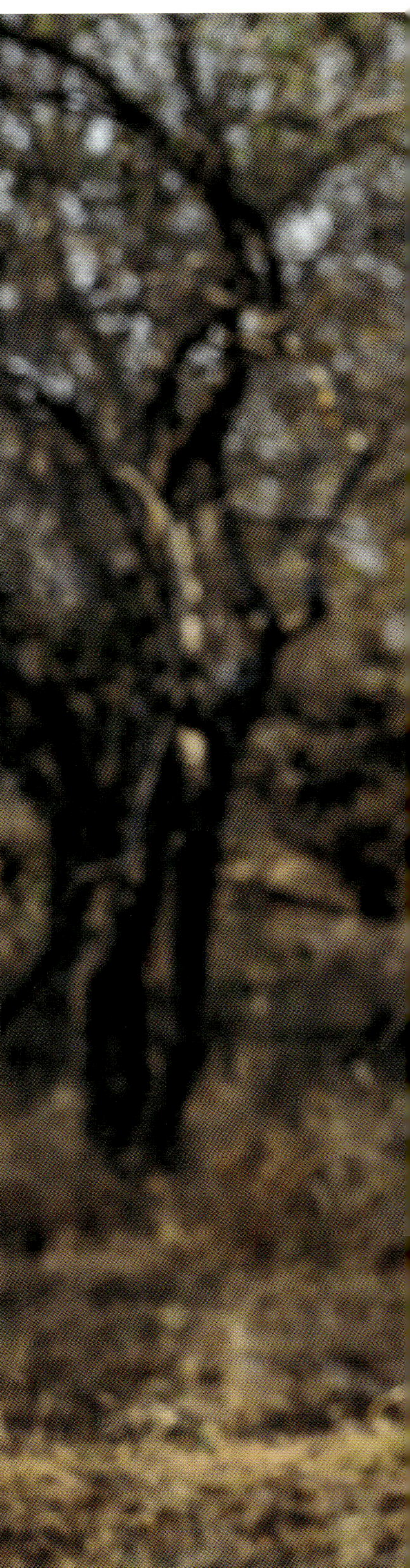

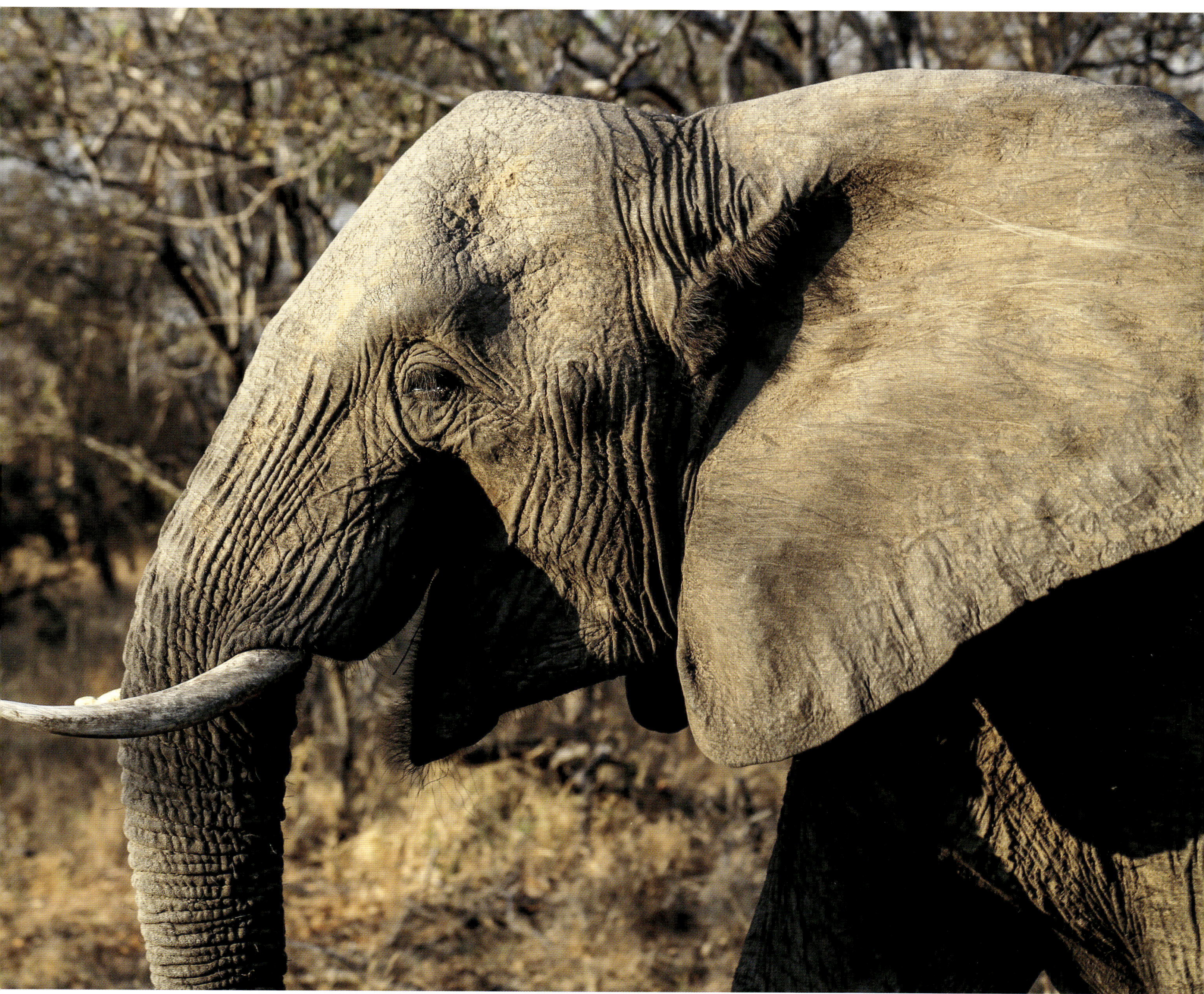

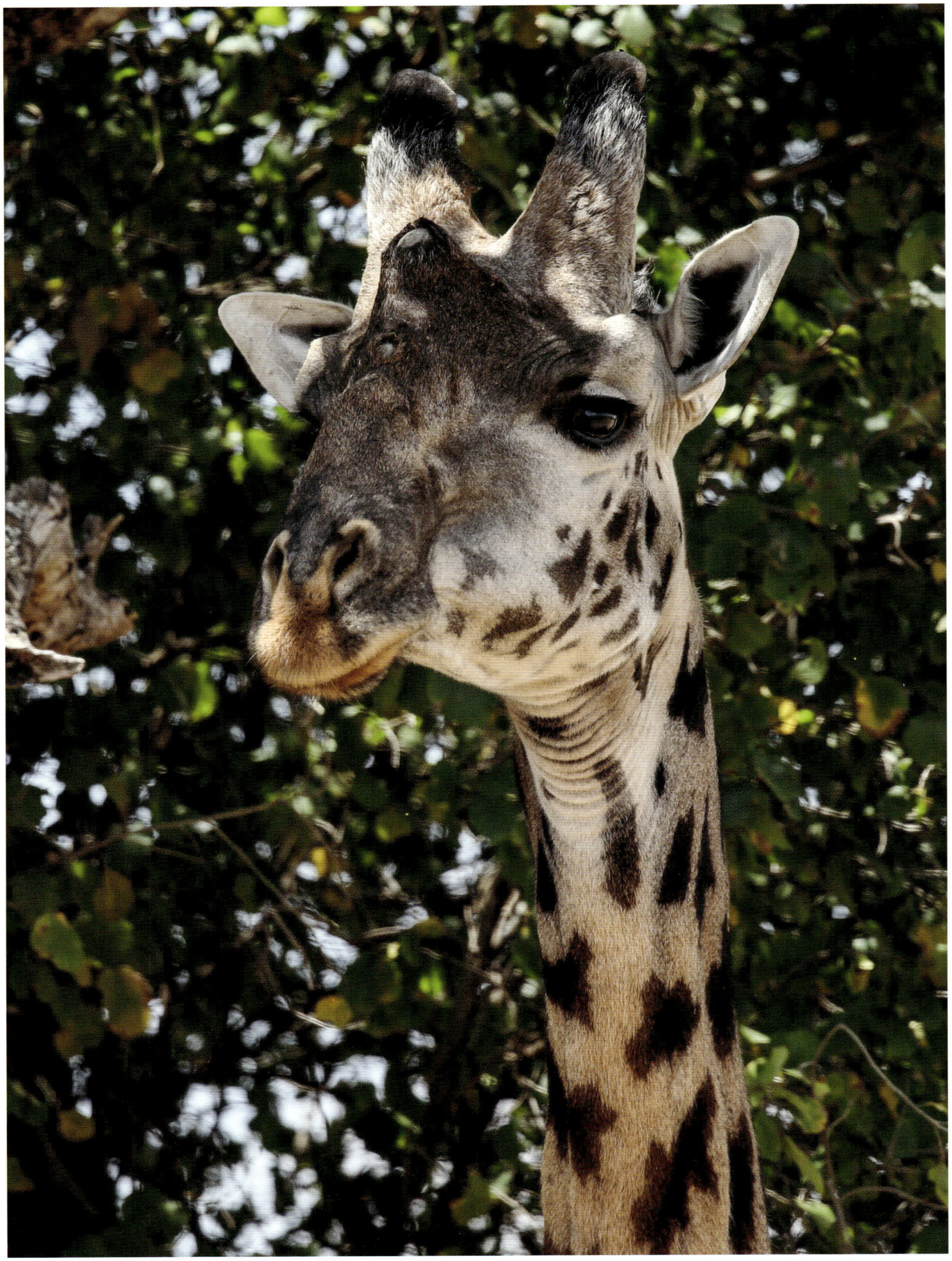

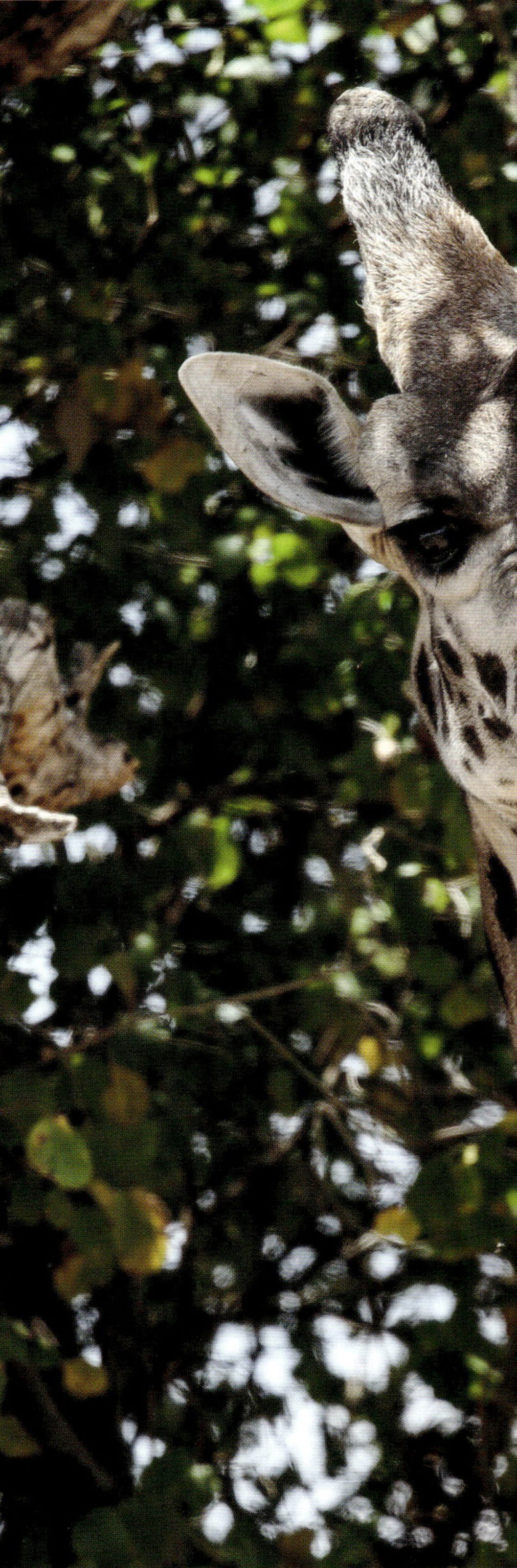

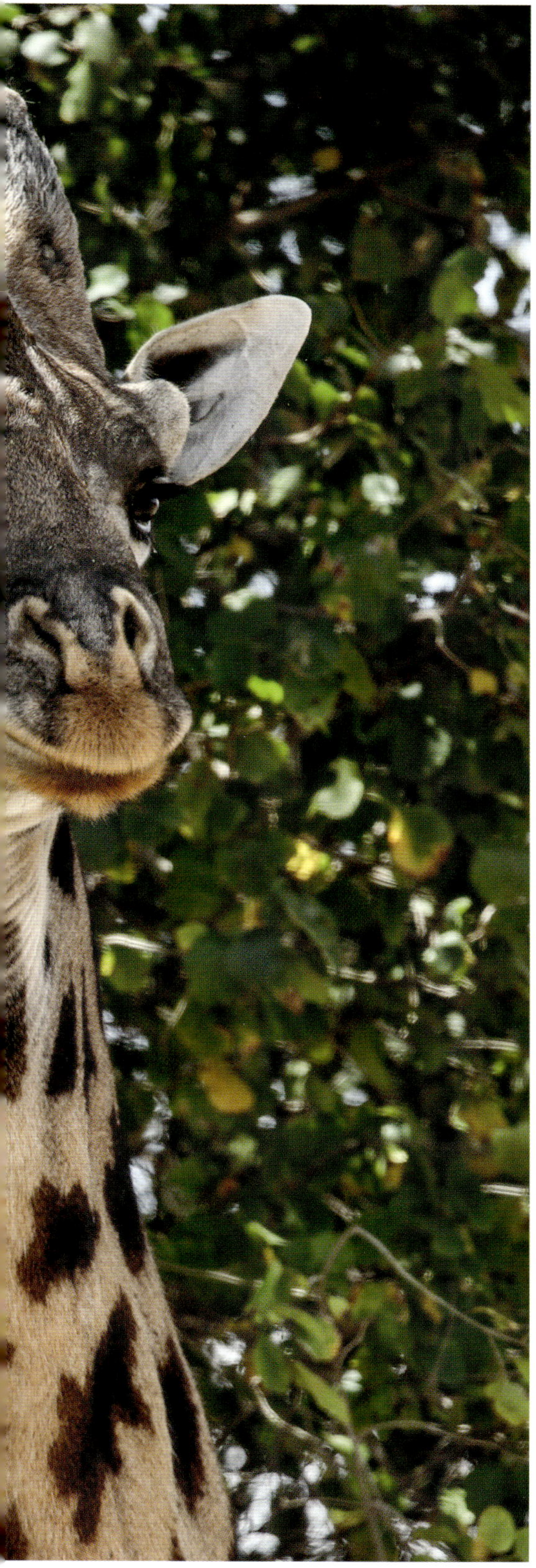

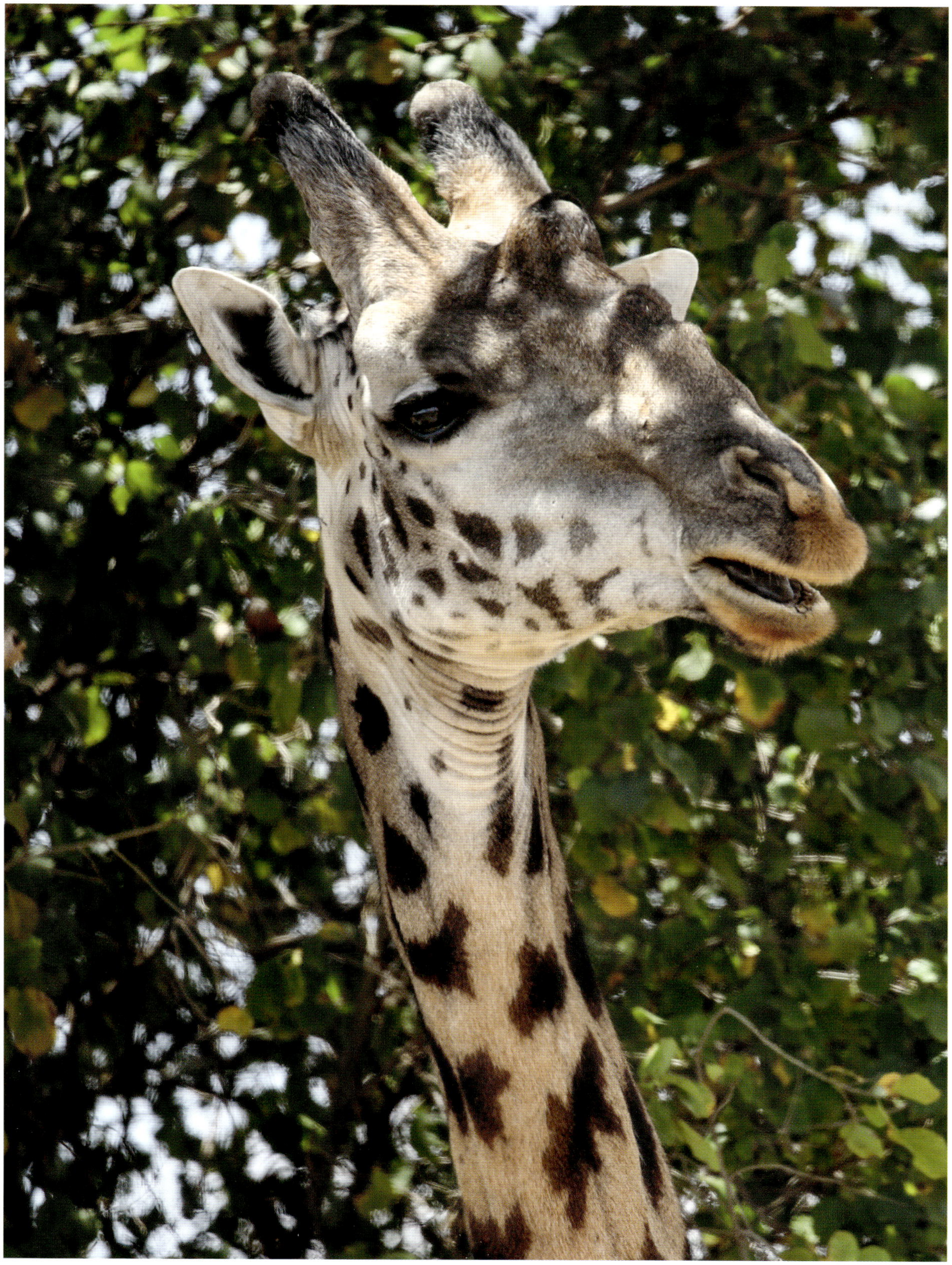

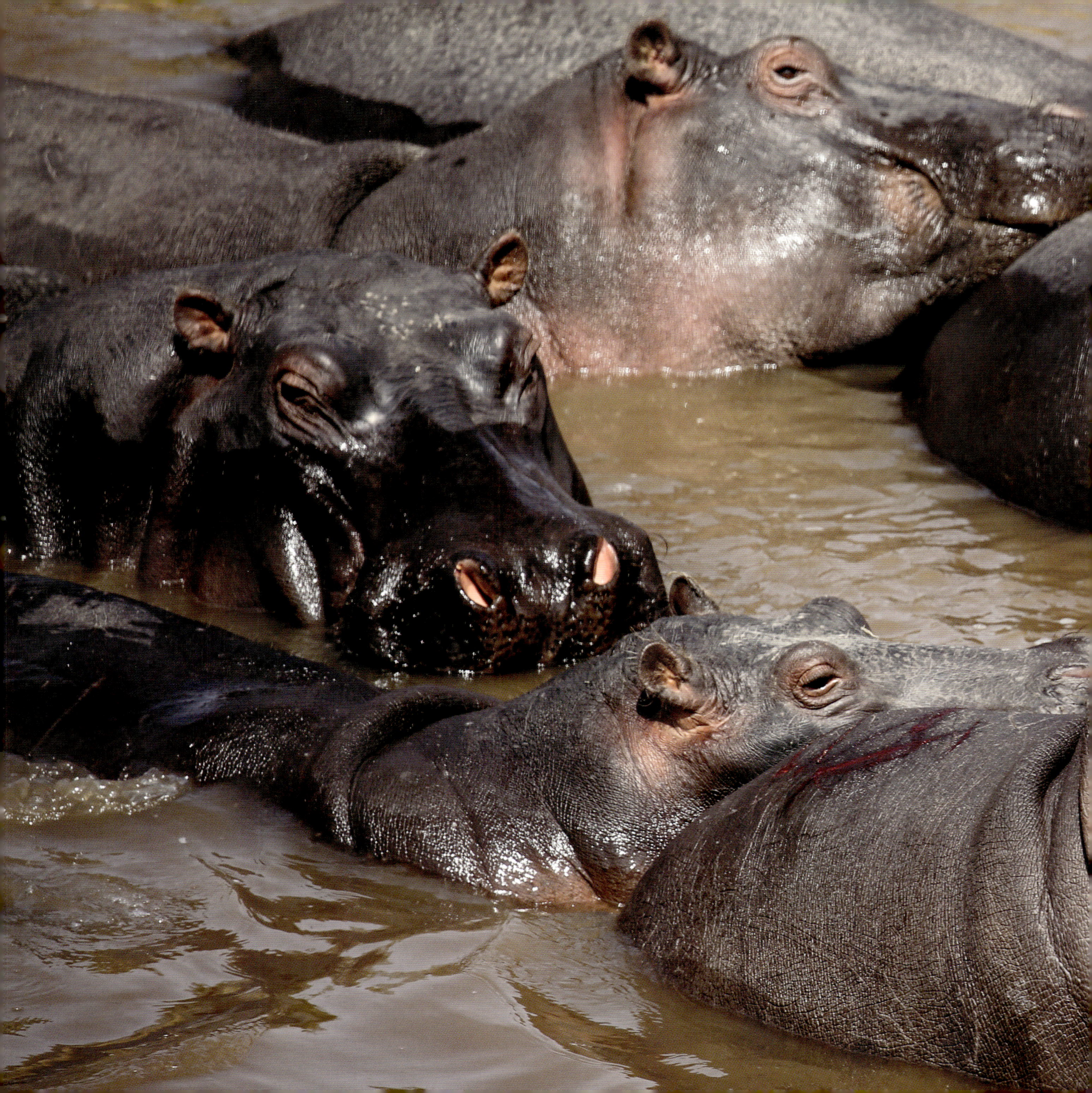

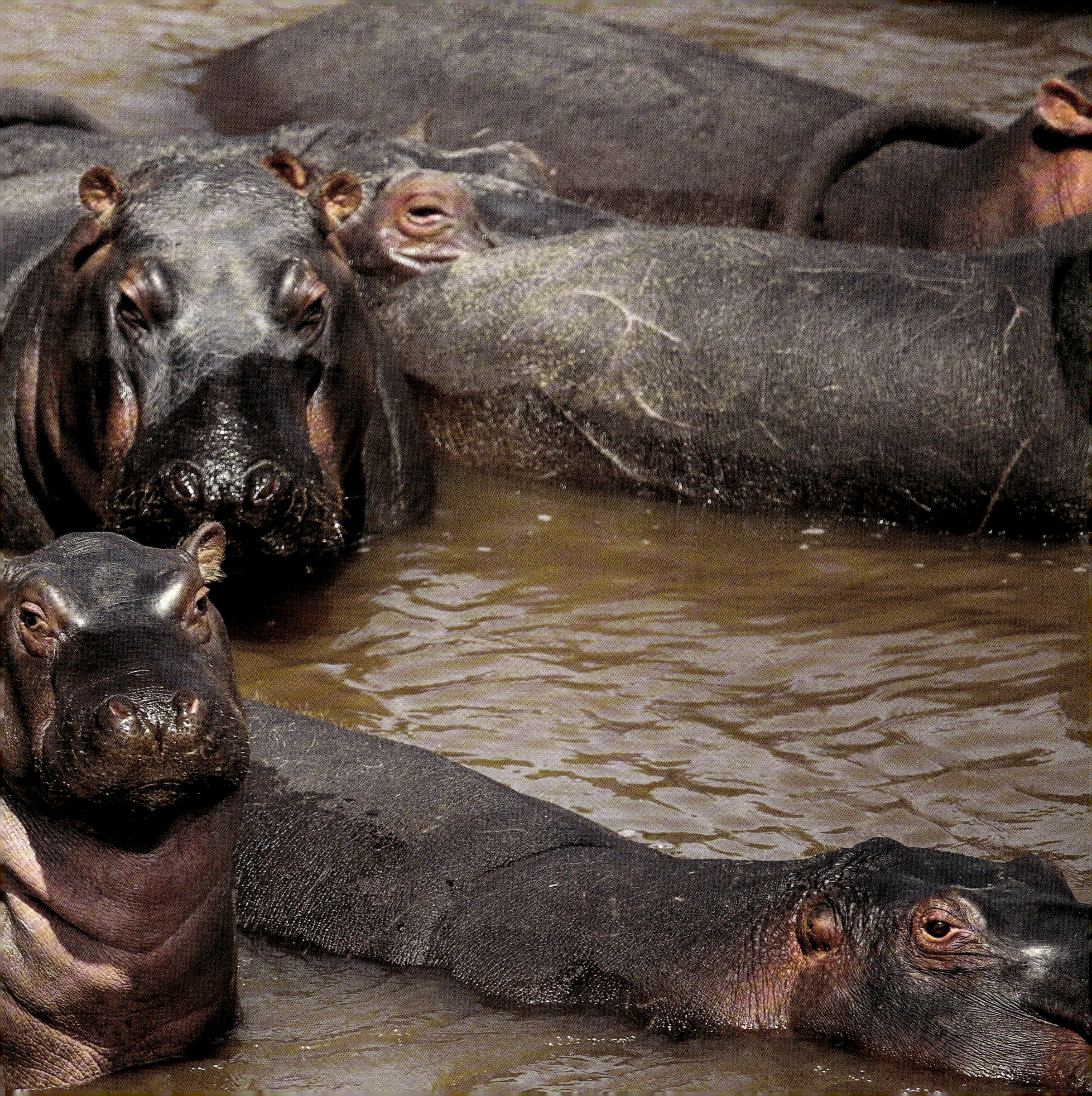

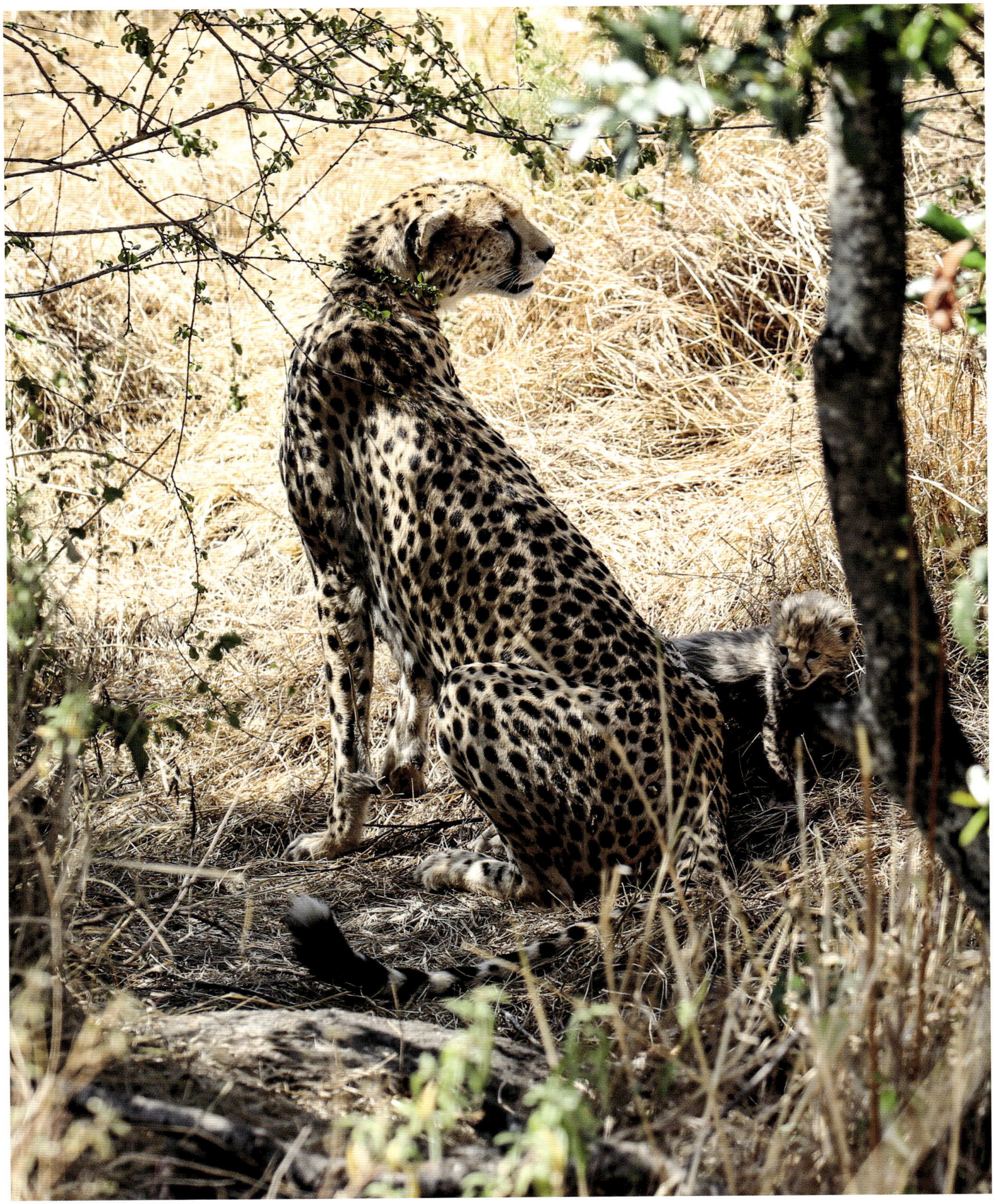

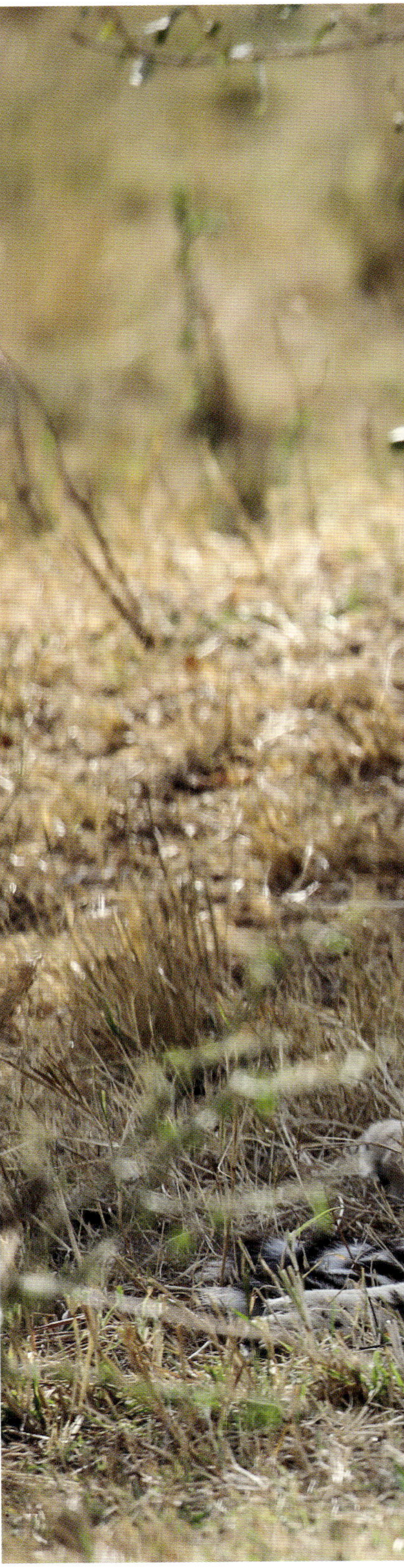

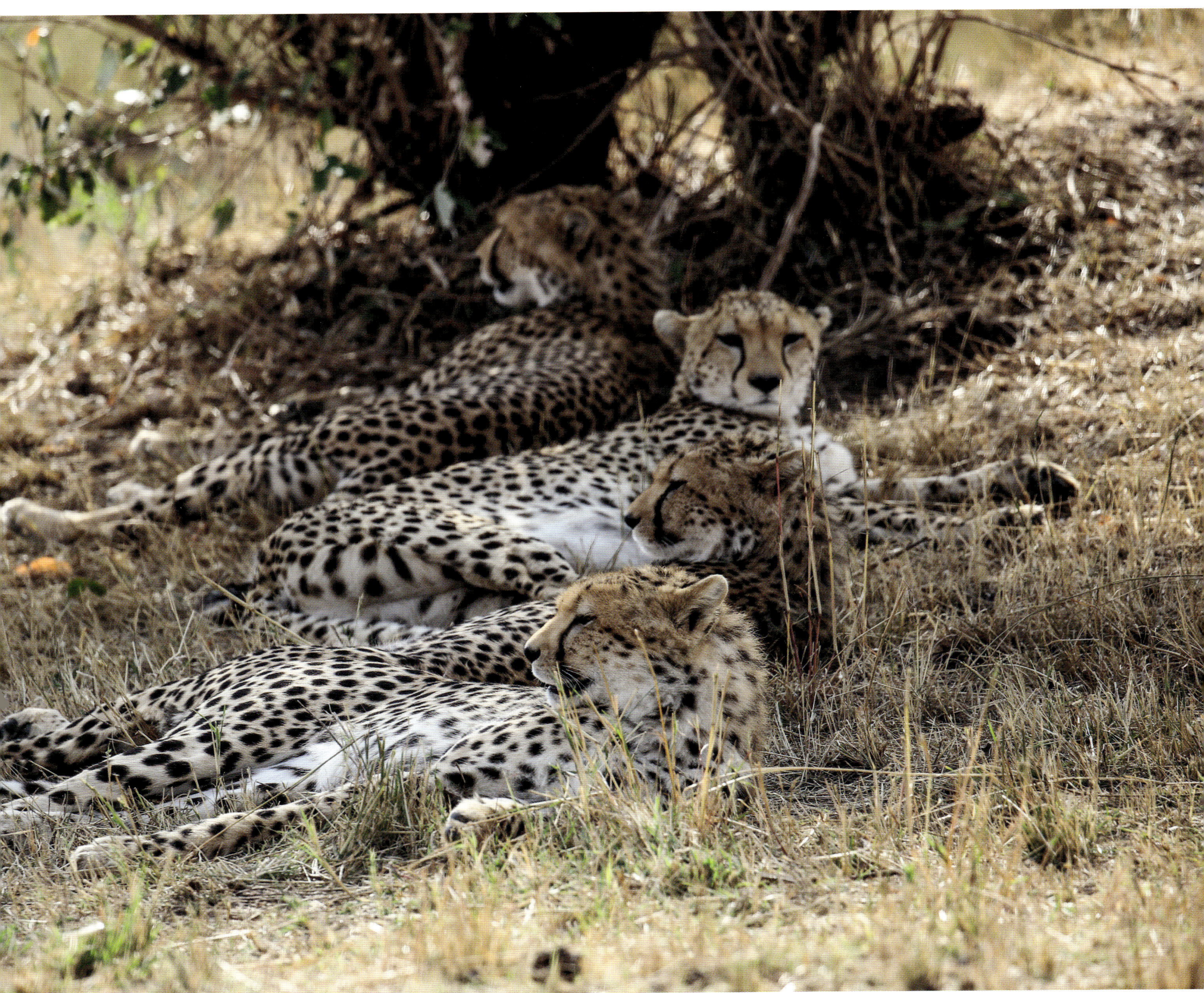

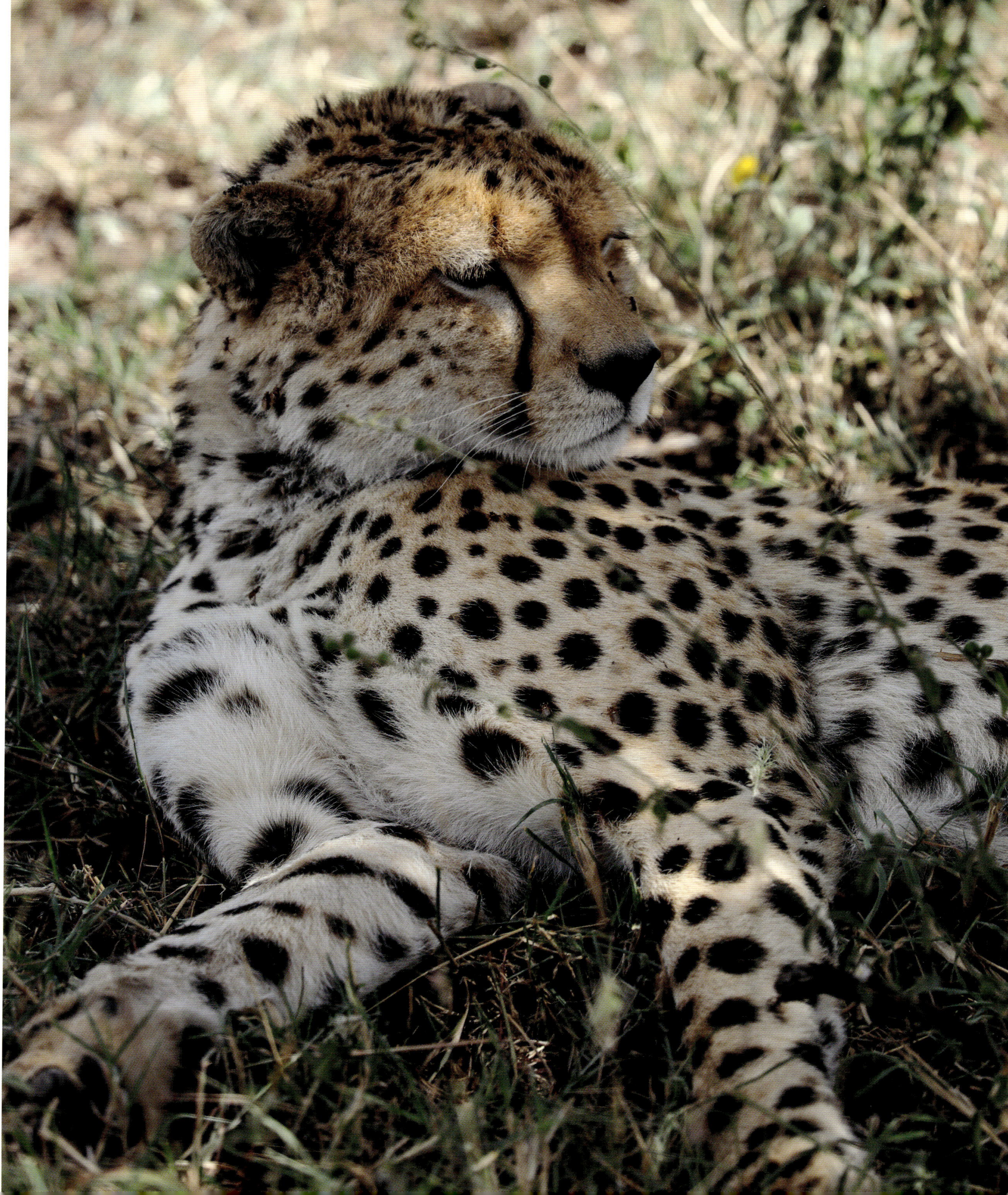

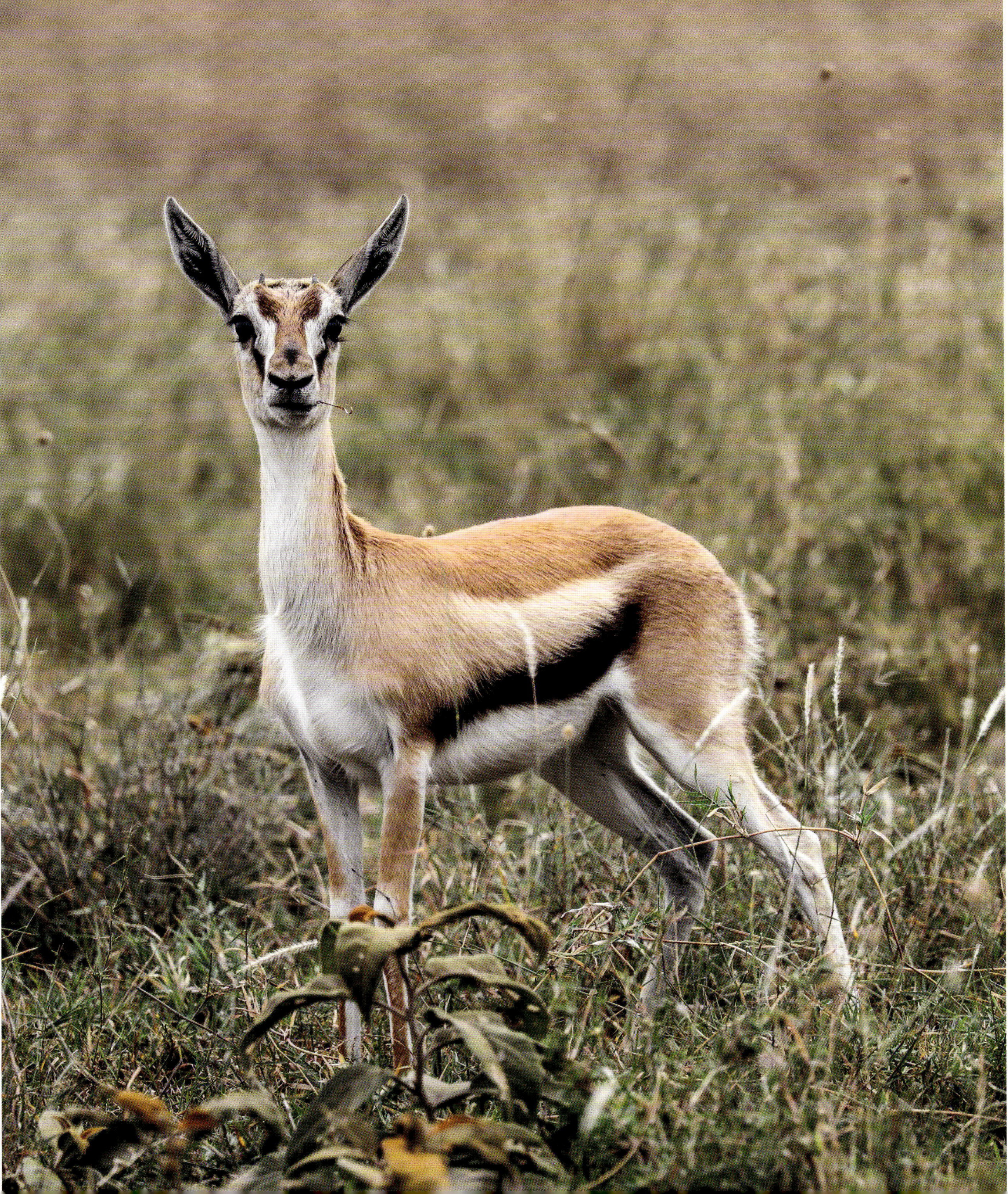

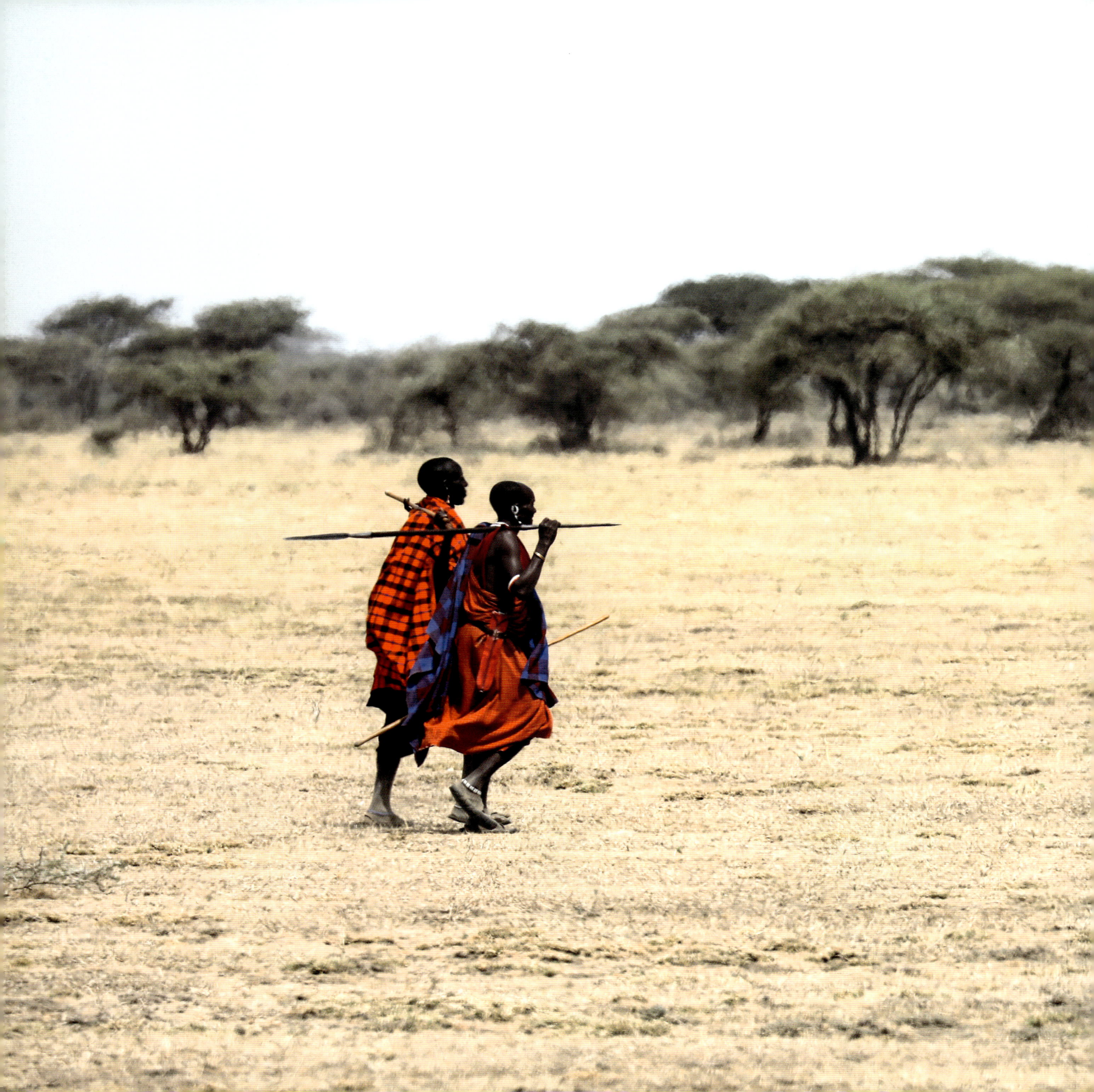

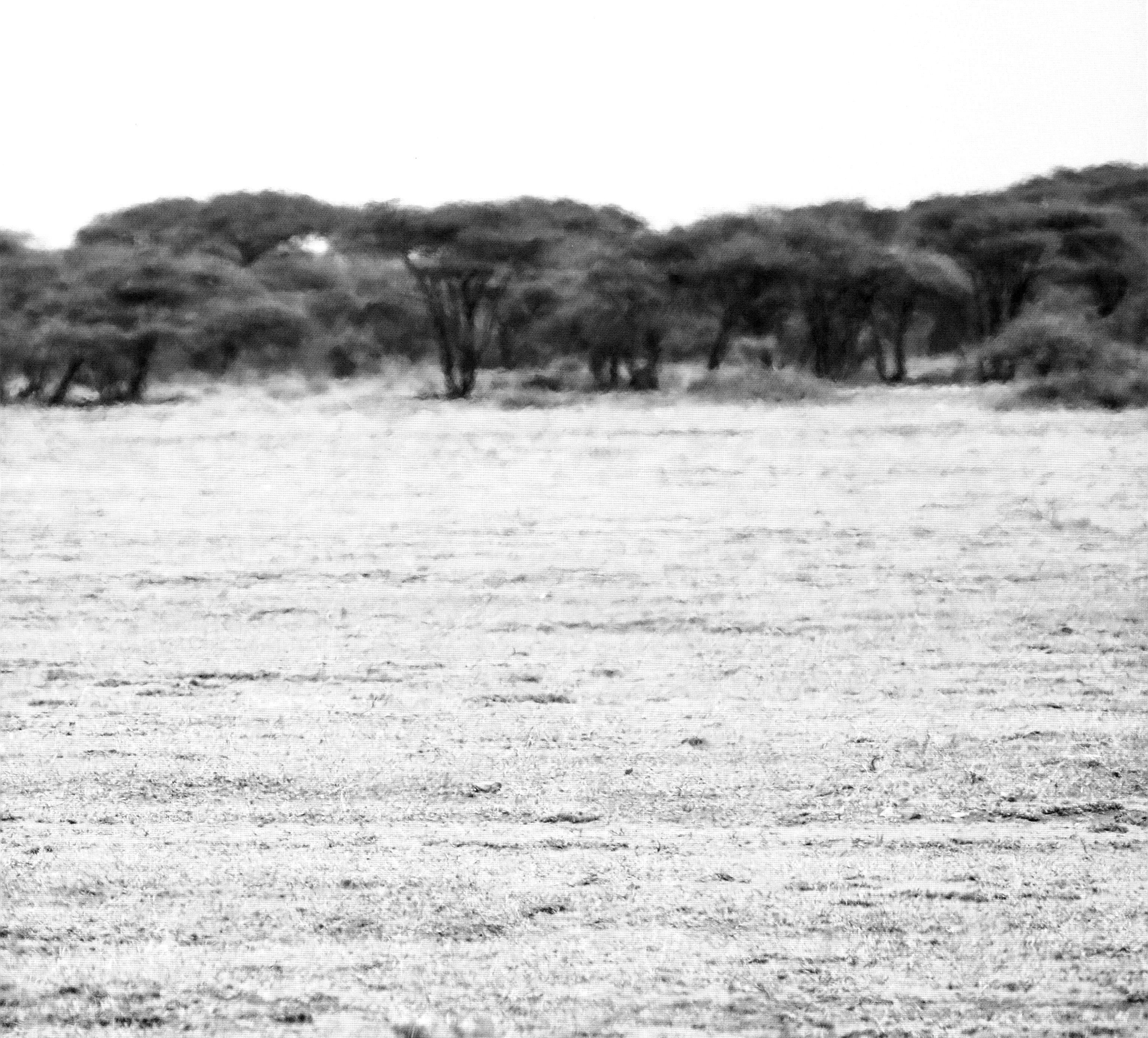

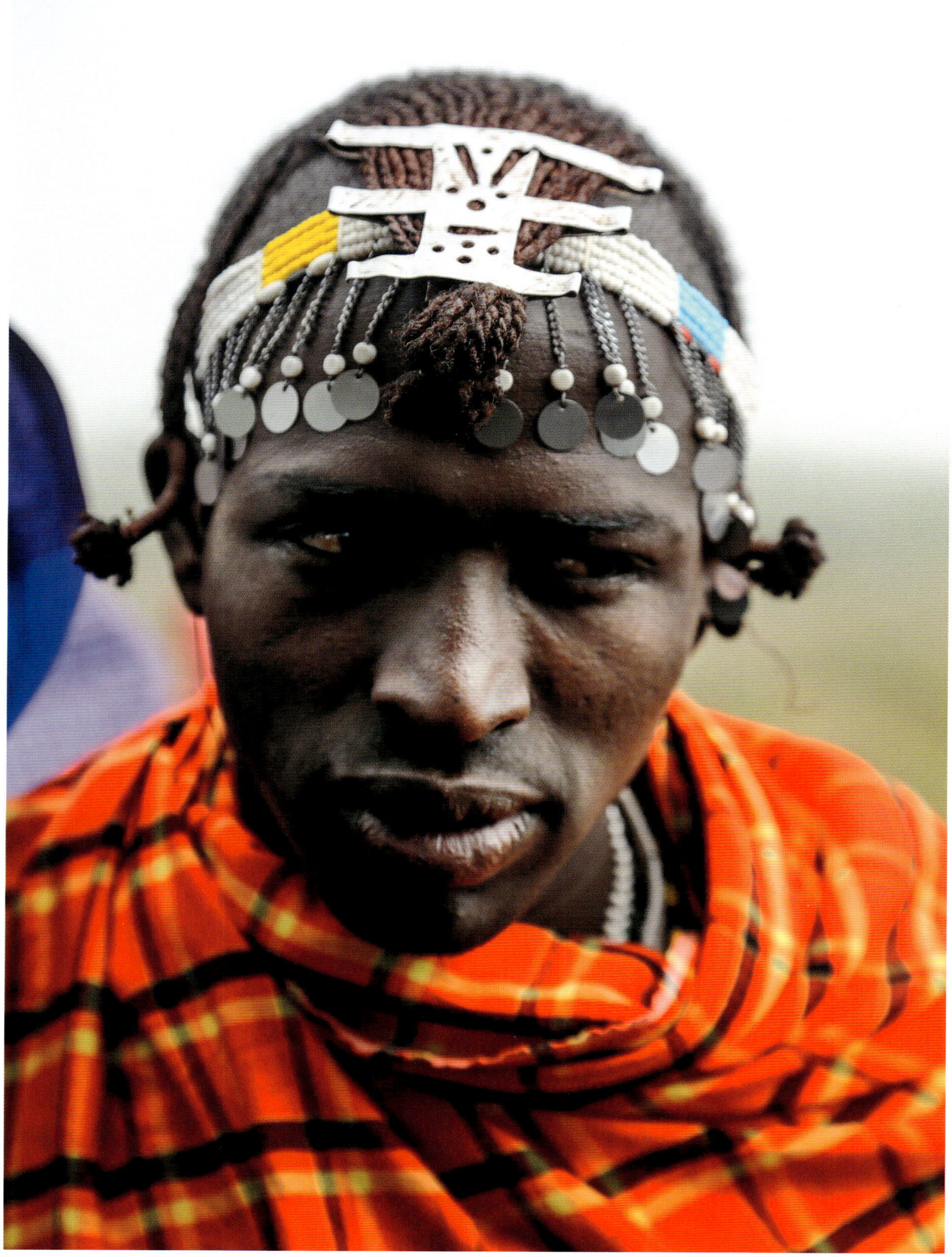

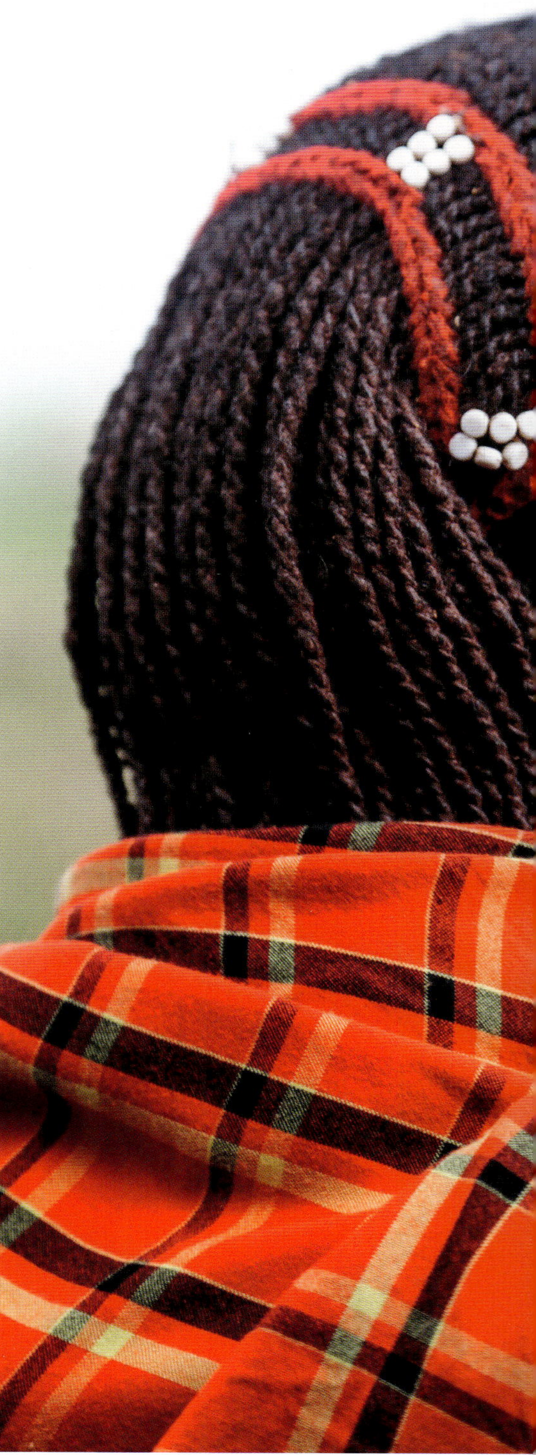

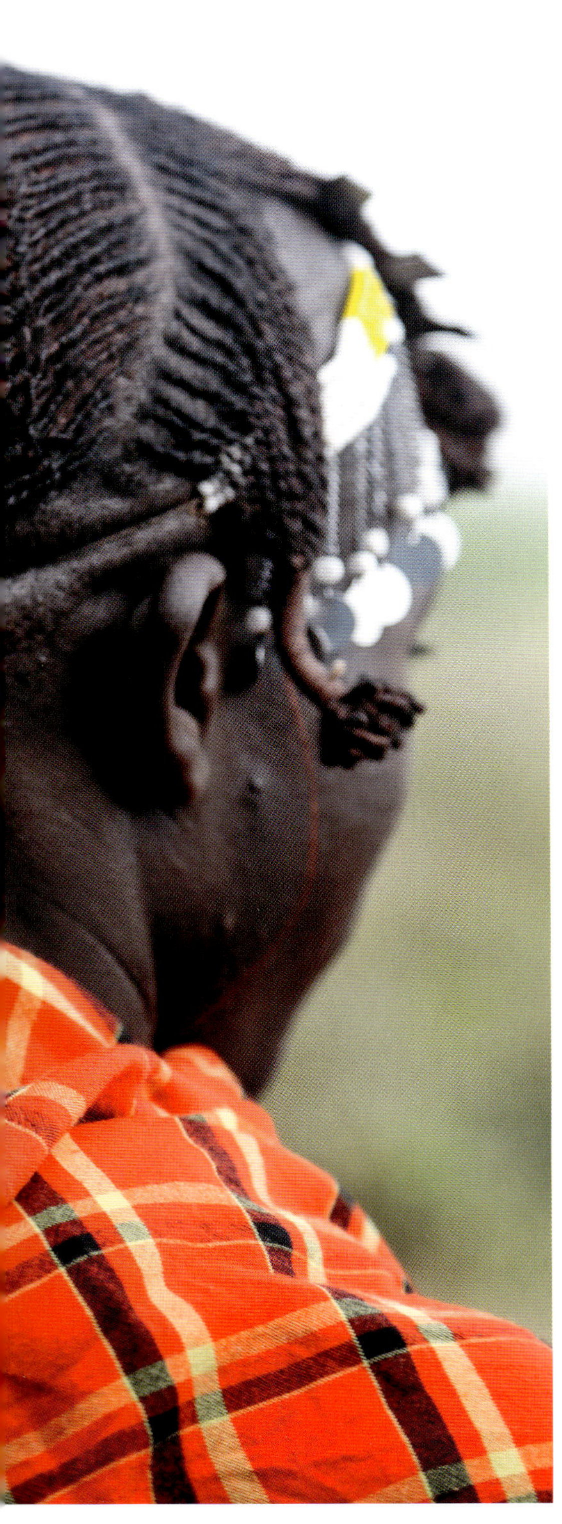

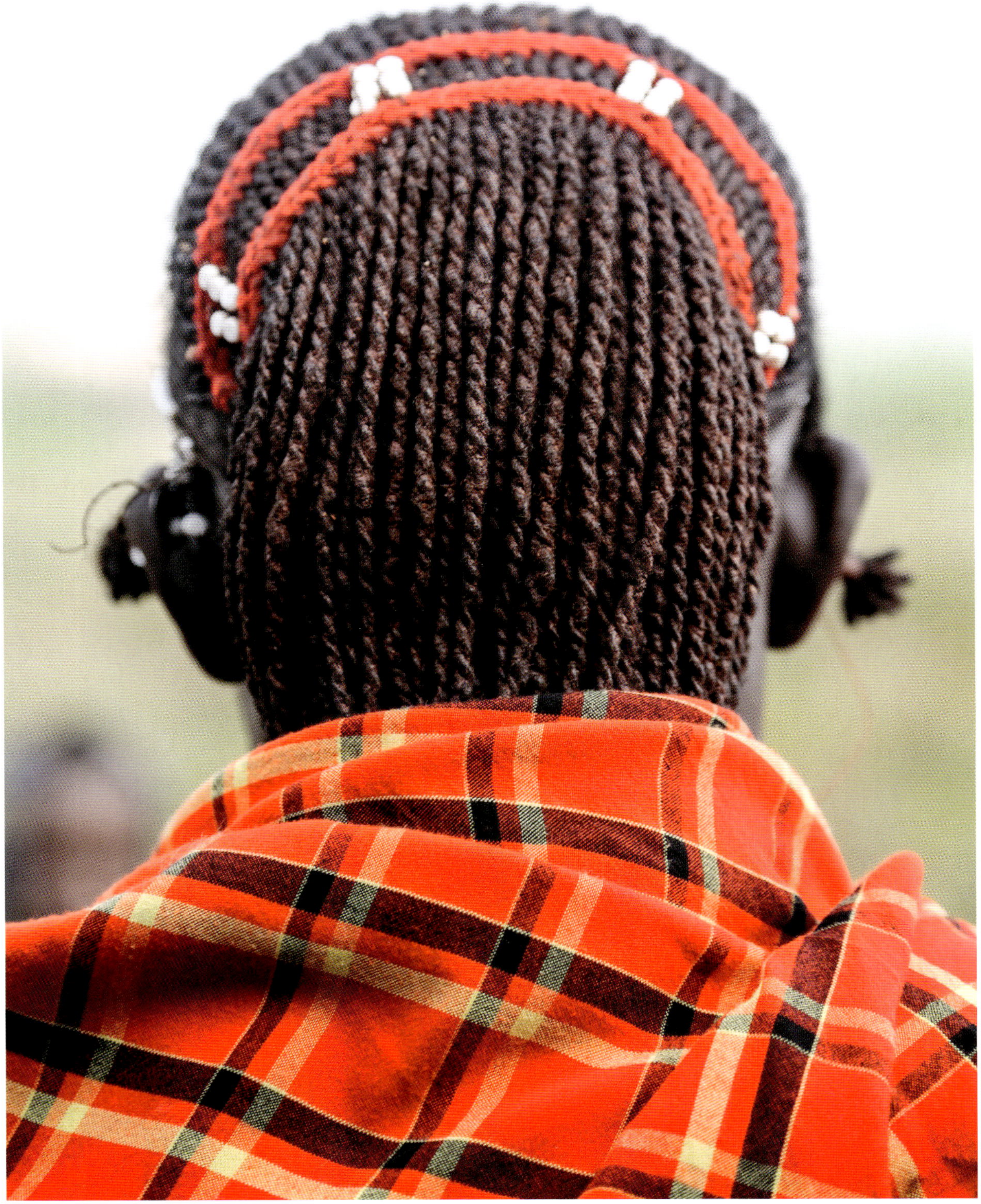

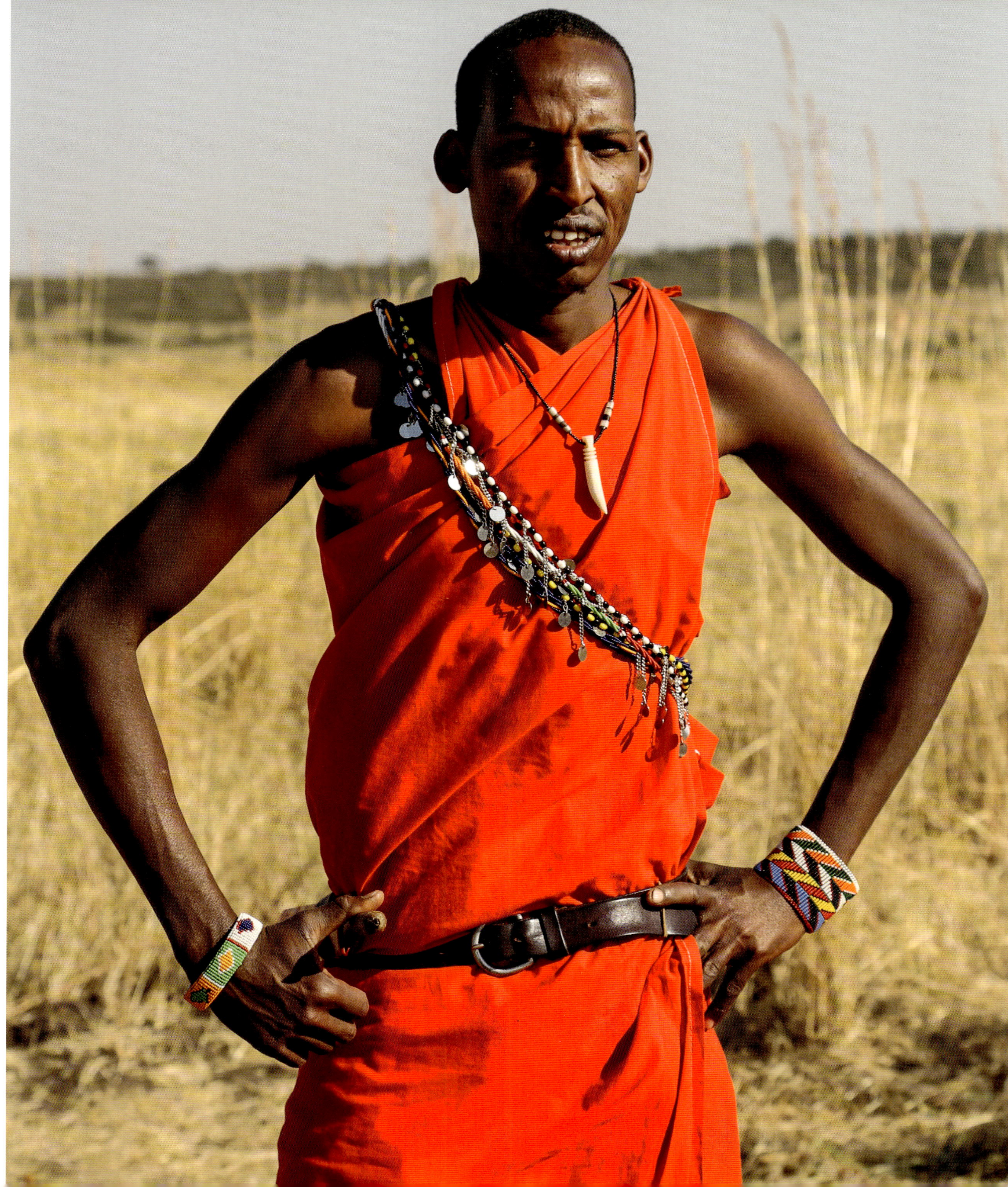

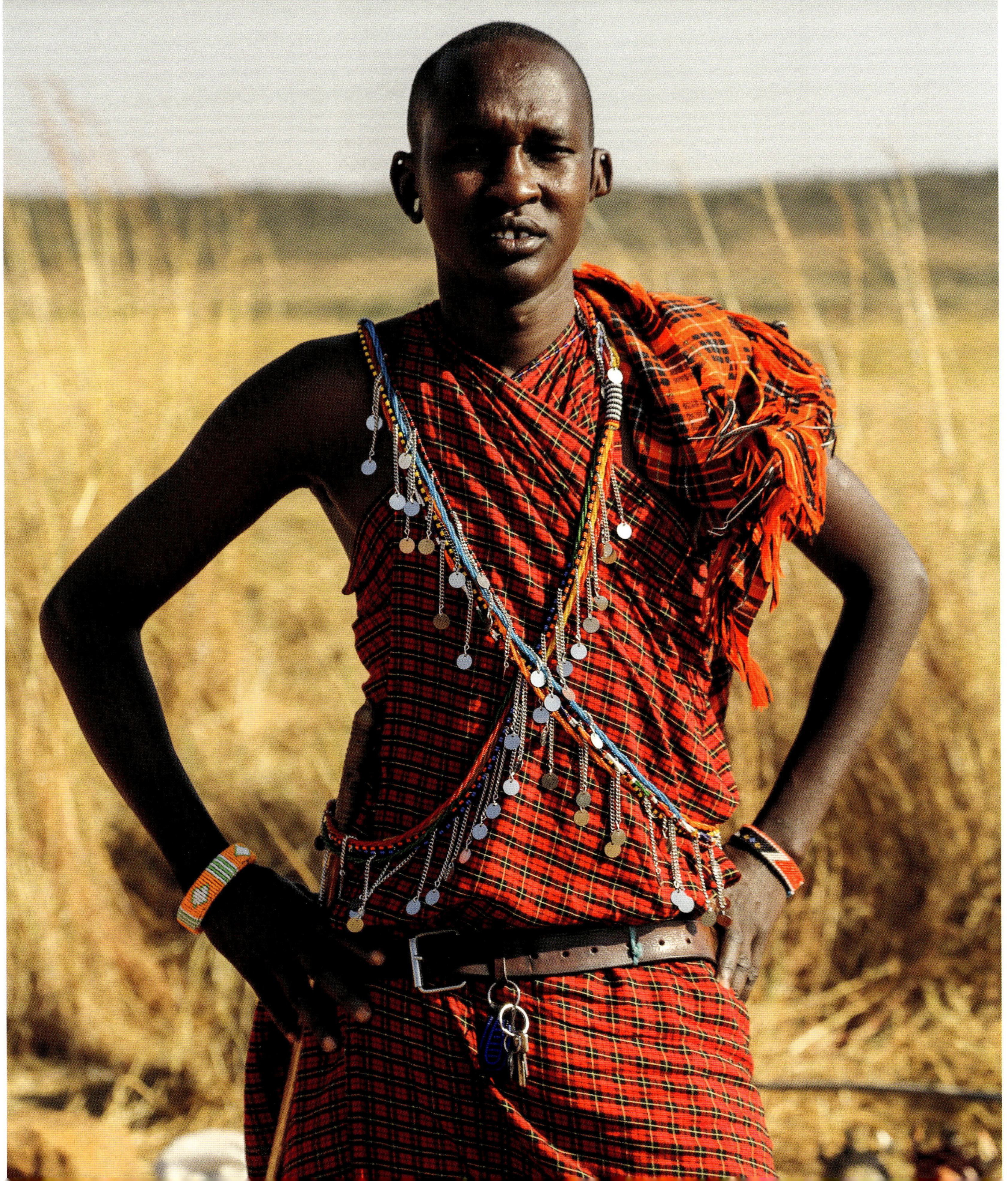

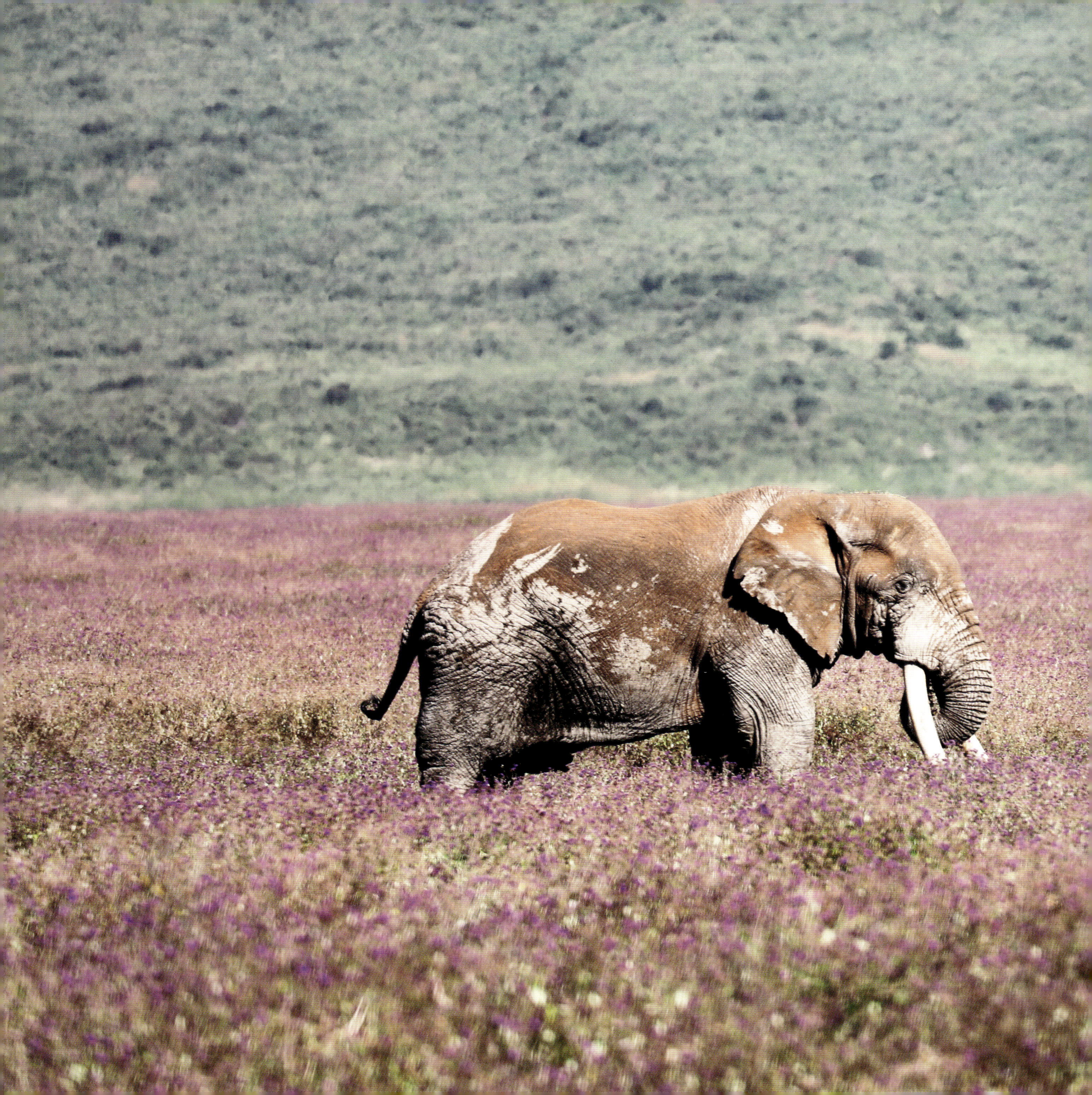

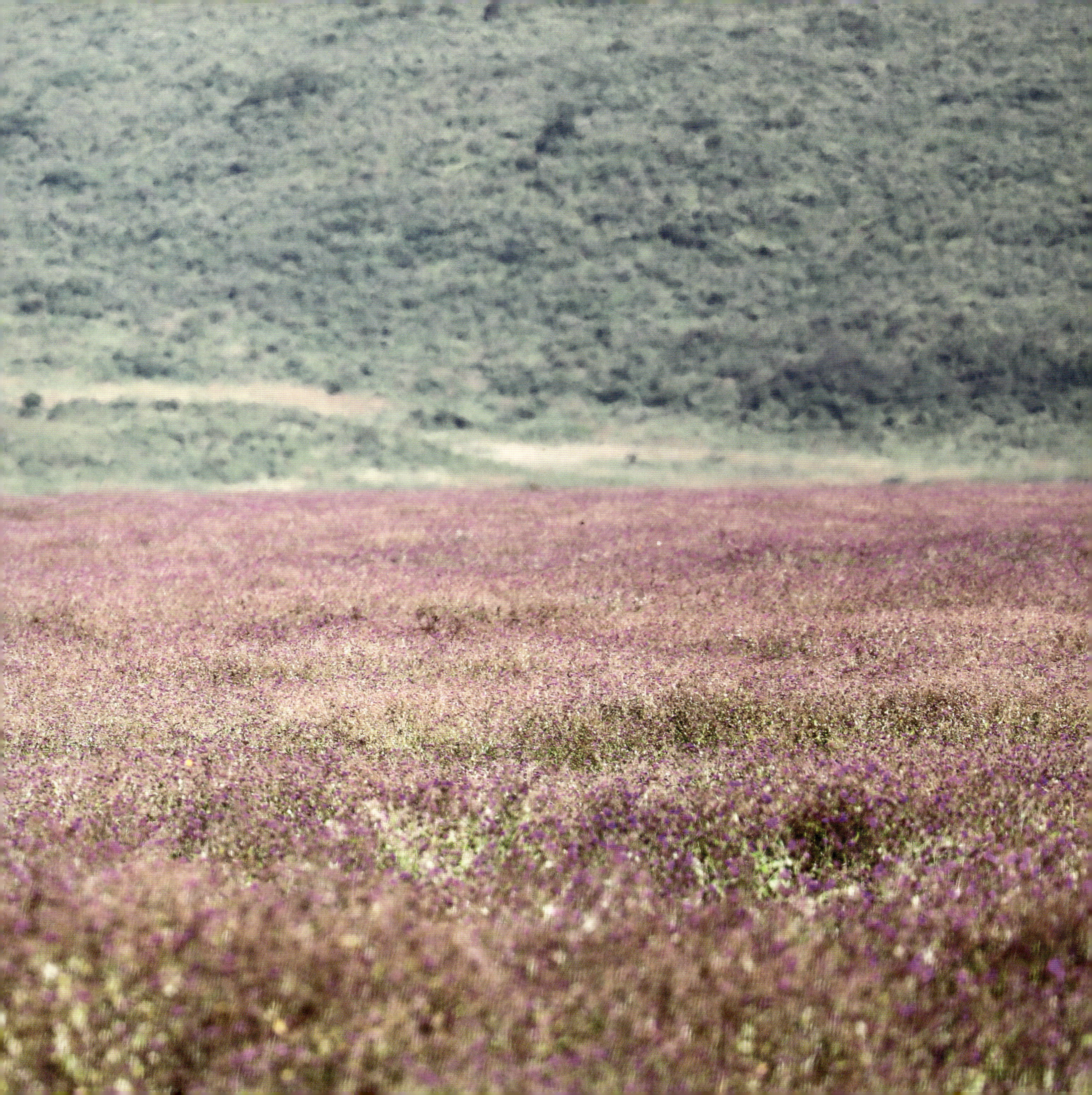

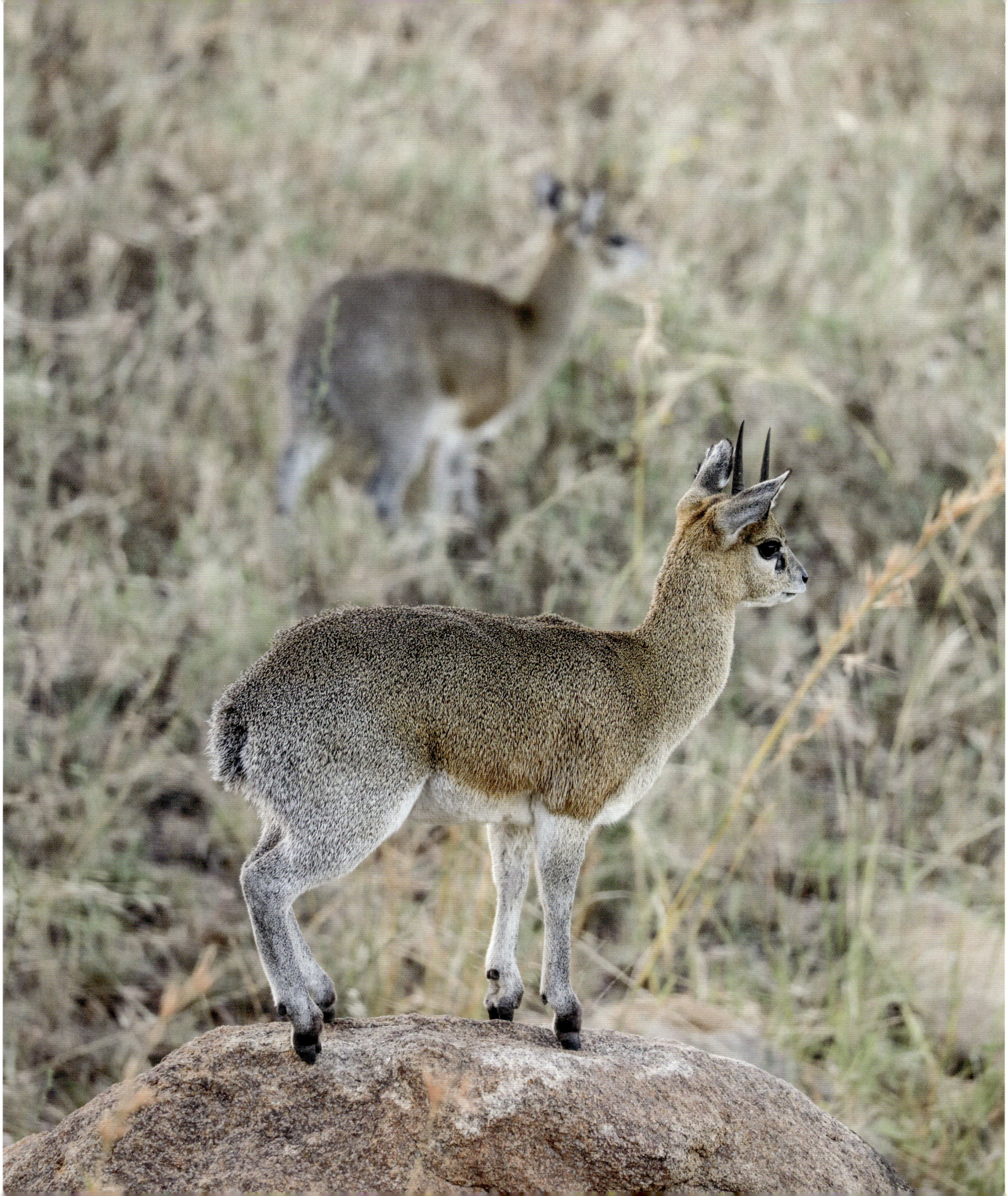

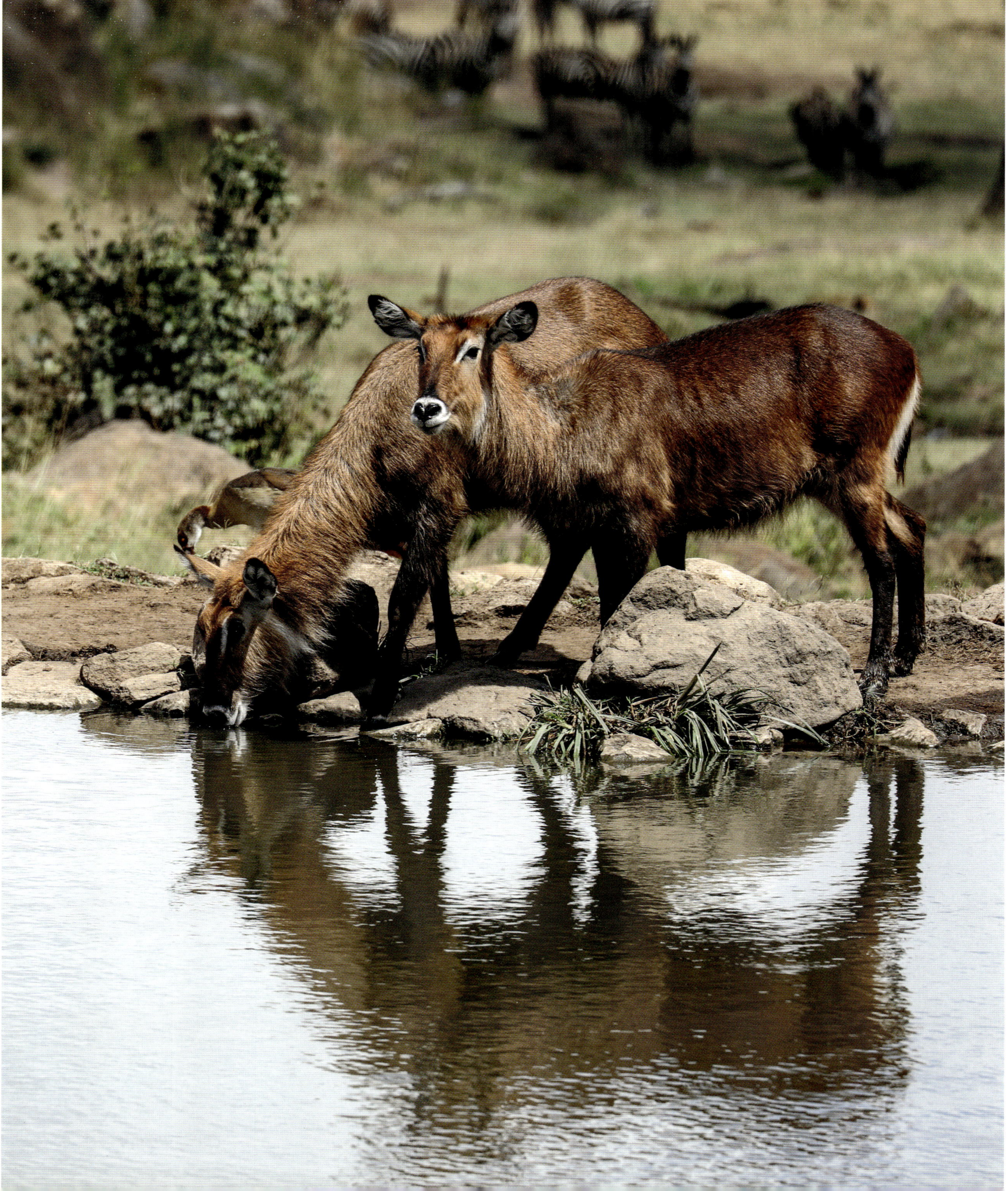

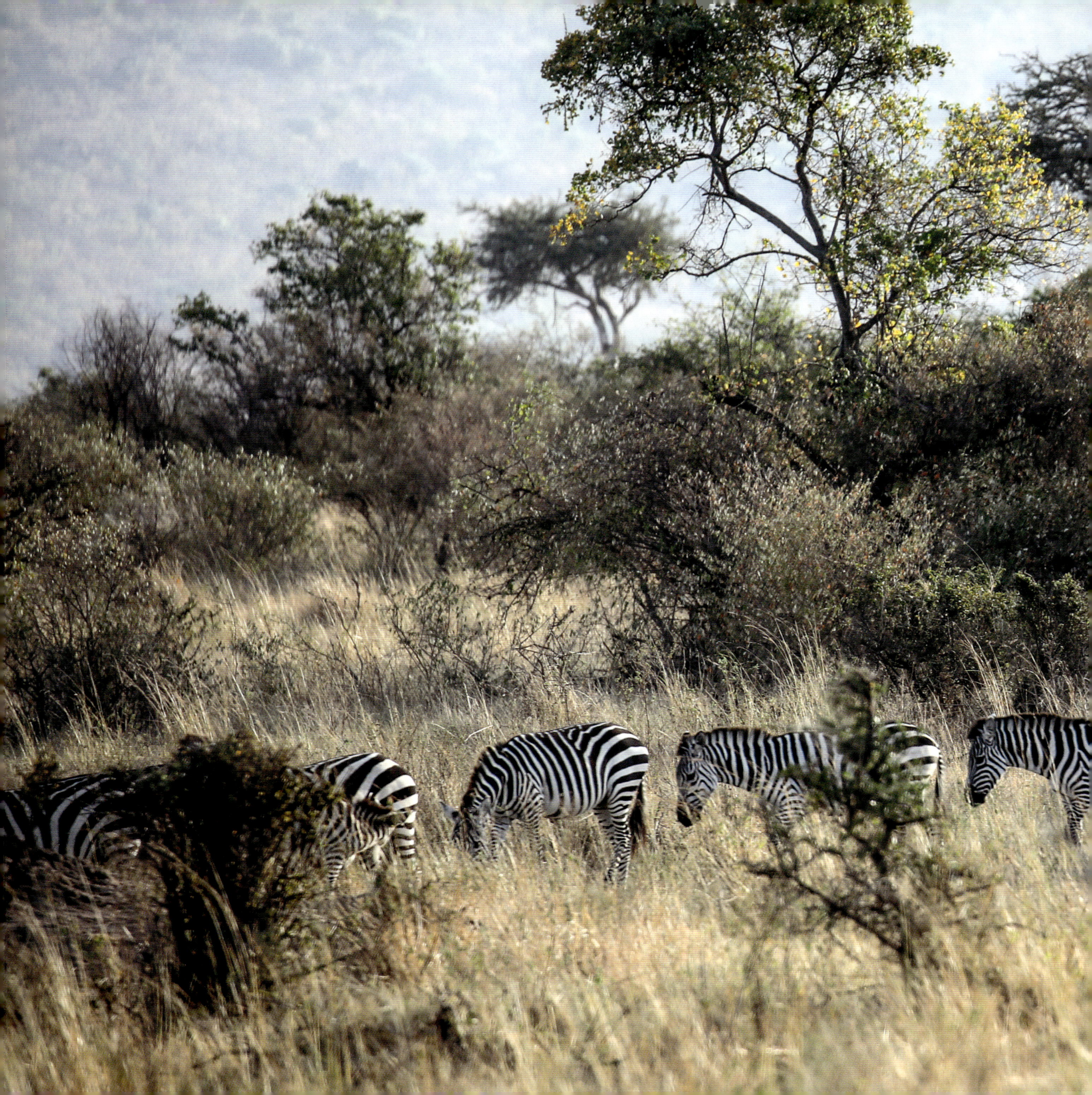

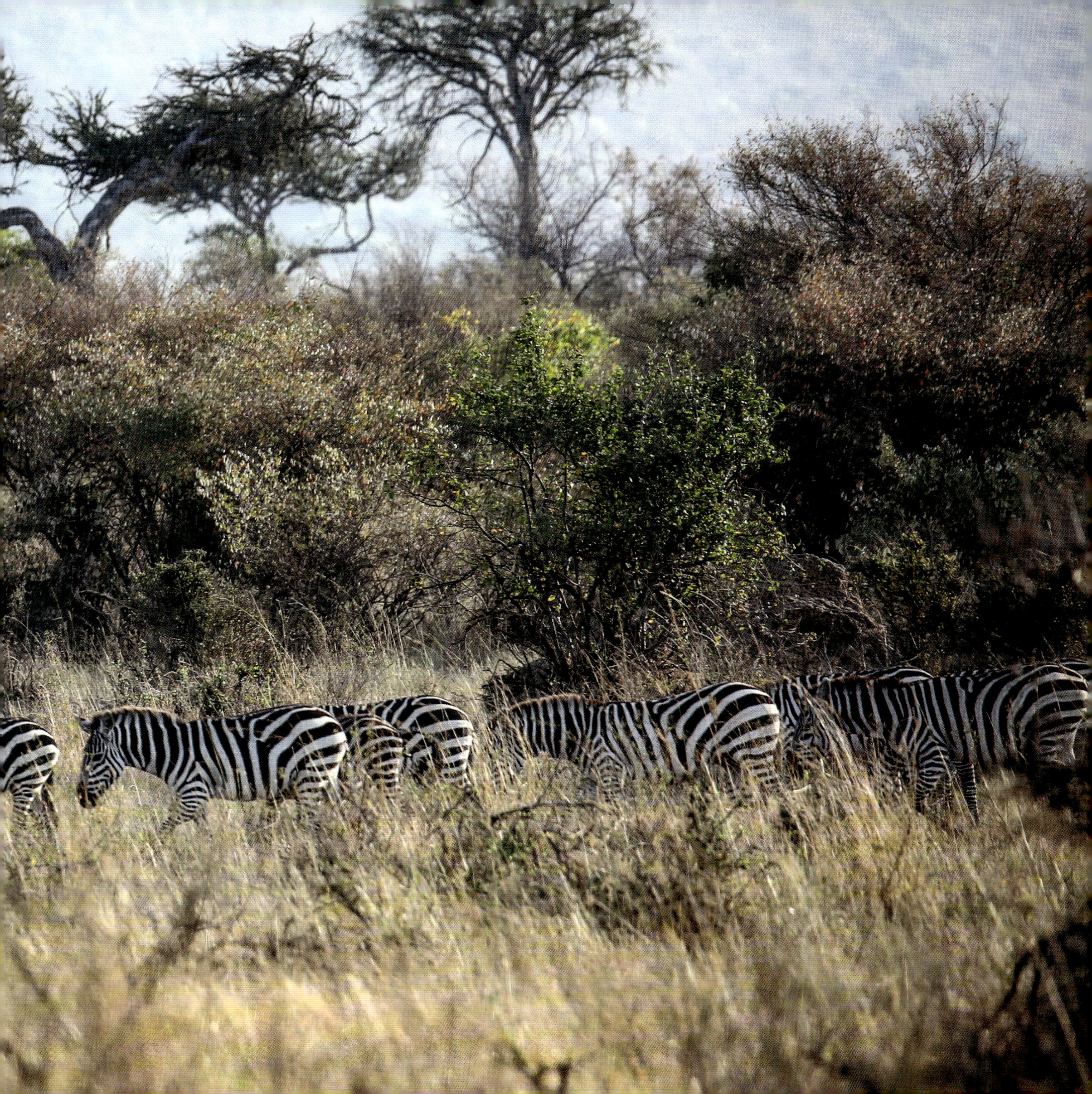

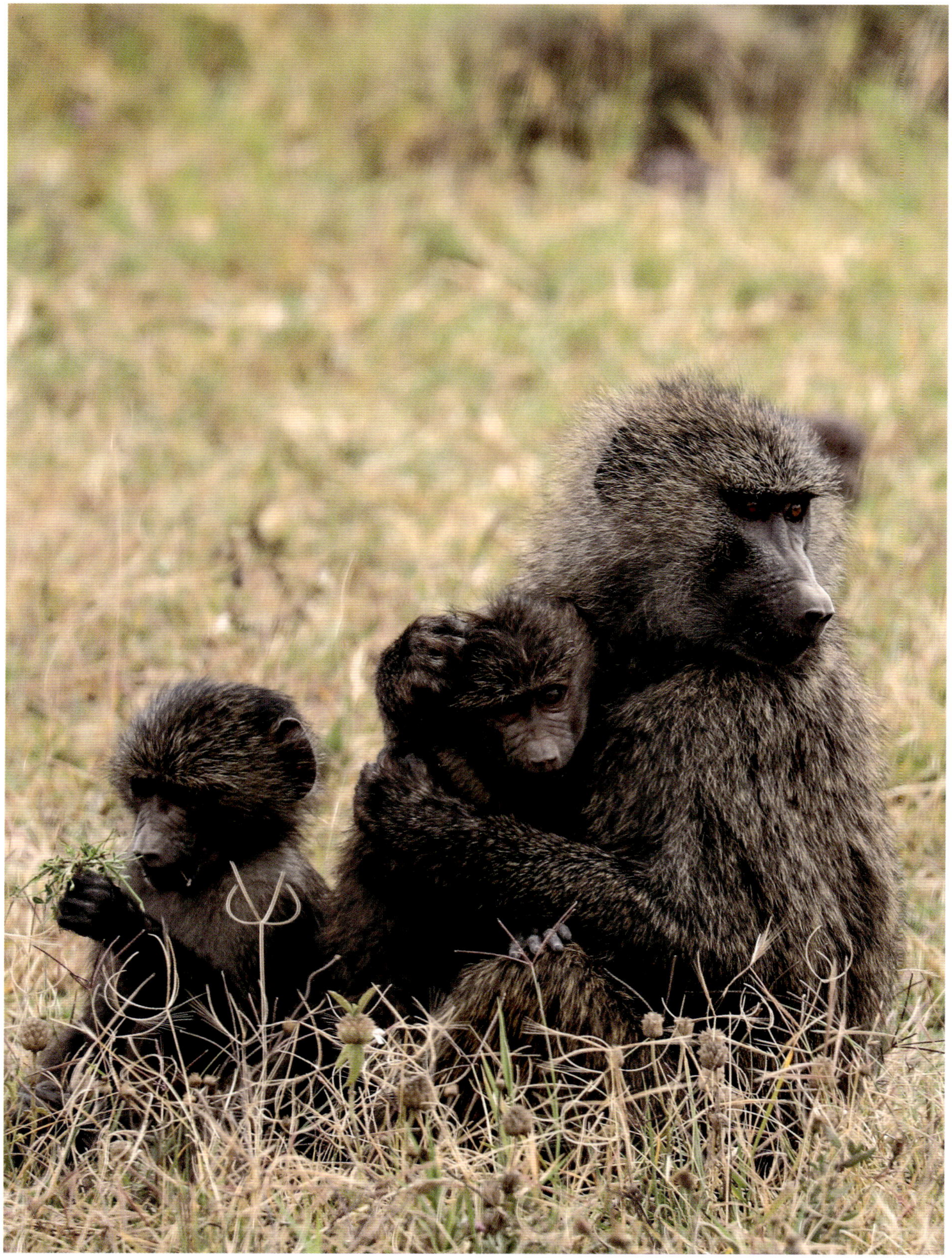

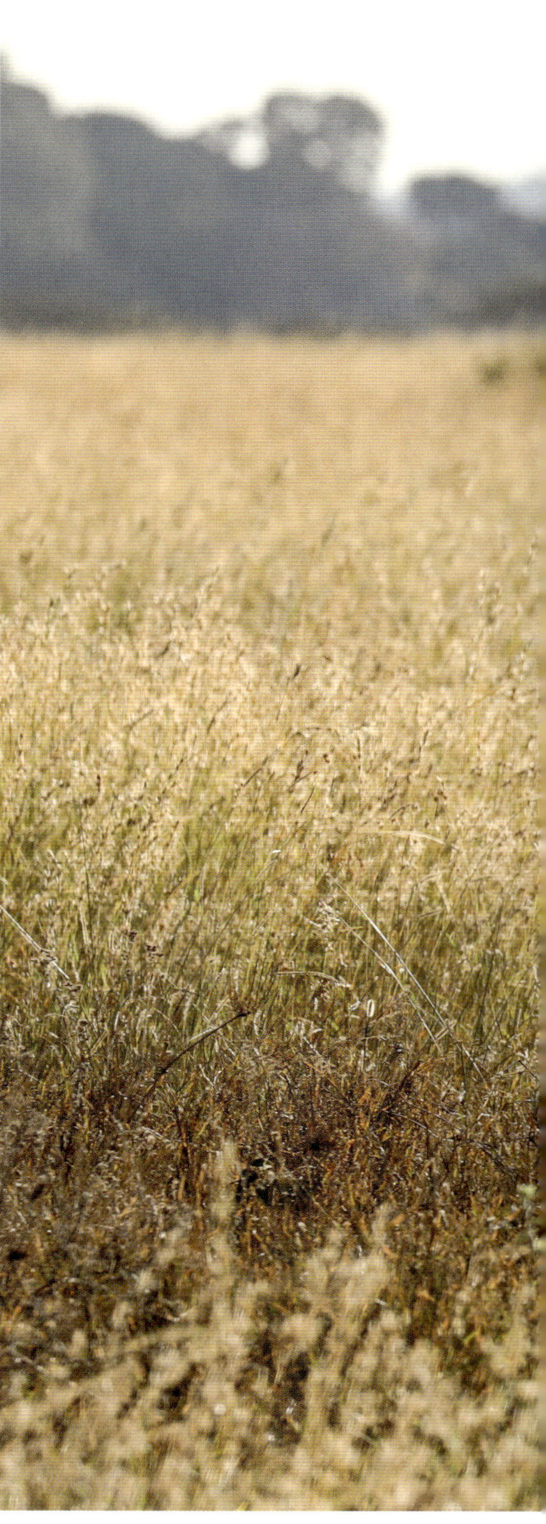

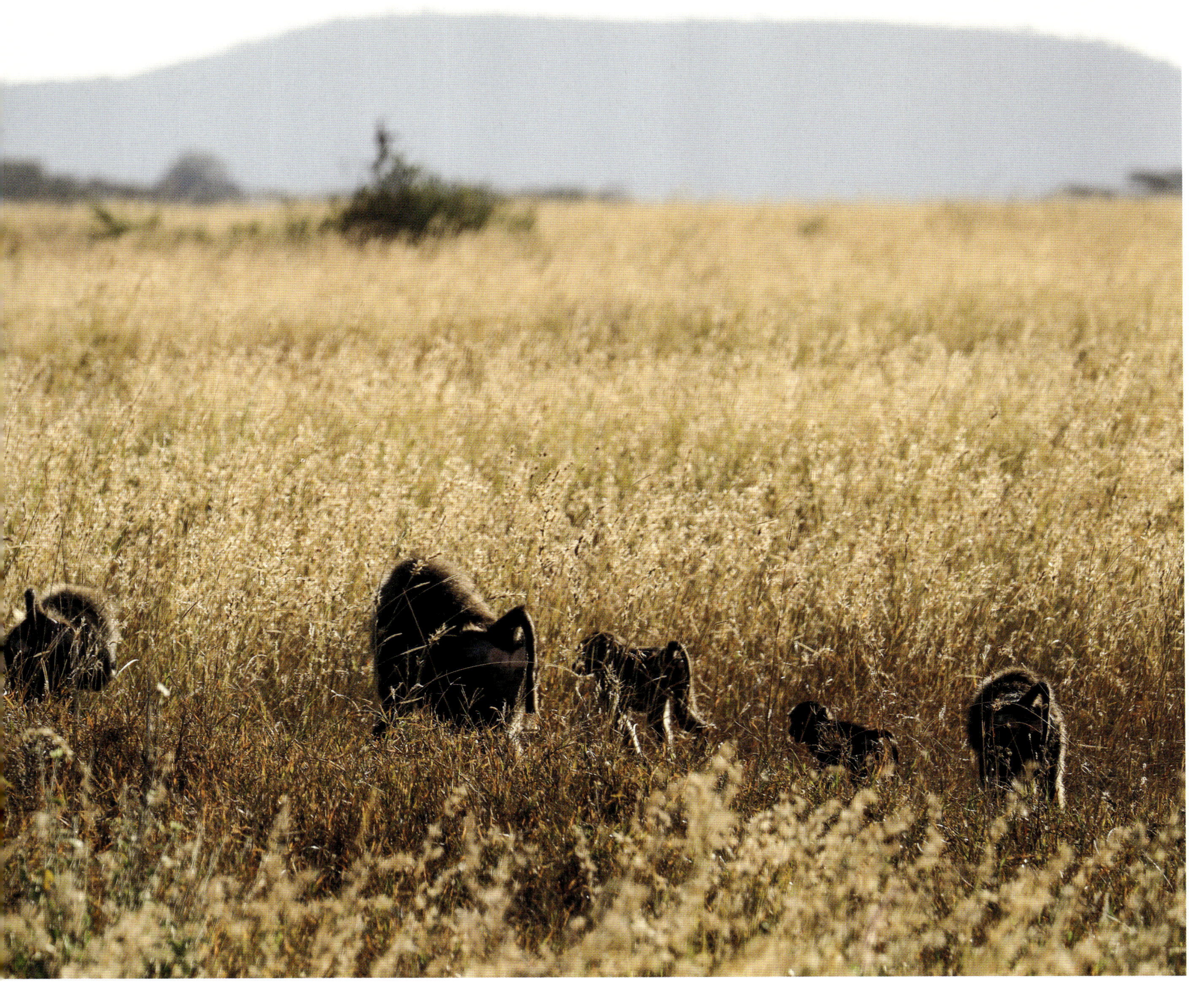

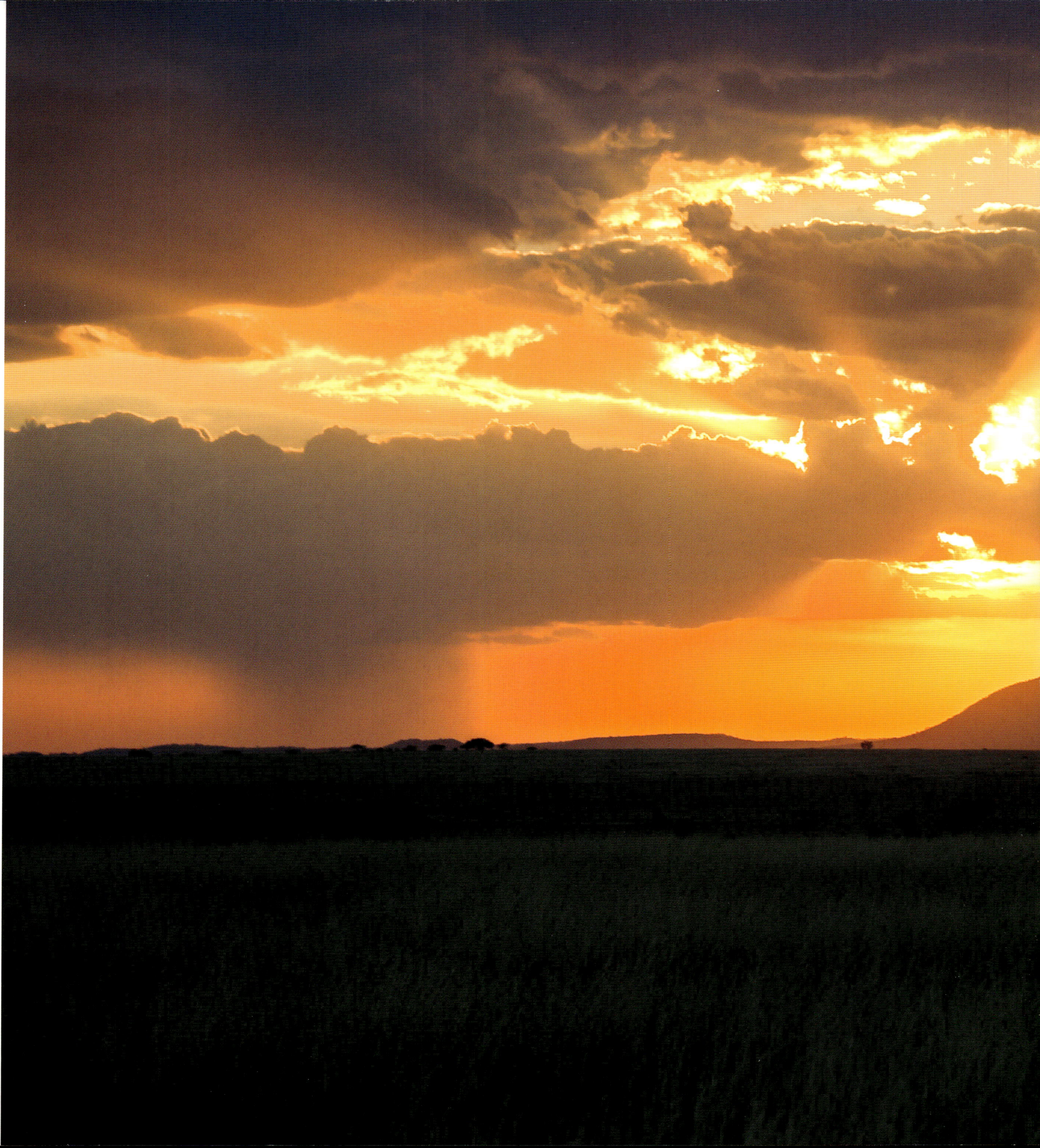

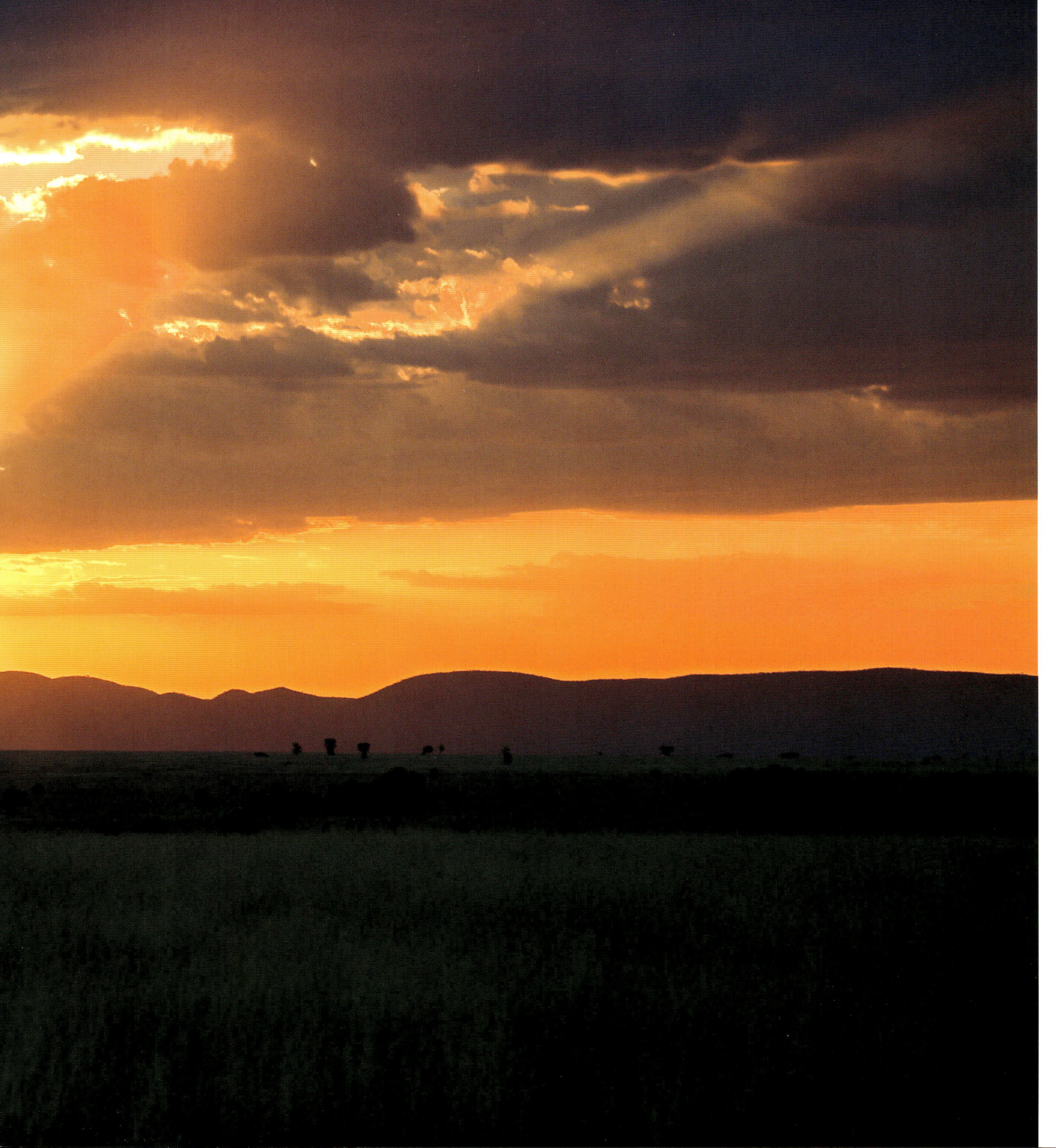

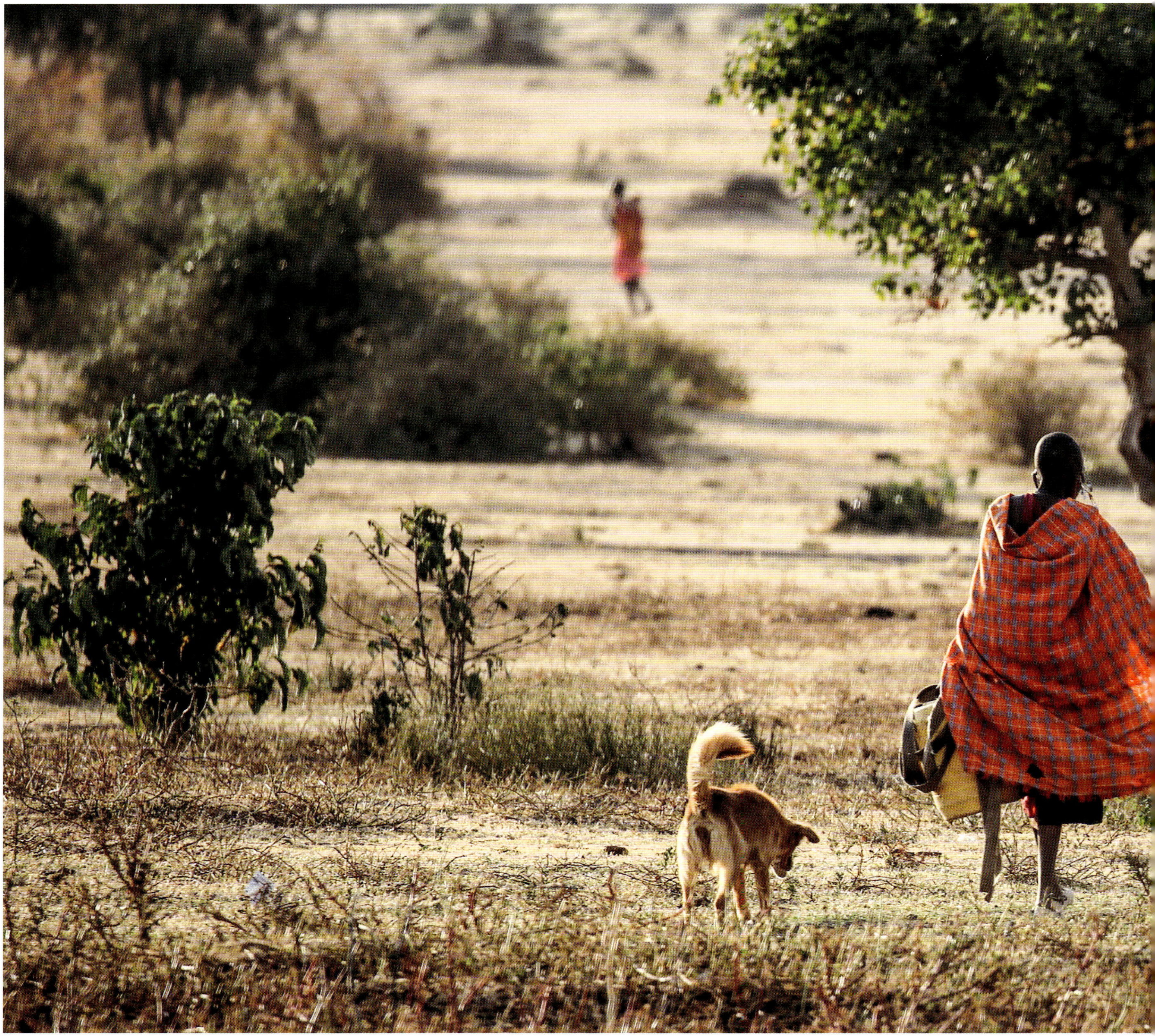

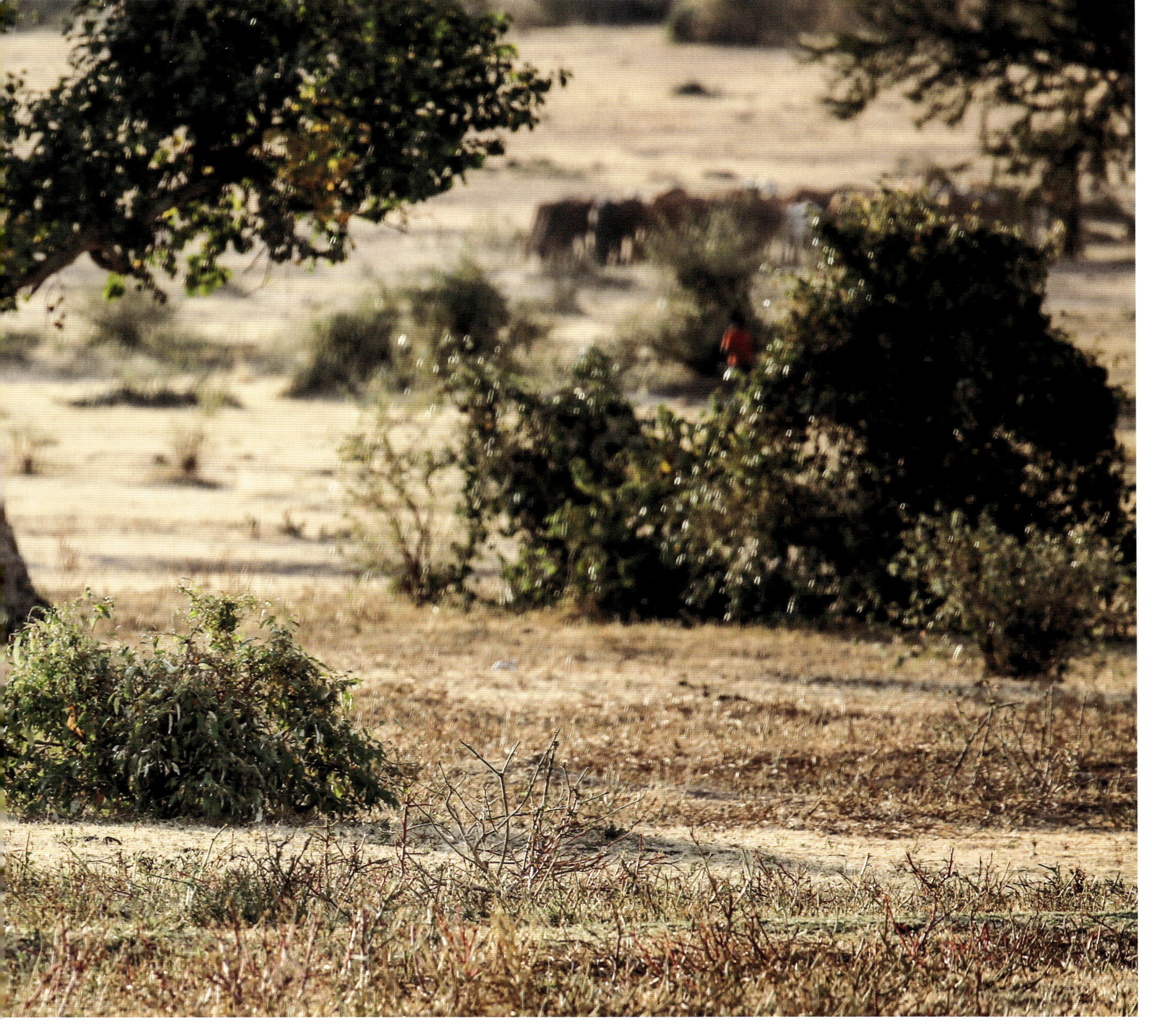

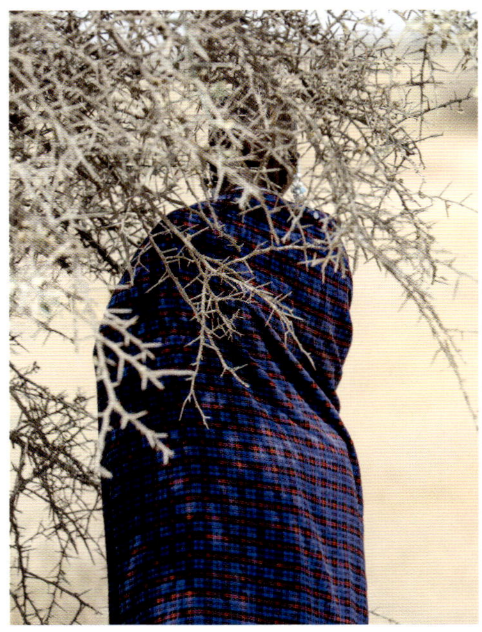

ACKNOWLEDGEMENTS

I wish to thank Philip Vergeylen and Paolo Moschino for believing in this book and for introducing me to David Shannon, the editor, without whom this dream could not have come true. Thanks to his patience and dedication during a whole year the book reached the quality that I desired.

Thanks to my sister Lucita, my brother-in-law Angelo Porcella and my nieces Maria Luz Haggar and Serena Safa for so many ideas and advices that were implemented during this endeavour.

I also thank my niece Carolina Bonfiglio, Isabel Falkenberg, David Langford, Mark Murphy, Lisa Garbarino and Simone Falcetta for their invaluable suggestions.

I am especially grateful to Beatriz Ordovas for her great support both in the graphic, literal and moral aspects. Also for her unwavering belief in my work.

Finally, I want to thank all those who look after natural reserves, true heroes that keep the beauty and diversity of this land. They provided the canvas for my photography.

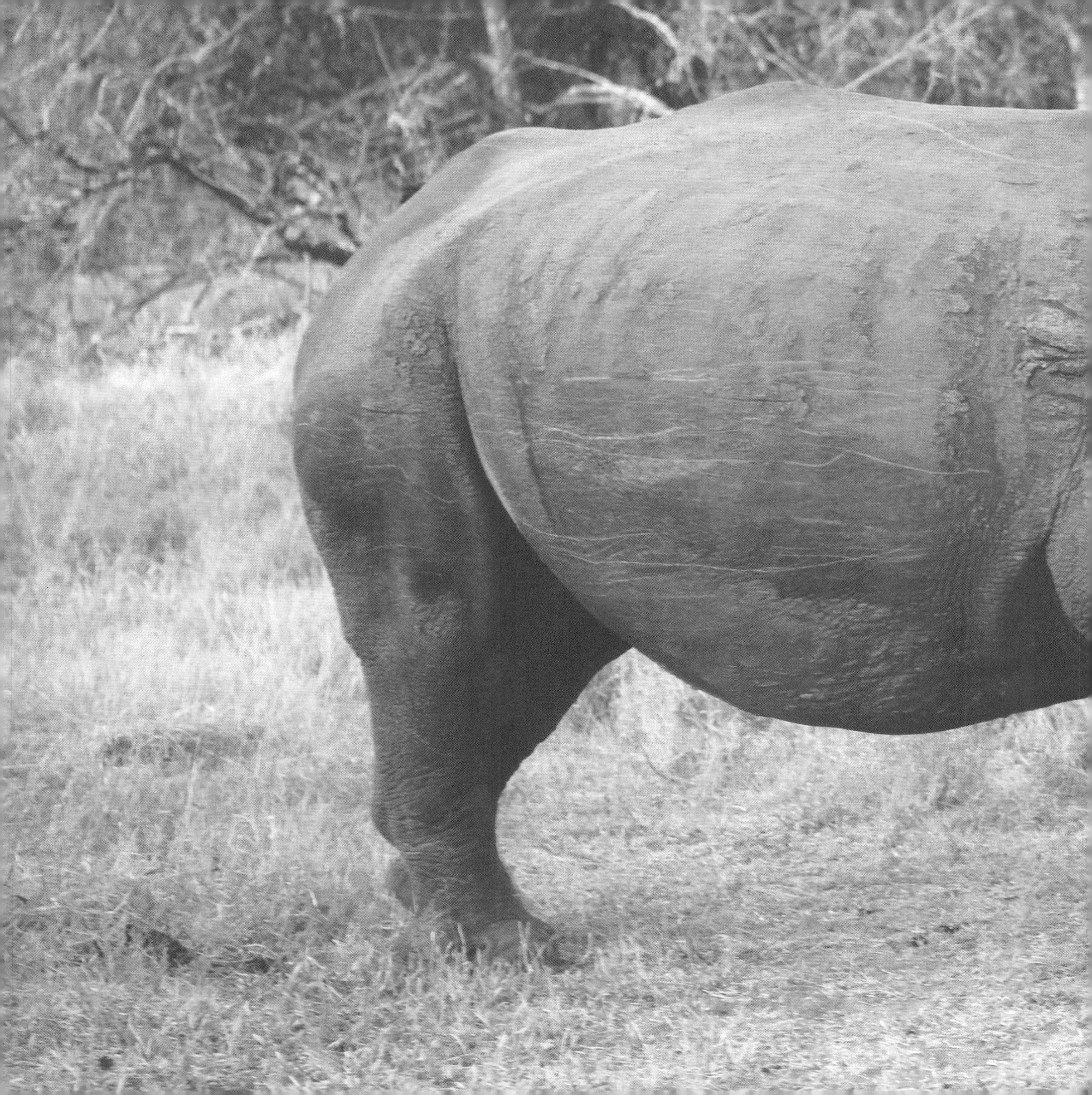